T0144167

INTRODUCTION TO
COGNITIVE RADIO NETWORKS
AND APPLICATIONS

INTRODUCTION TO
COGNITIVE RADIO NETWORKS AND APPLICATIONS

EDITED BY

GEETAM TOMAR
ASHISH BAGWARI
JYOTSHANA KANTI

CRC Press
Taylor & Francis Group
Boca Raton London New York

CRC Press is an imprint of the
Taylor & Francis Group, an **informa** business

A CHAPMAN & HALL BOOK

CRC Press
Taylor & Francis Group
6000 Broken Sound Parkway NW, Suite 300
Boca Raton, FL 33487-2742

© 2017 by Taylor & Francis Group, LLC
CRC Press is an imprint of Taylor & Francis Group, an Informa business

No claim to original U.S. Government works

Printed on acid-free paper
Version Date: 20160728

International Standard Book Number-13: 978-1-4987-6298-4 (Hardback)

Library of Congress Cataloging-in-Publication Data

Names: Tomar, Geetam, author. | Bagwari, Ashish, author. | Kanti, Jyotshana, author.
Title: Introduction to cognitive radio networks and applications / Geetam Tomar, Ashish Bagwari, and Jyotshana Kanti.
Description: Boca Raton : Taylor & Francis, a CRC title, part of the Taylor & Francis imprint, a member of the Taylor & Francis Group, the academic division of T&F Informa, plc, [2017] | Includes bibliographical references and index.
Identifiers: LCCN 2016015501 | ISBN 9781498762984 (alk. paper)
Subjects: LCSH: Cognitive radio networks.
Classification: LCC TK5103.4815 .T66 2017 | DDC 621.3845/6--dc23
LC record available at https://lccn.loc.gov/2016015501

Visit the Taylor & Francis Web site at
http://www.taylorandfrancis.com

and the CRC Press Web site at
http://www.crcpress.com

Printed and bound in the United States of America by
Edwards Brothers Malloy on sustainably sourced paper

Dedicated to our real God "Our Parents," Baba Kedarnath, Anshul, and Anuskha.

Ashish Bagwari and Jyotshana Kanti

Contents

Part I   Introduction

Part II   Spectrum Sensing in CRN

Part III   Collaborative Sensing Techniques
in Cognitive Radio Networks

Part IV   Routing Algorithms and Layers in CRN

Part V   Challenges in Cognitive Radio Networks/ Energy Utilization in Cognitive Radio Networks

Part VI   Applications of Cognitive Radio Networks

Preface

In recent years, radio networks have played an important role in human life. The importance of a radio network is well known in various fields of engineering. It is therefore necessary for an electronic, computer science, IT, and networking engineer to know the fundamentals of a wireless radio network system or model.

According to IEEE, the bandwidth of a radio network is limited while the number of users is increasing day by day, so there may be the chance of bandwidth crises occurring in the future of the radio network. The cognitive radio network (CRN) is one solution for the bandwidth crisis problem. The concept of CRN is given by Dr. Joseph Mitola III, which defines that radio users utilize the licensed band of primary radio users. The Federal Communication Commission (FCC) defines the characteristics and parameters of CRN. Nowadays, most researchers are working in this direction and thousands of research papers are available. Therefore, we have introduced this book on CRNs to discuss state-of-the-art knowledge from cognitive radio to networking cognitive radios. This book was inspired by the overwhelming response to the syllabus offered by various Indian universities, as well as abroad.

This book has been prepared carefully with each topic giving suitable practical illustrations and detailed explanations of each given step, making it easy for researchers to understand complicated derivations.

In every section of each chapter, the important basic concepts are highlighted by key points, which is a notable feature of this book. The references are added in each chapter, which help students to refer and understand the theory in great depth. This book has been divided into six parts and 16 chapters.

We would like to thank Mr. Pradeep Bagwari and Mrs. Saraswati Bagwari, who have been encouraging and supporting us during the preparation of the manuscript for this book, and the grace of Baba Kedarnath to achieve this goal. We also wish to acknowledge our family members for their continuous support, help, and encouragement: without them this work would not have been completed in time. Last but not least, special thanks to Mr. Anshul Semwal and Ms. Anushkha Gaur for their true love.

We hope that this book will prove to be very useful, not only for researchers, but also for subject faculties. The authors have not intentionally omitted anything and possibly have nothing more to cover at this time, but we welcome any suggestions for the improvement of this book.

Prof. Geetam Singh Tomar
MIR Labs
India

Ashish Bagwari
India

Jyotshana Kanti
India

MATLAB ® is a registered trademark of The MathWorks, Inc. For product information, please contact:

The MathWorks, Inc.
3 Apple Hill Drive
Natick, MA 01760-2098 USA
Tel: 508-647-7000
Fax: 508-647-7001
E-mail: info@mathworks.com
Web: www.mathworks.com

Editors

Dr. Geetam Singh Tomar received his UG from Institute of Engineers Calcutta, PG from REC Allahabad, and PhD from RGPV Bhopal in electronics engineering and he has also completed Post-Doctoral in computer engineering from the University of Kent, Canterbury, UK. He is the director of THDC Institute of Hydropower Engineering and Technology (Government of Uttarakhand), Tehri, India and is also the director of Machine Intelligence Research Labs, Gwalior, India. Prior to this, he served in the Indian Air Force, MITS Gwalior, IIITM Gwalior, and other institutes. He also served at the University of Kent, UK, and University of West Indies, Trinidad. He is a senior member of IEEE, Fellow of IETE and IE(I), and Member of ACM, CSI, and ISTE. He received the International Plato award for academic excellence in 2009 from the International Biographical Centre (IBC), Cambridge, UK. He was listed in the 100 top academicians of the world in 2009 and 2013 and was also listed in Who's Who in the World for 2008 and 2009. He has organized more than 20 IEEE International conferences in India and other countries. He is a member of IEEE/ISO working groups. He has delivered the keynote address in many conferences abroad. He is the chief editor of 5 International Journals, has filed 1 patent, published 79 research papers in international journals, 85 papers in IEEE conferences, has written six books, and contributed five book chapters in CRC and IGI USA. He has more than 100 citations per year. He is associated with many other universities abroad as a visiting professor.

Ashish Bagwari received B. Tech. (Hons.), M. Tech. (Hons. and gold medalist), and PhD degrees in electronics and communication engineering in 2007, 2011, and 2016, respectively. He is currently head of Electronics and Communication Engineering Department, Women's Institute of Technology (WIT) Dehradun, Constituent College of Uttarakhand Technical University (State Government Technical University), Dehradun, India. He has more than 7.5 years' experience in industry, academic, and research. He received the Best WIT Faculty award in 2013 and 2015 and Best Project Guide Award in 2015. Dr. Bagwari also received the Corps of Electrical and Mechanical Engineers Prize from the Institution of Engineers, India (IEI), in December 2015 and was named in Who's Who in the World 2016 (33rd Edition). Dr. Bagwari has published more than 60 research papers in various international journals (including ISI/SCI indexed) and IEEE international conferences. His current research interests include robust spectrum-sensing techniques in cognitive radio networks. He is a member of IEEE USA, MIR Laboratories India, IETE, ACM, and IAENG. He has also been an editor, an advisor, and a reviewer of several well-known international journals published by IEEE, Taylor & Francis, Springer, Elsevier, IJCCN, ISTP, IJATER, JREEE, JCSR, and JNMS, CICN-2011, 2013, 2015, 2016, CSNT-2014, 2015, ICMWOC-2014, I4CT'2014, and ICEPIT-2014. Dr. Bagwari has filed one patent. He has written one book and a few book chapters in CRC Press publications.

Jyotshana Kanti received B. Tech. (Hons.) and M. Tech. degrees in computer science and engineering from Uttarakhand Technical University, Dehradun, India. She has published three research papers in reputed international journals (Indexings SCI/ISI indexed) and conferences, including the IEEE international conferences.

Contributors

Taufik Abrão
Electrical Engineering Department
State University of Londrina (DEEL-UEL)
Londrina, Brazil

Fakir Mashuque Alamgir
Department of Electrical and Electronics
    Engineering
East West University
Dhaka, Bangladesh

Weng Chon Ao
Department of Electrical Engineering
University of Southern California
Los Angeles, California

K. V. Arya
Atal Bihari Vajpayee Indian Institute
    of Information Technology and
    Management
Gwalior, India

Mohd Dani Baba
Centre for Computer Engineering Studies
Faculty of Electrical Engineering
Universiti Teknologi MARA
Selangor, Malaysia

Ashish Bagwari
Head of Department of Electronics and
    Communication Engineering
Women's Institute of Technology
Uttarakhand Technical University
Dehradun, India

Robin Singh Bhadoria
Discipline of Computer Science and
    Engineering
Indian Institute of Technology Indore
Indore, India

Vimal Bhatia
Discipline of Electrical Engineering
Indian Institute of Technology Indore
Indore, India

P. T. V. Bhuvaneswari
Department of Electronics Engineering
Madras Institute of Technology
Anna University
Chennai, India

Rajib Biswas
Department of Physics
Tezpur University
Tezpur, India

Kwang-Cheng Chen
Graduate Institute of Communication
    Engineering
National Taiwan University
Taipei, Taiwan

Pin-Yu Chen
Department of Electrical Engineering
    and Computer Science
University of Michigan
Ann Arbor, Michigan

Shin-Ming Cheng
Department of Computer Science and
    Information Engineering
National Taiwan University of Science
    and Technology
Taipei, Taiwan

Fábio Renan Durand
Universidade Tecnológica Federal do
    Paraná (UTFPR)
Cornélio Procópio, Brazil

Harwati Hashim
Faculty of Education
Universiti Kebangsaan Malaysia
Selangor, Malaysia

Aislan Gabriel Hernandes
Electrical Engineering Department
State University of Londrina (DEEL-UEL)
Londrina, Brazil

Hui-Yu Hsu
Department of Computer Science and
Information Engineering,
National Taiwan University of Science and
Technology
Taipei, Taiwan

Izwah Ismail
Faculty of Electrical Engineering
Universiti Teknologi MARA
Selangor, Malaysia

Rachit Jain
Department of Electronics and
Communication Engineering
Institute of Technology and Management
(ITM) Group of Institutions
Gwalior, India

Toni Janevski
Faculty of Electrical Engineering and
Information Technologies
Ss. Cyril and Methodius University
Skopje, Macedonia

A. Jayanthiladevi
Jain University
Bangalore, India

Animesh Kumar Jha
School of Computer Science and Informatics
University College Dublin
Dublin, Ireland

G. M. Kadharnawaz
Department of Computer Applications
Sona College of Technology
Salem, India

Jyotshana Kanti
Department of Computer Science and
Engineering
Uttrakhand Technical University
Dehradun, India

Ricardo Tadashi Kobayashi
Electrical Engineering Department
State University of Londrina (DEEL-UEL)
Londrina, Brazil

Manish Mandloi
Discipline of Electrical Engineering
Indian Institute of Technology Indore
Indore, India

Lailun Nahar
Link3 Technologies Ltd.
Dhaka, Bangladesh

Vladimir Nikolikj
Faculty of Electrical Engineering and
Information Technologies
Ss. Cyril and Methodius University
Skopje, Macedonia

A. Dinesh Prasanna
Reva University
Bangalore, India

Lucas Sampaio
Computer Science Department (CCE)
State University of Londrina
Londrina, Brazil

Rinki Sharma
Department of Computer Science and
Engineering
Faculty of Engineering and Technology
M.S. Ramaiah School of Advanced
Studies
Bangalore, India

Shikha Singhal
Department of Computer Science
Jaypee Institute of Information
Technology
Noida, India

Adwitiya Sinha
Department of Computer Science
Jaypee Institute of Information Technology
Noida, India

F. Takawira
School of Electrical and Information
    Engineering
University of the Witwatersrand (WITS)
Johannesburg, South Africa

M. N. Thippeswamy
Department of Computer Science and
    Engineering
Nitte Meenakshi Institute of Technology
Bangalore, India

Geetam Singh Tomar
Director, THDC Institute of Hydropower
    Engineering and Technology
Tehri, Garhwal
Uttarakhand, India

Rhoma Erma Zaini
Electrical and Electronic Department
Institut Latihan Perindustrian Ipoh
Ipoh, Malaysia

Part I

Introduction

1

Fundamental Concepts of Cognitive Radio Networks

Shikha Singhal and Adwitiya Sinha

CONTENTS

1.1 Introduction

In the past decade, the global market has witnessed a rapid increase in the availability of wireless devices, which has greatly boosted their applications. This has created a huge demand in developing several innovations for optimized utilization of sparse capacity of the wireless networks, especially in the license-free bands. The major challenges faced by wireless networks include underutilization, wastage of bandwidth, and allocation of spectrum. Cognitive radio (CR) technology equipped with software-defined radio (SDR) aims to address these challenges by utilizing the scarce and limited natural resources efficiently without causing excessive interference to the official band users [1].

Cognitive radio network (CRN) deals with spectral scarcity in the wireless domain through configurable radios and efficient application-based protocol stack, offering solutions for cross-layer issues and challenges. CR is considered a highly potential and prospective technological innovation that would enhance and redefine the concept of resource sharing in the forthcoming wireless era. It enables programmable wireless devices to sense and observe their surrounding environment and adapt dynamically to it. It also enhances the channel assignment method, resource allocation, and networking protocols, which are deliberated for better connectivity and high quality of service [2,3].

1.2 Cognitive Radio Networks

CRN enhances the utilities of wireless network services by configuring the radio model, dynamically allocates bands to users, and empowers electronic devices to logically adapt to the demands of wireless communication.

1.2.1 Significance of CRNs

Two cardinal goals associated with the CR include

1. High reliability, authenticity, and communication feasibility over spatio-temporal domain
2. Proficient utilization of available radio spectrum

Spectrum bands can be categorized as official and unofficial bands. Official wireless users are the ones with legal permissions and are given the highest priority to access the channel without any interference, while unofficial users are supposed to use the band without disturbing the official users. In addition, official users have spectrum mobility to communicate whenever and wherever they want. Unofficial users first need to detect the conceivable vacant bands, determine the channel, and eventually adjust their parameters to maintain the live communication. These stages are defined as spectrum sensing, decision, and handoff. Figure 1.1 illustrates all these sets of activities as CR cycle, which include spectrum sensing, decision making, sharing, and mobility as its important phases [4–6].

1.2.1.1 Advantages of CRNs

1. It is an adaptive learning network.
2. It is a self-organized network.
3. It performs its operations in real time.
4. It has an ability to tolerate faults in the network.

1.2.2 Architectural Dynamics of a CRN Simulating the Human Brain

This section describes the architecture of CRN in context with the human brain and behavior, and how this information processing paradigm makes decisions during allocation of spectrum bands.

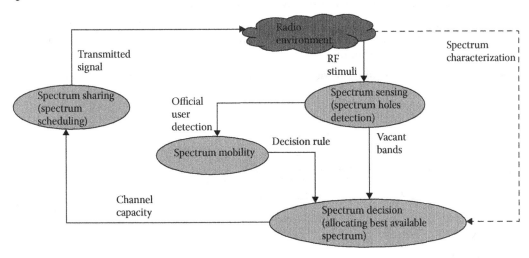

FIGURE 1.1
Cognitive radio cycle.

1.2.2.1 Human Brain

Conceptually, functioning of CR can be compared to that of the human brain. The human brain is a collection of interconnected neurons, with each neuron operating as a cell using biochemical reactions to receive processes and transmit information. The three-stage system of human brain consisting of receptors, coordinator, and effectors is highlighted in Figure 1.2.

A receptor organ processes the network inputs and sends the sensory data to the brain through neurons, simultaneously conveying the information to the network. The coordinator processes this information and sends signal to the effectors to perform actions such as movement, sight, etc. To a large extent, CRN simulates neuronal activities while performing tasks and making decisions regarding simple or complex issues. For instance,

- First step involves perceiving, i.e., identifying the current environment or running status of jobs.
- Second step requires learning and storing the information in buffer (brain), along with the knowledge of the current environment.
- Third step is to initiate some control to invoke new actions to help ongoing jobs or tasks to run uninterruptedly.
- Fourth step is to maintain the coordination among different activities.
- Last step includes storage of acquainted observations, which can eventually help to set the objectives for next higher complex-level tasks or decision making.

CRN is one of the most sophisticated and complicated multiuser cordless communication systems which is capable of adopting the desired behavior of operating devices. It epitomizes the following operations:

- Sensing: to *perceive* the radio environment (i.e., outside world) in real time and sense the status of the current working environment
- Learning: to *remember* the perceived information acquired from the sensing environment and *improve* the performance of each communicating devices operating in the current environment
- Forwarding: to *promote* continuous communication by maintaining the coordination among multiple users

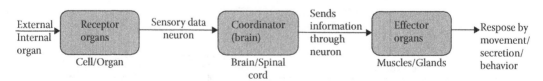

FIGURE 1.2
Human brain functionalities.

- Rules management: to *supervise* the coordination among communicating processes and competing devices (users) via efficient resource allocation algorithm

Therefore, CR closely resembles the human brain in dealing with the problems of wireless networks. Figure 1.3 shows the major components, modules and functioning of CR. CR addresses the spectrum underutilization problem in the following ways:

- Sensing radio environment to find spectrum holes in the available band, based on both time and location
- Reusing the spectrum holes for unofficial users proficiently by checking all possible constraints in the current scenario

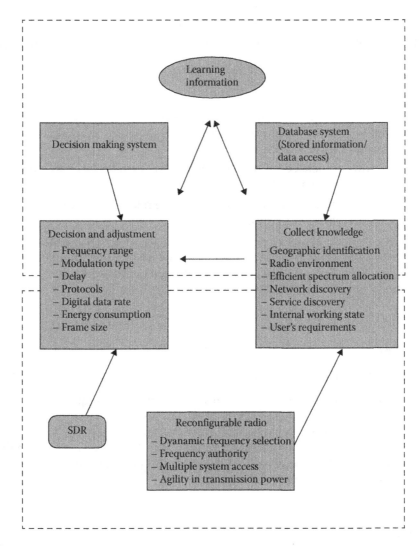

FIGURE 1.3
Functioning of cognitive radio.

1.2.3 CRN Usage and Amenities

Cognitive usage and amenities consolidated to enable more competent and efficient usage of the spectrum include the following aspects:

- Capability of CR-enabled devices to transform functioning frequency and improve the usage toward adapting to the environment.
- Selection of ideal operation environment on the basis of perceived signals from the neighboring transmitters.
- Ability to identify its own as well as other cognitive devices location that are using the same spectrum so that operating parameters of the radio environment can be improved by enhancing the spectrum reuse.
- Efficiency to support the utilization of radio spectrum.
- Real-time applicability of advanced algorithms allowing rearrangement of vacant bands in the spectrum.
- Intelligence technology to manage control actions corresponding to the perceived environment.
- Effective decision-making strategies to share the available spectrum with interference-tolerant communication among official and unofficial users, without affecting the quality of service.
- Mobility feature associated with the CR empowers the users to avail network services anywhere they want.
- CR-based devices have adequate capacity to store relevant information, similar to the human mind, for taking future decisions
- Capability to learn about its nearby objects and associated activities by using certain learning rules helps the CR-based devices to eventually identify the requirements of new users to promote flexibility and reliability in spectrum utilization.

1.3 Terminal Potentiality of CRNs

Utilities of CR can be deduced based on different application requirements. Important characteristics of CR include the ability to perceive current environment status (cognitive capability), analyze, observe, and learn from the sampled sensory information (self-organized potentiality), and adapt to the operating parameters from running environment (reconfigurable potentiality). Sections 1.3.1 through 1.3.3 describe each of these characteristics and their related prospects [7–12].

1.3.1 CRN Capability

There are several aspects that enhance the capability of the CR technology, which include sensitivity, spectrum allocation, geographic identification, network, and service discovery, etc.

1.3.1.1 Sensitiveness to the Environment

The CR terminal monitors and detects the vulnerable spots, also known as "spectrum holes" or "vacant bands," which can be eradicated based on the official usage of spectrum band and considering the factor of interference in frequency bands.

1.3.1.2 Efficient Spectrum Allocation

Spectrum sharing arrangements between the official users and third party on an ad hoc or a real-time basis can improve the efficiency and throughput of the CRN [12–15]. This can be achieved by sharing the bandwidth with the guaranteed quality of service at a given time, especially to the highly prioritized primary users (PUs).

1.3.1.3 Geographic Identification

A CRN is aware of the geographic location of each terminal and its corresponding neighboring node. Based on the appropriate operating parameters of the geographic location, power and frequency are allocated and assigned to each node. In satellite downlink communication, belonging to the receive-only category, geographic location sensing helps to avoid interference with the nearby nodes.

1.3.1.4 Network/System Discovery

Network discovery is vital to ensure a reliable communication in CRNs. A terminal is responsible to assess the optimal path before establishing communication. Once communication is established, monitoring of the system throughput for all channels is also done by the CRN terminals. Throughout the network lifetime, CRN terminals are responsible for analyzing, monitoring, and deducing the optimal path for delivery with the least interference. For example, in an event when a CR-terminal needs to place a call request, it would sense the nearby global system for mobile communication (GSM), base transceiver stations (BTSs), and Wi-Fi access point (AP) spectrum environment. Based on the information gathered during the discovery phase, an optimal path is deduced that ultimately connects the terminal and GSM BTS/Wi-Fi AP. Attempts are made to establish the shortest communication link with minimum set of terminals involved, but at times, the communication channel can also be multihops in which an array of terminals support the communication link for a seamless delivery.

1.3.1.5 Service Discovery

Service discovery is performed to assess the nature of communication link during the discovery process. The network serves as a backbone to cater to the requirements of communication, but the infrastructure may differ depending on the nature of communication. The terminals determine the communication path and link, based on the availability and feasibility of the operator's infrastructure. This step is accomplished during the network/system discovery process.

1.3.2 Reconfigurable Potentiality

CR extends several possibilities to improve the network performance and potential by allowing reconfiguration of certain features, including independency in the choice of frequency band, switching between the desired transmission power levels, and multiple user access, etc. Sections 1.3.2.1 through 1.3.2.5 illustrate some of these issues in detail.

1.3.2.1 Frequency Authority

Based on the environment of the access network, the terminals can choose to change the operational frequency of the radio. This capability is usually accompanied with a dynamic selection method to opt for the right frequency. This helps the CRN to recover from high-interference channels and improve the communication quality.

1.3.2.2 Dynamic Frequency Selection

The dynamic selection process detects the signals from nearby systems operating at different frequencies, and accordingly applies measures to avoid interchannel interference with the established communication. The decision-making process is largely influenced by sensing, geographic location monitoring, and commands received from a network or device. Finally, an optimal decision is deduced to switch to a better frequency band for higher communication quality and system throughput.

1.3.2.3 Adaptive Modulation/Coding

For a more efficient usage of the spectrum, adaptive modulation techniques were introduced. These techniques enable modification of parameters involved in the transmission process with optimized waveforms to provide improved spectrum access, and allow the CRN to take a more extensive approach toward usage of spectrum by optimizing through the available channels and bandwidth utilization. To maintain interoperability among systems, appropriate modulation is adapted by the radio for compatibility with neighboring terminals and nodes in the networking infrastructure.

1.3.2.4 Agility in Transmission Power

The terminal radio is endowed with a transmission power control feature that facilitates the electronic devices to dynamically switch between appropriate transmission power levels, thereby allowing a seamless data transmission and delivery process. The transmission can be tweaked or allowed in a fraction of time whenever required. Moreover, the transmitter power can be reduced to a lower level for better sharing, especially when high-power operations are not required.

1.3.2.5 Multiple System Access

A CR-terminal can be configured in a manner that a single node can expedite multiple communications with networks running different protocols with distinct set of calibrations. Concurrency in running multiple systems efficiently helps the terminals to be more effective toward cross-compatibility and interoperability, thus boosting overall efficiency of the communication system.

1.3.3 Self-Organization and Management

1.3.3.1 Spectrum/Radio Resource Management

The vulnerabilities identified during sensing and discovery stage yield vital information about spectrum holes, which is further processed and scrutinized to fulfill the optimal resource management and spectrum requirements. Spectrum resource and radio infrastructure need to be allocated in an optimal manner and a good spectrum management scheme is necessary to cater to all communication needs [16].

1.3.3.2 Mobility and Connection Management

Wireless environment is often considered to be highly heterogeneous in terms of hardware and communication stack of the neighboring CRNs. Each network might involve different routing and topology management strategies, as a result of which optimal route selection becomes even more complicated. Good mobility and connection management helps in maintaining cross-compatibility and is responsible for an effective neighborhood discovery with WAN/LAN access detection to assess the feasibility of vertical handoffs.

1.3.3.3 Trust/Security Management

Owing to the heterogeneous nature of CRN-based devices in any established communication link, security evolves as a challenge. Also, due to involvement of large numbers of mobile operators in communication process, ensuring hassle-free, uninterrupted, and reliable handoffs becomes important. The intensity of ensuring confidentiality and integrity of the communication link varies with the nature of communication and is a matter of prime importance. Since CRNs are generally operated by multiple operators, establishing grounds for trust becomes a prerequisite for secured operations. Both legal and operational safeguards are considered of high priority, however, it varies according to the scope and nature of the communication agreement.

1.4 CRN Architecture

CRN architecture includes various heterogeneities in networks. Such diversity may exist within the interconnections of CR terminals, base station (BS) utilities, hardware modules of APs and mobile terminals (MTs), and networking protocols, etc. CR mainly carries out sensing of the spectrum holes and accordingly applies the spectrum reuse. Figure 1.4 shows the modeling of CR architecture. Variety of wireless access technologies are available to be used by terminals and wide range of service providers [17]. CR technology empowers the users to access the channel anytime, anywhere with tolerable levels of interruptions. Moreover, the system operators are vested with the liability of delivering better services to mobile users. The operators also manage the highly constrained radio resources and other network utilities, necessary for delivering more packets per unit bandwidth in a suitable way [18–22].

CRNs can be designed in three ways to solicit the official as well as unofficial applications. Key constituents of CRNs are MTs, BS/APs, and *backbone networks*. Three categories of CRNs architecture include infrastructure-based, ad hoc, and mesh architectures. These are described in this section.

1.4.1 Infrastructure-Based Architecture

In infrastructure-based architecture, BSs or APs are accessed by MTs either in direct or multihop manner (Figure 1.5). MTs can communicate with other corresponding terminals

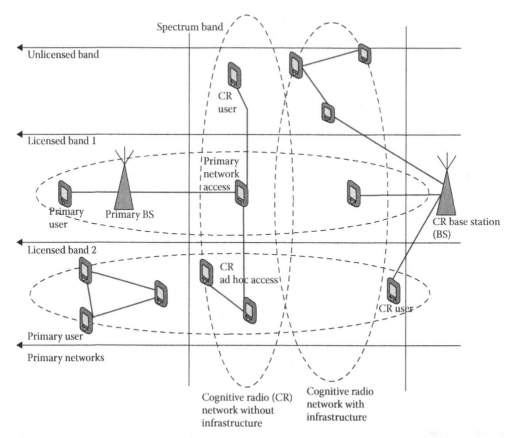

FIGURE 1.4
Cognitive radio architecture.

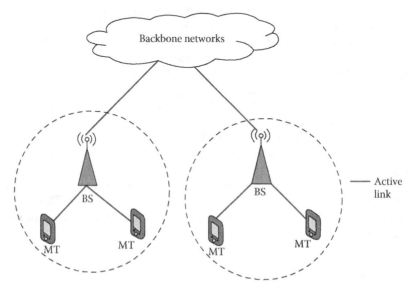

FIGURE 1.5
Infrastructure-based architecture.

through the BS within the same transmission range. To meet the demands of MTs, networking protocols are executed by BS/APs at different layers of protocol stack. Routing of packets among different cells is managed by backbone networks to make the communication feasible among MTs belonging to distinct APs. Various application domains and networking systems can be built from the infrastructure-based model.

1.4.2 Ad Hoc Architecture

Ad hoc architecture is constructed for the special purpose applications where fixed infrastructure is not practical (Figure 1.6). Communication between two or more cognitive terminals is coordinated by several networking protocols and standards, such as Wi-Fi, GSM, Bluetooth, or using spectrum holes dynamically. It is an interconnection of MTs in which if any terminal perceives signal from the nearby terminal, they can set up a temporary connection with each other by using specific networking technologies.

1.4.3 Mesh Architecture

The combination of both, infrastructure-based and ad hoc–based architectures, is referred to as the mesh architecture (Figure 1.7). It allows wireless connection among MTs, APs, and BSs. Each terminal acts as a transmitter as well as a router to manage the packet forwarding. Therefore, MTs can approach the BS/APs directly or by relaying via intermediate terminals in multiple hops. Moreover, BS/APs often work as gateways to connect the wireless and wired backbone networks together. Therefore, it becomes more cost effective and reliable with improved architectural setup compared to the infrastructure- and ad hoc–based setups. BS/APs perceive spectrum holes for communicating with each other. They possess cognitive potentiality so that the spectrum holes can be used to fulfill demands of MTs and serve as a wireless backbone.

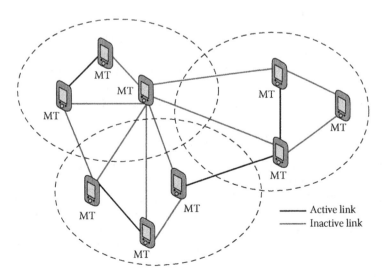

FIGURE 1.6
Ad hoc–based architecture.

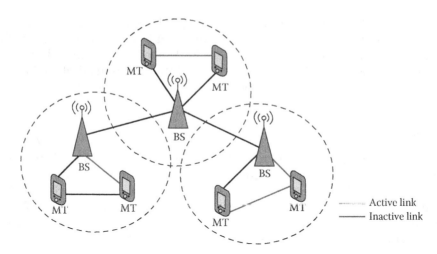

FIGURE 1.7
Mesh architecture.

1.5 Issues in CRNs

This section encompasses several issues in cognitive networks at the spectrum-sensing level. Significantly, CRN needs to be efficient during the handoff process so that the PUs are serviced without delays. For this purpose, radio resource needs to be managed in a manner so that the requirements of PUs could be prioritized over the secondary users to avoid interference in the primary stream of service. Interferences can be mainly caused either due to the temperature exceeding a certain level of threshold or because of the multiple users accessing the spectrum simultaneously [15].

1.5.1 Interference Temperature Measurement

The system mostly operates in ultrawide band (UWB) frequency, where secondary cognitive users generally coexist with the PUs. Secondary users can transmit in spectrum holes and white bands with low-power communication link with critical monitoring of the temperature level, which restricts the secondary users from causing interferences and distortion in the communication link of the primary licensed users.

1.5.2 Spectrum Sensing in Multiuser Networks

CR must be able to sense the demand from PUs and differentiate communication links established by PUs to secondary users. PUs must always be given a high priority route clearance and the CRN must ensure that the communication link remains free from any interference by any secondary user or co-channel disturbances. The vital process of primary receiver detection is deduced on the principle of the primary receiver's local oscillator leakage power. For this purpose of assertion, the following two techniques are preferably used:

- *Primary transmitter detection*: This is achieved through energy detection when there is no prior knowledge of primary signal energy. Match filter methodology is used to maximize the output signal-to-noise ratio (SNR).

- *Cooperative techniques*: This allows mapping of coordinates in a centralized controller–receiver architecture in a CRN.

Certain challenges faced during multiuser access are described as follows:

1. *Uncertainty in allocating the channel resource*: Inconsistency in the received signal strength (RSS) due to channel fading can cause the CR to make wrong decision, which leads to violation of cognitive policies laid out for reasoning and learning from the communication environment. Highly sensitive radio devices can differentiate between faded primary signals and white spaces. The decision-making process is often challenged when the fading effect is severe and the results are nonconclusive. In such circumstances, local readings of all the neighboring CRs are collated and processed to deduce the signal strength, frequency, and PU channels. Adaptive learning and sophisticated reasoning algorithms help the radio to allocate appropriate channels, thereby establishing seamless communication links to the primary licensed users.

2. *Noise and attenuation uncertainty*: Communication signal in the environment is susceptible to noise and attenuation losses. The factor of attenuation may vary in CRN, therefore the impact of noise needs to be reduced for quality interpretation of signal in a consistent and coherent manner. Therefore, SNR is deduced, which compares the level of desired signal strength to random noise.

3. *Uncertainty due to aggregated interference*: Communication links of CRs are affected by the interference caused by different environmental variables present in the surrounding vicinity. Hence, inconsistency produced from the immediate environment can hamper the quality of communication of the PUs. Also, owing to the learning capability of CRs, aggregated interference deduced by a set of radios in the neighborhood having a similar set of environmental variables may lead to incorrect detection of the PU frequency, and may eventually cause trouble in sensing the entire network of cognitive users. The only solution here is to calibrate the sensitivity of the radios and compensate for the difference of aggregate interference at each radio or at the controller.

4. *Interference limit*: A couple of major cases contributing to this context are localization difficulty and listen-only mode. In first case, when the geographic location of the licensed receiver is unknown to the secondary user, the aggregate interference and compensation fail to be suitably analyzed. In the second case, the PU is calibrated to be in a listen-only mode, in which no feedback or communication could be acquired from the receiver radio to the PU. In such scenario, one-way communication takes place, as a result of which the primary transmitter/controller fails to deduce the aggregate interference at the receiving end. The preceding two cases inhibit the analysis of interference limits that could further lead to disturbances in communication link of the PUs.

1.6 Attacks and Threats

Attack can be described as an action that violates the security of the CRN, and threats are the possible dangers that might exploit the security mechanisms of the network.

In network security management, main types of attacks and threats that can pose hindrance to the security of network are as follows:

1. Attack on confidentiality—unauthorized access of information
2. Attack on integrity—delay and modify the real information
3. Attack on availability—destroy server or pretend the server is not in a working mode
4. Attack on authenticity—unauthorized user intervention

Security is the main concern at every stage of the cognitive cycle. Owing to the nature of services imparted by CRNs, security attacks and threats become more challenging. To avoid malicious attacks and unauthorized access, the following security measures are considered at large:

1. Secure mechanism in implementation of SDR
2. Secure and trustworthy design of CR
3. Implementation of OSI security architecture in cognitive network
4. Implementation of authentic protocols in network
5. Usage of encryption/decryption mechanisms

Employing spectrum holes in the frequency band can lead to better utilization of the available spectrum without causing interference among the official users. Further, handling fallacious or deceptive detection in services offered to official users may involve critical security issues. Fallacious detection of official users is referred to as the attack made by malicious users who pretend to be an official user by sending strong signals to CR PUs. To protect from such attacks, security mechanisms in spectrum sensing are required to be highly resilient and ethical.

From an even broader perspective, CRN attacks and threats can be categorized specific to different operational layers, including physical, data link (medium access control), network, and transport layers [3]. A diagrammatic analysis of such attacks along with the relative instances is shown in Figure 1.8.

1.6.1 Attack on Physical Layer

At the physical layer, there are three types of threats and attacks that can hamper the security of CR. These can be classified and elaborated as follows:

1. *Primary user emulation (PUE) attack*: CRs are required to detect the spectrum holes or official users before occupying a specific channel (Figure 1.9). If a PU is detected then the CR immediately switches the channel to allow the PUs to carry out their services without a drop in performance. However, if a cognitive user finds the vacant band used by other users with same priority, then the spectrum sharing mechanism is used. A PUE attack is conducted by those who pretend to be an authentic user with legal rights to acquire resources/services without sharing it with other users. This often makes other licensed users to believe the attacker as a PU and hence channel access is allowed. This attack is further subdivided into selfish and malicious PUE attacks. In selfish PUE attack, two attackers are involved. They establish a link between them at a given time to

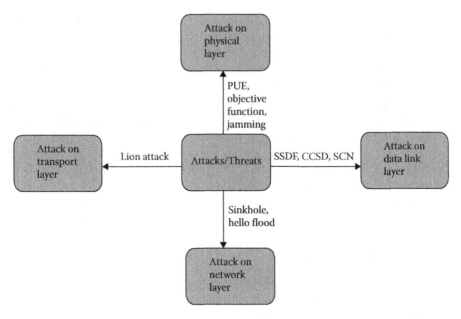

FIGURE 1.8
Attacks and threats in a cognitive radio network.

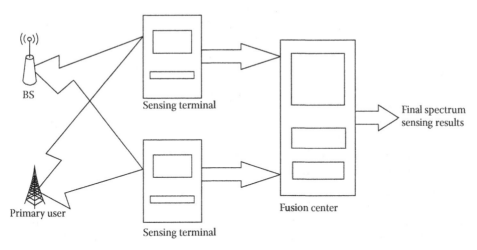

FIGURE 1.9
Primary user emulation.

increase their shared spectrum resources. In a malicious PUE attack, the attacker prevents the transmission of a cognitive user without accessing the vacant band.

2. *Objective function attack*: A CRN employs a cognitive engine that is vested with the responsibility to adjust radio parameters to address the essential user requests, e.g., high transmission or reception data rates, low energy consumption, less delay, and high security level. These radio parameters include baud rate, energy consumption, wave-type deviation, center frequency, digital data rate, medium access control (MAC) protocols, routing schemes, channel access protocols, encryption mechanisms, and frame size. These parameters are computed by the cognitive

engine in the CRN for solving one or more objective functions. While the cognitive engine is operating in an environment to calculate or adjust the radio parameters, the attacker can make changes in the results, hence corrupting the actual parameters. Such an attack that targets to alter objective kernels and contaminate system parameters is termed as objective function attack.

3. *Jamming*: Jamming is considered to be one of the most common attacks in the radio frequency environment. In this attack, the attacker can send strong signals to hinder a legitimate user during an ongoing communication session. Malicious user may access the available channels by jamming to interrupt the communication between CR users. In such cases, the attacker creates denial of service (DoS) so that normal communication cannot be performed between CRs and hence, they are jammed by a malicious user in the same channel. This type of attack is further divided into four types: constant, deceptive, random, and reactive jamming.

1.6.2 Attack on Data Link Layer

The data link layer deals with different attacks categorized as spectrum sensing data falsification attack, control channel saturation with DoS attack, and selfish attack. Each of these attacks is explained in the following section.

1. *Spectrum sensing data falsification (SSDF)*: This attacking phenomenon is also referred to as a Byzantine attack. The threat involves the attacker transmitting fake spectrum sensing results (i.e., false presence of a spectrum hole) to its neighboring MTs. This would result in authentic users eventually making bad spectrum sensing decisions in the network. This attack is mainly aimed to exploit the administrative features of centralized as well as distributed CRNs.

2. *Control channel saturation denial of service attack (CCSD)*: Multiple CR users communicate to each other simultaneously by sharing a common control channel. This shared channel can only be used for supporting a limited number of synchronous channels. This feature can be utilized by an attacker for generating fake MAC control packets with the sole objective of clogging a shared control channel, thereby degrading the network performance due to high congestion and packet collisions.

3. *Selfish channel negotiation (SCN)*: In a multihop CRN, transfer of large files to other devices is denied by the CR host to conserve its energy and increase its own throughput. This will result in a selfish channel covering. An attacker (i.e., selfish host) has the ability to modify the medium access characteristics of CR-based devices. This would compel the host to decrease the size of its back-off window, therefore illegally imposing channel expense on other hosts. Selfish attacks ultimately lead to degradation of the network throughput and efficiency of CR-based devices.

1.6.3 Attack on Network Layer

At the network layer, CR users often confront sinkhole and flood attacks. These are detailed as follows:

1. *Sinkhole attacks*: An attacker broadcasts the "best route" to reach a particular destination between a pair of nodes. On receiving the broadcast message, all nodes consider the attacker's route to be the best route for forwarding packets.

This causes overburdening of a specific route leading to congestion in the network. This type of attack is known as a sinkhole attack. Sometimes another method is used to perform a similar type of attack called selective forwarding. In this scheme, an attacker has the ability to alter or dispose packets from any node that lies in the intermediate path toward destination. Apparently, these types of attacks pose enormous threat especially to mesh architectures where the whole network traffic passes through a BS.

2. *Hello flood attacks*: A hello message is transmitted by an attacker to all other nodes in the network with strong signals for convincing them that it is arriving from one of their neighboring devices. This type of attack is called a hello flood attack. Such attack often disturbs the topological information stored by any device in the network.

1.6.4 Attack on Transport Layer

The normal functioning of the transmission layer in cognitive networks is often interrupted by a lion attack [3]. It is generally identified as a cross-layer attack which aims at disrupting transport layer operations by illegitimately emulating an authorized transmission. This enforces the cognitive network to experience frequent handoffs, therefore degrading the transmission control protocol (TCP) performance.

1.6.5 Preventive Measures

A few preventive measures are applied relevant to different layers to minimize or completely restrict the impact of the attacks.

1.6.5.1 Prevention at Physical Layer

To prevent PUE attack at the physical layer, two approaches are proposed, namely the distance ratio test (DRT) and the distance difference test (DDT). The DRT utilizes the RSS statistics and measurements, while the DDT involves the phase difference in signaling. These two approaches are based on a transmitter verification procedure and are capable to defend against a jamming attack.

1.6.5.2 Prevention at Link Layer

Decision fusion techniques are used to protect the network from SSDF attack. For instance, a specified value between 1 and number of sensing terminals is randomly chosen. If this value is greater than or equal to a certain threshold, the sensing result is "active," i.e., it represents the presence of an official signal; otherwise the spectrum band is considered to be "inactive," i.e., it represents the absence of an official signal [3]. By adopting the trusted architecture, CCSD and SCN can be alleviated and any dubious CR host is observed and computed by its neighbor nodes. Upon surveying the observed parameters, a neighboring node is able to make a final decision about whether the network is misconducting or not.

1.6.5.3 Prevention at Network Layer

It is difficult to defend against a sinkhole attack because the design of routing protocol and network architecture is exploited by it. To defend against a hello flood attack, a common key (called a symmetric key for encryption/decryption) can be shared by a trusted BS.

The trusted BS will act as a trusted third party to provide the mechanism for establishment of connection between two communicating parties by using the session key in the network.

1.6.5.4 Prevention at Transport Layer

The TCP connection parameters can be fixed by CRN devices during frequency handoffs. As post-handoff activity, CRN devices could adapt to those parameters for new network conditions. To secure control data from an attacker, a group of keys can be used by CRN members for encryption, decryption, and authentication. Cross-layer IDSs could be further employed to detect the attack source, if it exists.

1.7 Applications

With the capabilities of CRNs, the performance of many networks and communication systems can improve and coordinate with other nodes in the networks effectively. Several applications of CR in real time are illustrated as follows.

1.7.1 CRNs as a Military Network

A military network operates under very similar conditions to a CRN: avoidance of interference between official users, sensing spectrum holes or vacant bands for better utilization of spectrum, localization of other neighboring devices, etc. Decision-making logic in CR is very helpful for military networks by deciding the parameters such as frequency selection, waveform, and networking protocols. Military networks need all the features of CRNs so they can easily implement and improve the performance and efficiency of their network.

1.7.2 Machine Learning

A CRN has an ability to get self-organized and perceive information on its own. It possesses learning power, i.e., potential to perceive information from the running environment and act according to the sensed information. These capabilities can be incorporated in machine learning.

1.7.3 TV White Spaces Applications

Television white spaces are the main application of CRN. In the TV spectrum, the frequencies between the channels are either used or left unused. A CRN is one of the keys to adjust the change in frequencies and improve the performance of such networks. This would lead to increased utilization of the TV spectrum in an efficient manner. CRNs as radio equipment must be able to recognize the spectrum holes and allow these holes to be used by other users so that they can maintain an effective and reliable usage of the spectrum.

1.7.4 Multimedia

Multimedia can also be considered as a prospective application area of CRNs. CR features such as interference avoidance and spectrum mobility mainly attract the multimedia domain. If a user wants to execute any multimedia file while running or driving across a lane, CR-enabled technology allows the user to perform such actions anywhere and anytime without any interruption. A CRN facilitates sensing capability and adapts to the operating parameters of the current working environment. Having improved network performance, the user simply enjoys CR-based embedded multimedia technologies.

1.7.5 Emergency Network

An emergency network is one of the most common applications supported by CRN. Such applications need CRN abilities that prominently include location determination, sensing spectrum use by nearby devices, changing frequency, and dynamically adjusting the output power.

1.7.6 Leased Network

In leased network, CR can be applied for determining the spectrum holes and provide spectrum facility to both the users, official and unofficial, without service intervention. They can utilize all the services provided by the network in an efficient manner.

1.7.7 Monitoring Network Applications

For the networks used to closely examine the status of aircraft engines or engaged in other critical industrial monitoring, a CRN could be an ultimate choice. By monitoring the vibrations and sounds in engines, the network is able to perceive the problem and take some new action to control them.

1.8 Benefits of CRNs

1.8.1 Self-Organization

The CRN has an ability to self-organize and represent the sensed information perceived from the environment accordingly. The CR terminals sample relevant information from the environment and perform network reorganization dynamically according to the gathered information.

1.8.2 Adaptive Learning

A CRN has the potential to adapt to its environment by observing the communication pattern and user requirements. It is also capable of taking control actions based on the learning information acquired from the environment for avoiding interference between multiple users.

1.8.3 Real-Time Operation

A CR terminal primarily takes control decisions according to real-time sensed information and performs tasks accordingly. It strictly operates under the constraint of avoiding intervention between official and unofficial users at real time.

1.8.4 Fault-Tolerance Capability

CR technology possesses the capability to tolerate service disruptions without degrading the performance of the overall network. Also, it has the ability to respond to major damages and take precautionary actions to overcome network faults, thereby maintaining spectrum utilization.

References

1. Venkateswari, S., and R. Muthaiah. 2012. An overview of cognitive radio architecture: A review. *Journal of Theoretical and Applied Information Technology* 41 (1): 20–25.
2. Yu, Y.-C., L. Hu, H.-T. Li, Y.-M. Zhang, F.-M. Wu, and J.-F. Chu. 2014. The security of physical layer in cognitive radio networks. *Journal of Communications* 9 (12): 916–922.
3. Khare, A., M. Saxena, R. S. Thakur, and K. Chourasia. 2013. Attacks and preventions of cognitive radio network—A survey. *International Journal of Advanced Research in Computer Engineering & Technology (IJARCET)* 2 (3): 1002–1006.
4. Clancy, T. C., and N. Goergen. 2008. Security in cognitive radio networks: Threats and mitigation. In *International Conference on Cognitive Radio Oriented Wireless Networks and Communications (CrownCom)*, Singapore, pp. 1–8.
5. El-Hajj, W., H. Safa, and M. Guizani. 2011. Survey of security issues in cognitive radio networks. *Journal of Internet Technology* 12 (2): 181–198.
6. Sampath, A., H. Dai, H. Zheng, and B. Y. Zhao. 2007. Multi-channel jamming attacks using cognitive radios. In *Proceedings 16th International Conference on Computer Communications and Network, IEEE*, Honolulu, HI, pp. 352–357.
7. FCC, ET Docket No 03-222 Notice of proposed rule making and order. December 2003.
8. Jin, Z., S. Anand, and K. P. Subbalakshmi. 2009. Detecting primary user emulation attacks in dynamic spectrum access networks. In *Proceedings IEEE International Conference on Communications*, Dresden, Germany. pp. 1–5.
9. Karlof, C. and D. Wagner. 2003. Secure routing in wireless sensor networks: Attacks and countermeasures. In *Proceedings of the First IEEE International Workshop on Sensor Network Protocols and Applications*, Berkeley, CA. pp. 113–127.
10. Akyildiz, I. F., W. Y. Lee, M. C. Vuran, and S. Mohanty. 2006. NeXt generation/dynamic spectrum access/cognitive radio wireless networks: A survey. *Computer Networks* 50 (13): 2127–2159.
11. Akan, O. B., O. B. Karli, and O. Ergul. 2009. *Cognitive Radio Sensor Networks*. Next generation Wireless Communications Laboratory (NWCL), Department of Electrical and Electronics Engineering, Middle East Technical University, Ankara, Turkey. 060531.
12. Akyildiz, I. F., W.-Y. Lee, and K. R. Chowdhury. 2009. CRAHNs: Cognitive radio ad hoc networks. *Ad Hoc Networks, Elsevier* 7 (5): 810–836.
13. Akyildiz, I. F., W. Y. Lee, and K. Chowdhury. 2009. Spectrum management in cognitive radio ad hoc networks. *IEEE Network* 23 (4): 6–12.
14. Mathur, C. and K. Subbalakshmi. 2007. *Security Issues in Cognitive Radio Networks, Cognitive Networks: Towards Self-Aware Networks*. New York, NY: Wiley. pp. 284–293.
15. Chen, K. C., Y. J. Peng, N. R. Prasad, Y. C. Liang, and S. Sun. 2008. Cognitive radio network architecture: Part I—General structure. In *Proceedings of the 2nd International Conference on Ubiquitous Information Management and Communication*, Suwon, South Korea. pp. 114–119.
16. Reddy, Y. B. 2013. Security issues and threats in cognitive radio networks. *AICT 2013: The Ninth Advanced International Conference on Telecommunications*, Rome, Italy.
17. Akyildiz, I. F., X. Wang, and W. Wang. 2005. Wireless mesh networks: A survey. *Computer Networks ISDN System* 47 (4): 445–487.

18. Tabaković, Ž. 2000. A survey of cognitive radio systems. Croatian Post and Electronic Communications Agency, Jurišićeva 13, Zagreb, Croatia.
19. Haykin, S. 2008. Cognitive radio: Research challenges. Paper presented McMaster University Hamilton, Ontario, Canada, (VTC, Calgary, Sept. 23/08 (Haykin)).
20. Joshi, G. P., S. Y. Nam, and S. W. Kim. 2013. Cognitive radio wireless sensor networks: Applications, challenges and research trends. *Sensors* 9: 11196–11228.
21. Arshad, K., R. MacKenzie, U. Celentano, et al. 2014. Resource management for QoS support in cognitive radio networks. *IEEE Communications Magazine* 3: 114–120.
22. Jiang, T., T. Li, and J. Ren. 2012. Towards secure cognitive communications in wireless networks. *IEEE Wireless Communications* 19 (4): 82–88.

2

Basics of Cognitive Radio Networks: An Appraisal

Rajib Biswas

CONTENTS

2.1 Introduction

When we look for the meaning of the word "cognition," it shows the mental process of knowing, including aspects such as awareness, perception, reasoning, and judgment. Similarly, when we frame the name "cognitive radio" (CR), the best definition in Haykin's words can be quoted as,

> Cognitive Radio is an intelligent wireless communication system that is aware of its surrounding environment and uses the methodology of understanding-by-building to learn from the environment and adapt its internal states to statistical variations in the incoming RF (radio frequency) stimuli by making corresponding changes in certain operating parameters in real-time.

The number of mobile users is increasing day by day in the current wireless communication domain, which is apt to create a bandwidth crisis due to limited spectrum availability. CR is a future technology capable of solving the spectrum scarcity problem. It provides a solution by which efficient spectrum utilization is possible by applying the optimistic spectrum sharing techniques [1]. Mitola is considered as the pioneer who brought the concept of CR into existence. In synchrony with the name, CR is capable of detecting dynamically varying environments. Once it senses any changes in the surroundings, it adapts its communication variables such as carrier frequency, bandwidth, power, coding schemes, and modulation scheme in an intelligent way. In this chapter, we basically deal with the fundamental aspects of CR, which include its properties (based on spectrum sensing), an outline of a CR transceiver, and other architectures.

2.2 Properties of CRs

Generally, CR is considered to possess two important characteristics which are completely based on its spectrum-sensing capability. These are as follows.

2.2.1 User Centric

The framework of CR is based upon radio knowledge representation language (RKRL). It manifests itself like a small physical world. It uses and disseminates information with adaptable changes in unison with the surrounding environment, albeit keeping track of the user over different timescales which do not resemble each other. As it involves many sensors, it first gathers knowledge from its neighborhood and then employs relevant software. With their help, CR gets access to databases and makes contact with other sources of information. It clearly shows that CR is a unique electronic aid for the developer. Owing to its versatile operability, it will not be an exaggeration to say that CR provides assistance in day-to-day life irrespective of the fact whether its owner realizes it or not. It is often looked upon as a small part of a huge physical world, using and providing information over different timescales [1–11].

2.2.2 Technology Centric

With the advent of advanced spectrum sharing systems, there is a need to implement higher version of algorithms. To do that, lots of tactics are to be executed by the CR. For example, suppose an access mode is already sharing a portion of the spectrum. Corresponding to the demand of the user, CR first inspects the data rate and then the mode of transmission. To accomplish its own mode of transmission, it starts searching space allocations (spectrum) which are redundant. In such circumstances, CR is presumed to have specific features such as self-location (information about its own location) and self-awareness (knowing its ability). In addition to that, it should have knowledge of accessible base stations. To overcome interference, it has to find out other active signals in the neighboring bands, and must have knowledge of their transmission standards [11]. Consequently, a CR should be in possession of a location sensor as well as an intelligent monitoring system to keep an eye on its spectral environment [11] (see Figure 2.1).

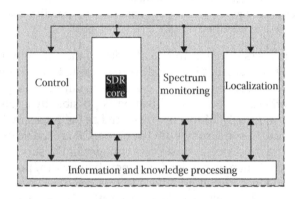

FIGURE 2.1
Technology centric radio. (From Jondral, F.K., *EURASIP J. Wirel. Commun. Netw.*, 3, 275–283, 2005. With permission.)

2.3 CR Transceiver

Software-defined radio (SDR) possesses a unique transceiver, which can be reconfigured, unlike the conventional one (see Figure 2.2). The reconfiguration and standard operational efficiency of CR are achieved by a control bus, which creates processing parameters for the desired standard of CR. Hence, the system is named as parameter-controlled SDR. Chiefly, an SDR terminal is composed of front-end radio, base-band processing, and data-processing modules [3,4]. The process is as follows.

The analog RF signal is first transformed into its digital complex baseband representation and then band-pass filtered, followed by amplification. An additional RF is locally generated. A two-way splitter is adapted to mingle the radio frequency with the signal. The entire mode of modulation is based on quadrature modulation. The main components I and Q undergo low-pass filtering and analog-to-digital conversion. In the process of analog-to-digital conversion, the sampling rate is optimized to match the signals standard. This is done so that signal processor operates at the least possible rate [11]. During sampling, the rate of digitization should be uniform for all the signals to be processed. This is in accordance with Shannon's sampling theorem. Prior to the adaptation of sampling rate to that of signal standard, another crucial factor was figured out. During the signal processing, signal mixer, filter, and analog-to-digital converter induce impairments in two-branch signal processing owing to their inherent mechanism. To circumvent this problem, corrections [5] are introduced before adapting sampling rate to the signal standard. The minimum rate of digitization is dependent on the chip rate. Generally, sampling rate is

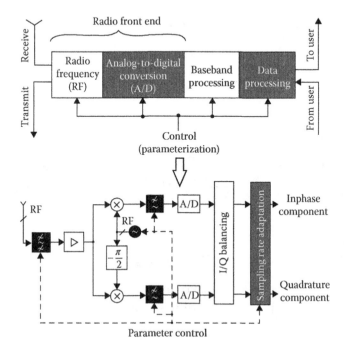

FIGURE 2.2
CR transceiver. (From Mitola, J., III., *1999 IEEE International Workshop on Mobile Multimedia Communications (MoMuC '99)*, San Diego, CA, 1999. With permission.)

kept as four times the chip rate, which is sufficient for the subsequent processing. Once it is precisely synchronized, there occurs a diminution by a factor of four.

In Section 2.4, a general model of CR is presented.

2.4 General Model of CR Networks

In general, CR acts as a multitasking platform. The modus operandi of CR can be visualized with a model elaborated in this section.

Figure 2.3 illustrates the simplified model of CR interactions devoid of the symbols used herein. Generally, each CR has its own goal. This goal-centric CR reacts to the external environment within its chosen adaptation (or waveform). In chosen adaptation, CR makes a proximal connection to its goal irrespective of its structure, content, etc. Whatever CR is going to observe at any given point of time is decided by the passive network. As constituents of the passive operating environment, channel conditions and interference environment along with the adjacent CR are taken into account. However, goal-centric adaptation plays an important role. Here, we present some general symbols and conventions that actually characterize the features of the CR environment.

Suppose there are J number of CRs in the network designated by l, m particular devices. Each one is linked to an available set of actions represented by B_l. In general, CR possesses limited number of sets which try to contain all prevalent adaptations. These adaptations are

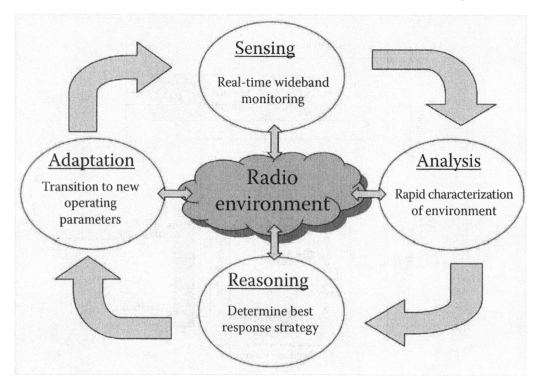

FIGURE 2.3
General model of CR network.

found to be influenced by several parameters, for example, power levels, center frequency, modulation, and source coding schemes. As a result, B_l becomes multidimensional, which is not affected by time. This can be interpreted as the reluctance of the CR to learn new actions during their very short span of adaptations. Consider B as the action space constructed by the Cartesian product of each radio action set, $B = B_1 \times B_2 \times B_3 \times \ldots \times B_l$. Similarly, if we use b as a particular set of action in B space pertaining to a specific lth CR, we can write b_l, which denotes its contribution. Again, P denotes the outcomes corresponding to outside world; p_l in similitude to this implies an observation associated with or furnished to radio l. Lastly, we introduce two additional parameters: p as a vector space inclusive of observed outcome and d_l designating the decision rule as updated by radio l on the basis of observation.

Specifically, d_l assumes the form e_d: $p_l \rightarrow B_l$. Since, there is statistical coverage of observed outcome by the action vector, each decision rule becomes a function, i.e., d_l: $B \rightarrow B_l$.

For different types of CRs, there is an explicit definition of decision rules, subjected to selection of *locally optimal action* or *selfish action*. Again, when the CR's goal is practically implemented, numbers with the radio's observed outcome, p_l, need to be associated. The detailed description is beyond the scope of this chapter.

2.5 Architecture of CR Network

The whole framework of CR is generally a mapping from spectrum sensing to spectrum utilization. CR inspects the available networks and communication systems which are in its immediate vicinity. A CR network is composed of various types of communication systems and networks. Consequently, the whole configuration can be regarded as networks characterized by heterogeneity. This is apparent in every single component of a CR's network. It includes the service providers, user terminals, etc. [10]. The true objective behind the design of cognitive radio network (CRN) architecture is to make optimal utility of network, which overshadows its other prime target of linking spectral efficiency. When we use network utilization, we actually mean that the users can complete their demand regardless of their location and time. Similarly, from the operator's viewpoint, it provides the operators a platform to provide maximal packets per bandwidth efficiently. There are several ways in which CRN can be framed. To name two, distributed and ad hoc are some of the significant ones. They actually contain licensed and unlicensed applications.

2.6 Conclusion and Future Directions

In this chapter, we provide a basic review of CRNs. Outlining the properties of CR, we have documented the fundamentals related to the CR transceiver and its functioning. Moreover, the general model of CR has also been presented. Although so far CR has come a long way since its invention, there are still some hurdles which need to be overcome. For an effective CR, better rates among transceivers are stressed, which necessitates incapacitating many practical engineering aspects. For example, an efficient coding scheme is of major importance. Another future direction for effective implementation is scaling this behavior to large networks. In a given network with cognitive nodes, one important aspect is to find the extent of collaboration among them for efficient distribution of their respective messages.

Acknowledgments

We thank our parents for their support and motivation.

References

1. Jondral, F. K., R. Machauer, and A. Wiesler. 2002. *Software Radio—Adaptivität durch Parametrisierung.* Weil der Stadt, Germany: J. Schlembach Fachverlag.
2. Jondral, F. K. 2005. Software-defined radio—Basics and evolution to cognitive radio. *EURASIP Journal on Wireless Communications and Networking* 3: 275–283.
3. Mitola, J., III. 1999. Cognitive radio for flexible multimedia communications. *1999 IEEE International Workshop on Mobile Multimedia communications (MoMuC '99)*, San Diego, CA. pp. 3–10.
4. Mitola, J., III. 2000. Cognitive Radio: An Integrated Agent Architecture for Software Defined Radio. PhD Diss., Royal Institute of Technology, Stockholm, Sweden.
5. Neel, J. 2006. Analysis and Design of Cognitive Radio Networks and Distributed Radio Resource Management Algorithms. PhD Diss. Virginia Polytechnic Institute and State University, Blacksburg, VA.
6. Rykaczewski, P., D. Pienkowski, R. Circa, and B. Steinke. 2005. Signal path optimization in software defined radio systems. *IEEE Transaction on Microwave Theory and Techniques* 53 (3): 1056–1064.
7. Jondral, F. K. 2002. Parametrization—A technique for SDR implementation. In *Software Defined Radio—Enabling Technologies*, 232–256. Edited by W. Tuttlebee. London, UK: John Wiley & Sons.
8. Wiesler, A., and F. K. Jondral. 2002. A software radio for second- and third-generation mobile systems. *IEEE Transaction on Vehicular Technology* 51 (4): 738–748.
9. Mitola, J., III, and G. Q. Maguire. 1999. Cognitive radio: Making software radios more personal. *IEEE Personal Communication* 6 (4): 13–18.
10. Gao, X., G. Wu, and T. Miki. 2004. End-to-end QoS provisioning in mobile heterogeneous networks. *IEEE Wireless Communications* 11 (3): 24–34.
11. Öner, M., and F. K. Jondral. 2004. Air interface recognition for a software radio system exploiting cyclostationarity. In *Proceedings 15th IEEE International Symposium on Personal, Indoor and Mobile Radio Communications (PIMRC '04)*, vol. 3. Barcelona, Spain. pp. 1947–1951.

3

Introduction and Applications of Software-Defined Radio

A. Jayanthiladevi and G. M. Kadharnawaz

CONTENTS

3.1 Overview

A cognitive radio (CR) is a software-defined radio (SDR) that senses its surrounding conditions and enables a user to keep track of different types of alterations and respond upon identification. A CR is an autonomous component in a communication atmosphere that often interchanges data with the links it is capable of acquiring, and communicates with other CRs. In our opinion, a CR is a reconfigured SDR which is precisely software-defined and shows the further progress of next-generation radio technologies [1,2].

SDR communication systems can sense their immediate surroundings or those situated within their limits, and can make decisions about their radio functions to perform activities based on this data, which also includes location information connected to the radio communication systems.

CR uses adaptive radio, SDR, and other technologies to routinely change its actions or functions to accomplish the desired purpose. A radio transmitter and/or receiver employs a technology that allows radio frequency (RF) functioning including, but not restricted to, modulation type, output power, or frequency range to be modified or set by the software, changes to operating parameters which occur during normal predetermined and preinstalled operation of radios according to a standard radio or system specification, primarily defined in software which supports a broad range of frequencies and can be reconfigured for user-specified requirements.

If SDR technology is properly applied, it will facilitate the single platform design to provide a path toward realization of concepts such as reconfigurability (single platform concept), run-time reconfiguration (run-time bug fixes), and eventually self-governed learning (cognitive) radios that can seamlessly handle a range of frequencies, modulation techniques, and encoding schemes.

SDR products are characterized by their adaptability to various applications and easy availability in the market. They also have the capability to combine radio systems to make interoperability possible between potential systems which are otherwise incompatible. Current technology can work only on assured frequencies, whereas SDR gives commercially feasible and usable frequencies.

SDRs are based on a technology in which the software components are successively placed on a standard hardware platform used to generate radio signals to be communicated at the transmitter-end (modulation) and detect/tune the received radio signal (demodulation) at the receiver-end.

A radio contains a transmitter in which the function parameters of the transmitter, including modulation type, frequency range, and maximum radiated or conducted output power, can be modified by making changes to hardware without changing the software. It reduces the life-cycle cost, renders uniform communication across commercial, civil, military, and federal organizations, and helps downloading data as well as software for new services and features. However, debugging is impossible for mobile terminals once they are sold.

3.1.1 What Is SDR?

In general, SDR refers to a radio design that uses a computer and a controlling software to "define" that radio's operation. Most of the modern ham rigs incorporate at least some level of software definition into their operational modes [3–5].

A true SDR has very little hardware and virtually every aspect of its operation is performed by the controlling software. In fact, in SDR the entire physical layer is software-defined, contrary to older radios where all of their functionality is determined by hardware.

3.1.2 Necessity for SDR

Ease of design: Reduced design-cycle time, quicker iterations.

Ease of manufacture: Digital software reduces testing and manufacturing costs of radios.

Operation in multimode: SDR can operate in multiple modes by loading the relevant software into memory.

Advanced signal processing techniques: Permits execution of new receiver configurations and signal-handling techniques.

Use of discrete components: Digital processes can be implemented such as synchronization, demodulation, error correction, and decryption.

Flexibility to incorporate additional functionality: Can be modified to correct problems and to upgrade.

3.1.3 Evolution of CR

The term "software-defined radio" was devised by Joseph Mitola in 1991, who published the first paper on this subject in 1992. Since late 1970s, SDR has been used in the defense sector in both the United States and Europe. One of the first open software radio initiatives was a US military project named Speakeasy, the main goal of which was to use programmable handling to compete with the existing military radios, operating in frequency bands between 2 and 2000 MHz. The project was developed to easily combine new coding and modulation principles, so that the military communications can keep up with the improvements in coding and modulation techniques in future.

Transceivers are considered as software radios since their communication tasks can be checked as programs running on an appropriate processor. Different transmitter/receiver algorithms with the same hardware, which usually describe transmission principles, are applied in the transceiver software.

A software radio transceiver is a collection of all the layers of a communication system, generally connected with the physical layer. The baseband signal processing of a digital radio (DR) is continuously performed by a digital processor. A model software radio openly clarifies the antenna output. SDR is an experimental SR in which the received signals are trialed subsequently at proper band choice riddle. SDR is currently considered as a reliable type of software radio. However, analog-to-digital converters (ADCs) facilitating high-level sharing that can be engaged in SRs are not available till now. SDR development allows spectrum deregulation as shown in Figure 3.1.

3.1.4 SDR Basics

SDR software communication architecture fundamentally defines the software mechanisms and, in particular, interfaces used in the radio. It has two main advantages: (1) It facilitates

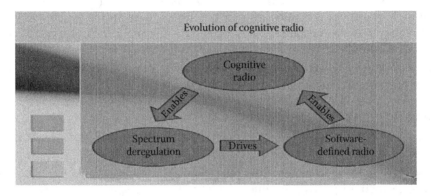

FIGURE 3.1
Evolution of cognitive SRD.

software elements or modules to be written by different organizations and transported together. (2) It allows reuse of some modules, thereby refining interoperability and providing substantial cost savings. SDR software communication architecture falls into one of the three classifications as discussed in the next section. It is useful to classify them because they need to be controlled in slightly different ways, as some can be reused across quite a lot of platforms and others cannot be. The three SDR classifications are as follows:

Management: Software adopted for this SDR classification is used to control the radio scheme. It consists of a number of applications such as deployment, configuration, and plug and play.

Node: This software can incorporate solicitations, e.g., access to hardware and bootstrapping.

Application: This is typically used for indication of processing. Examples of this include modulation, demodulation, waveform generation, and frequency translation.

3.2 Software CR Properties

A radio that employs model-based reasoning to achieve a specified level of competence in radio-related domains is called a CR based on a smart wireless communication method that is responsive to its adjacent locality (i.e., the external world), and uses the technique of accommodating-by-construction to sense the surroundings and regulate its internal conditions to arithmetical deviances according to the incoming RF thereby providing assembly reliable deviations in guaranteed effective restrictions (e.g., transmit-power, carrier frequency, and modulation scheme) in actual, with two leading concepts in attention.

SDRs are used whenever and wherever highly consistent communications are needed with efficient utilization of the radio spectrum. RF technology senses the spectrum information of the main users' location and time, allocates the accessible resources (frequency, time, and space), and regulates optimal transmission [latency, bandwidth, and quality of service (QoS)] by embedded acumen based on the main users' behavior.

Renewable: Airwaves used for broadcasting can be reused after the transmission is completed.

Technology: When required, maximum natural resources can be collected manually, although inefficiently. Spectrum is in the atmosphere and is functional because technology has been established to deal with the properties of electromagnetic waves for sound, data, and video broadcast.

Domestic asset with worldwide rules and regulations: Most of the domestic uses of spectrum are assigned to bands through the International Telecommunication Union, an agency of the United Nations; the satellites for broadcasting are governed by a worldwide agreement.

Administered: To avoid interference from challenging transmission broadcasts, frequency assignments are accomplished by standard experts.

The coexistence of heterogeneous air interfaces naturally occurs where SDR devices adapt to their respective air interface and dynamic spectrum access strategies to their QoS requirements. In particular, devices operating in a context-aware environment offload huge data streams to one or several different air interfaces selected on the basis of their availability and QoS. Uncertainties regarding the efficiency of resource usage strategies in user devices and/or network equipment create significant problems for both industry and regulators. These topics will be studied to determine the feasibility of developing standards in this area.

3.3 Software Radio Classification

3.3.1 Tier 0: Hardware Radio

No changes can be made to the system by software.

3.3.2 Tier 1: Software-Controlled Radio

Controller task can be executed in the software, but variation of features such as frequency band and modulation cannot be done without altering the hardware.

3.3.3 Tier 2: SDR

In addition to implementing software, SDR is proficient in covering considerable frequency range to deliver changes in the varied or narrow bands, modulation techniques, and transport network safety and to meet routine necessities of appropriate legacy systems, and is capable of keeping large number of air interfaces or waveforms, or add new ones by downloading the software. System software is proficient in relating the original or additional components for new functionality or in virus repairs without loading full set of software again. It has a discrete antenna system which monitors wideband descriptive, amplification and down-conversion, proceeding to obtain analog-to-digital (A/D) conversion. The communication sequence offers reverse function of digital-to-analog (D/A) conversion, filtering, analog up-conversion, and amplification.

3.3.4 Tier 3: Ideal Software Radio

It has complete competences of an SDR, but diminishes analog amplification and socializing proceeding to A/D-conversion and after D/A-conversion.

3.3.5 Tier 4: Ultimate Software Radio

This is a perfect software radio in a chip, needs no external antenna, and has no limitations on operational frequency. It can perform a wide range of adaptive services for user, and is intended for comparison purposes rather than implementation as illustrated in Figure 3.2.

3.4 Technologies That Will Facilitate Future SDR Systems

Antennas: Receiving antennas will be easily accessible to undertake wide-range-band routine than communications. Original fractal and plasma projections are estimated in the next 5–10 years that will be less significant and wider in range.

Waveforms: Organization and variety of numerous waveforms. Termination transporters and pulse defining are comparatively different techniques.

Analog-to-digital converter: Its speed reduces every 6–8 years; therefore if the ADC shows a sustainable growth, perhaps ~500 MHz of bandwidth might be digitized in future.

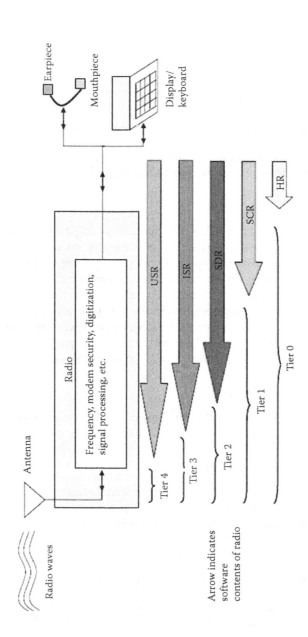

FIGURE 3.2
Illustrating the future: shift from tier 0 to 4. HR, hardware radio; ISR, ideal software defined radio; SCR, software controlled radio; USR, ultimate software radio.

Digital signal processing (DSP): Large quantities of transistor pairs have to be replaced every 18 months. When will this step slow down? Some specify this step is only supportable for a few years. More specific purpose DSPs are required.

Batteries: More and more power is needed (need to focus on more efficient use of power). Fuel cell development is underway and will take another 5–10 years until it becomes viable for handhelds.

Terrain databases: Offers the most recent peer group of terrain data for prevention, interference prediction, and environment awareness.

Cognitive science: A vital specific drive to recognize how several CRs can work with each other and separately.

Resources: Radio access technologies, frequency bands, and channels, wherein frequency bands cover multiple channels.

3.5 Illustration of Advanced SDR Applications

Advanced SDR applications are as follows: Enable and improve efficiency of joint functions (cooperation between separate troops) both national and international; enable and improve efficiency of interoperability (connections between different systems); and implement new features and systems without procuring new equipment. However, SDR is profoundly lacking in many applications.

3.5.1 Military Applications of SDR

Military applications are not explored fully due to the legal complications in interoperability, very large number and different types of systems to be communicated among the dissimilar armed forces, and different components of the armed forces in different countries (navy, air, security forces, and land forces).

The method involves spectrum backing of locations from backpacks to ships. The subordinate advantages are ad hoc peer-to-peer wireless networking (ad hoc p2p), also recognized as mobile mesh network. Ad hoc p2p works by captivating a group of mobile terminals (such as handheld devices and vehicular systems) that communicate directly with each other without conventional infrastructure. Ad hoc networking provides a self-healing and self-organizing network configuration. It uses multi hop terminals acting as routers which transmit for each other, and spread the range and communications links between different soldiers, troop transports, and command hubs. This is illustrated in Figure 3.3.

3.5.2 Ground Guidance

Ground guidance guides militaries to mark the right direction while sidestepping the complications. Ground control ranges from road maps to inflight pictures, to determine obstacles and produce directions. This helps the commanding officer to cordon off the dangerous areas and determine safe regions. This also relieves the commander from supplying turn-by-turn information, as in the past they had to use paper maps, issue turn-by-turn directions, and propose blocked routes for independent handoffs as illustrated in Figure 3.4.

(a)

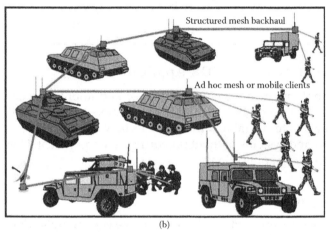

Structured mesh backhaul

Ad hoc mesh or mobile clients

(b)

FIGURE 3.3
Battlefield forces with (a) infrastructure network and (b) ad hoc network.

FIGURE 3.4
Target handoff.

3.5.3 Monitoring System

Wireless patient intensive care is an important element in eliminating the consequences and depressing the healthcare charges. Over low-cost, wireless devices, widespread intensive care can be prolonged for maximum, if not all, patients in many hospitals. By way of such universal intensive care, ups and downs in a patient's illness can be standardized for the initial period and suitable use of equipment can be determined. By getting liberated of wires and their association, the related risks of septicity are complete. Additionally, it increases the patient's ease and flexibility, improves the value of care supporters, and increases the value of medical choice. Patient movement is an essential feature during rescue operations. The new system will be able to study each aircraft, soldier, and vehicle as a portion of a node of a tactical network that will share information with each other, and send and receive the classified information on the battle ground as illustrated in Figure 3.5.

3.5.4 Disaster Management

Avoiding natural and technological disasters requires a solid understanding of science and technology, speedy implementation of research information into disaster-decrease programs and applications, and resourceful access to diverse information from both public and private units, as shown in Figure 3.6.

3.5.5 Deep Space Communications

The role of an SDR in commercial applications is not yet clear and some possible applications include next generation multimedia satellites, the only (economical) way to introduce new services or systems to orbiting satellites. SDR complies with the latest standards for satellite communications, and its flexibility can guarantee the safety of present and future space missions as illustrated in Figure 3.7.

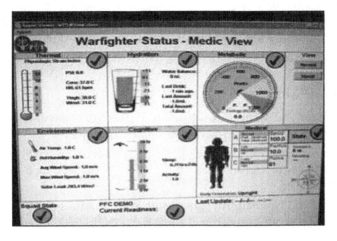

FIGURE 3.5
Monitoring system.

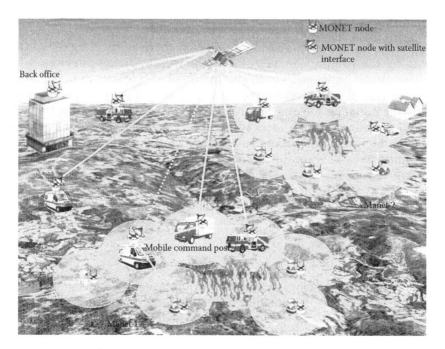

FIGURE 3.6
Disaster scenario.

3.6 Hardware and Software SDR Terminal

3.6.1 Hardware SDR Terminal

An analog phase consists of synthesizers, mixers, amplifiers, DACs, and ADCs with different RF specification, such as carrier bandwidth, frequency, transmission power, and modulation scheme. Digital phase contains CPU, application specific integrated circuits (ASICs), and I/O interfaces (e.g., digital filters and modems, digital up/down converters, digital filtering, signal generation, frequency mixing, channel codec, and speech codec).

3.6.2 Software's SDR Terminal

Radio function libraries: These groups define basic radio encompassing filter platforms for modem suites for the hardware commands controller.

Operating system and device driver: The operating system is completely track-to-switch with device driver platforms for each hardware controller such as a synthesizer, amplifier, and ADC.

Application platform: This platform complies the exact radio standard, such as global system for mobile communication (GSM), IS-95, or IMT-2000.

3.6.3 SDR Security

SDR safety is becoming increasingly important as both military wirelesses and commercial radio systems need to confirm that the communications are safe. Using SDR gives an

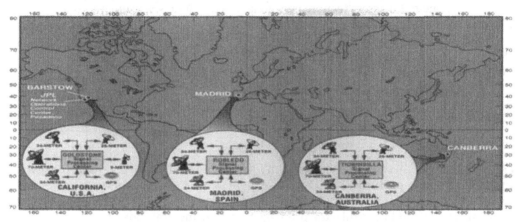

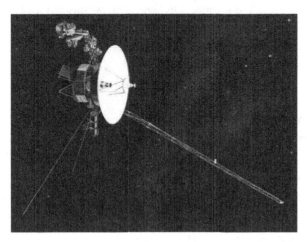

FIGURE 3.7
Space-communication scenario.

additional amount of safety, i.e., software surrounding the radio is very secure. SDRs can use the Internet as an intermediate medium to bring themselves up to date. However, this opens the SDR to malicious software that might revise the process of the radio or prevent it completely. Consequently, SDR software safety needs to be measured against malwares.

3.7 Conclusion

SDR works on a technology that will eventually bring an unlimited, compact traceability and adaptability to the upcoming systems. It defines system architecture for the optimization of wireless resource procedure and spectrum access and standardizes protocols for a later stage to enhance efficiency, measurements, and effectiveness within varied wireless networks in which devices operate on various air interfaces, using spectrum bands at maximum by means of next-generation radio capabilities. It provides instantaneous connection to more than one radio access technologies to access dynamic spectrum and disseminates decision making for radio resource in licensed and unlicensed bands. As many benefits as it provides, the technology still has a long way to go before it finds its way to cellular handsets that can use the absolute potential of SDR. SDR serves as an enabling technology for intelligent radios and multiple inputs multiple outputs (MIMOs).

Acknowledgments

I, A. Jayanthiladevi, would like to extend my gratefulness to the editor, Ashish Bagwari, who gave me this opportunity and Dr. P. Raj Chelliah, who suggested I write this chapter. I would also like to express gratitude to my research supervisor for his valuable guidance. At the outset, I would like to take the privilege to convey my gratitude to God, my parents, my husband, and my lovable daughter, Diyasre, who supported and cooperated a lot with me to complete this work on time.

References

1. Buddhikot, M. M., P. Kolody, S. Miller, K. Ryan, and J. Evans. 2005. DIMSUMNet: New directions in wireless networking using coordinated dynamic spectrum access. In: *Proceedings IEEE on Worlds of Wireless Mobile and Multimedia Networks, 2005*, Taormina, Greece. pp. 78–85. 9. O. Ileri, D. Samardzija,
2. Mandayam, N. B. 2005. Demand responsive pricing and competitive spectrum allocation via a spectrum server. In: *Proceedings IEEE Dynamic Spectrum Access Network, 2005*, Baltimore, MA. pp. 194–202.
3. The Institute for Telecommunications Sciences. (2008). *The History of SDR*. Available at: faculty .wiu.edu/Y-Kim2/ZL.ppt. Retrieved 9 December 2008.
4. Wikimedia Foundation Inc. (2008). *Software Defined Radio Wikipedia*. Available at: slideplayer .com/slide/6936109/. Retrieved 7 December 2008, from GNU Licensing.
5. Youngblood, G. (2002). *A Software Defined Radio for the Masses, Part I*. Available at: faculty.wiu .edu/Y-Kim2/ZL.ppt. Retrieved 9 December 2008.

Part II

Spectrum Sensing in CRN

4

Spectrum-Sensing Techniques in Cognitive Radio Networks: Achievements and Challenges

Aislan Gabriel Hernandes, Ricardo Tadashi Kobayashi, and Taufik Abrão

CONTENTS

4.1 Introduction

The usage of wireless communication resources, mainly energy and spectrum, has increased tremendously in the recent past. Considering its scarcity and misuse, spectrum becomes an even more important and challenging resource to deal with. Spectrum is a natural resource that has suffered even more limitation thanks to the growth of numerous services such as social networks, video streaming, and cloud storage. Another contributing factor is the geographical location of services. Indeed, there are many geographical areas where communication systems do not make usage of specific bandwidths (BWs) and/or these BWs are only partially used, featuring a misuse or inefficient use of the spectrum.

   One of the most important parameter related with the use of spectrum is the spectrum efficiency (SE). In the last few years, many techniques and methods have been proposed to improve the SE, including the capacity and performance of the wireless systems. A promising solution for this challenge is the cognitive radio (CR) concept [1] that allows licensed or primary users (PUs) and nonlicensed or secondary users (SUs) to share the same spectrum. In this scheme, SU accesses the spectrum of PU without causing harm to the PU operation; it is called the *underlay* scheme. Alternatively, the SU can occupy the licensed spectrum when the PU is absent, which is known as the *overlay* scheme; in this context, the SU is seen as an opportunistic user. CR has been one of the promising access methods for future 5G communications; it is an intelligent radio that can be reconfigured dynamically and basically operates in sensing and sharing the spectrum.

   Spectrum sensing (SS) is the ability of the radio systems to detect an idle portion of the spectrum or any busy licensed band that allows its usage for SU, depending on the constraints of the PU. Spectrum sharing is the momentary utilization of a portion of spectrum by SU without causing interference to the PU [2].

   During sensing, the CR must reliably detect the presence of PUs without causing any interference to them. There are many ways to detect the presence or absence of a PU in a portion of spectrum, starting with a hypothesis, constructing a statistic test, and, based on this, comparing the signals at a threshold level. The simplest and low computational complexity SS is by *energy detection*. The main disadvantage of the energy detection method is its high noise sensitivity. There are many other kinds of detectors, such as coherent detector [matched filter (MF)], feature detector [cyclostationary (CS)-based sensing], covariance matrix detector, and eigenvalue-based detector [3,4].

   Another important task carried out by CRs is the *spectrum handoff* (SH) [5]. Whenever a PU returns to its operation, the SU using the PU band must switch its channel to a free one, to avoid interfering the PU. This procedure should be implemented carefully to avoid disturbance to SU communication. There are two types of SHs: *reactive* and *proactive* [3]. In the reactive handoff, SU would sense other available channels when the PU returns and waste some time sensing the spectrum again. On the other hand, in the proactive handoff the SU has a list of candidate channels to access once the PU returns, i.e., the SU constructs a list of available channels and accumulates data records about the behavior of the PUs in order to predict which channels are going to be available for future access. The SH in CRNs depends on the behavior of the PUs. This is a major challenge since the PUs, behavior is random.

We can expand the concept of singleband CRNs (SB-CRNs) to multiband CRNs (MB-CRNs) [3]. MB-CRNs have recently received much attention from several research organizations, as they can significantly enhance the SUs throughput. With MB-CRNs, the SU not only has a set of candidate channels, but can also reduce handoff frequency and data interference due to the return of PUs.

MB-CRNs sensing can be proceeded by *serial-SS* or *parallel-SS techniques* [3]. In serial spectrum sensing (SS), any singleband (SB) detector using a reconfigurable bandpass filter (BPF) or a tunable oscillator sweeps the entire spectrum sequentially. In parallel SS, a filter and detector band structure working in parallel allows it to sense the entire spectrum more rapidly. In this chapter, we focus on the following MB-SS techniques: *angle-based sensing* (AS), *compressed sensing*, and *wavelet sensing*, which have gained more research interest and attention in the last few years [3].

Two hybrid schemes that can be used jointly with CRNs are *cooperative relays* [6] and *cooperative SUs* [3], which provide spatial diversity, i.e., analogous to multiple inputs multiple outputs (MIMOs). Through the use of cooperative networks, destructive effects of wireless channels, such as fading, path loss, and shadowing can be minimized. Spatial diversity of cooperative networks is called macrodiversity, since the distance between relays and/or SUs is in order of meters. On the other hand, spatial diversity of MIMO is called microdiversity because the distance between antennas is comparable with wavelengths, considering the carrier frequency.

There are many schemes and protocols in cooperative communication such as *relays, cooperative secondary users (coop-SUs)*, and *cooperative spectrum sensing (CSS)* [3]. The frequently used ones are *amplify-and-forward (AF)* and *decode-and-forward (DF)* [3] in the relay network, and *hard* and *soft* combined with *or-and-majority* rules in coop-SUs scheme. The AF relay is the simplest scheme which receives a signal version of the source node in a first time-slot, while an amplified version of it is sent by the relay node to the destination node in a second time-slot. This scheme is known as *transparent relaying protocol* because the relay does not modify the information represented by a known waveform. In contrast, the DF relay scheme decodes the received signal at relay node coming from the source node, and then re-encodes and retransmits it to the receiver node. This scheme is known as *regenerative relaying protocol* because the information (bits) or waveform (samples) is modified before being retransmitted by the relay node. This procedure requires digital baseband operations and thus more powerful hardware. The advantage of the AF relay scheme is its simplicity, but the disadvantage is the amplification of the input noise along with the source signal. The DF relay scheme has the advantage of decoding; therefore the noise is not amplified. The disadvantage of the DF relay scheme is that if the signal received by the source node is not decoded correctly, the cooperative communication has to be instantly interrupted.

In CSS scheme, *hard combiner* is simply the sum of decision of all SUs in the network, i.e., the SUs send the final one-bit decision to the other SUs. In *soft combining*, the SU shares its original sensing information or original statistical test weighted by a factor that matches the importance of the decision of each SU.

One of the most used transmission systems in conjunction with CR method is the *orthogonal frequency division multiplexing (OFDM)* because it allows more flexibility for spectrum allocation. OFDM technique splits a user data stream into several substreams, which are sent in parallel to several subcarriers, obtained by splitting the total BW in narrower channels. The OFDM for multiple access called *orthogonal frequency division multiple access (OFDMA)*, also known as multiuser OFDM (MU-OFDM), allows choosing which users will be allocated to which subcarriers in each time-slot. Currently, OFDMA technique is the basis of many operating technologies, e.g., IEEE 802.16 (WiMax) and 3GPP LTE-Advanced used in 4G systems [7,8].

Another important issue in current and future efficiency-based communication systems and methods is the *energy efficiency* (EE). In CRNs, improving EE poses a challenging problem, because it focuses on optimizing SE and EE jointly. What parameter needs to be sacrificed for the overall system to achieve satisfactory EE: QoS, fairness, PU interference increasing, network architecture, security?

In the CRN context, it is noteworthy that on the one hand, PUs put strict requirements on the interference and channel usage by the SUs; on the other hand, the SUs expect high QoS from the operator at a lower cost; finally, the operator desires to operate at low-operating and low-management costs [9], which represent a challenging and complex optimization problem.

The rest of this chapter is organized as follows. In Sections 4.2 through 4.2.3, the main concepts and principles associated with CRNs are explored. The main SB-SS detectors are discussed and compared in Section 4.3. Recent MB-CRNs concepts and methods are examined in Section 4.4, while cooperative CRNs are put into perspective in Section 4.5. Final remarks and perspectives are offered in Section 4.6. Lists of symbols and acronyms used across this chapter are shown in Tables 4.1 and 4.2, respectively.

TABLE 4.1

List of Symbols

Symbol	Note
α	Cyclic frequency
B	Bandwidth
C	Capacity
F	Frequency
Γ	Signal-to-noise ratio (SNR)
G	Effective throughput
$h_{r,d}$	Channel coefficient between relay and destination
$h_{s,d}$	Channel coefficient between source and destination
$h_{s,r}$	Channel coefficient between source and relay
H_0, H_1	Free and occupied channel hypotheses, respectively
Λ	Threshold
$n_{s,d}$	Addictive Gaussian noise between source and destination
$n_{s,r}$	Addictive Gaussian noise between source and relay
N	Number of samples
σ_n^2	Noise power
P	Power
P_d	Detection probability
P_f	False-alarm probability
ρ_{max}	Maximum eigenvalue
ρ_{min}	Minimum eigenvalue
S	Signal
$T(\cdot)$	Statistic test

TABLE 4.2

List of Acronyms

Acronym	Expansion
AF	Amplify-and-forward
AWGN	Additive white Gaussian noise
CS	Compressive sensing
CRN	Cognitive radio network
CWT	Continuous wavelet transform
CSS	Cyclic spectral density
DF	Decode-and-forward
ED	Energy detector
EE	Energy efficiency
MF	Matched filter
MIMOs	multiple inputs multiple outputs
MME	Maximum–minimum eigenvalue ratio
MB	Multiband
OFDM	Orthogonal frequency division multiplexing
OFDMA	Orthogonal frequency division multiple access
QoS	Quality of service
PSD	Power spectral density
PU	Primary user
ROC	Receiver operating characteristic
SB	Single band
SE	Spectral efficiency
SNR	Signal-to-noise ratio
SH	Spectrum handoff
SS	Spectrum sensing
SU	Secondary user
WMM	Wavelet modulus maxima
WMP	Wavelet multiple product
WMS	Wavelet multiple sum
WSS	Wavelet spectrum sensing

4.2 Spectrum Sensing: Concepts and Principles

Spectrum idles must be sensed by the SU for opportunistic spectrum access. Successful SS allows the overlay access scheme. Let us first consider the most simple case of SS, in which the channel can be used by its PU. From a given observation, the SU must determine whether or not the spectrum is occupied [3,4,10], which implies two hypotheses, i.e., when the channel is free and when it is occupied:

$$\begin{cases} H_0 : y = \eta \\ H_1 : y = x + \eta \end{cases} \tag{4.1}$$

When the channel is free, only additive noise will be observed on the SU side, i.e., $y = \eta$, characterizing the hypothesis H_0. However, if the channel is being used, the SU will sense the PU signal x plus the noise η, hence hypothesis H_1 will be taken. It is noteworthy that x

contains the message of the PU and effect of the wireless channel on it. To decide between the two hypotheses, the SU receiver evaluates a test statistics $T(y)$ based on its observed signal and compares it with a specific *threshold* λ:

$$\begin{cases} H_0 : T(y) < \lambda \\ H_1 : T(y) \geq \lambda. \end{cases} \qquad (4.2)$$

Thus, spectrum idles are identified when $T(y)$ is above its threshold and is considered free otherwise.

Although SS may seem a simple task, it still remains a challenging area for CRNs. Important and remaining open issues on SS include the following:

- A more reliable detector than the traditional detectors is required, because any missed-detection creates unacceptable interference among SUs and PUs.
- To identify a spectrum hole a wider BW needs to be sensed, e.g., 4G mobile communications use up to 20 MHz BW and one channel less than this cannot be used. Thus, different bands experience different signal propagation characteristics, while the design of a detector with suitable performance becomes a challenging task.
- The classical sensing/detection techniques may fail in CRNs, because the knowledge of PUs, parameters at SUs is restricted, while computational complexity and implementation cost are the other restricted factors.

4.2.1 SB-Sensing versus MB-Sensing Techniques

SB-sensing technique allows the SU to detect a PU in an SB-spectral sensing environment, with the possibility to use this band to transmit. This provides a better use of available spectrum, since it is a scarce resource nowadays. MB-sensing technique is the extension of SB sensing to many bands (Figure 4.1). The main benefit in operating under MB-SS is the increased system throughput while reducing the SH, which is challenging in CRNs. Indeed, when an SU needs higher throughput or has to maintain a certain quality of service (QoS), it may naturally transmit over a larger BW available by accessing multiple bands.

In MB sensing, the wideband spectrum is divided into M nonoverlapping subbands as shown in Figure 4.1. For simplicity, one can assign the same BW value for all subbands,

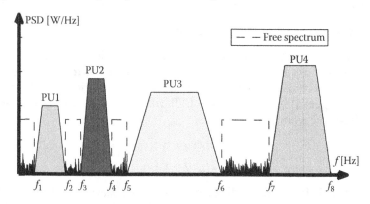

FIGURE 4.1
Multiband spectrum, considering $M = 8$ and unequal subband sizes, i.e., $B_m \neq B_n$.

$B_1 = B_2 = \cdots = B_M$. The main task for the SU sensing is to determine which subchannels are available for the spectrum access. This is, in general, a challenging task, since the available bands are not necessarily contiguous, and the activity of the PUs might be correlated across these bands.* In addition, each particular band is considered occupied even if only a small portion of it is being used.

In Figure 4.1, the wideband spectrum is divided into unequal subband (or subchannel) sizes. Thus, the problem becomes an MB detection problem. Hence, when an SU needs to minimize the data interruptions due to return of PUs to their respective priority bands, a seamless handoff from one band to another becomes a vital feature to guarantee QoS. As a consequence, in MB-CRN the SUs are provided with backup channels, since such channels have already been accessed. Hence, under MB-CRNs, SUs do not only have a set of candidate channels, but MB mode also allows handoff rate reduction.

4.2.2 Noncooperative versus Cooperative Sensing Techniques

- CSS is conceived and implemented to enhance the performance of SB noncooperative detectors. In CSS, the SUs help the network, sensing the spectrum and sharing the sensing results with other SUs. Cooperative sensing scheduling is the case where sensing scheduling is performed in a way that leverages the sensing performance by selecting the best set of cooperating SUs for each channel. On the other hand, in noncooperative wireless networks the SS procedure may be impaired because of the fading channel effects or due to unknown noise. There are many methods to combine the signals arriving at the receiver. In this chapter we discuss two classes of cooperative schemes: cooperative relay and cooperative SS.

- The cooperative relay scheme allows increasing the diversity using relay node, which retransmits the signal to the destination. Such methods boost the probability of detection and lower the probability of false alarm by utilizing the diversity of the measurements from multiple SUs. In addition, *or-and-majority* rules with hard or soft combining are usually deployed to construct hypothesis testing in CSS.

- Even considering the large number of channels to be sensed and the minimum number of sensing SUs for each channel, plenty of SUs should perform sensing all over the service area at any time. However, if almost all SUs perform sensing continuously, enormous energy expenditure is expected, reducing the SU battery lifetime. Therefore, the channels to be sensed as well as the set of SUs that should sense each channel must be selected carefully [11]. Cooperative sensing procedures are responsible to do this selection effectively in order to improve the performance of the CRNs. Cooperative and relay cooperation techniques for SS are treated in more details in Section 1.5.

4.2.3 Spectrum Handoff

In the context of CRNs, the SH consists band changing by the SUs due to return of PUs at the licensed band that was being momentarily used by the SUs. When this happens, there are two possible scenarios. First, the SU remains in the band on silent mode until the PU evacuates the band. Second, the SU moves to another channel. The first scenario is inefficient

---

* For instance, the primary users in wireless local area networks (WLAN) and broadcast television.

because the SU does not know how long the PU would be active. In the second scenario, two different methods can be implemented for sensing the band: reactive and proactive.

In the reactive method, the SU would again sense to detect other available channels when the PU returns. This way the SU wastes some time sensing the spectrum even if the sensing occurs instantaneously. The target channels are sensed in a demand manner. In the proactive method, the SU makes the target channel ready for SH before transmitting any information. In this method, the SU periodically observes all channels to obtain channel statistics and detects the possible candidate set of idle channels.

In the context of CRNs, the SU throughput and handoff delays are two major parameters of interest for comparing different handoff techniques. The main feature of the spectrum searchers is to initiate a fast and smooth handoff, to avoid performance degradation while reducing the time during SH, namely handoff delay.

Another way to define SH is the cell-based SH, i.e., in the macroview context. There are two major types of SHs in the cell-based type: *intracell* SH and *intercell* SH. The intracell SH occurs commonly in the wireless regional area networks' (WRANs) internal cell, when the PU appears or when the SU QoS decreases in a specific band. On the other hand, the intercell SH generally occurs when the mobile cognitive user (SU) is moving from one WRAN cell to another WRAN cell.

Efficient schemes for fast and smooth handoff are discussed in [5,12]. Generally, the SH degrades SUs performance because of the interruptions that cause delay in the transmissions. Maheshwari and Singh [5] discuss new techniques that allows a fast and smooth SH, such as those based on *queueing theory, fuzzy-based, neural networks, support vector machines* (SVMs), and *hidden Markov model* (HMM).

4.3 SB-SS Detectors

This section explores the fundamentals of SB-SS, covering the most widespread sensing techniques found in literature, including energy detector (ED), MF, covariance detector, CS detector, and eigenvalue detector. The features, operation, and performance are covered under these classical SS techniques. Sensing performance will be discussed through Monte Carlo simulations and theoretical performance will be presented, whenever it is available considering, for simplicity, additive white Gaussian noise (AWGN) channels.

For this section, let us consider the following model for SS

$$\begin{cases} H_0 : & \mathbf{y}(n) = \boldsymbol{\eta}(n) \\ H_1 : & \mathbf{y}(n) = \mathbf{x}(n) + \boldsymbol{\eta}(n) \end{cases}, \tag{4.3}$$

where $\mathbf{y}(n)$ is a vector containing N observations made at distinct times by the SU receiver, $\mathbf{x}(n)$ is the PU signal, which is probably affected by the channel between the PU and SU, and $\boldsymbol{\eta}(n)$ is the zero mean, variance σ^2, n-power AWGN on the SU receiver. In this case, the terms on Equation 4.3 are

$$\mathbf{y}(n) = [\mathrm{y}(n)\mathrm{y}(n-1)\mathrm{y}(n-2)...\mathrm{y}(n-N+1)]^T,$$

$$\mathbf{x}(n) = [\mathrm{x}(n)\mathrm{x}(n-1)\mathrm{x}(n-2)...\mathrm{x}(n-N+1)]^T, \tag{4.4}$$

$$\boldsymbol{\eta}(n) = [\eta(n)\eta(n-1)\eta(n-2)...\eta(n-N+1)]^T.$$

Hence, SS is carried out by the SU through its observations $\mathbf{y}(n)$, which will be compared with a specific threshold λ

$$\begin{cases} H_0 : T\big(\mathbf{y}(n)\big) < \lambda \\ H_1 : T\big(\mathbf{y}(n)\big) \geq \lambda \end{cases}, \tag{4.5}$$

where H_0 implies on free spectrum and H_1 on occupied channel. When the threshold is reached, i.e., $(y(n) > \lambda$, there are two possible outcomes in an SS:

- $P_f = \Pr\big(\mathbf{y}(n) > \lambda \,|\, H_0\big)$, the false-alarm probability, i.e., the probability of an SU not detecting an idle channel. Misleading spectrum detection comes, mainly, from noisy measurements
- $P_d = \Pr\big(\mathbf{y}(n) > \lambda \,|\, H_1\big)$, detection probability, i.e, correct detection probability

The detector performance can be characterized by curves. Hence, it is straightforward that a spectrum sensor should operate with a high detection and low false-alarm probabilities. The most common way of characterizing an SS technique is through receiver operating characteristic (ROC), which is a $P_d \times P_f$ curve. Given the definitions of P_f and P_d, one can conclude that it is very desirable that an ROC curve converges to a step function.

In the following section, the main SS detectors are characterized and compared in terms of ROC curves. Hereafter, for the sake of simplicity, let us drop the discrete time index (n), resulting in $y(n) = y$, $x(n) = x$, and $\boldsymbol{\eta}(n) = \boldsymbol{\eta}$.

4.3.1 Energy Detector

When the SU does not have prior knowledge of the PU's transmitted signal, the ED is a suitable choice. It simply computes the energy of the received signal over a time period associated with N samples and within the predefined BW. This detector does not require the channel gains and other parameter knowledge or estimates, while holds a low design cost, as shown in Figure 4.2. However, its performance degrades substantially with noise power and/or increasing interference, i.e., when the ED operates in a low SNR region.

4.3.1.1 Statistic Test and Threshold Level

The test statistics for a typical ED is expressed as [3]

$$T^{ED}\big(\mathbf{y}\big) = \frac{\|\mathbf{y}\|_F^2}{\sigma_n^2}, \tag{4.6}$$

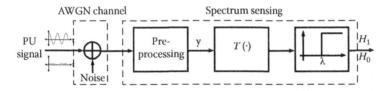

FIGURE 4.2
General singleband detection topology for spectral sensing purpose.

where $\|y\|_F^2$ is the Frobenius norm, N is the number of samples, and σ^2 is the noise power. The numerator of Equation 4.6 represents the received energy power, ε_y. In practice, one cannot dispose off the actual received energy power. Instead, the ED uses the following approximation [13]

$$\hat{\varepsilon}_y = \frac{1}{N}\sum_{k=1}^{N}|y(k)|^2,$$

where as the number of samples N becomes large, by the law of the large numbers, $\hat{\varepsilon}_y$ converges to ε_y. After evaluating the $T^{ED}(\mathbf{y})$, it is compared with a threshold to satisfy a given target false-alarm probability P_f and a given SNR γ

$$\lambda^{ED}(\mathbf{y}) = \left[Q^{-1}(P_f) + 1\right]\gamma, \tag{4.7}$$

where $Q^{-1}(\cdot)$ is the inverse Q function.

4.3.1.2 Performance Analysis

Considering AWGN channels and a given threshold λ, specified by SNR, the number of samples N and target false-alarm probability P_f, the theoretical detection probability can be described as [4]

$$P_d^{ED} = \frac{\Gamma\left(NB, \dfrac{\lambda}{2}\right)}{\Gamma(NB)}, \tag{4.8}$$

where B is the total BW, the function $\Gamma(\cdot,\cdot)$ is the incomplete Gamma function. However, through the central limit theorem, the detection probability can be simplified to

$$P_d^{ED} = Q\left(\frac{1}{\sqrt{2\gamma+1}}\left[Q^{-1}(P_f) - \sqrt{N}\gamma\right]\right). \tag{4.9}$$

The performance of ED in SS applications under SNR $\in [-30; -15]$ [dB] is depicted in Figure 4.3. One can observe that with $N = 1000$ samples, the ROC curve (a) is far from the ideal, even for SNR $= -15$ [dB]. It should be remarked that spectrum sensors should operate reliably under low SNR, in order to avoid interference in case of misleading SS. In Figure 4.3(b), it can be seen that high detection probabilities are reached for SNR values superior to -10 [dB]; hence, more samples are required if the detector is to operate under lower SNR values. Finally, in Figure 4.3(c) it can be pointed out that, setting a low false-alarm probability, the ED requires around $N = 10^4$ samples to reach high detection probability, when operating under SNR values higher than -15 [dB].

4.3.2 Matched Filter

When the SU has a perfect knowledge of PU signal structure, e.g., modulation type, code, and wave shape, it can correlate the receive signal with a known copy of the PU signal. In this scenario, the MF or coherent receiver is the optimal detector which maximizes the SNR in the presence of AWGN. However, its computational complexity is excessively high while its performance decreases as the channel response changes quickly, i.e., under short coherence time in fading channels scenarios.

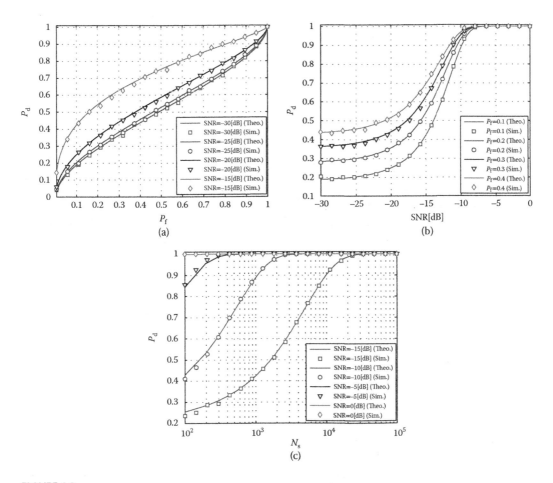

FIGURE 4.3
Energy-detector performance in terms of detection and false-alarm probabilities, as well as number of samples N, operating under AWGN channels. (a) ROC @ $N = 1000$; (b) $P_d \times$ SNR, @ $N = 1000$; (c) $P_d \times N$, @ $P_f = 0.1$.

4.3.2.1 Statistic Test and Threshold Level

To determine whether or not the spectrum is occupied, the MF evaluates the following test [3]

$$T^{MF}(\mathbf{y}) = \Re\left[\mathbf{x}^H \mathbf{y}\right], \tag{4.10}$$

which correlates the transmitted signal with the received one, where $\Re[\cdot]$ is the operator real part and $(\cdot)^H$ is the Hermitian operator. After calculating $T^{MF}(\mathbf{y})$, the detection sensing compares it to a specific threshold for the MF, which is defined, for AWGN, as

$$\lambda^{MF} = Q^{-1}(P_f)\sqrt{N\gamma}. \tag{4.11}$$

Thus, the MF threshold is a function of the number of samples N, SNR γ and the target false-alarm probability P_f. Figure 4.2 depicts a general topology for the MF detection, with statistical test and threshold given by (10) and (11), respectively.

4.3.2.2 Performance Analysis

If the the MF-SS detector operates under AWGN scenarios, the theoretical detection can be expressed by [4]

$$P_d^{MF} = Q\left(\frac{\lambda^{MF}}{\sqrt{N}\gamma}\right).$$

(4.12)

Figure 4.4 shows the MF performance considering different perspectives, i.e., graphs of the ROC, $P_d \times$ SNR and $P_d \times N$. In these figures, continuous lines represent the theoretical performance, while markers represent simulated performance. In (a), one can observe that the ROC converges rapidly to its optimal point, e.g., with a SNR $\gamma = -20$ [dB] the probability of detection is higher than 90%, while the probability of false alarm is just 5%. In (b), it can be observed that the probability of detection converges to 1 around $\gamma = -20$ [dB], considering only $N = 1000$ samples. Also, (c) shows that $N = 1000$ samples are enough to perform reliable SS in such a way that false-alarm probability is quite low.

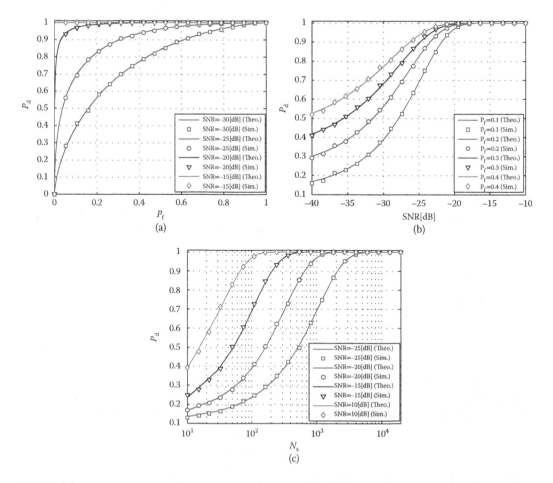

FIGURE 4.4
Matched-filter performance operating under AWGN channels. (a) ROC @ $N_s = 1000$; (b) $P_d \times$ SNR, @ $N_s = 1000$; (c) $P_d \times N_s$, @ $P_f = 0.1$.

4.3.3 CS Feature Detector

To perform a reliable SS, the CS detector takes advantage of the knowledge of the second moment statistics of the PU signal. If the PU signal presents periodic statistical properties, i.e., periodic mean and autocorrelation, the received signal on the SU side also features periodic properties in the CS sense. Since white noise is, generally, uncorrelated in time, this detector can easily verify if a CS signal is present on a given spectrum band. However, if the noise is correlated in time, CS detection may require a higher sample rate, which is a concerning drawback, as it increases the sensing complexity. Hence, if the PU signal is known to present statistical periodicity, CS detection can be used to perform SS in a CRN.

In order to determine whether or not a signal is CS, the spectral correlation density or cyclic spectral density (CSD) function must be evaluated. The evaluation of CSD is based on the cyclic autocorrelation of the signal y

$$R_y^\alpha(\tau) = \mathbb{E}\left[\mathbf{y}(t)\mathbf{y}(t)e^{j2\pi\alpha n}\right], \tag{4.13}$$

which forms the following Fourier transform pair

$$S_y^\alpha(f) = \int_{-\infty}^{\infty} R_y^\alpha(\tau)e^{-j2\pi f\tau}\, d\tau, \tag{4.14}$$

where S_y^α is the power spectral density (PSD) of $\mathbf{y}(t)$. Alternatively, the SCD function can be obtained, for example, using the FFT accumulation method (FAM) [14], which uses two FFT blocks to estimate the SCD of a given signal in order to get a better SCD approximation.

4.3.3.1 Statistic Test and Threshold Level

The CS statistics test and threshold for the SS problem under AWG noise are given, respectively, by [15]

$$T^{CS}(\mathbf{y}) = \max\left(S_y^\alpha(f)\right), \tag{4.15}$$

and

$$\lambda^{CS} = \sqrt{\frac{\sigma_n^4}{2\sigma_x^2}\ln\left(\frac{1}{P_f}\right)}, \tag{4.16}$$

where σ_x^2 is PU signal variance and σ_n^2 is the noise variance.

4.3.3.2 Performance Analysis

The detection probability is defined as [15]

$$P_d^{CS} = Q_m\left(\frac{\max\left(S_y^\alpha(f)\right)}{\sigma_1}, \frac{\lambda^{CS}}{\sigma_1}\right), \tag{4.17}$$

where $Q_m(\cdot,\cdot)$ is the generalized Marcum Q-function [16] and variance

$$\sigma_1^2 = \frac{\sigma_n^4}{2\sigma_x^2}\left(1 + \frac{S_x\left(f+\frac{\alpha}{2}\right)}{\sigma_n^2} + \frac{S_x\left(f-\frac{\alpha}{2}\right)}{\sigma_n^2}\right).$$

Figure 4.5 shows the CS-simulated performance considering different parameters, i.e., graphs of ROC, $P_d \times$ SNR and $P_d \times N$. In (a), the ROC considering $\gamma = -15$ dB and $P_f = 0.1$ shows a probability of detection $P_d \simeq 0.53$. Besides, in (b) if the $P_f = 0.1$ and $\gamma = -15$ dB, the probability of detection is around $P_d \simeq 0.5$, and for a SNR $\gamma \leq -15$ dB the performance decreases rapidly, becoming very poor around $\gamma \approx -30$ dB. Finally, in (c) the CS detector shows that it must operate under $N = 10^5$ samples for a SNR of $\gamma = -15$ dB in order to achieve a near-optimal performance, i.e., operate with greater number of samples and excessive computational processing.

4.3.4 Covariance Matrix Detector

Covariance sensing determines whether or not the channel is being occupied, based on the covariance matrix of the observed signal, considering L temporal lags. In this case

$$\begin{cases} H_0 : \hat{\mathbf{y}}(n) = \hat{\boldsymbol{\eta}}(n) \\ H_1 : \hat{\mathbf{y}}(n) = \hat{\mathbf{x}}(n) + \hat{\boldsymbol{\eta}}(n) \end{cases}, \tag{4.18}$$

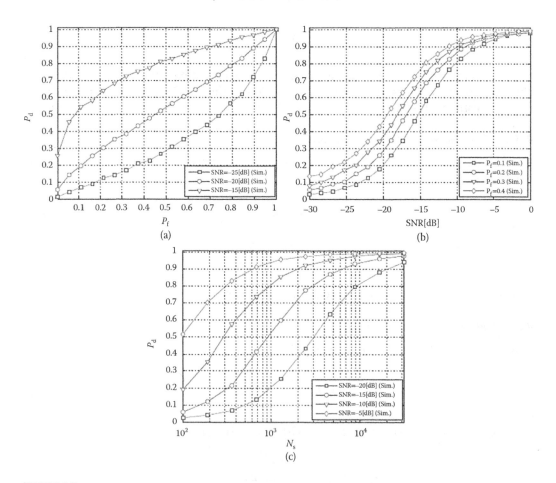

FIGURE 4.5

Cyclostationary-detector performance under AWGN channels. (a) ROC @ $N_s = 1000$; (b) $P_d \times$ SNR, @ $N_s = 1000$; (c) $P_d \times N_s$, @ $P_f = 0.1$.

where $\hat{y}(n)$, $\hat{x}(n)$ and $\hat{\eta}(n)$ are windowed versions, of length* $N \leq L$, of the received SU signal, PU signal x and the SU side noise η. More specifically

$$\hat{\mathbf{y}}(n) = \left[y(n)\ y(n-1)\ y(n-2),\ldots,y(n-L+1) \right]^T,$$

$$\hat{\mathbf{x}}(n) = \left[x(n)\ x(n-1)\ x(n-2),\ldots,x(n-L+1) \right]^T, \qquad (4.19)$$

$$\hat{\mathbf{n}}(n) = \left[\eta(n)\ \eta(n-1)\ \eta(n-2),\ldots,\eta(n-L+1) \right]^T.$$

Since SS is proceeded with a finite number of samples, the covariance matrix of $\mathbf{y}$ can only be estimated. The reason for windowing $\mathbf{y}$ into $\hat{\mathbf{y}}$ is to obtain a better covariance matrix estimate just for L lags, instead of a poor covariance matrix over N lags. Hence, L is associated with the covariance matrix estimation quality and is usually referred as the smoothing factor. Considering these observations, we define the following estimated covariance matrices

$$\mathbf{R}_y(N) = \frac{1}{N} \sum_{n=L-1}^{L-2+N} \hat{\mathbf{y}}(n)\hat{\mathbf{y}}(n)^H, \qquad (4.20)$$

and

$$\mathbf{R}_x(N) = \frac{1}{N} \sum_{n=L-1}^{L-2+N} \hat{\mathbf{x}}(n)\hat{\mathbf{x}}(n)^H. \qquad (4.21)$$

Finally, taking the noise as uncorrelated in time

$$\mathbf{R}_y = \mathbf{R}_x + \sigma_n^2 \mathbf{I}_L. \qquad (4.22)$$

It is known that x is probably correlated in time,[†] thus $\mathbf{R}_x$ is not diagonal. Hence, covariance-based detection verifies if the covariance matrix of the received signal is diagonal or not.

4.3.4.1 Statistic Test and Threshold Level

Based on the previous observations, a straightforward test is

$$T^{\text{COV}}(\mathbf{y}) = \frac{T_1}{T_2}, \qquad (4.23)$$

where the expressions for T_1 and T_2 are given by

$$T_1 = \frac{1}{L} \sum_{\substack{n=1 \\ m=1}}^{L} |r_{nm}|, \qquad (4.24)$$

and

$$T_2 = \frac{1}{L} \sum_{n=1}^{L} |r_{nn}|. \qquad (4.25)$$

Thus, if $T_1/T_2 \geq \lambda^{\text{COV}}$ the spectrum is occupied and if $T_1/T_2 < \lambda^{\text{COV}}$ it is idle. Finally, given a target false-alarm probability, the threshold can be obtained as

---

* Since $\hat{\mathbf{y}}(n)$ is a windowed version of y, $L \leq N$.
† Mainly due to the carriers of transmitted signals and due to time dispersion introduced by the channel (multi-tap channel).

$$\lambda^{COV} = \frac{1+(L-1)\sqrt{(2/N\pi)}}{1-Q^{-1}(P_f)\sqrt{(2/\pi)}}.$$ (4.26)

4.3.4.2 Performance Analysis

Though many analytical formulas for covariance SS performance are available in the literature, unfortunately, such formulas are just approximated expressions. Zeng [17] proposed the following approximation for the probability of detection of covariance detector

$$P_d^{COV} \cong 1 - Q\left(\frac{\frac{1}{\lambda^{COV}} + \frac{\gamma Y_L}{\gamma+1} - 1}{\sqrt{2/N}}\right),$$ (4.27)

where

$$Y_L = \frac{2}{L}\sum_{l=1}^{L-1}\frac{(L-l)\mathbb{E}\left[x(n)x(n-l)\right]}{\sigma_x^2},$$ (4.28)

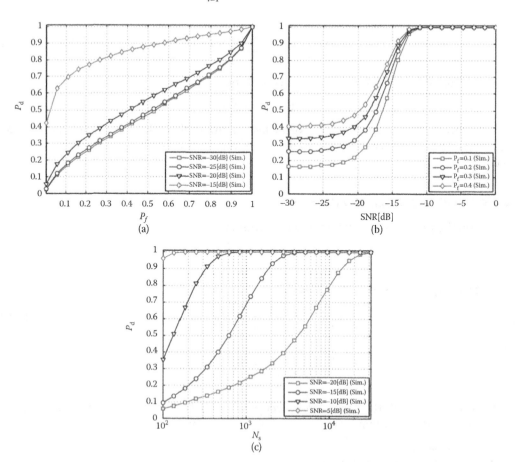

FIGURE 4.6
Covariance detector performance. (a) ROC @ $N_s = 1000$; (b) $P_d \times$ SNR, @ $N_s = 1000$; (c) $P_d \times N_s$, @ $P_f = 0.1$.

is a measure of temporal correlation of the PU signal. Since the analytical performance available in the literature is inaccurate, next section will present only simulation results. Figure 4.6 depicts the performance of the covariance detector. First, it can be observed in (a) and (b) that the detection probability may not be as high as expected for SNR lower than $\gamma = -15$ [dB]. It should be pointed out that the covariance detector does not require SNR estimates; however, if the second statistical moment is poorly estimated, the performance of the covariance detector will be impacted negatively. Through Fig. 4.6(c) one can see that $N = 2000$ samples are enough to reach a high detection probability (≥ 0.9), given 10% of false alarm and $\gamma = -15$ [dB].

4.3.5 Eigenvalue Detector

The eigenvalue detector can exploit the eigenvalue structure of the covariance matrix of PUs signals. The ratio between the maximum and minimum eigenvalue of the covariance matrix of receiver signal vector (PUs signal vector) is compared with a specific threshold. Nevertheless, if the correlation of the PUs signal is zero (white noise feature), the detection may fail.

The eigenvalues of a covariance matrix of a signal can reveal some of its characteristics. If the eigenvalues are similar, it is very likely that the matrix is well-behaved, tending to a diagonal matrix. The eigenvalue detector exploits this feature, i.e., for the idle channel, a diagonal $\mathbf{R_y}$ matrix will be generated due to white noise temporal decorrelation feature for lags other than zero.

4.3.5.1 Statistic Test and Threshold Level

First, the SU must estimate the correlation matrix of $\mathbf{y}$ using Equation 4.20. Then the eigenvalues of $\mathbf{R_y}$ are evaluated in order to proceed with the test, which is given by the maximum–minimum eigenvalue (MME) ratio

$$T^{\text{MME}}\left(\mathbf{y}\right) = \frac{\rho_{\max}}{\rho_{\min}}, \tag{4.29}$$

where $\rho_{\max}$ is the maximum and $\rho_{\min}$ is the minimum eigenvalue of covariance matrix of the received signal. Fixing a target false-alarm probability, the threshold for this sensing technique is written as [18]

$$\lambda^{\text{MME}} = \left(\frac{\sqrt{N}+\sqrt{L}}{\sqrt{N}-\sqrt{L}}\right)^2\left(1+\frac{\left(\sqrt{N}+\sqrt{L}\right)^{-\frac{2}{3}}}{(NL)^{\frac{1}{6}}}F_1^{-1}\left(1-P_f\right)\right), \tag{4.30}$$

where $F_1(\cdot)$ is the cumulative distribution function (CDF) of Tracy–Widom distribution.*

4.3.5.2 Performance Analysis

For the MME test, the detection probability is given by

$$P_f^{\text{MME}} = 1 - F_1\left(\frac{\lambda^{\text{MME}}\left(\sqrt{N}-\sqrt{L}\right)^2-\mu}{\nu}\right), \tag{4.31}$$

---

* Tracy–Widom distribution is the limiting law of the largest eigenvalues of random matrices and has no closed form for the CDF function [19,20].

where $\mu = \left(\sqrt{N-1} + \sqrt{L}\right)^2$ and $\nu = \left(\sqrt{N-1} + \sqrt{L}\right)\left(\dfrac{1}{\sqrt{N-1}} + \dfrac{1}{\sqrt{L}}\right)^{1/3}$. Numerical results performance for eigenvalue detector are presented in Figure 4.7. It can be observed through Figure 4.7(a) and (b) that the detection probabilities converge rapidly for $\gamma \geq -15$ [dB], while (c) corroborates that $N = 1000$ samples are enough to perform a reliable SS, given a target false-alarm probability as low as 10%.

4.3.6 Performance Comparison of SB-SS Methods

- There is no detector to confirm that the performance is better than others in all channel and system scenarios. The choice of the detector depends on many factors, such as how much information SU has about the PU signal, SNR level, and signal processing resource availability.

- ED is highly indicated when no prior knowledge about the PU is available and when the performance is not much affected by uncertain noise, i.e., the system

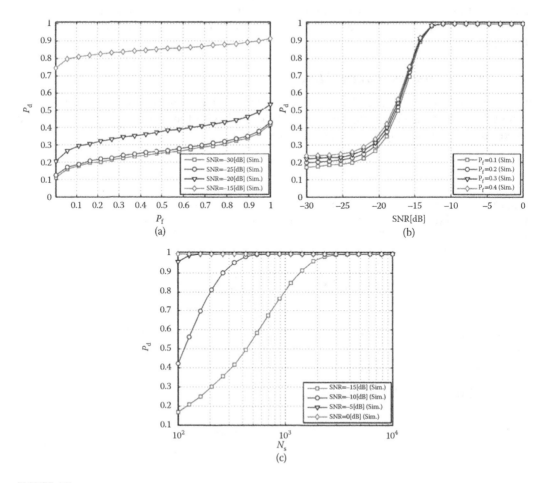

FIGURE 4.7
Eigenvalue detector numerical simulation performance under AWGN channels. (a) ROC @ N_s = 1000; (b) $P_d \times$ SNR, @ N_s = 1000; (c) $P_d \times N_s$, @ P_f = 0.1.

operates in not-so-low SNR. This detector results in low computational complexity compared with other SS detectors analyzed in this chapter.

- The MF (coherent detector) is used when the SU has full knowledge of the PU signal, i.e., when the SU knows about modulation, wave format, codification, and other PU features.

- A CS detector is used when the SNR is quite low and knowledge regarding the PU signal is partial. In this situation, the CS detector has better performance and robustness, substituting ED with advantage in performance. However, this detector has a high computational complexity and some parameters must be known by the detector, such as cycle prefix or cycle frequency. In addition, the PU signal must present the CS statistical properties.

- Covariance matrix (cov) detector is based on the estimated covariance matrix of the PU signal. Similar to CS, eigenvalue, and MF detectors, the cov spectral sensing detector has the ability to distinguish the PU signal from other signals, such as other SUs. No other information a priori of signal, channel, and noise is necessary.

- Eigenvalue detector is also based on the estimated covariance matrix of PU signal. The difference between (cov) detector is given by the statistic test. The statistic test of eigenvalue detector is determined only by the ratio of maximum and minimum eigenvalues. Table 4.3 summaries the main characteristics of the principal SB-SS methods in CRNs.

Figure 4.8 shows the numerical performance analysis comparing all the SB detectors treated in this chapter. In (a), the sample number is $N = 1000$ and SNR is fixed as $\gamma = -15[dB]$ which are realistic values that can be deployed in practical scenarios of CRNs. One can observe that the ED has the worst performance among all the detectors until $P_f = 0.6$. On the other hand, the eigenvalue detector has better performance than the covariance detector until $P_f = 0.15$, when the covariance detector is replaced by better performance than the eigenvalue detector. The covariance detector has better performance than ED for all values of P_f. As expected, the MF detector has the optimal performance, because the system is operating under AWGN scenarios.

TABLE 4.3

Singleband Spectrum-Sensing Detector Comparison

SS detectors	Required Knowledge		Identify PU From		Remark
	σ_n^2	PU Signal, x	Noise	Other Signals	
Energy	✓		Limited by SNR		Simple method
MF		✓	✓	✓	Max. SNR under AWGN
Cyclostationary		✓	✓	✓	High sensing time
Covariance			✓	✓	Require reliable estimates of covariance matrix
Eigenvalue			✓	✓	Performance similar to COV detector

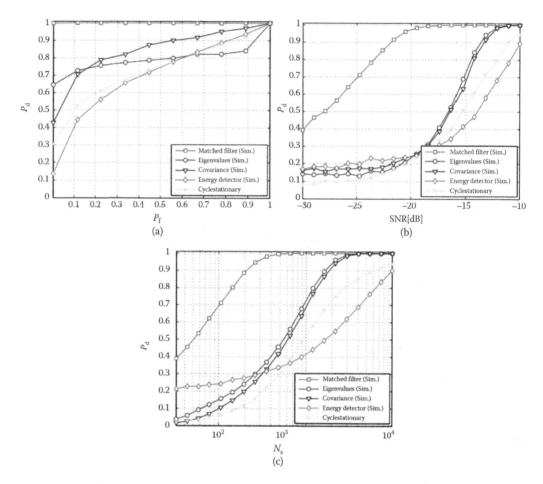

FIGURE 4.8
Comparison of spectrum-sensing techniques operating under AWGN channels. (a) ROC @ N_s = 1000, SNR = −15 dB; (b) $P_d \times$ SNR, @ N_s = 1000, P_f = 0.1; (c) $P_d \times N_s$, @ P_f = 0.1, SNR = −15 dB.

In Figure 4.8(b), sample number is N = 1000 and false-alarm probability is fixed as P_f = 0.1, which are the real parameter values found in a practical system configurations. Until γ = −20 dB the ED is slightly better than the covariance detector, which in turn is better than eigenvalue detector. After SNR = −20 dB, ED becomes the worst detector and the eigenvalue and covariance present equivalent performance, with eigenvalue slightly better than covariance detector. Once again, the MF has the best performance, even for very low SNR values, demonstrating satisfactory operation for a wide range of low SNR values, i.e., $\gamma \geq$ −22 [dB].

In Figure 4.8(c), the false-alarm probability is fixed as P_f = 0.1 and the SNR in γ = −15 dB; indeed, we are interested in determining the minimum number of samples with which SS detectors can operate satisfactorily. For these parameters, the CS, eigenvalue, and covariance detectors give poor performance under a lower number of samples $N \in$ [300; 500] samples, but the ED results in a better performance in terms of detection probability. For medium–high values of samples, $N \in$ [700; 2000], the ED gives the worst performance among all. The eigenvalue and covariance have approximate performances, with the eigenvalue being slightly better than the covariance detector. For high values of samples,

$N = 3000$, the eigenvalue, covariance, and even CS detector result in good performance. The best performance is obtained with MF with lower number of samples $N_s = 500$. For each chosen parameter ($P_{f,\,SNR}$), the number of samples (N) impacts on the performance and complexity of the detector.

4.4 MB Cognitive Radio Networks

MB-CRNs have recently caught the attention of several researcher organizations, since MB techniques can significantly enhance the SU's throughput. For example, the *ultrawideband* (UWB) channel can be divided in multiple subchannels and the sensing problem becomes an MB detection problem. Alternatively, MB sensing can be seen in an OFDMA perspective, where each subchannel is treated as subband sensing.

Another advantage of MB-CRNs is that they provide simultaneous sensing to the SUs and access to multiple channels, reducing the handoff frequency, i.e., diminishing the SUs, transmission interruptions. In addition, with MB-CRNs, the SU not only has a set of candidates channels, but reduces handoff frequency which generates data interference upon return of the PU.

CRNs deploy MB mode when the SUs aim is to achieve higher throughput or keep the QoS without interfering the PUs.

4.4.1 MB Sensing Problem

Spectrum idles must be sensed by the SU for opportunistic spectrum access by expanding spectrum-sensing techniques to MB mode. Let us consider a classical binary hypothesis testing problem

$$\begin{cases} H_{0,m} : \mathbf{y}_m = \mathbf{n}_m \\ H_{1,m} : \mathbf{y}_m = x_m + \mathbf{n}_m \end{cases}, \tag{4.32}$$

where m is the individual subchannel of a wideband consisting M subchannels in total and $\mathbf{y}_m = [y_m(1), y_m(2), ..., y_m(N)]^T$ is the N number of samples of the received signal at the SU receiver in subband m; transmitted PU signal in the same subband m is $\mathbf{x}_m = [x_m(1), x_m(2), ..., x_m(N)]^T$; and $\mathbf{n}_m$ is the AWGN noise vector sample with $n_m \sim N(0, \sigma^2; {}_n I)$.

In order to decide between absence or presence of PU signal hypotheses, H_0 and H_1 on subchannel m, one can compare a test statistics $T(\mathbf{y}_m)$ with a default threshold λ

$$\begin{cases} H_{0,m} : T(\mathbf{y}_m) < \lambda \\ H_{1,m} : T(\mathbf{y}_m) \geq \lambda \end{cases}. \tag{4.33}$$

Spectrum idles are identified when $H_{0,m}$ is true. When the PU signal is detected, the hypothesis $H_{1,m}$ is true.

There are many techniques to use MB-CRNs in sensing, such as serial spectrum-sensing techniques, parallel spectrum-sensing techniques, wavelet sensing, compressed sensing, and AS. However, few important issues still remain open in MB-CRNs, such as trade-off between sensing time and throughput [3]. In the next section, we will discuss the last three techniques.

4.4.2 Wavelet Spectrum Sensing

Continuous wavelet transform (CWT) in the spectrum-sensing context was firstly deployed by Tian and Giannakis (2006) [21], who showed how to identify the edges (or boundaries) of subchannels and how to estimate the PUs allocated to each subchannel of a wideband spectrum [22–26].

This mode of spectrum sensing is employed when the SU has no knowledge of the number of subbands M, associated with subbands $B_1, B_2, \ldots, B_M$ B_2 B_M, and the correspondent localization of frequencies $f_1, f_2, \ldots, f_M$, where the mth subband is defined as $B_m = f_m - f_{m-1}$ (Figure 4.1). In this kind of sensing, the CWT [27] is deployed due to its suitable properties, which is enabled to search the boundaries of spectral occupancy of PU signals across the entire subband set.

CWT has the ability to construct a time–frequency representation of a signal that offers a very good simultaneous localization of time and frequency. If $y_m(t)$ is a received signal, $s > 0$ and r are the scaling and shifting factors respectively, with $s \in R^+$ and $r \in R$, the CWT is defined as [27]

$$w_{y_m} = \frac{1}{\sqrt{|s|}} \int_{-\infty}^{\infty} y_m(t) \psi\left(\frac{t-r}{s}\right) dt, \tag{4.34}$$

where $\psi(t)$ is a continuous function called the mother function with $s = 1$ and $r = 0$. Daughter functions are originated from the mother function with $s \neq 1$ and $r \neq 0$, i.e., functions built from scaled and shifted version of the mother function. There are many types of mother functions available in the literature, which include beta, hat mexican wavelet, and Gaussian continuous wavelet functions. However, the most used wavelet function in spectrum sensing is the Gaussian wavelet function that shows recurrent regularity which can be written as

$$\psi(t) = \frac{d^n \exp\left(\dfrac{-t^2}{2}\right)}{dt^n}. \tag{4.35}$$

Figure 4.9 depicts the continuous Gaussian wavelet functions of order $n = 1$–6. It is to be noted that there is a preference for nonorthogonal smoothing function, e.g., Gaussian wavelet function in SS, because orthogonal wavelet families can degrade the performance in detecting the limit of subband occupancy, i.e., orthogonal wavelet function can smooth the edges. Being capaable of determining the boundaries of occupied subbands, CWT allows singularities detection in the wideband spectrum in wavelet sensing. Wavelet sensing is also called edge detection and while analyzing the power spectrum density (PSD), the SUs are able to determine which subchannel is vacant for access. In this technique, the sensing PSD should be smooth in order to obtain reliable ROC.

PSD is smooth and almost flat within each subband B_m, but exhibits discontinuities from its neighboring bands B_{m-1} and B_{m+1}. Hence, irregularities in PSD appear only at the edges of the those subbands. PSD of the mth received signal can be written as

$$S_{y_m}(f) = \sum_{m=1}^{M} \alpha_m^2 S_{x_m}(f) + S_{n_m}(f), \tag{4.36}$$

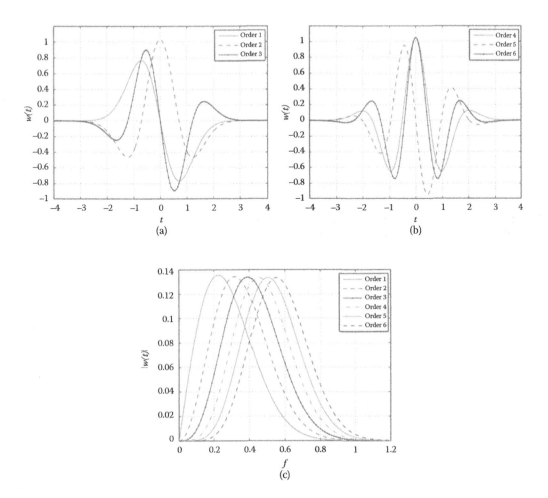

FIGURE 4.9
Continuous Gaussian wavelet functions of order $n = 1, 2$, and 3 (a) and 4, 5, and 6 (b) in the frequency domain.
(c) Frequency representation.

where α_m^2 indicates the signal power density within the mth band; furthermore, in the absence of noise, $S_{x_m}(f)$ represents the normalized (unknown) power spectral shape within each band B_m, satisfying three conditions:

$$S_{x_m}(f) = 0, \quad \forall f \neq B_m \tag{a}$$

$$w_{y_m} = \int_{f_{m-1}}^{f_m} S_{x_m}(f) df = f_m - f_{m_1} \tag{b} \tag{4.37}$$

$$S_{x_m}(f) = \begin{cases} 1, & \forall f \in B_m \\ 0, & \text{otherwise} \end{cases} \tag{c}$$

Condition (c) holds true since PSD within each subband B_m is smooth and almost flat; PSD of the mth PU signal defined by $\alpha_m^2 S_{x_m}(f)$ and $S_{n_m}(f)$ is the noise PSD that can be described as AWGN noise, i.e., $S_{x_m}(f) = N_0/2$.

CWT of the PSD of received signal is given as

$$W_s(f) = S_{y_m}(f) * \Psi_s(f), \tag{4.38}$$

where $\Psi_s(f) = \dfrac{1}{s}\Psi\left(\dfrac{f}{s}\right)$ is the wavelet smoothening function with $\Psi(f)$ being the Fourier transform of $\psi(t)$, the $*$ is the convolution operator and $s = 2^j$ for $j = 1, 2, ..., J$ is the scale factor. Equation 4.38 is able to take a frequency interval and enlarge the details in the analysis of a specific subband. As a consequence, to obtain the subband edges, derivatives of $W_s(f)$ can be deployed in order to allow a better identification of edges in the PSD signal.

4.4.2.1 Wavelet Modulus Maxima Method

In the wavelet modulus maxima (WMM) method, the edges of the subchannels f_n can be determined by first and second derivatives of wavelet signal $W_s(f)$. Setting as local variation point of $S_{y_m}(f)$ smoothed by $\Psi_s(f)$, the local maxima (LM) is obtained via the first derivative of wavelet $W_s(f)$ as follows

$$f_n = \max_f \left| W_s'(f) \right|, \tag{4.39}$$

where f_n is the nth edge frequency. Another criterion based on derivative is the zero crossing (ZC) rule. It is obtained from the second derivative of wavelet $W_s(f)$

$$f_n = \left\{ f \mid \left| W_s''(f) \right| = 0 \right\}, \tag{4.40}$$

where $W_s'(f)$ and $W_s''(f)$ are the first and second derivatives of the wavelet smoothing function with scale factor s, given respectively by

$$W_{s=2^j}'(f) = s\frac{d}{df}(S_{y_m} * \Psi_s)(f) = S_{y_m} * \left(s\frac{d\Psi_s}{df} \right)(f), \tag{4.41}$$

$$W_{s=2^j}''(f) = s^2\frac{d^2}{d^2 f}(S_{y_m} * \Psi_s)(f) = S_{y_m} * \left(s^2\frac{d^2\Psi_s}{d^2 f} \right)(f). \tag{4.42}$$

The LM- and ZC-based WMM methods have the same objective, to determine the edges, i.e., allow to identify the occupancy of mth subchannel B_m associated to the edge frequencies f_m and f_{m-1}.

4.4.2.2 Wavelet Multiscale Product Method

Wavelet multiscale product (WMP) method uses the first PSD wavelet derivative. It is simply the product of J first order derivatives of the frequency-scaled wavelet

$$\mathcal{U}_j^p = \prod_{j=1}^{J} W_{s=2^j}'(f), \tag{4.43}$$

where the derivative of the smoothed PSD of the received signal is given in Equation 4.41.

The desired local maxima of wavelet modulus are tracked by their propagation to multiple coarse scale $s = 2^j$ for $j = 1, 2, ..., J$ with the goal of decreasing the noise effect in the spectrum sensing, where false edges caused by noise are very common in the WMM method.

The WMP approach is intended to enhance multiscale peaks due to edges or singularities, while suppressing noise. Boundaries of consecutive frequencies bands $\{f_m\}$ can be acquired from $\mathbf{y}_m$ picking the LM of the multiscale product, which can be written as

$$f_m = \max_f |U_j^p|, \, f \in [f_0; f_M]. \tag{4.44}$$

4.4.2.3 Wavelet Multiscale Sum Method

In the wavelet multiscale sum (WMS) method again the first derivative of the PSD wavelet is deployed. The difference is that the product is replaced by the sum of the PSD wavelet derivative

$$U_j^s = \sum_{j=1}^{J} W'_{s=2^j}(f). \tag{4.45}$$

The problem in applying the WMP method to narrowband spectral sensing is a subband signal appears with slow variation on the PSD signal. This slow variation could result in edge detection fault, because they are attenuated when the multiplication method of Equation 4.43 is used. This problem can be solved using the WMS method that replaces the product by the sum.

4.4.3 Compressive Sensing

The compressive sensing (CS) method uses the concept of compressive sampling (CS) [3,28]. The CS method allows reducing the sampling rate below the Nyquist rate when the signal is sparse in a certain domain. A signal is sparse when it has low PSD, i.e., when the signal produces a white space. Therefore, a wideband spectrum is underutilized when the wideband is sparse in the frequency domain. This fact can be exploited in the MB-CRNs SS context.

Suppose a hypothetical model [29] $Q \leq M$, where Q is a subset of the M subbands of a wideband system. The received signal of a SU can be given by

$$y(t) = \sum_{q=1}^{Q} a_q x_q(t) \exp(j2\pi f_q t) + n(t), \tag{4.46}$$

where t is the time index, a_q is the amplitude of the qth primary signal, x_q is the baseband representation, f_q is the carrier frequency of the qth primary signal and also is the center frequency of one of the occupied subbands, and $n(t)$ is the AWG noise. If the sampling rate is defined as f_y, suppose this frequency is much higher than the date rate of each source, i.e., the Nyquist rate is obeyed. Then, the data sample in the SU can be defined as

$$y\left(\frac{n}{f_y}\right) = \sum_{q=1}^{Q} a_q x_q\left(\frac{n}{f_y}\right) \exp\left(j2\pi f_q \frac{n}{f_y}\right) + n\left(\frac{n}{f_y}\right), \tag{4.47}$$

where $n = 1, 2, ..., N$ and N is the number of samples.

Following the previous description the discrete-time signal received vector $\mathbf{y}_m$ with dimension $N \times 1$ can be written in a matrix form as

$$\mathbf{y}_m = \mathbf{B}_{am} + \mathbf{n}_m,$$ (4.48)

where $\mathbf{B}$ is a matrix defined as

$$\mathbf{B} = [\mathbf{b}_1, \mathbf{b}_2, \ldots, \mathbf{b}_Q],$$

with each vector given by

$$b_q = \left[x_q \left(\frac{1}{f_y} \right) \exp \left(\frac{j2\pi f_q}{f_y} \right), \ldots, x_q \left(\frac{N}{f_y} \right) \exp \left(\frac{j2\pi f_q N}{f_y} \right) \right]^T,$$ (4.49)

where $q = 1, \ldots, Q$, $\mathbf{a}_m = \left[a_{1_m}, \ldots, a_{Q_m} \right]$ and $\mathbf{n}_m = \left[n_{1_m} \left(\frac{1}{f_y} \right), \ldots, n_{Q_m} \left(\frac{1}{f_y} \right) \right]^T$.

For a sparse representation of the previous signal, a basis must be considered that represents the signal. Therefore, considering Π is the sparsity basis matrix that must be written in terms of all possible channel occupancy states [29]. Let $\left[\hat{f}_1, \ldots, \hat{f}_M \right]$ be a sampling set of the frequencies of M subbands that matches the frequency components of the received signal [29]. The received signal can be represented in a sparse form as follows

$$\mathbf{y}_m = \Pi \mathbf{s}_m + \mathbf{n}_m.$$ (4.50)

The sparsity basis matrix can be constructed as $\Pi = \left[\mathbf{b}\left(\hat{f}_1 \right), \mathbf{b}\left(\hat{f}_2 \right), \ldots, \mathbf{b}\left(\hat{f}_M \right) \right]$ where

$$\mathbf{b}\left(\hat{f}_i \right) = \left[x_q \left(\frac{1}{f_y} \right) \exp \left(\frac{j2\pi \hat{f}_i}{f_y} \right), \ldots, x_q \left(\frac{N}{f_y} \right) \exp \left(\frac{j2\pi \hat{f}_i N}{f_y} \right) \right]^T.$$ (4.51)

Making the following change of variables $\mathbf{z}_m = \mathbf{Y}\mathbf{y}_m = \mathbf{Y}\Pi \mathbf{s}_m + \mathbf{Y}\mathbf{n}_m$ where $\mathbf{z}_m$ is the measurement vector with dimension $L \times 1$ and $\mathbf{Y}$ is a measurement matrix with dimension $L \times N$ that can be choosen by considering that the correlation between $\mathbf{Y}$ and Π must be low, a good choice for $\mathbf{Y}$ is a totally random matrix [29]. Then $\mathbf{z}_m$ is called L-sparse if $L \ll N$ and $\mathbf{y}_m$ is compressible.

CS problem can be defined as a stable matrix $\mathbf{Y}$, where the signal $\mathbf{y}_m$ is transformed into $\mathbf{z}_m$ without losing signal information that characterizes the transformation of sparse domain $R^{N \times 1}$ into compressed domain $R^{L \times 1}$.

The reconstruction of the sparse signal can be described as an optimization problem. The analysis of the sparsity measure can be done by the p-norm, where $p \in [0,2]$ [29]. The optimal sparsity measure is done by a pseudonorm, called 0-norm, defined as [30]

$$\underset{\mathbf{z}_m}{\text{minimize}} \quad \|\mathbf{z}_m\|_0$$

$$\text{s.t.} \quad \mathbf{z}_m = \mathbf{Y}\mathbf{y}_m = \mathbf{Y}\Pi \mathbf{s}_m + \mathbf{Y}\mathbf{n}_m$$ (4.52)

where the 0-norm is defined for a vector x as [30]

$$\|x\|_0 = n(i \mid x_i \neq 0), \tag{4.53}$$

where n is the number or quantity and 0-norm is number of nonzero elements in a vector.

The 0-norm sparsity performance is a challenge, because the optimization problem is not convex and makes it a nondeterministic polynomial time hard problem (NP-hard problem). An alternative approach is to formulate the optimization problem as 1-norm, called *basis pursuit* (BP) [31]. Hence, the linear convex problem is written as [30]

$$\underset{z_m}{\text{minimize}} \ \|\mathbf{z}_m\|_1$$

$$\text{s.t.} \quad \mathbf{z}_m = \mathbf{Y}\mathbf{y}_m = \mathbf{Y}\prod\mathbf{s}_m + \mathbf{Y}\mathbf{n}_m \tag{4.54}$$

where $\|x\|_1$ is the 1-norm of $\mathbf{z}_m$.

The signal reconstruction and sparsity measurement can also be defined and calculated by other criterion and algorithms in the literature, such as matching pursuit (MP), LASSO, and AIC [10].

4.4.4 Angle-Based Sensing

AS can exploit the available spectrum in a space dimension, similar to a MIMO system, by increasing the spatial diversity. The major feature in AS is that not all subchannels occupy the same physical space for PUs. For example, if an SU is aware of the azimuth angle* of the PUs, then when the PUs transmit in a certain direction, the SU can simultaneously transmits in another direction using the same band in the same geographical area without interference.

The AS problem is capable of determining the *direction of arrival* (DoA) or *angle of arrival* (AoA), wherein each PU is transmitting. The main techniques described in literature to realize the AS include the *MUltiple SIgnal Classification* (MUSIC), Bartlett, Root MUSIC, Capon, and *estimation of signal parameters via rotational invariance technique* (ESPRIT) [32,33]. In this chapter, we only describe the MUSIC technique [34], which is one of the most important techniques to determine array angle and direction. MUSIC is a technique based on eigen space methods used for the signal and noise separation in different subspaces during signal processing which simplifies the signal analysis.

The system considered herein represents the array distribution with their directions, according to the Figure 4.10, modeled as [34,35]

$$\mathbf{y}_m = \mathbf{A}(\theta)\mathbf{x}_m + \mathbf{n}_m, \tag{4.55}$$

where $\mathbf{y}_m$ is the received signal at the mth subband B_m; the transmitted signal $\mathbf{x}_m$ by the array configuration with dimension $N \times 1$, and $\mathbf{n}_m$ is AWGN vector with dimension $N \times 1$, with statistical distribution $\mathbf{n}_m \sim N(0, \sigma^2 \mathbf{I})$. In this model, the sources (PUs) are considered

---

* Azimuth angle is the angular measurement formed between a reference and a line from the observer until a point of interest is reached in the same horizontal plane.

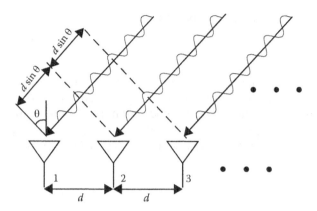

FIGURE 4.10
Schematic representation for the DoA analysis.

independent and the noise is uncorrelated. The $N \times D$ matrix $\mathbf{A}(\Theta)$ is called the steering matrix corresponding to the angles of distribution of arrays, and defined as [34]

$$A(\theta) = \left[a(\theta_1), a(\theta_2), \ldots, a(\theta_D) \right], \tag{4.56}$$

where $\mathbf{a}(\theta_i)$ is the steering vector with dimension $N \times 1$ defined as the angle, and the direction of PUs transmission are as follows

$$a(\theta_i) = \left[1, \exp\left(\frac{-j\omega d \sin\theta_i}{c} \right), \ldots, \exp\left(\frac{-j\omega(N-1)d \sin\theta_i}{c} \right) \right], \tag{4.57}$$

where d is the distance between antennas and c is the speed of light.

Under this model, the correlation matrix of the received signal with dimension $D \times D$ is readily obtained as follows

$$\begin{aligned}
\mathbf{R}_{\mathbf{y}_m} &= \mathbb{E}\left[\mathbf{y}_m \mathbf{y}_m^H \right] \\
&= \mathbb{E}\left[\mathbf{A}(\theta) \mathbf{x}_m \mathbf{x}_m^H \mathbf{A}(\theta)^H \right] + \mathbb{E}\left[\mathbf{n}_m \mathbf{n}_m^H \right] \\
&= \mathbf{A}(\theta) \cdot \mathbf{A}(\theta)^H + \sigma^2 \mathbf{I}_D \\
&= \mathbf{R}_{\mathbf{x}_m} + \sigma^2 \mathbf{I}_D,
\end{aligned} \tag{4.58}$$

where $\mathbf{R}_{\mathbf{x}_m}$ is the correlation of the transmitted signal and $\mathbf{X} = \mathbb{E}\left[\mathbf{x}_m \mathbf{x}_m^H \right] = \mathrm{diag}\left(\sigma_1^2, \ldots, \sigma_N^2 \right)$.

4.4.4.1 MUSIC Algorithm

MUSIC algorithm [34] estimates the angle or direction content of a signal autocorrelation matrix using an eigenspace method. In this method, the detector needs to know the array spatial distribution.

The correlation matrix $\mathbf{R}_{\mathbf{x}_m}$ can be related to its ith eigenvector $\mathbf{q}_m$ associated with its ith eigenvalue

$$\mathbf{R}_{\mathbf{x}_m} \mathbf{q}_m = A(\theta) \cdot A(\theta)^H \mathbf{q}_m = 0. \tag{4.59}$$

Hence,

$$\mathbf{q}_m^H \mathbf{A}(\theta) \cdot \mathbf{A}(\theta)^H \mathbf{q}_m = 0. \tag{4.60}$$

Finally, from Equation 4.60 and assuming that $\mathbf{A}(\theta)$ is positive definite, it follows that the steering matrix is orthogonal to the eigenvector of $\mathbf{R}_{x_m}$

$$\mathbf{A}(\theta)^H \mathbf{q}_m = 0. \tag{4.61}$$

Equation 4.61 implies that all $N-M$ eigenvectors $\mathbf{q}_m$ of the matrix $\mathbf{R}_{x_m}$ corresponding to the zero eigenvalues are orthogonal to all M signal steering vectors. This is the principle of the MUSIC technique which allows to separate the signal from the noise.

Now, let us consider $\mathbf{U}_N$, a $N \times (N-M)$ subspace of the noise eigenvectors. Then, the MUSIC *pseudospectrum* can be defined as [34]

$$P^{\text{MUSIC}} = \frac{1}{\mathbf{a}^H(\theta)\mathbf{U}_N\mathbf{U}_N^H\mathbf{a}(\theta)}. \tag{4.62}$$

In the CRN context, the important information of angle and direction is obtained by applying the following operation [36]

$$\theta^{\text{MUSIC}} = \arg\min_\theta \mathbf{a}^H(\theta)\mathbf{U}_N\mathbf{U}_N^H\mathbf{a}(\theta). \tag{4.63}$$

As a consequence, the following statistic test can be applied

$$T^{\text{MUSIC}}(y) = \frac{1}{180°}\sum_{\theta=-90°}^{90°} P^{\text{MUSIC}}, \tag{4.64}$$

where P^{MUSIC} is the spatial spectrum, also called pseudospectrum at time t.

4.4.5 Comparison of MB-SS Methods

The main characteristics of the MB-SS methods are summarized in Table 4.4. The MB-SS remains challenging in CR implementations; hence, further promising MB techniques should be evolved in the future to improve this branch.

Wavelet sensing is deployed when the SUs do not know the frequency limits of the subbands. Wavelet is a technique which is common in image processing and is used to determine the image edges. Similarly, in the SS context, the wavelet sensing has the same properties, i.e., this technique is able to determine the edges of the occupied portion of spectrum. However, the wavelet-based detector is affected by the noise and can produce false-edges detection, which disrupts the SUs opportunities and can generate an interference in PUs.

TABLE 4.4

Performance Comparision—MB Sensing

MB–SS Detector	Advantages	Disadvantages
Wavelet	Unknown MB limits	False edges
Compressed	Low sampling rate	Known $\prod$ and Υ
Angle	New dimension to explore	MIMO system

Compressed sensing can be used when the signal is sparse, i.e., in the case of a major part of the spectrum in communication systems. This technique is able to reconstruct the signal using a subsample information. This fact makes the processing less complex and helps increase the EF. The main challenge in this technique is that the SUs must know the sparsity basis **matrix** Π and measurement matrix Υ.

In AS technique, a new dimension is explored, providing new forms of diversity to the system, such as angle and space diversities. However, in this case, multiple antennas must be used to detect the directions and angles of the PU's transmission, increasing the complexity of the applications.

4.5 Cooperative CRNs

Cooperative CRNs work in two ways: relays networks and CSS. CSS schemes provide spatial diversity, increased coverage, ubiquitous connectivity, and network throughput.

Cooperative CRNs can provide diversity in environment subject to fading, shadowing, and path-loss channel effects, which can degrade the SS performance substantially.

SU cooperative sensing has two methods for SS: *hard* and *soft* combining. There are some rules that allow to choose the best threshold for each application and channel scenario, called *or-and-majority* rules.

Furthermore, considering the context of the relay cooperative sensing, there are two main and widely deployed protocols: AF and DF.

The binary decision of cooperative SS can be formulated as same as SB SS. The next section desribes the principle of CSS with the main rules to construct the threshold λ.

4.5.1 Cooperative Spectrum Sensing

Detection of transmissions from licensed (or primary) users is challenging in CRN environment due to a few uncertainties, such as (a) channel uncertainty, i.e., dynamic variations in the channel fading and shadowing conditions; (b) aggregated-interference uncertainty, when there are too many unlicensed users in the same CRN, who interfere with each other; (c) and finally, the noise uncertainty which can affect the detection sensibility and ROC performance.

Aiming to mitigate the uncertainties in SS, a CSS approach can be deployed in CRN context. CSS offers diversity gain, which can remarkably improve the detection probability performance of an unlicensed (secondary) user. Multiple unlicensed users cooperatively sense the target spectrum and share the SS results with each other. Figure 4.11 depicts a general topology of CRN with CSS. Indeed, each SU is responsible to sense a small portion of the spectrum and sends the results to the fusion center (FC), which constructs and broadcasts an updated map of availability of spectrum rules to all CRN nodes [37].

One advantage of CSS is that unlicensed user SU_1 may not be able to detect transmission from licensed user PU_1 due to channel fading. If SU_1 (source node) starts transmission, it will interfere with data reception at the licensed user, say PU_1. However, if unlicensed user SU_1 senses the spectrum and reports the presence of licensed user PU_1 to the FC, SU_2 can be notified by the FC and will defer its transmission to avoid any interference to the licensed user PU_2.

Alternatively, the cooperative cognitive networks can deploy multiple relay users to forward the signal received from a PU to an SU aiming to improve the performance of SS

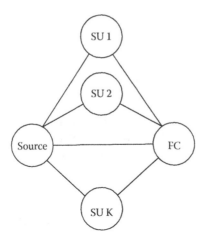

FIGURE 4.11
Cooperative CR scheme with K secondary users, one source node, and a fusion center.

while taking advantage of the spatial diversity [38]. In this mode, CSS is used to combat the noise and channel uncertainties, and therefore, the probability of misdetection and false alarm decreases substantially. Additionally, cooperative mode for SS reduces the sensing time while improving the accuracy. However, CSS implies higher complexity and energy consumption.

In CSS based on decision fusion, each cooperative partner makes a binary decision based on its local observation and then forwards one bit of the decision to the common receiver in FC. Let $d_k \in \{0,1\}$ denote the local SS result of the kth CR, including SUs and in some schemes relay nodes. Hence, $d_k = 0$ indicates that the CR infers the absence of the PU in the observed band. In contrast, $d_k = 1$ implies the PU operation in that band. At the common fusion receiver, all 1-bit decisions are fused together according to a specific logic rule [39].

FC uses different techniques for combining the SS results coming from different unlicensed SUs to make a decision in CSS. The simplest method is to use an OR operation among the received sensing results. Moreover, combining techniques based on maximal ratio combining (MRC) and equal gain combining (EGC) have been investigated in [40]. Following section briefly discusses the *hard combining*, *soft combining* and *or-and-majority* rules.

4.5.1.1 Hard Combining

In hard combining SS, K cooperative SUs are sensing the spectrum and the final decision is given for the following metric

$$T(y) = \sum_{k=1}^{K} d_k, \tag{4.65}$$

where the d_k is the decision of kth SU and $d_k \in \{0,1\}$, being $d_k = 0$ if PU is absent, or $d_k = 1$ if PU is present in the band.

4.5.1.2 Soft Combining

In soft combining SS, the metric is given as weight sum of the observations states for each SU's contribution. Hence, the most important contributions are associated to higher weight, but the other less important contributions are also considered. The associated test statistic in the soft combining method is simply written as follows

$$T(y) = \sum_{k=1}^{K} c_k T_k(y),\tag{4.66}$$

where c_k is the weight coefficient and $T_k(y)$ is the test statistics of the kth SU. Taking $c_k = 1$ the soft combining becomes the classical EGC diversity combine. Besides, if c_k is proportional to SNR at the kth SU, the rule gets closer to the classical MRC.

4.5.1.3 Or-And-Majority Rules

The *or-and-majority* rules allow to describe different ways to construct the threshold λ in a CSS scheme; in summary

- *Or* rule: $\lambda = 1$. The rule *Or* ensures minimum interference to the PUs. The PU is considered present in a band, if only a single PU sends 1 to FC in its decision, i.e., if test statistic of an SU adds one. It can be seen that the Or rule is very conservative for CRs to access the licensed band. As such, the chance of causing interference to the PU is minimized.

- *And* rule: $\lambda = K + 1$, where K is the number of collaborative nodes sensing the same subband. It is much less conservative, ensuring a high rate of transmission to the SUs. The PU is considered present in the band, if all CRs sense the presence of a PU in the band.

- *Majority* rule: $\lambda = \left(\dfrac{K+1}{2}\right)$. The PU is considered present in the band, if the majority of SUs send 1 to the decision center.

4.5.2 Relay CSS

In this kind of CSS, one or more relay(s) help to realize the SS. There are many relay protocols in the communication systems, but the most important are AF and DF protocols. In the following sections, the AF and DF protocols are introduced.

4.5.2.1 AF Relaying Protocol

In the AF protocol, the relay scales the received version of the signal and retransmits it to a second time-slot, an amplified version of it, to the destination node. In the first time-slot, the signal transmitted from the source is received at both the relay and the destination, which respectively are [6,41]

$$y_{s,r} = \sqrt{P} h_{s,r} x + n_{s,r},\tag{4.67}$$

$$y_{s,d} = \sqrt{P} h_{s,d} x + n_{s,d},\tag{4.68}$$

where P is the RF transmit power deployed by the source node in the first time-slot; x is the transmitted signal; h_r^s and h_d^s are the channel fading coefficients between the source–relay and source–destination paths, respectively.

In the AF protocol, the relay node does the simple scaling on the received signal by a factor inversely proportional to the received power given as

$$\beta = \frac{\sqrt{P}}{\sqrt{P|h_{s,r}|^2 + N_0}}. \tag{4.69}$$

As a consequence, the signal transmitted by the relay node to the destination node in the second time-slot is scaled by $\beta \cdot y_r^s$.

SNR at the destination node is the sum of SNRs from the source node and relay node, as a result of the macro-diversity gain offered by cooperative source–relay–destination scheme. SNR from the source node is given as follows

$$\gamma_{s,d} = \frac{P}{N_0}|h_{s,r}|^2. \tag{4.70}$$

4.5.2.2 DF Relaying Protocol

In DF relaying, the receiver signal is detected at relay node, re-encoded, and then retransmitted to the receiver node. The DF relaying scheme has an advantage over the AF relaying scheme in reducing the effects of additive noise at the relay node, but in a low SNR regime the decision errors of relay node propagates to the destination. On the other hand, if the relay is able to decode the transmitted symbol correctly, i.e., when relay node operates in medium and high SNR regimes, the relay retransmits the decoded symbol with power P to the destination node; otherwise the relay does not cooperate in the retransmission. This can be written as follows

$$y_{r,d} = \sqrt{P}h_{r,d}\hat{x} + n_{r,d}, \tag{4.71}$$

where $\hat{x}$ is the decoded signal x at the relay node.

4.5.3 Comparison among Cooperative SS Methods

A comparison of the principal CSS methods are summarized in Table 4.5. The hard combining method is based on the fact that the SUs perform the SS and each SU has a decision, which is shared among the other SUs. This method has a simple decision, i.e., the sum of the decision of each individual SU. The disadvantage of this technique is if the SU misses the detection, the error is propagated to the decision fusion, affecting other decisions.

The soft combining method has advantages over other methods, but does not disregard others as less reliable. This makes the final decision less wrong, but this depends on the hits of some SUs.

In the AF relaying protocol, the signal receives a gain before retransmission to the destination node. The disadvantage of this protocol is that the noise is amplified jointly to the signal and is received by the destination node.

In the DF relaying protocol, the signal is re-encoded in the relay node, which makes the signal free of noise amplified. The biggest problem is if the relay decodes wrong or the

TABLE 4.5

Method Comparison—Cooperative Sensing

CSS method	Advantages	Disadvantages
Hard combining	Simple decision of each user	Subject to error propagation
Soft combining	Weights the best performance	More complexity
AF relaying	Simple propagation with a gain	Propagates noise with a gain
DF relaying	Reduce noise propagation	If decoding fails, it does not work (low SNR)

signal contains errors, then the relay does not retransmit the signal and the destination node only depends on the direct link or direct node.

4.6 Conclusions and Perspectives

Concerning SB-SS, this chapter explored five basic techniques capaable of analyzing spectrum usage in a specific BW, namely ED, MF, CS feature detector, covariance detector, and eigenvalue detector. In terms of complexity, ED offers SS at low computational cost. However, ED also presents low performance, especially under very low SNR, along with requiring precise SNR knowledge, which is not always available, to perform proper SS. On the other hand, MF performs optimal spectrum, but also requires a detailed description of the PU signal characteristics, which, in some cases, can be an unreasonable requirement. Despite presenting a reasonable spectral sensing performance, the CS method may require embedding more features of the signal in order to improve cyclostationarity on the PU signal, e.g., a header signal or a periodic pulse. In this sense, PU signal should experience a reduction in SE in order to ease SS for PUs, which may not bring benefits to PUs if they do not take advantage on SUs. Finally, covariance and eigenvalue detections are based on measuring temporal correlation of the PU signal, being capable of robust SS, which is bounded to the number of lags considered for correlation calculus.

MB-SS expands the SS from an SB model to an MB model. Basically, this chapter deals with three MB methods: wavelet sensing, compressed sensing, and AS. There are other methods to sense the spectrum in a MB model, but the three methods discussed here are the most promising. Wavelet SS is used when the limits of the subbands are unknown. So, wavelet technique is able to determine these limits. There are three kinds of wavelet methods to determine the limits of subbands: WMM, WMP, and WMS. The first is the most simple method and determines the limits using an LM through first derivative or zero crossing that uses the second derivative of the wavelet PSD. The second derivative is an improvement of the first and uses the idea of the product of the first derivative of the wavelet increasing the scale and is able to reduce the false edges in the SS, which is a very common problem in WMM. Third method is a variation of the second method and is simply the change of the product by the sum. This change reduces the edge fault, due to slow variation of PSD in narrowband systems.

Compressed sensing is another way to deal with SS in the MB systems. This method uses the concept of sparsity of signal combined to a norm optimization problem that is capable of measuring the sparsity of a channel. The optimal measure depends on a 0-norm, which in essence results in a nonconvex optimization problem; so, it cannot be solved in a polynomial time. Based on that, other optimization metrics have been proposed, such as basis pursuit, match pursuit, and AIC.

The last SS method for MB-CRNs is angle sensing that provides another dimension to the MB-SS challenge. This method uses an algorithm to sense the DoA of a signal or a set of signals. A classical algorithm to deal with is MUSIC algorithm based on the signal separation from the noise subspace.

Another class of CRN is the cooperative CRNs. There are two ways in which the SUs can cooperate in a CRN. The first one is when one SU shares its sensing decision with another SUs through FC, or act as a relay helping the PU's transmission. In the first class, two options are avaliable to combine the information: hard and soft combining. First, the final decision is only the sum of all SU's decisions. The second one deploys weights that can act according to the importance of the decision. Another important rule is the *or-and-majority* rules that allow determining the threshold in a cooperative SS using different consensus rules. In the second class of CSS, two basic relay protocols arise: AF protocol and DF protocol. In the first class, the signal received by the destination node is only the signal of the source node with a gain. The problem with this method is that the noise is amplified along with the information. The second method decodes the signal coming from the source node and retransmits this signal to the destination without amplifying the noise. The problem with this method is if the signal contains decision error, basically due to SNR regime, the relay is unable to retransmit to the destination node.

CRNs is one of the techniques that will enable the future 5G communications. Due to scarcity of spectrum and high rates of 5G communications protocols, CRN is a candidate to operate under high spectral efficiency mode. The spectral sensing techniques addressed in this chapter can contribute to improving the performance, robustness, and efficiency of CRNs, till another promising technique appears to construct a solid knowledge area in the future.

References

1. Mitola, J., and Maguire, G. Q. (1999). Cognitive radio: Making software radios more personal. *Personal Communications, IEEE* 6 (4): 13–18.
2. Sharma, M., and Gupta, R. (2014). Comparative analysis of various communication systems for intelligent sensing of spectrum. In *2014 International Conference on Advances in Computing, Communications and Informatics (ICACCI)*, New Delhi, India, pp. 902–908.
3. Ibnkahla, M. (2014). *Cooperative Cognitive Radio Networks: The Complete Spectrum Cycle*. Boca Raton, FL: CRC Press.
4. Zhang, Y., Zheng, J., and Chen, H.-H. (2010). *Cognitive Radio Networks: Architectures, Protocols, and Standards*. Boca Raton, FL: CRC Press.
5. Maheshwari, P., and Singh, A. (2014). A survey on spectrum handoff techniques in cognitive radio networks. In *2014 International Conference on Contemporary Computing and Informatics (IC3I)*, Mysore, India, pp. 996–1001.
6. Dohler, M., and Li, Y. (2010). *Cooperative Communications: Hardware, Channel & PHY*. Chichester, West Sussex, U.K.; Hoboken, NJ: Wiley.
7. Parekh, P., and Shah, M. (2014). Spectrum sensing in wideband OFDM based cognitive radio. In *2014 International Conference on Communications and Signal Processing (ICCSP)*, Melmaruvathur, India, pp. 1476–1481.

8. Wang, N., Gao, Y., and Cuthbert, L. (2014). Spectrum sensing using adaptive threshold based energy detection for OFDM signals. In *2014 IEEE International Conference on Communication Systems (ICCS)*, Macau, pp. 359–363

9. Lunden, J., Koivunen, V., and Poor, H. (2015). Spectrum exploration and exploitation for cognitive radio: Recent advances. *IEEE Signal Processing Magazine* 32 (3): 123–140

10. Hattab, G., and Ibnkahla, M. (2014). Multiband spectrum access: Great promises for future cognitive radio networks. *Proceedings of the IEEE* 102 (3): 282–306.

11. Di Benedetto, M.-G., Cattoni, A. F., Fiorina, J., Bader, and Nardis, L. D. (2015). *Cognitive Radio and Networking for Heterogeneous Wireless Networks: Recent Advances and Visions for the Future* (1st edn). Volume 1 of Signals and Communication Technology. Switzerland: Springer International Publishing.

12. Feng, C. (2012). Cognitive learning-based spectrum handoff for cognitive radio network. *International Journal of Computer and Communication Engineering* 1 (4). 350–353

13. Kay, S. (1998). *Fundamentals of Statistical Signal Processing: Detection Theory.* Englewood Cliffs, NJ: Prentice-Hall PTR, p. 672.

14. Roberts, R., Brown, W., and Loomis, H. (1991). Computationally efficient algorithms forcyclic spectral analysis. *IEEE Signal Processing Magazine* 8 (2): 38–49.

15. Bhargavi, D., and Murthy, C. (2010). Performance comparison of energy, matched-filter and cyclostationarity-based spectrum sensing. In *2010 IEEE Eleventh International Workshop on Signal Processing Advances in Wireless Communications (SPAWC)*, Marrakech, pp. 1–5.

16. Gradshteyn, I. S., and Ryzhik, I. M. (2007). *Table of Integrals, Series, and Products.* Elsevier/Academic Press, Amsterdam, seventh edition. Translated from the Russian. Translation edited and with a preface by Alan Jeffrey and Daniel Zwillinger, with one CD-ROM (Windows, Macintosh and UNIX).

17. Zeng, Y., and Liang, Y.-C. (2009b). Spectrum-sensing algorithms for cognitive radio based on statistical covariances. *IEEE Transactions on Vehicular Technology*, 58 (4): 1804–1815.

18. Zeng, Y., and Liang, Y.-C. (2009a). Eigenvalue-based spectrum sensing algorithms for cognitive radio. *IEEE Transactions on Communications*, 57 (6): 1784–1793.

19. Tracy, C. A., and Widom, H. (1996). On orthogonal and symplectic matrix ensembles. *Communications in Mathematical Physics* 177: 727–754.

20. Tracy, C. A., and Widom, H. (2000). The distribution of the largest eigenvalue in the Gaussian ensembles: β. In *Calogero-Moser-Sutherland Models* (Montreal, QC, 1997), CRM Ser. Math. Phys. New York: Springer, pp. 461–472.

21. Tian, Z., and Giannakis, G. (2006). A wavelet approach to wideband spectrum sensing for cognitive radios. In *2006 1st International Conference on Cognitive Radio Oriented Wireless Networks and Communications.* Mykonos Island, pp. 1–5.

22. Devi, T., and Sagar, S. (2014). Discrete wavelet packet transform based cooperative spectrum sensing for cognitive radios. In *2014 First International Conference on Computational Systems and Communications (ICCSC)*, Trivandrum, pp. 226–231.

23. El-Khamy, S., Abdel-Malek, M., and Kamel, S. (2014). An improved reconstruction technique for wavelet-based compressive spectrum sensing using genetic algorithm. In *2014 31st National Radio Science Conference (NRSC)*, Cairo, pp. 99–106.

24. Jadhav, A., and Bhattacharya, S. (2014). A novel approach to wavelet transform-based edge detection in wideband spectrum sensing. In *2014 International Conference on Electronics and Communication Systems (ICECS)*, Coimbatore, India, pp. 1–5.

25. Jindal, S., Dass, D., and Gangopadhyay, R. (2014). Wavelet based spectrum sensing in a multipath Rayleigh fading channel. In *2014 Twentieth National Conference on Communications (NCC)*, Kanpur, India, pp. 1–6.

26. Zhao, Y., Wu, Y., Wang, J., Zhong, X., and Mei, L. (2014). Wavelet transform for spectrum sensing in cognitive radio networks. In *2014 International Conference on Audio, Language and Image Processing (ICALIP)*, Shanghai, pp. 565–556.

27. Daubechies, I. (1992). *Ten Lectures on Wavelets.* Philadelphia, PA: Society for Industrial and Applied Mathematics.

28. Hosseini, H., Syed-Yusof, S., Fisal, N., and Farzamnia, A. (2015). Compressed waveletpacket-based spectrum sensing with adaptive thresholding for cognitive radio. *Canadian Journal of Electrical and Computer Engineering* 38 (1): 31–36.

29. Liu, F. L., Guo, S. M., Zhou, Q. P., and Du, R. Y. (2012). An effective wideband spectrum sensing method based on sparse signal reconstruction for cognitive radio networks. *Progress in Electromagnetics Research C* 28: 99–111.

30. Hayashi, K., Nagahara, M., and Tanaka, T. (2013). A user's guide to compressed sensing for communications systems. *IEICE Transactions* 96-B (3): 685–712.

31. Chen, S., and Donoho, D. (1994). Basis pursuit. Technical report, Department of Statistics, University of California, Berkeley.

32. Dhope, T., and Simunic, D. (2012). On the performance of AoA estimation algorithms in cognitive radio networks. In *2012 International Conference on Communication, Information Computing Technology (ICCICT)*, Mumbai, India, pp. 1–5.

33. Dhope, T., and Simunic, D. (2013). On the performance of DoA estimation algorithms in cognitive radio networks: A new approach in spectrum sensing. In *2013 36th International Convention on Information Communication Technology Electronics Microelectronics (MIPRO)*, Opatija, pp. 507–512.

34. Schmidt, R. (1986). Multiple emitter location and signal parameter estimation. *IEEE Transactions on Antennas and Propagation* 34 (3): 276–280.

35. Roy, R., Paulraj, A., and Kailath, T. (1986). Direction-of-arrival estimation by subspace rotation methods—ESPRIT. In *IEEE International Conference on ICASSP '86 Acoustics, Speech, and Signal Processing* (Volume 11), ICASSP 86, Tokyo, pp. 2495–2498.

36. Liping, D., Feifei, L., and Yueyun, C. (2012). Time-angle spectrum sensing based on sliding window music algorithm. In *2012 Fourth International Conference on Multimedia Information Networking and Security (MINES)*, Nanjing, pp. 644–647.

37. Zhang, Y., Yang, W.-D., and Cai, Y.-M. (2007). Cooperative spectrum sensing technique. In *Proceedings of IEEE International Conference on Wireless Communications, Networking and Mobile Computing (WiCom)*, Shanghai, pp. 1167–1170.

38. Ganesan, G., Li, Y., Bing, B., and Li, S. (2008). Spatiotemporal sensing in cognitive radio networks. *IEEE Journal on Selected Areas in Communications* 26 (1): 5–12.

39. Letaief, K., and Zhang, W. (2009). Cooperative communications for cognitive radio networks. *Proceedings of the IEEE* 97 (5): 878–893.

40. Ma, J., and Li, Y. G. (2007). Soft combination and detection for cooperative spectrum sensing in cognitive radio networks. In *Proceedings of IEEE Global Telecommunications Conference (GLOBECOM)*, Washington, DC, pp. 3139–3143.

41. Hossain, E., Kim, D. I., and Bhargava, V. K. (2011). *Cooperative Cellular Wireless Networks*. New York, NY: Cambridge University Press.

5

Spectrum Sensing in Cognitive Radio Networks: A Survey

P. T. V. Bhuvaneswari

CONTENTS

5.1 Introduction

The scarcity of electromagnetic radio spectrum is due to its increasing usage day by day. However, the allocated spectrum is underutilized due to the conventional approach of spectrum allocation and management, and existing inflexibility in operating frequency bands. As most of the useable radio spectrums are already allocated, it is cumbersome to detect the vacant bands to either deploy new services or enhance the existing ones. To improve spectrum utilization, dynamic spectrum access (DSA) scheme [1] has been introduced. Cognitive radio network (CRN) technology, an outcome of DSA scheme, aims to address the issues related to spectrum underutilization in wireless communication.

5.1.1 Cognitive Radio Networks

Joseph Mitola first developed the idea of CRNs at the Defense Advanced Research Projects Agency (DARPA), United States. A CRN is also known as "Mitola radio" software. The Federal Communications Commission defines CRN as "a radio or system that senses its operational electromagnetic environment and can dynamically and autonomously adjust its radio operating parameters to modify system operation, such as maximize throughput, mitigate interference, facilitate interoperability, access secondary markets" [2].

In CRN, the users are classified into primary user (PU) and secondary user (SU).

- *Primary user* (PU): A user with higher priority or legacy rights on the usage of a specific part of the spectrum
- *Secondary user* (SU): A low-priority user exploiting the spectrum without causing interference to PUs

Thus, the primary goals of a CRN are to provide (1) highly reliable communication to all users in the network, wherever and whenever required and (2) cost-effective mechanism for efficient utilization of the radio spectrum.

5.1.2 Features of CRNs

CRN features which enable more efficient and flexible usage of the spectrum are as follows [3]:

- *Frequency agility*: It is the ability to adapt to changing operating frequency environment.
- *Dynamic frequency selection*: It is the ability to dynamically select the optimal frequency from the sensed spectrum.
- *Adaptive modulation*: It is the reconfiguration of transmission characteristics and waveforms to enable efficient spectrum usage.
- *Transmit power control*: The transmission power should be adaptive to enhance spectrum utilization.

5.1.3 Fundamental Requirements of CRNs

5.1.3.1 Coexistence of SUs with PUs

The fundamental requirement of a CRN is to tackle the coexistence of SUs with the PUs. It can be achieved through three different paradigms [4].

- *Interweave paradigm*: The SU is prohibited to access the band under usage by the PU to minimize the interference level.
- *Underlay and overlay paradigms*: The SU is permitted to concurrently access the band used by the PU, thus enabling coexistence of SU and PU. However, the interference caused is kept minimal. To achieve this, the SU must be aware of various channel side information (CSI), such as channel conditions and encoding mechanism of the PU network.

5.1.3.2 Spectrum Awareness

These access paradigms require reliable spectrum awareness to obtain information about the spectrum status. Spectrum awareness can be classified into two approaches:

- *Passive-based awareness:* In this approach, the SU acquires the information about the spectrum availability through external entities such as beacons or geo-location databases.
- *Active-based awareness:* In this approach, the SU performs local sensing to determine the spectrum status, commonly known as *spectrum sensing* (SS). In both the approaches, periodic monitoring of the spectrum sensed and occupied by the SU is mandatory, because the sudden reappearances of the PUs may degrade the quality of service (QoS) of the SU.

5.1.3.3 Sensing Reliability

Due to the stochastic nature of the wireless channel, SS performed by the SU can be incorrect and become unreliable, which may lead to degradation in the QoS of both PU and SU [5]. To combat the fading in wireless channels, cooperative communication is devised that provides spatial diversity gains by enabling multiple SUs to cooperate together in SS and access. This mechanism is called cooperative cognitive radio (CCR). A CRN includes SS, spectrum management, spectrum sharing, and spectrum mobility described as follows.

- *Spectrum sensing*: The task of obtaining awareness about the spectrum usage and existence of PUs in a geographical area.
- *Spectrum management*: The task of capturing the best available spectrum to meet the user's communication requirements.
- *Spectrum mobility*: The task of maintaining seamless communication requirements during the transition to better spectrum.
- *Spectrum sharing*: The task of providing fair spectrum scheduling method among the coexisting users.

This chapter details the issues and challenges in SS and also presents the state of art in SS algorithms.

5.2 Spectrum Sensing

SS is the ability to measure, sense, and be aware of various parameters related to the radio channel characteristics such as the availability of spectrum, transmit power, interference, noise, operating frequency of the radio, user requirements and applications, available networks and nodes, local policies, and other operating restrictions. It is done across frequency, time, geographical space, code, and phase. To allow a reliable operation of cognitive radios (CRs), the following tasks have to be carried out in SS [6].

5.2.1 Task of SS

1. Detection of the spectrum holes
2. Spectral resolution of each spectrum hole
3. Estimation of the spatial directions of incoming interferences
4. Signal classification

In practice, the secondary users (SUs), also known as unlicensed users, should continuously monitor the activities of PUs, also called licensed users, to identify the presence of the spectrum holes (SHs). This procedure is called spectrum sensing (SS). There are two types of SHs, namely temporal and spatial.

- *Temporal SHs:* Appears whenever PU transmission does not occur for a certain period of time, and SUs are allowed to use the spectrum for transmission.
- *Spatial SHs*: Appears whenever the PU transmission occurs within a certain geographical area, and the SUs are allowed to use the spectrum outside that area.

5.2.2 Principle of SS

Figure 5.1 illustrates the principle of SS, where the PU transmitter sends data to the PU receiver in their allotted licensed spectrum band, while a pair of SUs also intend to access the spectrum at the same instant. To protect the PU transmission, SS should be performed to detect the presence of the PU receiver present within the coverage of the SU transmitter.

5.2.3 Issues and Challenges in SS

This section discusses the various issues such as channel uncertainty, noise uncertainty, and sensing interference limit addressed by SS in CRNs [7].

- *Channel uncertainty*: In wireless communication networks, uncertainties in received signal strength (RSS) can arise due to channel fading or shadowing. In SS, the deep fade experienced by the PU signal may be wrongly interpreted as

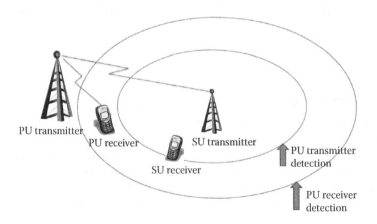

FIGURE 5.1
Principle of spectrum sensing.

white space by the SU. Then the SU transmission can become interference to the PU. Hence, cognitive radios have to be more sensitive to distinguish a faded or shadowed primary signal from a white space. Cooperative sensing is the mechanism devised to handle this issue, in which a group of cognitive radios share their local measurements and a collective decision can be taken on the occupancy status of the licensed band.

- *Noise uncertainty:* The detection sensitivity defined as the minimum signal-to-noise ratio (SNR) at which the PU signal can be accurately detected by the cognitive radio is given by

$$\gamma_{min} = \frac{P_p L(D+R)}{N} \tag{5.1}$$

where N is the noise power, P_p is the transmitted power of the PU, D is the interference range of the SU, and R is the maximum distance between primary transmitter and its corresponding receiver.

Limitation: Determining noise power is difficult in a practical scenario and needs to be estimated which may contain calibration errors due to change in thermal noise. Therefore, to calculate noise uncertainty, it is necessary to have a more sensitive detector.

- *Aggregate interference:* In future, the possibility of widespread deployment of SUs operating over the same licensed band increases; this may result in uncertainty known as aggregate interference. Even though the PU may lie outside the interference range of an SU, detection of white space may become faulty due to aggregate interference. In order to enhance the accuracy of detection, usage of more sensitive detectors becomes mandatory.

- *Sensing interference:* The primary goal of SS is to detect the spectrum status which may be either idle or occupied, so that access can be made by the unlicensed user. However, the crucial challenge faced in practice is the errors involved in the interference measurement. In order to compute the level of interference caused by the unlicensed user (SUs) to the licensed users (PUs), SUs need to be aware of the location of the PUs. However, when the PU device becomes passive, determination of location becomes cumbersome. These factors need to be given more attention while calculating the sensing interference limit.

5.2.4 SS Mechanism

The SS mechanism can be classified into narrowband and wideband sensing. This section deals with some of the common narrowband SS mechanisms and throws some light on the wideband SS mechanism.

The taxonomy of narrowband SS mechanism is illustrated in Figure 5.2. It can be broadly classified under two categories: cooperative detection technique and noncooperative detection technique [8].

5.2.4.1 Cooperative Detection

In this technique, a group of cognitive radios (SUs) share sensing information with each other to enhance the sensing accuracy. In this process, a group of SUs collect the channel occupancy information and represent it as a spectrum map. This information is then

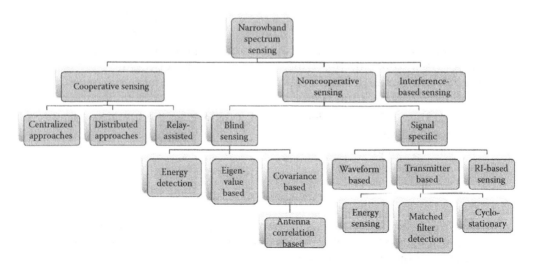

FIGURE 5.2
Taxonomy of narrowband SS mechanisms.

periodically transmitted to the central coordinator which determines the set of available ultra-high frequency channels by performing a bitwise-OR operation on the spectrum maps. Then the best available channel is selected and broadcasted back to the SU. This technique exploits the spatial diversity intrinsic to a multi-user network. It can be accomplished in a centralized or distributed fashion [9]. Cooperative SS adopts three approaches, namely centralized, distributed, and relay-assisted cooperative.

5.2.4.1.1 Centralized Approach

In this approach, the fusion center (FC) or central processor node collects sensing information from all the SU radios that are within its coverage, as shown in Figure 5.3. Based on the analyses performed over them, the optimal frequency of operation for the SU can be determined [10].

5.2.4.1.2 Distributed Approach

In this approach, the concept of central processing is not adopted. Instead, each cognitive radio can share the sensing information gathered by them with other radios that are within their coverage, as shown in Figure 5.4. Thus, an ad hoc approach is adopted which requires higher level of autonomy for each radio [11].

5.2.4.1.3 Relay-Assisted Cooperative

In this approach, relay cognitive radios are used between the SU and FC to mitigate the effect of fading in the wireless medium, as shown in Figure 5.5. This enhances the accuracy of SS.

Procedure involved in the cooperative sensing.

Cooperative sensing consists of two phases such as detection of PUs and reporting them to the FC.

- Detection of PU: In this phase, the SU attempts to detect primary unused channel.
- Reporting: In this phase, the detected information is reported to the FC for processing.

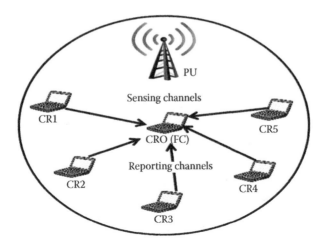

FIGURE 5.3
Centralized approach.

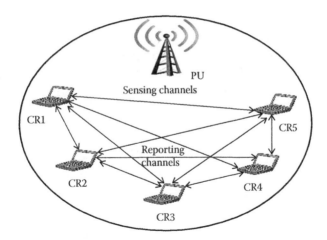

FIGURE 5.4
Distributed approach.

5.2.4.2 Noncooperative Detection

In this technique, individual radios locally perform spectrum occupancy measurements and analysis to detect the primary unused channel. Hence, each node is autonomous in nature. Noncooperative SS adopts two approaches, namely blind sensing and signal-specific sensing.

5.2.4.2.1 Blind Sensing

In this approach, no prior information related to PUs and noise power is required to perform SS. For a given number of observation samples of primary channels, statistical analysis is performed which reflects the channel condition. Based on the obtained result, the detection threshold value is computed. Through an efficient decision-making algorithm, SS is achieved. Some of the popular blind-sensing mechanisms are detailed in this section.

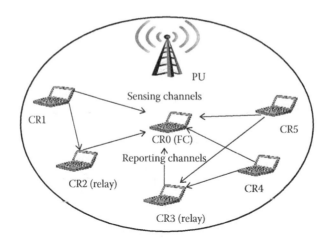

FIGURE 5.5
Relay-assisted cooperative approach.

5.2.4.2.1.1 Energy Detector-Based Sensing

Energy detector-based sensing, also known as radiometry or period gram, is the most popular SS method because of its low computational and implementation complexities [12]. In this approach, the receiver does not require any prior knowledge about the PU. The PU signal is detected by comparing the output of the energy detector with a threshold value which depends on the noise floor. However, a few challenges exist in this approach, which are as follows:

- Selection of adaptive threshold value to detect PUs
- Inability to differentiate interference from PUs and noise
- Poor performance under low SNR values and detection of spread spectrum signals

The block diagram of energy detector-based sensing approach is illustrated in Figure 5.6.
In this approach, the received signal obtained from the channel is passed through band-pass filter of the bandwidth W and is integrated over time interval. The output from the integrator block is then compared to a predefined threshold λ_E to discover the absence of the PU. The threshold value λ_E can be either fixed or variable based on the channel conditions.

Let $s(n)$ be the signal transmitted by the PU to be detected, $w(n)$ be the additive white Gaussian noise (AWGN) sample, and n be the sample index, then the received signal $y(n)$ can be expressed as

$$y(n) = s(n) + w(n) \tag{5.2}$$

Let N be the period over which the detection of spectrum occupancy is observed. Then the decision metric M made in the energy detector can be expressed as

$$M = \sum_{n=0}^{T} |y(n)|^2 \tag{5.3}$$

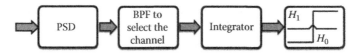

FIGURE 5.6
Energy detector-based sensing. BPF, band pass filter; PSD, power spectral density.

The decision on the occupancy of a band can be obtained by comparing the decision metric M against a fixed threshold λ_E. Two hypothetical conditions, namely H_0 and H_1, represent the status of the detection algorithm.

H_0: $y(n) = s(n) + w(n)$ indicates the presence of a PU.

H_1: $y(n) = w(n)$, when $s(n) = 0$, indicates the absence of a PU. Hence, the spectrum can be assigned to the SU. The performance of the energy detector–based sensing algorithm can be analyzed using metrics called probabilities:

- Probability of detection P_D
- Probability of false alarm P_F

P_D is the probability of detecting the presence of a PU signal when it is present. It can be formulated as

$$P_D P_r \left(M > \lambda_E \mid H_0 \right) \tag{5.4}$$

while PF is the probability of detecting the presence of PU signal in its absence.

$$P_F = P_r \left(M > \lambda_E \mid H_1 \right) \tag{5.5}$$

To prevent the underutilization of spectrum, it is necessary that P_F be kept as small as possible compared to P_D. The value of λ_E aids to achieve an optimum balance between P_D and P_F.

5.2.4.2.1.2 Eigenvalue-Based Sensing
In this approach, the eigenvalue of the covariance matrix of the received signal is used in detection of PU. The ratio of maximum-to-minimum eigenvalue is computed using the random matrix theory. Detection threshold value is chosen from this ratio [13,14].

5.2.4.2.1.3 Covariance-Based Sensing
It is a known fact that the statistical covariance matrices of the received signal and noise are normally different. By differentiating this difference, the desired signal component can be obtained from the background noise [15].

5.2.4.2.2 Signal Specific
This sensing approach requires prior knowledge of a PU signal.

5.2.4.2.2.1 Waveform-Based Sensing
In this approach, the prior knowledge of the PU signal pattern is obtained through various methods such as preamble, midamble, pilot signals, and spreading sequence. Preamble is a known sequence transmitted before each burst and midamble is a sequence transmitted

in the middle of a burst. It is also known as waveform-based sensing or coherent sensing. This approach outperforms energy detector–based sensing in terms of reliability and convergence time. Further, performance of this approach is enhanced when the length of the known signal pattern is increased [16].

The decision matrix M can be computed from the given expression:

$$M = \text{Re}\left[\sum_{n=1}^{T} Y(n) \times S(n)^{*}\right] \tag{5.6}$$

where $s(n)^{*}$ is the conjugate of $S(n)$.

In the absence of PU, the metric value becomes

$$M = \text{Re}\left[\sum_{n=1}^{T} W(n) \times S(n)^{*}\right] \tag{5.7}$$

Similarly, in the presence of a PU, it becomes

$$M = \sum_{n=1}^{T} |S(n)|^{2} + \text{Re}\left[\sum_{n=U}^{T} W(n) \times S(n)^{*}\right] \tag{5.8}$$

The decision on the detection of the presence of a PU signal is made by comparing the decision metric M with the fixed threshold λ_E. Since this approach requires a short observation period T, it is susceptible to synchronization errors.

5.2.4.2.2.2 Transmitter-Based Sensing

In this approach, SUs can detect the presence of the PUs in its vicinity. When the RSS of the PU with respect to the SU is weak, it can be considered to be located far away from the SU. Then, the sensed spectrum can be made available for the SU. The basic hypothesis for transmitter detection is given as follows:

$$x(t) = \begin{cases} s(t), & H_0 \\ n(t), & H_1 \end{cases} \tag{5.9}$$

where $x(t)$ is the received signal, $s(t)$ is the PU transmitted signal, $n(t)$ is AWGN, and h is the amplitude gain of the channel. As mentioned earlier, H_0 indicates the presence and H_1 indicates the absence of PU. This approach suffers under fading channel condition, as the distance between the PU and SU alone cannot be considered for RSS degradation.

The three main hypothesis-based transmitter detection approaches are described as follows:

- *Energy sensing*: Whenever information gathered about the PU signal becomes insufficient, and power of the random Gaussian noise is alone known, then SS can be done with an optimal energy detector. The operation of the energy sensing model is shown in Figure 5.7. This model is simple and can be implemented efficiently using a fast Fourier transform (FFT) algorithm [17].

- *Matched filter sensing*: A matched filter (MF) is a linear filter designed to maximize the output SNR for a given input signal. When the SU has a priori knowledge of the PU signal, MF detection can be applied. The operation of the MF-based sensing equivalent to correlation is illustrated in Figure 5.8.

The PU signal x is convolved with h, the impulse response of the MF which is the time-shifted version of a reference signal. The operation of MF detection is expressed as

$$Y(n) = \sum_{k=-\infty}^{\infty} h(n-k) \times x(k) \tag{5.10}$$

where x is the PU signal and h is the impulse response of MF. H_0 indicates the presence and H_1 the absence of a PU.

This approach is computationally efficient as it involves few samples and provides promising results when PU signal information is known to the SU [18]. However, it suffers from a few drawbacks such as accurate prior knowledge of every primary signal and dedicated receiver to acquire a signal from different types of PUs.

- *Cyclostationary-based sensing*: In this approach, the inherent cyclostationary features such as periodicity and spectral correlation of the received primary signal is exploited to sense the availability of the spectrum as shown in Figure 5.9. This approach uses cyclic spectral correlation function parameter to detect the presence of the PU signals. Due to noise rejection capability, this approach outperforms energy-detection method even in low SNR regions. It is more suitable for practical scenarios, when prior knowledge about the PU signal remains unknown.

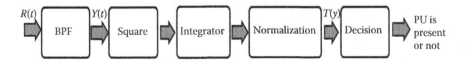

FIGURE 5.7
Energy sensing model.

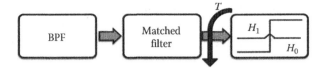

FIGURE 5.8
Matched filter based sensing.

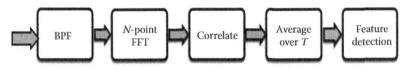

FIGURE 5.9
Cyclostationary-based sensing.

Moreover, the type of modulation scheme used by the PU signal can also be determined. However, this approach suffers drawbacks such as spectral leakage of high amplitude signals, nonlinearity, and high computational complexity [19].

5.2.4.2.3 Radio Identification–Based Sensing

From the sensing approaches discussed in the previous section, it can be clearly understood that the impact of interference between the transmitter (PU) and receiver (SU) plays a crucial role affecting the sensing accuracy. Hence, in this approach a study of interference with respect to the transmitter is analyzed. It is observed that by regulating the output transmission power and out-of-band emissions based on its location with respect to other users, the inference caused due to transmitter can be minimized [20].

5.2.4.3 Interference-Based Detection

In Section 5.3, the coexistence of SUs with PUs in CRNs has been discussed. The SS approaches fall under the category of interweave paradigm. However, in practical scenarios underlay and overlay paradigms also exist. In this section, two SS approaches are presented under this category.

5.2.4.3.1 Primary Receiver Detection

In a real-time wireless communication environment, the local oscillator (LO) present in the receiver emits leakage power from its front end while receiving data from the transmitter. Such leakage power may cause interference to the adjacent transceiver. In a CRN, this scenario can be experienced in an underlay or overlay paradigm. When the LO of the primary receiver emits leakage power while receiving the data from primary transmitter, it causes interference to other cognitive users within its vicinity. Therefore, to alleviate this problem, a low-cost sensor node is mounted close to the receiver of the PU to detect the leakage power emission. The local sensor node then reports the sensed information to the CR users from which spectrum occupancy status can be identified [21].

5.2.4.3.2 Interference Temperature Management

Similar to the previous approach, the basic idea behind the interference temperature management is to fix an upper interference limit for the given frequency band used by the CR user according to the geographic location, so that the interference caused by them when using a specific band in a specific area can be minimized. This is achieved by regulating the transmission power of the CR user transmitters based on their locations with respect to PUs. The interference caused by the CR user is measured at the receiver (PUs) [21]. Thus, coexistence of SUs with PUs is achieved by restricting the interference temperature level.

5.2.5 Comparison of SS Approaches

Figure 5.10 shows a comparison of various SS approaches. It can be inferred that waveform-based sensing approach is more robust when compared to both energy detector and cyclostationary-based sensing as it involves coherent processing using a deterministic signal component. However, it requires prior information about the characteristics of the PU in the form of pilot or pattern which adds complexity to the sensing module. The performance of energy detector–based sensing is not promising when noise is not stationary and its variance is not known. Further, the effects of baseband filter and spurious tones also influence the performance degradation. From the literature [19],

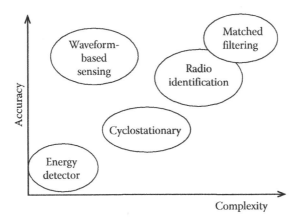

FIGURE 5.10
Comparison of various SS approaches.

it is observed that cyclostationary-based approach performance may be worse when compared to energy detector–based sensing, whenever noise happens to be stationary.

However, noise becomes nonstationary in the presence of cochannel or adjacent channel interferers. Under these circumstances the energy detector–based sensing approach fails, while the cyclostationary-based approach is not affected. On the other hand, cyclostationary features may be completely lost due to channel fading [22]. Hence certain trade-offs need to be considered while selecting an SS approach. The characteristics of the PUs are found to be a major design factor in selecting an SS approach. Other factors include required accuracy, sensing duration requirements, computational complexity, and network requirements.

5.2.6 Need for Wideband SS

The cooperative sensing adopted in narrowband SS exploits the spatial diversity of cooperative CR (SUs) focusing sensing of one frequency band in each round of cooperation. To determine the availability of the spectrum in multiple bands, the CR users have to switch to each band separately every time which may lead to synchronization problem. This process can incur significant switching delay and synchronization overhead. Wideband SS is an alternative approach, in which CR users can cooperatively sense multiple bands simultaneously involving less sensing time [23]. Wideband cooperative sensing has recently gained much attention in the literature. However, it raises many open research issues such as narrowband–wideband trade-off and signal classification. Although wideband sensing when compared to narrowband sensing reduces sensing time and channel switching overhead, it requires additional hardware to facilitate simultaneous detection of multiple bands. Hence, a trade-off between both sensing approaches has to be investigated in terms of various detection performance matrices such as sensing delay, complexity, and throughput. Several approaches exist in the literature [23]. However, it is beyond the scope of this chapter.

5.3 Conclusion

In this chapter, the fundamental concept and requirements of the CRN and its four primary functions, namely SS, spectrum management, spectrum sharing, and spectrum mobility, are discussed. Principles and various narrowband SS approaches are explained and a comparison is made. Finally, the need for wideband SS and its advantages and disadvantages is also discussed. This chapter helps as a base reference for future research.

Acknowledgments

I would like to thank my research scholars, Saraswathi Priyadharshini, A., Bino, J., and Ezhilarasi, S., for their support in writing this chapter.

References

1. Zhang, Y. 2008. Dynamic spectrum access in cognitive radio wireless networks. *Proceedings of IEEE International Conference on Communications,* Beijing. pp. 4927–4932.
2. Sahai, A., N. Hoven, S. M. Mishra, and R. Tandra. 2006. Fundamental tradeoffs in robust spectrum sensing for opportunistic frequency reuse. *IEEE Journal Selected Areas of Communications.* 1: 1–75
3. Mehta, T., N. Kumar, and S. S. Saini. 2013. Comparison of spectrum sensing techniques in cognitive radio networks. *International Journal on Electronics and Communication Technology* 4 (3): 33–37.
4. Hattab, G., and M. Ibnkahla. 2014. Multiband spectrum access: Great promises for future cognitive radio networks. *Proceedings of the IEEE* 102 (3): 282–306.
5. Biglieri, E., A. J. Goldsmith, L. J. Greenstein, and N. B. Mandayam. 2012. *Principles of Cognitive Radio.* New York, NY: Cambridge University Press.
6. Wang, W. 2009. Spectrum sensing for cognitive radio. *Proceedings of the IEEE Computer Society,* Nanchang. pp. 110–112.
7. Subhedar, M., and G. Birajdar. 2011. Spectrum sensing techniques in cognitive radio networks: A survey. *International Journal of Next-Generation Networks (IJNGN)* 3 (2): 37–51.
8. Jaiswal, M., A. K. Sharma, and V. Singh. 2013. A survey on spectrum sensing techniques for cognitive radio. *Conference on Advances in Communication and Control Systems,* D.I.T. Dehradun, India. pp. 647–660.
9. Sharan, V. and P. Wankhede. *Spectrum sensing for cognitive radio. International Journal of Communication Networks and Information Security (IJCNIS)* 4 (1): 14–22.
10. Cabric, A. D., S. Mishra, and R. Brodersen. 2004. Implementation issues in spectrum sensing for cognitive radios. *Processing of Asilomar Conference on Signals, Systems, and Computers,* vol. 1, Pacific Grove, CA. pp. 772–776.
11. Visotsky, E., S. Kuffner, and R. Peterson. 2005. On collaborative detection of TV transmissions in support of dynamic spectrum sharing. *Proceedings of IEEE DySPAN,* Baltimore, MD. pp. 338–345.
12. Digham, F. F., M. S. Alouini, and M. K. Simon. 2007. On the energy detection of unknown signals over fading channels. *IEEE Transactions on Communications* 55 (1): 21–24.
13. Pillay, N., and H. J. Xu. 2013. Eigenvalue-based spectrum sensing using the exact distribution of the maximum eigenvalue of a Wishart matrix. *IET Signal Processing* 7 (9): 833–842.
14. Wang, S., J. Bao, B. Shen, Q. Huang, and Q. Chen. 2014. Eigenvector based cooperative wideband spectrum sensing for cognitive radios. *Proceedings of IEEE International Conference on Ubiquitous and Future Networks,* TBD, Shanghai, China. pp. 346–351.
15. Zeng, Y., and Y.-C. Liang. 2009. Eigenvalue-based spectrum sensing algorithms for cognitive radio. *IEEE Transaction on Communications* 57 (6): 1784–1793.

16. Zeng, Y., and Y. C. Liang. 2009. Spectrum-sensing algorithms for cognitive radio based on statistical covariances. *IEEE Transaction on Vehicular Technology* 58 (4): 1804–1815.
17. Liu, X., M. Jia, X. Gu, and X. Tan. 2013. Optimal periodic cooperative spectrum sensing based on weight fusion in cognitive radio networks. *Sensors* 13: 5251–5272.
18. Akyildiz, I. F., B. F. Lo, and R. Balakrishnan. (2011). Cooperative spectrum sensing in cognitive radio networks: A survey. *Journal on Physical Communication* 4 (1): 40–62.
19. Sutton, P. D., J. Lotze, K. E. Nolan, and L. E. Doyle. 2007. Cyclostationary signature detection in multipath Rayleigh fading environments. *Proceedings of IEEE International conference on Cognitive Radio Oriented Wireless Networks and Communication*, Orlando, FL, USA. pp. 408–413.
20. Yucek, T., and H. Arslan. 2006. Spectrum characterization for opportunistic cognitive radio systems. *Proceedings of IEEE Conference of Military Communication*, Washington, D.C., USA. pp. 1–6.
21. Thanayankizil, L., and A. Kailas. 2008. *Spectrum Sensing Techniques (II): Receiver Detection and Interference Management*. White paper.
22. Yucek, T., and H. Arslan. 2009. A survey of spectrum sensing algorithms for cognitive radio applications. *Proceedings of the IEEE Communications Surveys and Tutorials* 11 (1): 116–130.
23. Bkassiny, M., and S. K. Jayaweera. 2014. Robust, non-Gaussian wideband spectrum sensing in cognitive radios. *IEEE Transactions on Wireless Communications* 13 (11): 6410–6421.

6

Spectrum-Sensing Techniques in Cognitive Radio Networks: A Review

Jyotshana Kanti, Ashish Bagwari, and Geetam Singh Tomar

CONTENTS

6.1 Introduction

Wireless communication has garnered a lot of attention nowadays and the cognitive radio network (CRN) is one of the future-based technologies in wireless communication systems. The idea of cognitive radio (CR) was first introduced in 1998 by Joseph Mitola III at KTH (the Royal Institute of Technology in Stockholm). CR is an intelligent wireless device that has cognitive, or unlicensed, or secondary users (SUs). These CRs sense the primary user's (PUs) licensed spectrum band in order to establish a communication link between radio nodes in real time. A CR comes under IEEE 802.22 Wireless Regional Area Network (WRAN)

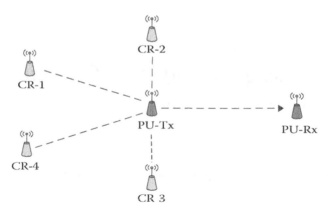

FIGURE 6.1
Cognitive radio network. Tx, transmitter; Rx, receiver.

standard and has the ability to detect channel usage, analyze the channel information, and make a decision whether and how to access the channel. The US Federal Communications Commission (FCC) gave a generalized definition: "cognitive radio: a radio or system that senses its operational electromagnetic environment, and can dynamically and autonomously adjust its radio operating parameters to modify system operation, such as maximize throughput, mitigate interference, facilitate interoperability, and access secondary markets." The basic goal of a CRN is to provide reliable communication connection anywhere, every time, and utilize the spectrum in an efficient manner. The requirements of current wireless communication technology are not fulfilled by static allocation scheme, and that is why dynamic spectrum is required for wireless networks. CR uses dynamic spectrum allocation scheme to mitigate bandwidth crises problem, senses the spectrum, and identifies the vacant frequency bands, thus CR users can use vacant frequency bands when the PUs are idle in order to avoid interference between PUs and SUs. The basic structure of a CRN is depicted in Figure 6.1. A PU is a licensed user that has been allocated a band of spectrum for exclusive use. A SU is an unlicensed user that does not have allocated band of spectrum. We use spectrum-sensing (SS) schemes to sense the licensed frequency band of a PU signal at low signal-to-noise (SNR), and then declare whether the frequency band is free or busy.

6.2 CRN Functions

Generally, CR users should be able to sense all spectrums, then select best vacant spectrum, share selected spectrum information to neighbor cognitive users, and finally, provide seamless connectivity during data transmission. To maintain such conditions, four basic functions are required in CRNs which include SS, spectrum decision/management, spectrum sharing/allocation, and spectrum mobility/handoff.

- *Spectrum sensing*: It identifies all the possible and available spectrum holes to avoid interference. SS determines which portion of the spectrum is vacant and senses the presence of licensed PUs.

- *Spectrum decision*: It captures the best available vacant spectrum holes among the detected ones.

- *Spectrum sharing*: It shares the spectrum related information among the neighboring nodes.
- *Spectrum mobility*: If the spectrum in use by a CR user is required for PU, CR leaves the present band and switches to another vacant spectrum band in order to provide seamless connectivity.

In a wireless communication system, few of the licensed spectrum bands are so busy and overloaded that longer wait times and interference are encountered. On the contrary, the rest of the bands are underused. The FCC acknowledges the variability in licensed spectrum usage. According to an FCC report, 70% of the allocated PU licensed spectrum band called white space/spectrum holes remains unused at any one point of time as shown in Figure 6.2. This surprising result is evident in the current static channel allocation scheme, which is unreliable, inefficient, and expensive. In a static allocation scheme, a fixed spectrum band is allocated to a single mobile user. However, nowadays, this scheme is not feasible and a fruitful solution of the bandwidth crises problem is required. In fact, an overhaul is required for the unlicensed spectrum/bands. Congestion resulting from the coexistence of heterogeneous devices operating in these bands is on the rise. For example, the license-free industrial, scientific, and medical (ISM) radio band is congested by wireless local area network equipment, such as cordless phones, microwave ovens, Bluetooth devices, and other radio users. Devices using unlicensed bands should have higher performance capabilities and better user quality of service. The selected availability of spectrum bands and inefficient use of existing RF resources require a new communication model to utilize radio spectrum band opportunistically with greater efficiency. The new model should support methods to ensure spectrum availability during traffic jams, reduce interference among users, and also make communications far more dependable. In the current scenario, the shortage of radio spectrum band can also be blamed for the cost and performance limits of current and legacy hardware. Software-defined radio (SDR) is the next-generation wireless technology that holds the key to promote better spectrum usage from an underlying hardware/physical layer perspective. SDR uses both embedded signal-processing algorithms to sift out weak signals and reconfigurable code structures to receive and transmit the new radio protocols. However, a CR is the system-wide solution.

In a typical CRN, there are two types of users, i.e., users of a given frequency band are classified into PUs and SUs. PUs are the licensed users having a licensed spectrum band allocated

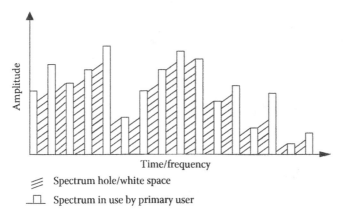

FIGURE 6.2
CRN concepts: spectrum holes.

to them, and SUs are the unlicensed users who do not have a licensed band and opportunistically access the spectrum of the PU when not in use. A CRN forms when SUs utilize spectrum holes in the licensed spectrum of the PU for communication. Generally, holes are white or gray spaces which are temporally unused sections of licensed spectrum and are free of PU signal. Figure 6.2 illustrates a scenario of PUs and SUs utilizing a frequency band.

In the other cognitive scenario, there are no allocated PUs for unlicensed spectrum. Since there are no license holders, all radio network entities have an equal right to access the spectrum. Multiple CRs coexist and communicate using the same portion of spectrum. The objective of the CR in these scenarios is a more intelligent and fair spectrum sharing to make open spectrum usage much more efficient. It will help in utilizing the unused channels to use the spectrum efficiently, and also includes better channel assignment and management policy.

6.3 Spectrum-Sensing Techniques

The main goal of CR is to resolve bandwidth crises problem by utilizing the natural resources well such as transmitted energy, time, and frequency. CR technology detects the available spectrum bands and identifies which bands are vacant and where. Detecting vacant band is only possible by using SS techniques which are useful to improve the spectral efficiency of a network. Unused frequencies can be considered as a spectrum pool from which frequencies can be assigned to cognitive radio users (CRUs), and a CR user can also directly use frequencies discovered to be vacant without gathering these frequencies into a common pool. Moreover, CR techniques can be used internally within a licensed network to improve the efficiency of the spectrum use. In a CRN, the CR users periodically observe the radio spectrum and opportunistically communicate over the white space or spectrum holes.

As shown in Figure 6.3, there are basically three types of SS techniques for detecting a PU licensed spectrum band [1–3].

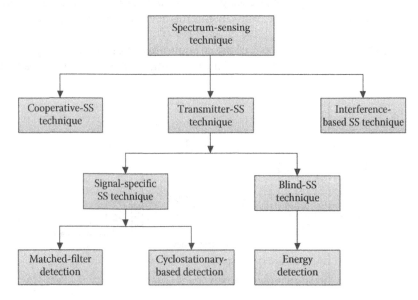

FIGURE 6.3
CRN spectrum-sensing techniques.

6.3.1 Cooperative Spectrum-Sensing Technique

In cooperative detection, all CR users work together to take a final decision that the licensed user's spectrum is free or not. There are basically two types of cooperative SS techniques named as centralized and distributed.

In centralized SS, there is one common center controller called the "fusion center" which receives local decision data from each radio user. Based on received data, a common central controller creates a spectrum occupancy map of the overall radio network, and makes a final decision regarding the status of the PU spectrum band.

On the other hand, in distributed SS technique, all the radio users share and exchange spectrum observations information among them, develop a spectrum occupancy map, and take the final decision individually.

Cooperative detection is one of the useful detection techniques, which increases the probability of detection of a PU signal by mitigating multipath fading and shadowing RF pathologies. Moreover, it also reduces hidden node problems in wireless communication networks, in which a CR has good line of sight of a receiving radio, but is not be able to detect a second transmitting radio in the same locality of the receiving radio due to shadowing, or because the second transmitter is geographically distant from it. Cooperation or collaboration between entire CR users can resolve this hidden node problem which will be discussed later.

6.3.2 Transmitter Spectrum-Sensing Technique

In this SS technique, CR identifies the free licensed spectrum bands if the PU is transmitting in its vicinity. To detect the PU signal, there is a mathematical hypothesis for received signal given as

$$x(n) = \begin{cases} w(n), & H_0 \\ s(n)h(n) + w(n), & H_1 \end{cases} \tag{6.1}$$

where $x(n)$ is the signal received by CR users, $s(n)$ is the licensed user signal, $w(n)$ is the additive white Gaussian Noise which has zero mean value, and if the variance is σ_w^2, the channel between PU and CR is considered the Rayleigh channel, having channel gain $h(n)$. H_0, known as the null hypothesis, shows the absence of a PU while H_1 is the alternative hypothesis and shows that the PU is present.

Transmitter SS technique can be divided into two categories: signal specific sensing technique and blind-sensing technique.

6.3.2.1 Signal-Specific Spectrum-Sensing Technique

This sensing technique requires prior knowledge of the PU signal. The detection techniques based on signal specific are called matched filter detection and cyclostationary-based detection.

6.3.2.1.1 Matched Filter Detection

This technique is also known as coherent detection and is an optimum spectrum detection method. Matched filter sensing technique maximizes SNR, but requires prior information of the PU such as modulation type, packet format, pulse shape, transmitting power, pilots, synchronization word, operational frequency, preambles, spreading codes, and bandwidth. In stationary Gaussian noise, matched filter works as an optimal detector. Figure 6.4 depicts the block diagram of a matched filter detector. The feature of matched filter is that it has lesser sensing time, but its main weakness is that it requires the PU's prior information which is not a preferable solution to detect the licensed band in a real world; also the implementation is computationally complex.

6.3.2.1.2 Cyclostationary-Based Detection

In cyclostationary-based detection, a signal is seen to be cyclostationary if its statistics, i.e., mean or autocorrelation, are a periodic function over a certain period. Because modulated signals are coupled with sinusoidal carrier waves, repeating spreading code sequences, or cyclic prefixes all of which have a built-in periodicity, their mean, and autocorrelation are periodic in nature which is considered as cyclostationary. Noise is a wide-sense stationary signal with no correlation. Using a spectral correlation function, it is easy to distinguish a noise signal from the modulated signal and hence, detection of the PU signal is simple. Cyclostationary detection has several advantages. It can differentiate noise power from signal power, more robust to noise uncertainty, and can work with a lower SNR. But it requires partial information of the PU which makes it computationally complex, along with a longer observation time. Figure 6.5 shows the block diagram of a cyclostationary-based detector.

6.3.2.2 Blind Spectrum-Sensing Technique

Blind sensing technique does not require any prior information of a PU signal, but detects the licensed users signal based on their energy level and that's why this technique is also known as the energy-detection technique.

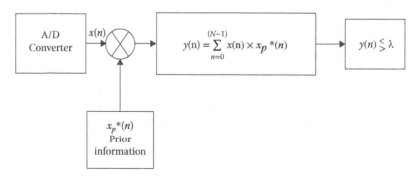

FIGURE 6.4
Matched filter detector.

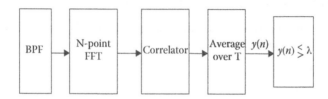

FIGURE 6.5
Cyclostationary-based detector.

6.3.2.2.1 Energy Detection

In CRNs, if an unlicensed user's receiver cannot collect sufficient information of a PU signal, only the power of random Gaussian noise can be used to detect or determine the presence of a PU signal, the optimal detector is called an energy detector (ED). ED's implementation and computation are easier than others. However, there are some limitations such as at low SNR its performance degrades, i.e., detector is not able to distinguish a noise signal from the user signal under low SNR, and is also not effective for signals whose signal power has been spread over a wideband.

Figure 6.6 depicts the block diagram of an ED, where an analog-to-digital converter converts an analog signal to digital waveform and passes to a square law device, which takes the square of incoming digital signal and feeds it to the summation device in order to calculate the energy of message signal, finally the signal $y(t)$ compares with threshold value (λ) and generates H_0 or H_1 based on the decision. If $y(n)$ is greater than λ it will decide H_0 (PU signal is absent or channel is free) else H_1 (PU signal is present or channel is busy).

There are some important parameters related to SS performance, e.g., probability of detection (P_d), probability of false alarm (P_f), and probability of miss-detection (P_m). P_d is the probability of accurately deciding the presence of PU signal; P_f refers to the probability that SUs incorrectly decide about the channel being idle when the PU is actually transmitting; and P_m refers to the probability of an SU missing the PU signal when the PU is transmitting.

6.3.3 Interference-Based Spectrum-Sensing Technique

In this technique, CRs focus on calculating the interference at the receiver terminal. FCC presented a new model of calculating interference mentioned as interference temperature. The proposed model handles interference at the receiver based on the interference temperature limit, which is the maximum amount of additional interference that the receiver can bear. The model accounts for the cumulative RF energy from multiple transmissions and sets a maximum cap on their aggregate level. As long as the transmissions of CR users do not exceed this limit, they can use a particular spectrum band. The major problem of the proposed model is that the CR users should know the exact location of the nearby PUs, otherwise it is difficult to measure the interference. Sometimes, the CR users deprive licensed users of their licensed spectrum bands. This occurs if the transmitting power of a CR is higher than the transmitting power of licensed users, and the licensed users exist near the CR users. This is a very serious problem with this model.

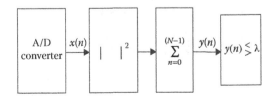

FIGURE 6.6
Energy detector.

6.4 Issues in CRNs

CRNs are a future-based wireless communication technology with various challenges or issues. In this chapter, we are dealing with a few major problems described as follows.

6.4.1 Spectrum-Sensing Failure Problem

In the ED-based SS technique, noise uncertainty [4] makes the perfect threshold level for CR difficult to be set due to which SS reliability reduces [5]. Moreover, this may not be optimum under low SNRs, where the performance of fixed threshold (λ_1)-based ED can significantly fluctuate from the desired targeted performance metrics.

In Figure 6.7, the x-axis shows the power level of signals and the y-axis shows the signals, probability. There are two curves depicting the PU signal and noise. According to the CRN scheme, it is very easy to detect the PU and noise if both the signals are separated from each other. For example if ED gets a PU signal it shows H_1, i.e., the channel is occupied, and if it gets a noise signal it shows H_0, i.e., the channel is unoccupied. But, if the PU signal and noise both intersect each other, it is very difficult to sense desired signals. In Figure 6.7, the area between the PU and noise curve, or under upper bound (λ_1) and lower bound (λ_2), is called the confused region, in which single threshold is not a fruitful solution to detect a PU signal.

6.4.2 Fading and Shadowing Problem

Multipath fading and shadowing is one of the reasons of increasing hidden node problem in carrier sense multiple accessing (CSMA). Figure 6.8 expresses the hidden node problem, where dashed circles indicate the operating ranges of the PU transmitter and the CR. The CR user is not able to sense the PU transmitter signal because of the location of node and creates unwanted interference to the PU receiver.

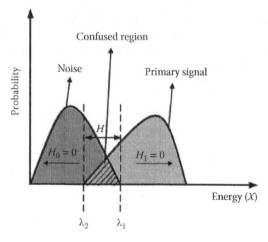

FIGURE 6.7
Energy distribution of primary user's signal and noise.

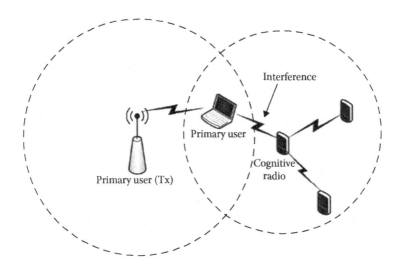

FIGURE 6.8
Hidden primary user's problem in CRNs. Tx, transmitter.

6.4.3 Spectrum-Sensing Time

The SS time defines the total time taken by the CR user to detect a PU signal. Suppose if SS time is increased, PU can utilize its spectrum in a better manner and the limit is decided where CR cannot interfere throughout the time. More PUs will be detected if the SS is high, due to which the level of interference will be less. The sensing time depends on the number of samples received by the CR user. More time is devoted to sensing and less for data transmissions, therefore, this phenomenon is called the sensing efficiency problem [6,7].

6.5 Related Works

6.5.1 Adaptive Spectrum Sensing

In this technique, we focus on two points: the first to improve local sensing and the second to improve cooperative SS for better data fusion results [8]. During cooperative SS in CRNs, each and every CR user sends their local decision to a common fusion center to take final decision about the presence or absence of PU signal [9]. In local SS, all the SUs make observations individually and the final decision is made individually. In literature, many improvements for local SS are proposed but there is still room for more improvement. Sensing a wideband spectrum is significant in CR; however, only a few researchers have worked on wideband SS in CRs. Two-stage SS is one of the techniques to deal with this issue. Hur et al. [10] proposed a two-stage wideband SS technique combining coarse and fine sensing. Coarse sensing exists in first stage and uses wavelet-transform-based multiresolution spectrum-sensing (MRSS) technique, where it performs over the entire frequency range with a wide bandwidth. In the first stage, occupied and candidate spectrum segments are identified. In the second stage, fine sensing is applied to the candidate spectrum segments to detect unique features of modulated signals. Confirmation of an unoccupied segment is done by careful fine sensing. Luo et al. [11] presented a two-stage dynamic spectrum access approach, in which first-stage coarse resolution sensing (CRS) is divided into equal-sized coarse sensing blocks (CSB) of equal bandwidth. Second-stage fine resolution sensing is done using ED applied on CSB to determine idle channel. Further, Maleki et al. [12] introduced another two-stage sensing scheme, where coarse sensing uses ED in the first stage, while cyclostationary detection is used in fine sensing in the second stage. Only if the coarse stage declares that the channel is free, the fine stage can be used for final decision. Otherwise, coarse sensing will give the final decision. Yue et al. [13] proposed a new sensing technique, known as two-stage SS scheme in which coarse detection carries ED, where the power in each channel detector decides the final decision, and the other stage, i.e., the fine stage, carries a one-order cyclostationary technique to detect weak signals. In all the afore-mentioned techniques, both stages perform SS, hence, increase the mean detection time. In this scheme, we considered only one of the detection techniques running during the two stages, based on the estimated SNR. In the worst case, mean detection time is equal to one-order cyclostationary detection. Although two stages are running in this scheme, the SNR of the channel can be estimated in advance and the history of channel SNR can be maintained to further decrease the mean SS time.

6.5.1.1 Limitations

The adaptive SS technique [8] presents a new scheme, where out of two stages only one of the detection technique runs at a time based on the estimated SNR [5]. Although this scheme reduces the mean sensing time, it does not consider SS failure problem [14].

6.5.2 Generalized Likelihood Ratio Test–Based Spectrum Sensing for CR

We know that current SS is inefficient in terms of any given location, time, and frequency band, where the radio spectrum is not utilized fully. Actually, in television broadcast-ing, which is a location-specific service, at a given location the incumbent licensed user may not use a specific spectrum channel at all but data transmission in that spectrum by other entities is still illegal. The concept of "spectrum sharing," "opportunistic spectrum access," or "cognitive radio" is defined as the coexistence of a CRN with a primary one that is the legal owner of the spectral band of interest [15]. There are several SS algorithms presented and studied in the literature, including, e.g., energy detection [16–19], matched filtering [18,20–22], and cyclostationary detection [23,24], but each one has merits and demerits, e.g., matched filter requires prior information of the waveform received from the primary transmitter and cyclostationary detection technique should know the cyclic frequency of the PU signal. But, energy detection does not require any kind of prior infor-mation of the PU signal to be detected and is fruitful for unknown dispersive spectrum channels. Energy detection is the best way for detecting independent and identically dis-tributed (i.i.d.) sequences [18], but does not work well to detect the presence of correlated signals, which is the case for most practical applications. In this scheme, we used the gen-eralized likelihood ratio test (GLRT) and considered certain parameters as unknowns in the probability distribution of the observations with and without the PU signal, and then making certain reasonable assumptions, resulting in a number of attractive algorithms for SS. These algorithms depend on the eigenvalues of the sample covariance matrix of the detected signal [15]. They require that one or both conditions should be satisfied, one is that the primary signal is nonwhite, and second that it reserves a vector space that is strictly a subspace of the detection signal space.

6.5.2.1 Limitations

The GLRT-based detection scheme [15] enhances the detection performance. This technique provides better results as compared to the conventional ED, whether noise variance is known or unknown. But, implementation is more complicated because it requires estimating the signal covariance matrix, and performs an eigen-decomposition on this estimate, the same way its mathematical expression is more complicated and also increases the system cost.

6.6 Proposed Scheme

6.6.1 Two-Stage Detector Comprising of Weighted-ED and Correlated-GLRT Detection Scheme

CR is used to detect situations to utilize the vacant spectrum band of licensed users when it is not used by them. SS techniques are used to allocate the spectrum to the SUs for a specific time period and geographical location [1]. SS is performed by the two-stage detector, which uses weighted-ED (W-ED) placed in first stage, and correlated-GLRT (C-GLRT) placed in the second stage [25]. When the noise variance is known, the W-ED acts as a simple ED [26,27]. However if we do not have exact knowledge of the noise variance, it leads to incorrect evaluation of the threshold and hence to an increase in the false-alarm probability [28]. When the noise variance is unknown, the eigenvalue-based spectrum detector GLRT will be used [15]. These detectors are based on the correlated multiple antennas and hence are suitable for the practical use.

In the proposed model, assume that the CR or SU is employed with M antenna, then the exponential correlation model is generally used to define the correlation among the antennas. The correlation matrix "C" of antennas is a symmetric toeplitz matrix, the components of which can be written as

$$C_{ij} = \begin{cases} \rho^{j-i}, & i \leq j \\ C_{ji}^*, & i > j \end{cases} \tag{6.2}$$

In the given Equation 6.2, $i, j = 1, 2, \ldots, M$, and $0 \leq \rho \leq 1$, ρ is the antenna correlation coefficient between two adjacent antennas; the mathematical expression is $\rho = \exp^{-23\Lambda^2\left(\frac{d}{\lambda_c}\right)^2}$. It depends on the angular spread (Λ), distance (d) between two adjacent antennas, and wavelength (λ_c). Angular spread (Λ) plays an important role to determine how spread out multipath power is across the horizon. The range of angular spread varies from 0 to 1, where 0 is representing the case of a single multipath component from a single direction, and 1 is representing no clear bias in the angular distribution of received power (Figure 6.9).

We assume the setup where multiple antennas are deployed at the single secondary node to detect the primary signal. The number of antennas which are used at the secondary node is represented by M. Therefore, to identify the licensed user signal with a very low SNR, various time instants have been considered, represented by N. First, consider the noise signal represented by $w(n)$ having Gaussian distribution with mean value zero and

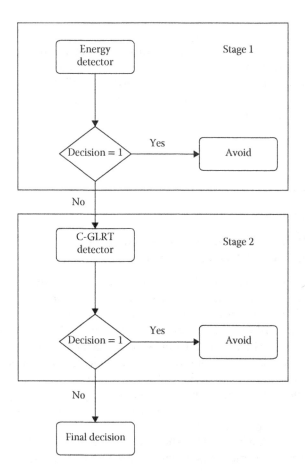

FIGURE 6.9
Flow chart of the proposed two-stage detector.

covariance matrix $\sigma_n^2 I$. The signal being transmitted by PU is represented by $s(n)$ and is complex phase shift keying modulated having an average power equal to p which we have assumed to be 1. The signal is transmitted over a channel which can be white Gaussian or Rayleigh fading channel. The channel gain is represented by $h(n)$ and a Gaussian distribution with zero mean value, and variance represented by σ_h^2. The detected signal is represented by $x(n)$. Since M antennas are considered at the SUs in this case, the received signal vector $x(n)$ is an $M \times 1$ vector. The entire received signal matrix is represented by $X(n)$ formed by considering the received signals at each antenna at different instants of time. Therefore $X(n)$ is given as

$$X(n) = \left[x(1) \; x(2), \ldots, x(N) \right] \tag{6.3}$$

The SS problem can be expressed based on two test hypotheses, H_0 and H_1. In H_0 we assume that we are receiving only the noise signal. Hence the received signal $x(n)$ is equal to the noise signal, i.e.,

$$H_0 : x_i(n) = w_i(n) \tag{6.4}$$

In H_1, it is expected that licensed signal and noise both are received. Hence the received signal here is given as

$$H_1 : x_i(n) = h_i(n) \times s(n) + w_i(n) \tag{6.5}$$

where $i = 1, 2, \ldots, M$, and $n = 1, 2, \ldots, N$.

Therefore, the distribution of $X(n)$ is given as

$$X \approx \begin{cases} C_N\left(0, \sigma_w^2 I\right) & \text{under } H_0 \\ C_N\left(0, P\sigma_h^2 C + \sigma_w^2 I\right) & \text{under } H_1 \end{cases} \tag{6.6}$$

Then, likelihood functions under H_0 and H_1 can be defined as

$$p\left(X | H_0, \sigma_w^2\right) = \prod_{n=1}^{N} \frac{1}{\pi^M \sigma_w^{2M}} \times \exp\left(\frac{-x(n)^H x(n)}{\sigma_w^2}\right) \tag{6.7}$$

$$p\left(X | H_1, \sigma_w^2\right) = \prod_{n=1}^{N} \frac{1}{\pi^M \det\left(P\sigma_h^2 C + \sigma_w^2 I\right)} \times \exp\left(-x(n)^H \left(P\sigma_h^2 C + \sigma_w^2 I\right)^{-1} x(n)\right) \tag{6.8}$$

Equations 6.7 and 6.8 show the likelihood functions under H_0 and H_1. The novelty of the proposed detection scheme is that it utilizes the property of both W-ED and C-GLRT detectors. Due to W-ED, it assigns the higher weight coefficients to the signal component, which corresponds to larger eigenvalues, while according to C-GLRT it considers the correlation effect of the multiple antennas being used at the SUs; hence this arrangement significantly improves the detection performance.

The ED being used at the first stage performs the coarse detection. If it declares that the channel is occupied, the result is simply accepted; however, if the ED declares the channel to be unoccupied the result is given to the other detector, i.e., the second stage of the detector. The C-GLRT forms the second stage of the detector which performs the final detection. The first-stage W-ED uses Neyman–Pearson (N–P) theorem when the noise variance is known, and is given as

$$L(X) = \frac{p\left(X | H_1, \sigma_w^2\right)}{p\left(X | H_0, \sigma_w^2\right)} \tag{6.9}$$

The test statistic is then given as

$$T_{\text{W-ED}}(X) = \ln L(X) \underset{H_0}{\overset{H_1}{\gtrless}} \varepsilon \tag{6.10}$$

In Equation 6.10, ε shows the decision threshold. In the first-stage detector, i.e., the W-ED detector, the detected signal $x(n)$ is first linearly converted into $y(n)$; further, the converted signal $y(t)$ component corresponding to the larger eigenvalue is used with a higher weight coefficient. If all antennas are independent, C defines a diagonal matrix, and all the eigenvalues are same, then the W-ED becomes the ED. When the constraint on probability of detection is known, the threshold decision (ε) can be calculated on the basis of probability of false alarm.

The false-alarm probability is given as

$$P_F^{ED} = P_r\{T_{ED} > \tau | H_0\} = 1 - F_{T_{ED}|H_0}(\tau) \tag{6.11}$$

The probability of detection is given as

$$P_D^{ED} = P_r\{T_{ED} > \tau | H_1\} \tag{6.12}$$

The second-stage C-GLRT-based technique calculates first the maximum likelihood estimate (MLE) of the unknown parameters, denoted by (θ) under H_0 and H_1. It further formulates the GLRT test statistic given as

$$L_G(X) = \frac{p(X|H_1, \theta_1)}{p(X|H_0, \theta_1)} \tag{6.13}$$

The MLE of σ_w^2 computed with the help of likelihood functions under H_0 and H_1 is

$$\sigma_{w0}^2 = \frac{1}{MN} \sum_{n=1}^{N} \frac{x(n)^H x(n)}{\sigma_w^2} = \frac{1}{M} \sum_{i=1}^{M} \lambda_{R_x}^i \tag{6.14}$$

where $\lambda_{R_x}^i$ defines the eigenvalue of the sample covariance matrix R_x defined as $R_x = 1/N X X^H$. The derivative is set to zero and the MLE of σ_w^2 is derived under H_1 as

$$\sigma_{w1}^2 = \max\left(0, \frac{1}{M} \sum_{i=1}^{M} \lambda_{R_x}^i - \frac{P\sigma_h^2}{M} \sum_{i=1}^{M} \lambda_i\right) \tag{6.15}$$

Using the MLE of σ_{w0}^2 and σ_{w1}^2 in the likelihood functions of H_0 and H_1 the test statistic of C-GLRT is derived as

$$T_{C\text{-}GLRT}(X) = \ln L_G(X) \underset{H_0}{\overset{H_1}{\gtrless}} \varepsilon \tag{6.16}$$

The false-alarm probability can be calculated as

$$P_F^{C\text{-}GLRT} = P_r\{T_{C\text{-}GLRT} > \tau | H_0\} \tag{6.17}$$

$$P_F^{C\text{-}GLRT} = 1 - F_{T_{C\text{-}GLRT}|H_0}(\tau) \tag{6.18}$$

The probability of detection is given as

$$P_D^{C\text{-}GLRT} = P_r\{T_{C\text{-}GLRT} > \tau | H_1\} \tag{6.19}$$

In the proposed two-stage detection scheme, the overall false-alarm probability is computed by using the false-alarm probabilities of both W-ED and C-GLRT detectors. False decision is made when the decision statistic is greater than the threshold under H_0 and when the decision statistic is smaller than the threshold under H_1. When the W-ED makes a false decision the result is given to the C-GLRT; based on this the decision of the second stage becomes the final result.

6.7 Simulation Results and Analysis for Two-Stage Detector Scheme

In the presented system model, we assumed that the transmitted power is taken as P which is assumed to be 1 and the channel parameter is taken as 1. The number of samples considered are 20 and number of antennas used are 6. The constraint on the false-alarm probability is 0.01. The detection performance of the proposed two-stage detector is analyzed with existing ED, GLRT, and adaptive spectrum sensing (ASS) detectors.

The probability of detection describes how often PU is susceptible to potential interference from the CR. In CRN, P_d is one of the important parameters to compute the performance of system. According to the IEEE 802.22 WRAN standard, the value of P_d should be as maximum as possible under the constraint of probability of false alarm.

Figure 6.10 illustrates the graph between the probability of detection and SNR. Simulation results indicates that the proposed two-stage detector scheme optimizes detection performance and outperforms the GLRT, ASS, and ED sensing techniques by 6.0%, 23.0%, and 63.0% at −5 dB SNR, respectively.

6.8 Conclusions and Future Work

In this chapter, we presented a review study of various SS techniques. As we discussed earlier, there are various sensing techniques but three of them are mainly used, namely matched filter detection, energy detection, and cyclostationary detection. Each sensing technique has its merits and demerits, e.g., matched filter detection improved SNR, but required the PU's prior information. Energy detection did not require prior information, but degraded performance under low SNR. On the other hand, cyclostationary detection

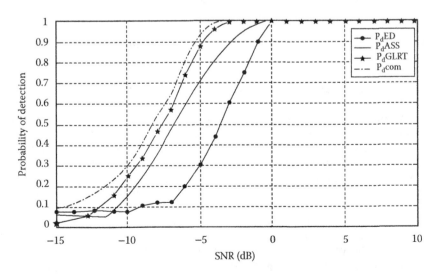

FIGURE 6.10
Detection performance comparison of ED, GLRT, ASS, and proposed two-stage detector.

performed better than both, but required PU information. We further discussed and explained the functions of a CRN, and challenges related to it. Moreover, we have proposed a two-stage detector, the detection performance of which is analyzed with the existing ED, GLRT, and ASS and that the proposed detector performance is better than other existing detectors, i.e., it outperforms the GLRT, ASS, and ED sensing techniques by 6.0%, 23.0%, and 63.0% at −5 dB SNR, respectively. All results conclude that the proposed detection technique exhibits better performances than existing sensing techniques. Hence, it is suitable to be used in present conditions. In future, we will try to further improve the quality of the proposed system in terms of detection.

Acknowledgments

We thank our parents for their support and motivation, for without their blessings and God's grace this chapter would not be possible. This work is dedicated to Anushka Gaur and Anshul Semwal for their true and valuable love.

References

1. Bagwari, A., and B. Singh. 2012. Comparative performance evaluation of spectrum sensing techniques for cognitive radio networks. In *2012 Fourth IEEE International Conference on Computational Intelligence and Communication Networks (CICN-2012)*, Mathura. pp. 98–105.
2. Cabric, D., S. M. Mishra, and R. W. Brodersen. 2004. Implementation issues in spectrum sensing for cognitive radios. In *Proceedings 2004 Asilomar Conference Signals, Systematic, Computer, vol. 1*, Pacific Grove, CA. pp. 772–776.
3. Zeng, Y., Y.-C. Liang, A. T. Hoang, and R. Zhang. 2010. A review on spectrum sensing for cognitive radio: Challenges and solutions. *EURASIP Journal on Advances in Signal Processing* 2010: 1–15.
4. Song, C., Y. D. Alemseged, H. N. Tran, G. Villardi, C. Sun, S. Filin, and H. Harada. 2010. Adaptive two thresholds based energy detection for cooperative spectrum sensing. In *Proceedings 2010 IEEE CCNC*, NJ, USA. pp. 1–6.
5. Tandra, R., and A. Sahai. 2008. SNR walls for signal detection. *IEEE Journal of Selected Topic in Signal Processing* 2 (1): 4–16.
6. Lee, W. Y., and I. F. Akyildiz. 2008. Optimal spectrum sensing framework for cognitive radio networks. *IEEE Transactions on Wireless Communications* 7 (10): 3845–3857.
7. Liang, Y. C., Y. Zeng, E. Peh, and A. T. Hoang. 2008. Sensing-throughput tradeoff for cognitive radio networks. *IEEE Transactions on Wireless Communications* 7 (4): 1326–1337.
8. Ejaz, W., N. U. Hasan, and H. S. Kim. 2012. SNR-based adaptive spectrum sensing for cognitive radio networks. *International Journal of Innovative Computing, Information and Control* 8 (9): 6095–6105.
9. Akildiz, F., B. F. Lo, and R. Balakrishan. 2011. Cooperative spectrum sensing in cognitive radio networks: A survey. *Physical Communication* 4: 40–62.
10. Hur, Y., J. Park, W. Woo, K. Lim, C.-H. Lee, H. Kim, and J. Laskar. 2006. A wideband analog multi-resolution spectrum sensing (MRSS) technique for cognitive radio (CR) systems. *IEEE Proceedings of ISCAS*, Kos, Greece. pp. 4090–4093.
11. Luo, L., N. M. Neihart, S. Roy, and D. J. Allstot. A two-stage sensing technique for dynamic spectrum access. *IEEE Transaction on Wireless Communication*, 8: 3028–3037.

12. Maleki, S., A. Pandharipande, and G. Leus. 2010. Two-stage spectrum sensing for cognitive radios. *IEEE International Conference on Acoustic Speech and Signal Processing*, Dallas, TX. pp. 2946–2949.
13. Yue, W., B. Zheng, Q. Meng, and W. Yue. 2010. Combined energy detection and one-order cyclostationary feature detection techniques in cognitive radio systems. *The Journal of China Universities of Posts and Telecommunications* 17 (4): 18–25.
14. Fehske, A., J. D. Gaeddert, and J. H. Reed. 2005. A new approach to signal classification using spectral correlation and neural networks. In *Proceedings of IEEE DySPAN*, Baltimore, MD. pp. 144–150.
15. Lim, T. J., R. Zhang, Y. C. Liang, and Y. Zeng. 2008. GLRT-based spectrum sensing for cognitive radio. In *Proceedings IEEE Global Telecommunication Conference*, New Orleans, LA. pp. 1–5.
16. Urkowitz, H. 1967. Energy detection of unknown deterministic signals. *Proceedings of the IEEE* 55 (4): 523–531.
17. Sonnenschein, A., and P. M. Fishman. 1992. Radiometric detection of spread spectrum signals in noise of uncertainty power. *IEEE Transaction on Aerospace and Electronic Systems* 28 (3): 654–660.
18. Kay, S. M. 1998. *Fundamentals of Statistical Signal Processing: Detection Theory*, vol. 2. Lebanon, IN: Prentice Hall.
19. Tandra, R., and A. Sahai. 2005. Fundamental limits on detection in low SNR under noise uncertainty. In *WirelessCom 2005*, Maui, HI.
20. Sahai, A., and D. Cabric. 2005. Spectrum sensing: Fundamental limits and practical challenges. In *Proceedings IEEE International Symposium New Frontiers in Dynamic Spectrum Access Networks (DySPAN)*, Baltimore, MD.
21. Chen, H. S., Gao, W., and Daut, D. G. 2007. Signature based spectrum sensing algorithms for IEEE 802.22 WRAN. In *Proceedings of IEEE International Conference on Communication (ICC)*, Glasgow, Scotland. pp. 6487–6492.
22. Cabric, D., Tkachenko, A., and R. W. Brodersen. 2006. Spectrum sensing measurements of pilot, energy, and collaborative detection. In *Military Communication on Conference (MILCOM)*, Washington, DC. pp. 1–7.
23. Gardner, W. A. 1991. Exploitation of spectral redundancy in cyclostationary signals. *IEEE Signals Proceedings of Magazine*, 8: 14–36.
24. Han, N., S. H. Shon, J. O. Joo, and J. M. Kim. 2006. Spectral correlation based signal detection method for spectrum sensing in IEEE 802.22 WRAN systems. In *International Conference Advanced Communication Technology*, Phoenix Park.
25. Luo, L. P., P. Zhang, G. C. Zhang, and J. Y. Qin. 2011. Spectrum sensing for cognitive radio networks with correlated multiple antennas. *Electronics Letters* 47 (23): 1297–1298.
26. Lu L., X. Zhou, U. Onunkwo, and G. Y. Li. 2012. Ten years of research in spectrum sensing and sharing in cognitive radio. *EURASIP Journal on Wireless Communications and Networking* 2012 (28): 1–16.
27. Bagwari, A., and G. S. Tomar. 2014. Cooperative spectrum sensing with multiple antennas using adaptive double-threshold based energy detector in cognitive radio networks. *Springer Journal of the Institution of Engineers (India): Series B* 95 (2): 107–112.
28. Wang, P., J. Fang, N. Han, and H. Li. 2010. Multi antenna-assisted spectrum sensing for cognitive radios. *IEEE Transactions on Vehicular Technology* 59 (4): 1791–1800.

Part III

Collaborative Sensing Techniques in Cognitive Radio Networks

7

Novel Collaborative Spectrum-Sensing Technique Based on Estimated SNR with Adaptive Threshold in Cognitive Radio Networks

Ashish Bagwari, Jyotshana Kanti, and Geetam Singh Tomar

CONTENTS

7.1 Introduction

The number of mobile users is increasing day by day in the current wireless communication scene, which may certainly create bandwidth crises due to limited spectrum availability. Cognitive radio (CR) is a future technology capable of solving the spectrum scarcity problem. In a cognitive radio network (CRN), the unlicensed CR users use the unused licensed band of primary users (PUs) while a PU is not active. The available sensing methods to detect the spectrum are matched filter detector, energy detector (ED), and cyclostationary feature detector [1–7]. Both matched filter and cyclostationary feature detections provide better performing results under low signal-to-noise ratio (SNR) in wireless communication systems but they require the PU's prior information. An ED is one of the most popular detectors for spectrum sensing (SS), also known as the blind SS technique. This technique does not require the prior information of a PU's signal and has low computational complexity, but does not perform well at a low SNR. Similarly, there are also some other limitations in a CRN such as the SS failure problem, sensing time, hidden terminal problem and shadowed effect by severe multipath fading. To resolve these problems, we proposed a sensing scheme known as estimated SNR with adaptive threshold where we sense the PU signal under low SNR, mitigate the sensing failure problem, and have a quick sensing time. In addition, using the collaborative sensing scheme with the proposed estimated SNR sensing, we resolve the hidden terminal problem and shadowing effects.

7.2 Problems in CRNs

The CRN follows the IEEE 802.22 standards for wireless regional area networks (WRANs). There are various problems or challenges related to SS in the CRN which are given as follows:

1. SS failure problem
2. SS time
3. Fading and shadowing problem

In this chapter, we devise an SS technique which is helpful to resolve the aforementioned problems.

7.3 Related Works

7.3.1 Adaptive SS

In a CRN implementation, SS is one of the most important aspects. Researches in a CRN focus over two main parts, one is to improve the local sensing, and second is the cooperative SS for better data fusion results [8]. In cooperative SS, all the CRs work together to get better performance results. Here, all the CRs send their local decision (LS) to a common fusion center (FC), which takes the final decision to declare the presence or absence of a PU in a spectrum [9]. In local SS, all the SUs made the observations individually and the final decision is also made individually. In literature, many improvements for local SS are proposed but there is still room for improvement. Sensing a wideband spectrum is significant in the CR; however, only a few researchers have worked on the wideband SS in CRs. Two-stage SS is one of the techniques to deal with this issue. Hur et al. [10] introduced a two-stage wideband SS scheme, the proposed scheme combined coarse and fine sensing. Coarse sensing exists in the first stage and is performed over the complete frequency band with a wide bandwidth, while fine sensing has a wavelet transform-based multi-resolution spectrum sensing (MRSS) technique. In the first stage, the occupied and candidate spectrum segments are recognized. In the second stage, fine sensing is applied on the candidate spectrum segments to detect the unique features of the modulated signals. Confirmation of an unoccupied segment is done by a careful fine sensing. Luo et al. [11] presented a two-stage dynamic spectrum access scheme which carries a preliminary coarse resolution sensing (CRS) followed by a fine-resolution sensing (FRS). In CRS, the whole spectrum band is divided into equal-sized coarse sensing blocks (CSBs) of equal bandwidth. One of the CSBs is selected randomly and checked for at least one idle channel by applying an ED of a bandwidth equal to that of the CSB. FRS is then applied on that CSB, using an ED equal to the bandwidth of the channel to determine an idle channel. Further, Maleki et al. [12] described another two-stage sensing technique where coarse sensing uses an ED and fine sensing uses a cyclostationary detection for SS. If a channel is announced as unoccupied in the coarse stage, then the final decision will be taken by the fine stage, otherwise, coarse sensing will provide the global decision. Furthermore, Yue et al. [13] presented a two-stage SS technique where coarse detection uses energy detection. Based on the power level in each channel, it sorts the channels in an ascending order. In the fine stage, a one-order cyclostationary sensing detection technique is applied on the channel with the lowest power level to identify the weak PU signals. In all the aforementioned techniques, both stages perform the SS; hence, an increased mean detection time. In this scheme, the authors considered that only one of the detection techniques will run during the two stages, based on the estimated SNR. Under the worst case, the mean detection time is equal to one-order cyclostationary detection. Although two stages are running in this scheme, the SNR of the channel can be estimated in advance and its history can be maintained to further reduce the mean sensing time.

7.3.1.1 Limitations

In the adaptive SS technique, Ejaz et al. [8] presented a new scheme, where out of the two stages only one of the detection techniques is running at a time based on the estimated SNR [5]. Although this scheme reduces the mean sensing time it does not consider the SS failure problem [14].

7.3.2 Two-Stage Detection Scheme

In CRNs, large portions of the licensed spectrum band of the PUs remain underutilized [15]. The CRs identify the vacant bands of the licensed spectrum, and utilize these spectrum bands to meet the regulatory constraints of the limiting harmful interference to the licensed users. For a CRN, sensing the licensed spectrum is one of the biggest challenges. In particular, (1) determining the presence or absence of the PU signal reliably and (2) sensing the multiple licensed spectrum bands has to be done as quickly as possible. The two detection schemes commonly used are energy detection [5,16] and cyclostationary detection [17,18]. Energy detection is easy to implement, but its performance is not good at low SNRs, whereas the cyclostationary detection scheme provides a better detection, but is computationally complex and requires more sensing time. Maleki et al. [12] introduced a two-stage sensing approach based on energy detection and cyclostationary detection. To detect the PU signal, the energy detection is performed in the first stage. If the calculated signal energy is above a certain threshold level λ, the channel is announced to be busy. Else, second stage cyclostationary detection is performed. If the decision metric in this stage is above a certain threshold level γ, the channel is again announced to be busy. Else, it is announced to be free and can be used by the CRs. The proposed technique analyzed the performance of the system in terms of the probabilities of detection, false alarm, and the mean detection time. Thresholds λ and γ that enhance the probability of detection under this approach, with the probability of false alarm being constrained, are also determined.

7.3.2.1 Limitations

The two-stage detection scheme [12] enhances the detection performance. This technique carries two detectors: the first stage consists of an ED and the second stage consists of a cyclostationary detector to give a better sensing performance, but it requires a longer sensing time and is computationally more complex.

7.4 Proposed Scheme

7.4.1 SNR Estimation-Based SS Scheme

Figure 7.1 shows a proposed SNR estimation-based spectrum sensing (ESNR_ADT) scheme. CR receiver receives the PU signal and calculates the SNR value (S_e) using the following mathematical formulas. Now, compare the values of S_e with decided threshold (γ) in order to select the detector for the PU signal detection. If the value of the estimated SNR is greater or equal to the threshold then the ED will be used. Otherwise, ED with ADT will detect the PU signal.

In Figure 7.1, assuming $S_e \geq \gamma$, the ED is selected which calculates the energy of the PU signal (X), and compares (X) with the threshold (λ_1) to indicate the PU is present or absent. On the other hand, if S_e is smaller than γ, then the ED with ADT is selected, which calculates the energy of the received PU signal Z and compares it with the thresholds λ_{A1} and λ_{A2} by using an adaptive threshold scheme. Finally, compare the output value Y of ED with ADT, i.e., Y to threshold λ_2 under a fixed P_f, i.e., 0.1, to identify the presence or absence of a PU spectrum. The proposed model chooses one detector between ED and ED with ADT using the mathematical expression given as

$$\text{Selection of detector} = \begin{cases} \text{ED,} & S_e \geq \gamma \\ \text{ED\_ADT,} & S_e < \gamma \end{cases} \tag{7.1}$$

- Probability of false alarm of ESNR_ADT detector is

$$P_F^{\text{ESNR\_ADT}} = P_r \times P_f^{\text{ED}} + (1 - P_r) \times P_f^{\text{ED\_ADT}} \tag{7.2}$$

$$P_F^{\text{ESNR\_ADT}} = P_r \left(P_f^{\text{ED}} - P_f^{\text{ED\_ADT}} \right) + P_f^{\text{ED\_ADT}} \tag{7.3}$$

- Probability of detection of ESNR_ADT detector is

$$P_D^{\text{ESNR\_ADT}} = P_r \times P_d^{\text{ED}} + (1 - P_r) \times P_d^{\text{ED\_ADT}} \tag{7.4}$$

$$P_D^{\text{ESNR\_ADT}} = P_r \left(P_d^{\text{ED}} - P_d^{\text{ED\_ADT}} \right) + P_d^{\text{ED\_ADT}} \tag{7.5}$$

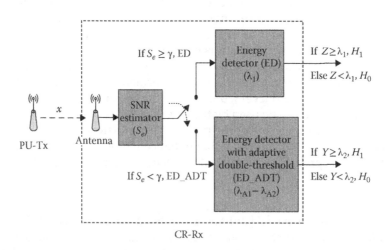

FIGURE 7.1
Proposed model: SNR estimation-based spectrum sensing detector (ESNR_ADT). Tx, transmitter; Rx, receiver.

where P_d^{ED} and $P_d^{ED\_ADT}$ are the probabilities of detection throughout ED and ED_ADT detectors, respectively, P_f^{ED} and $P_f^{ED\_ADT}$ are the false-alarm probabilities of ED and ED_ADT detectors, respectively. Probability factor is denoted by P_r where a channel would be reported to the ED and thus, the probability that a channel would be reported to the ED_ADT detector will be $(1 - P_r)$. P_r depends on the SNR of the channels to be sensed, i.e., if $P_r < 0.5$ shows the channel is very noisy, and $P_r \geq 0.5$ shows the channel is less noisy or has a good SNR. Hence, the overall false-alarm and detection probabilities directly depend on the P_r ($0 \leq P_r \leq 1$).

- Total SS time of the ESNR_ADT detector is as follows:

$$T = T_{ED} + T_{ED\_ADT} \tag{7.6}$$

where T is the total SS time of the CR user. T_{ED} and T_{ED_ADT} are the ED and ED_ADT detectors, respectively. Therefore, the ED sensing time can be calculated as follows:

$$T_{ED} = E[K_1] \times T_1 \tag{7.7}$$

where $E[K_1]$ denotes the mean number of channels reported to the ED.

$$T_1 = \frac{N_E}{2 \times W} \tag{7.8}$$

where T_1 defines the mean sensing time, wherein the number of samples during the observation interval is denoted by N_E. and the channel bandwidth by W. K_1 is a random variable following the binomial distribution and depends on the number of detected channels M and probability factor P_r that a channel would be informed to the ED. Therefore, the detection time of ED is as follows:

$$T_{ED} = M \times P_r \times T_1 \tag{7.9}$$

Similarly, the ED_ADT detector sensing time can be calculated as follows:

$$T_{ED\_ADT} = E[K_2] \times T_2 \tag{7.10}$$

where $E[K_2]$ denotes the mean number of channels reported to the ED_ADT detector:

$$T_2 = \frac{N_{ED\_ADT}}{2 \times W} \tag{7.11}$$

where T_2 defines the mean sensing time, wherein the number of samples during the observation interval is denoted by N_{ED_ADT}, and the channel bandwidth by W. K_2 is a random variable following the binomial distribution and depends on the parameters M and probability factor $(1 - P_r)$ in which a channel would be informed to the ED_ADT detector. Hence, the detection time of the ED_ADT detector is as follows:

$$T_{ED\_ADT} = M \times (1 - P_r) \times T_2 \tag{7.12}$$

Thus, the overall SS time is calculated by substituting Equations 7.9 and 7.12 in Equation 7.6

$$T = M \times P_r \times T_1 + M \times (1 - P_r) \times T_2 \tag{7.13}$$

$$T = M \times [P_r \times T_1 + (1 - P_r) \times T_2] \tag{7.14}$$

Equation 7.14 shows the final mathematical expression of the overall SS time for an ESNR_ADT detector.

7.4.1.1 Energy Detector with Single Threshold ED

ED plays an important role in a CRN to detect the PU signal due to its simplicity and easy implementation [19]. It measures the energy of PU signal and compares it to a threshold (γ) to determine whether the PU signal is present or absent. Signal energy is determined by a mathematical formulation as follows [20]:

$$Z = \frac{1}{N} \sum_{n=1}^{N} |x(n)|^2 \tag{7.15}$$

where $x(n)$ is the received PU signal, N is the number of samples, and Z is the total energy of $x(n)$. The value of threshold is set to meet the desired target P_f as per the power of noise signal. The detection probability can be calculated and the expression for P_d and P_f can be defined as follows [21]:

$$P_d = Q\left(\frac{\lambda - N(\sigma_S^2 + \sigma_\omega^2)}{\sqrt{2N(\sigma_S^2 + \sigma_\omega^2)^2}}\right) \tag{7.16}$$

$$P_f = Q\left(\frac{\lambda - N\sigma_\omega^2}{\sqrt{2N\sigma_\omega^4}}\right) \tag{7.17}$$

where σ_ω^2 and σ_S^2 represent the noise and signal variances, respectively. $Q(\ )$ denotes the Gaussian tail probability Q-function. The total probability of error is the addition of the false alarm (P_f) and missed-detection alarm (P_m). Thus, the total error rate is given by

$$P_e = P_f + (1 - P_d) \tag{7.18}$$

where ($1 - P_d$) is the probability of missed-detection alarm (P_m). Figure 7.2 shows the internal architecture of an ED with a single threshold (γ). The square law device (SLD) receives the PU licensed signal and produces the detected signal energy (X), then compares with the single threshold to make a final decision to announce whether the PU channel is free or not.

The mathematical expression of LS rule generated by ED with a single threshold can be computed as follows:

$$LF = \begin{cases} 1, & \gamma \leq X \\ 0, & X < \gamma \end{cases} \tag{7.19}$$

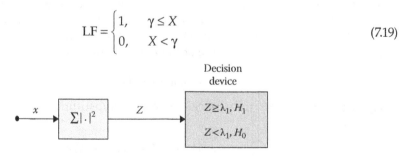

FIGURE 7.2
Energy detector having single threshold ED.

7.4.1.2 *Energy Detector with Adaptive Threshold (ED with ADT)*

This is a simple type of ED circuit without a fixed threshold. In this model, we used an adaptive threshold instead of fixed as in the single threshold detection. Suppose the PU signal is not detected at first stage; the second-stage detector will try to detect it. Figure 7.3 depicts the internal model of an ED with ADT in which the SLD first receives the sensed PU signal and then computes the signal energy (X). On the basis of the value of X, the ED_ADT choses the appropriate threshold and compares with X to decide whether the PU is present or absent. Further, the SLD has two parts. In the upper part, if the detected energy values $X \geq \lambda_1$, it will show H_1 (i.e., the signal present), and if less than λ_2, it will show H_0 (i.e., the signal absent). But, if the detected energy values (X) fall between λ_1 and λ_2, then it will consider the lower part and follow the quantization process to produce its respective decimal values (DVs) if $P_f > 0.1$.

If the calculated energy values (X) of a detected PU signal fall outside or within λ_1 and λ_2, then the proposed ED_ADT model generates the values of m or n expressed as follows:

$$m = \begin{cases} 0, & X \leq \lambda_2 \\ 1, & \lambda_1 \leq X \end{cases} \quad (7.20)$$

$$n = \{DV, \ \lambda_2 < X < \lambda_1 \quad (7.21)$$

where m and n are the output decisions of the upper and lower parts, respectively. Further, adder device is used to add the values of m and n:

$$Y = m + n \quad (7.22)$$

Finally, using Equations 7.20 through 7.22 the LS of the second stage or ED_ADT is expressed as follows:

$$LS = \begin{cases} 1, & \lambda \leq Y \\ 0, & Y < \lambda \end{cases} \quad (7.23)$$

Equation 7.23 equates the resultant value (Y) to threshold (λ) to maintain the overall system probability of false alarm (P_f) 0.1. If $Y \geq \lambda$, then the signal is present, otherwise absent.

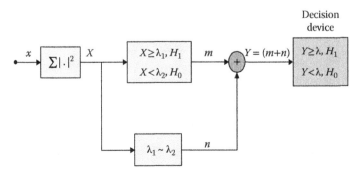

FIGURE 7.3
Internal circuitry of an energy detector with adaptive double-threshold (ED_ADT).

7.4.1.3 Adaptive Threshold Schemes for Spectrum Sensing

Most of the EDs [22] are based on the fixed single threshold scheme, in which the detected PU signal compares with the threshold to identify whether the PU is present or not. The aforementioned sensing detectors create problems when the noise uncertainty grows for a CR, which reduce its sensing reliability; moreover this may not be perfect in case of a low SNR where the performance of the single threshold (γ)-based detector can vary from the targeted performance metrics substantively.

Bagwari and Tomar [23] have shown the curve of the PU and noise signals, and discussed that the detection of the PU signal from noise signal is easy if both the signals do not overlap each other. Suppose the detector receives a PU signal, then it is H_1, i.e., the channel is occupied, and if it gets a noise signal, it is H_0, i.e., the channel is unoccupied. But, if both the PU and noise signals intersect each other, it is very difficult to sense the desired signals. The area between λ_1 and λ_2 is known as the confused region [23]. λ_1 is called the upper bound and λ_2 is lower bound.

The PU signal and noise are difficult to recognize in the confused region using a single threshold. The adaptive two-threshold scheme is capable to resolve this problem. The mathematical expression to explain the LS at the CR user following the logic function rule (LR) can be described as follows:

$$LR = \begin{cases} H_0 = 0, & X \leq \lambda_2 \\ H = M, & \lambda_2 < X < \lambda_1 \\ H_1 = 1, & \lambda_1 \leq X \end{cases} \tag{7.24}$$

where M is the quantization decision and X denotes the received PU signal energy by the CR user.

There is another double-threshold-based scheme proposed by Sun et al. [24] to reduce the average number of sensing bits to the receiver. But, the deductions are achieved at the expense of some sensing performance loss which is known as sensing failure problem. Two threshold schemes (λ_1 and λ_2) are helpful to resolve this issue. Figure 7.4 shows that the entire confused region is divided into four equal levels using the quantization

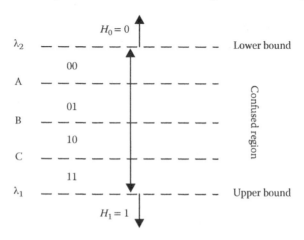

FIGURE 7.4
Four parts of the confused region using the quantization method.

process, and each level is represented by a combination of unique two-bits. These levels are $\lambda_2 A$, AB, BC, and $C\lambda_1$, where λ_2, A, B, C, and λ_1 are subthresholds (STs) and can be calculated as follows:

$$ST = \begin{cases} A = \lambda_2 + D \\ B = A + D \\ C = B + D \\ \lambda_1 = C + D \end{cases} \tag{7.25}$$

$$D = \frac{(\text{Upper bound} - \text{Lower bound})}{\text{No. of Quantization intervals}} = \frac{(\lambda_1 - \lambda_2)}{4} \tag{7.26}$$

$$M = \begin{cases} 00, & \lambda_2 < X \le A \\ 01, & A < X \le B \\ 10, & B < X \le C \\ 11, & C < X < \lambda_1 \end{cases} \tag{7.27}$$

Now, the false-alarm probability (P_f) of a conventional ED with a single threshold can be calculated as follows [21]:

$$P_f = Q\left(\frac{\lambda - N\sigma_\omega^2}{\sqrt{2N\sigma_\omega^4}}\right) \tag{7.28}$$

where $Q(\ )$ is called the Gaussian tail probability Q-function, and σ_ω^2 is known as the noise variance. Given the target false-alarm probability $\overline{P_f}$ the threshold λ can be calculated as

$$\lambda = Q^{-1}\left(\overline{P_f}\right) \times \sqrt{2N\sigma_\omega^4} + N\sigma_\omega^2 \tag{7.29}$$

In Equation 7.29, the inverse Gaussian tail probability Q-function is denoted by $Q^{-1}(\ )$. Assume that in the wireless communication network environment; the noise uncertainty is described as $[1/\rho\sigma_\omega^2, \rho\sigma_\omega^2]$, where ρ defines a constant parameter that computes the size of the uncertainty, $\rho > 1$. In the double-threshold decision, the value of maximum noise variance defines the value of upper threshold λ_1, and the lower threshold λ_2 is defined by the minimum noise variance value. Hence

$$\lambda_1 = Q^{-1}\left(\overline{P_f}\right) \times \sqrt{2N\rho\sigma_\omega^4} + N\rho\sigma_\omega^2 \tag{7.30}$$

$$\lambda_2 = Q^{-1}\left(\overline{P_f}\right) \times \sqrt{2N/(\rho\sigma_\omega^4)} + N/(\rho\sigma_\omega^2) \tag{7.31}$$

Suppose that x_i is the normalized version of the received sample $x(n)$, the cumulative distribution function of ED_ADT can be calculated as

$$f_{Yi}(y) = P_r\left(|x_i|^2 \le y^{\frac{2}{p}}\right) \tag{7.32}$$

In Equation 7.32, p is an arbitrary constant and has a value of two. The zero-mean primary signal $s(n)$ with an average power σ_s^2 is independent of the circularly symmetric complex Gaussian noise $w_i(n)$ with a variance σ_w^2, and $h_i(n)$ denotes the Rayleigh faded channel that is independent of $w_i(n)$. Hence, $|h_i(n)|$ is the Rayleigh distribution with a variance of $\sigma_h^2 / 2$. Thus, the probability distribution function (PDF) of the ED_ADT detector for H_j (where $j = 0, 1$) is given as follows:

$$f_{Yi|H_j}(y) = \left[\frac{2 \times y^{\left(\frac{2-p}{p}\right)}}{p}\right] \times f_{|x_i|^2|H_j}\left(y^{\left(\frac{2}{p}\right)}\right) \tag{7.33}$$

where $f_{|x_i|^2|H_0}$ and $f_{|x_i|^2|H_1}$ are exponentially distributed as follows:

$$f_{|x_i|^2|H_0}(y) = \exp[-y], \quad y \geq 0 \tag{7.34}$$

$$f_{|x_i|^2|H_1}(y) = \left[\frac{1}{(1+\gamma)}\right] \times \exp\left[-\frac{y}{(1+\gamma)}\right], \quad y \geq 0 \tag{7.35}$$

Note that $y = \left(\sigma_h^2 \times \sigma_s^2\right) / \sigma_n^2$ represents the average SNR of the SS channel. Finally, using Equations 7.33 and 7.34, we have

$$f_{Yi|H_0}(y) = \left[\frac{2 \times y^{\left(\frac{2-p}{p}\right)}}{p}\right] \times \exp\left[y^{\left(\frac{2}{p}\right)}\right], \quad y \geq 0 \tag{7.36}$$

Now, the false-alarm probability for ED_ADT can be calculated as follows:

$$P_f^{\text{ED\_ADT}} = \int_{\lambda_2}^{+\infty} f_{Yi|H_0}(y)\,dy \tag{7.37}$$

$$P_f^{\text{ED\_ADT}} = \int_{\lambda_2}^{+\infty} \left[\frac{2 \times y^{\left(\frac{2-p}{p}\right)}}{p}\right] \times \exp\left[y^{\left(\frac{2}{p}\right)}\right] dy \tag{7.38}$$

$$P_f^{\text{ED\_ADT}} = \exp\left(-\lambda_2^{2/p}\right) \tag{7.39}$$

Using Equations 7.33 and 7.35, PDF of the ED_ADT detector for H_1 is computed as

$$f_{Yi|H_1}(y) = \left[\frac{2 \times y^{\left(\frac{2-p}{p}\right)}}{p \times (1+\gamma)}\right] \times \exp\left[-\frac{y^{\left(\frac{2}{p}\right)}}{(1+\gamma)}\right], \quad y \geq 0 \tag{7.40}$$

Now the probability of detection for ED_ADT can be obtained as follows:

$$P_d^{\text{ED\_ADT}} = \int_{\lambda_2}^{+\infty} f_{Yi|H_1}(y)\,dy \tag{7.41}$$

$$P_d^{ED\_ADT} = \int_{\lambda_2}^{+\infty} \left[\frac{2 \times y^{\left(\frac{2-p}{p}\right)}}{p \times (1+\gamma)} \right] \times \exp\left[-\frac{y^{\left(\frac{2}{p}\right)}}{(1+\gamma)} \right] dy \tag{7.42}$$

$$P_d^{ED\_ADT} = \exp\left(-\frac{\lambda_2^{2/p}}{1+\gamma} \right) \tag{7.43}$$

Similarly, the total error rate (P_e) for ED_ADT can be calculated as

$$P_e^{ED\_ADT} = P_f^{ED\_ADT} + (1 - P_d^{ED\_ADT}) \tag{7.44}$$

where $(1 - P_d^{ED\_ADT})$ shows the probability of missed-detection alarm, denoted by $(P_m^{ED\_ADT})$. If sensed signal's calculated energy lies within any one of the quantized interval, it produces its respective DV given as

$$DV = \begin{cases} \text{If } M = 00, & \text{respective decimal value is 0} \\ \text{If } M = 01, & \text{respective decimal value is 1} \\ \text{If } M = 10, & \text{respective decimal value is 2} \\ \text{If } M = 11, & \text{respective decimal value is 3} \end{cases} \tag{7.45}$$

Equation 7.45 indicates the DV that compares thresholds (λ_1, λ_2, and λ) in order to provide the LS under a fixed P_f, i.e., 0.1. Beyond the confused region, the proposed model produces a binary bit, i.e., either 0 or 1 depending on the signal position.

Algorithm 1: Proposed ESNR_ADT SS scheme

1. Given $\{x_1, x_2, x_3, \ldots, x_N\}$
2. Given $\{\gamma\}$
3. Given $\{\lambda_1, \lambda_2\}$
4. Distribute uniformly $\{\lambda_2, \lambda_1, \lambda_{A1}, \lambda_{A2}\}$
   as $\{\lambda_{A2} < A < B < C < \lambda_{A1}\}$
5. Define Range $DR_0 = \{\lambda_{A2}, A\}$, $DR_1 = \{A, B\}$,
   $DR_2 = \{B, C\}$, $DR_3 = \{C, \lambda_{A1}\}$,
6. Values for Ranges $n = \{0, 1, 2, 3\}$ for
   $\{DR_0, DR_1, DR_2, DR_3\}$
7. Calculate estimated SNR value $\{S_e\}$
8. if $S_e \geq \gamma$
9. $Z = 0$;
10. for $i = 1, 2, \ldots, N$
    $Z = Z + x_i^2$;
    endfor
11. if $Z \geq \lambda_1$
    $LF = H_1$;
    else if $Z < \lambda_1$

  LF $= H_0$;

  endif

  else

12. $X = 0$;

13. for $i = 1, 2, ..., N$

  $X = X + x_i^2$;

  endfor

14. if $X \geq \lambda_{A1}$

  $m = H_1$;

  else if $X < \lambda_{A2}$

  $m = H_0$;

  else

  for $j = 0, 1, 2, 3$

  if $X \in R_j$

  $n = j$;

  endif

  endfor

15. $Y = m + n$;

16. if $Y \geq \lambda_2$

  LS $= H_1$;

  else

  LS $= H_0$;

  endif

  endif

  endif

7.5 Simulation Results and Analysis for ESNR_ADT Scheme

In this model, we assumed that the number of samples $(N) = 1000$, $P_f = 0.1$, threshold $\gamma = -6$ dB, $P_r = 0.5$, and the SNR varies from -20 dB to 0 dB. Quadrature phase shift keying (QPSK) modulation is considered in the Rayleigh fading channel.

  The detection probability describes how often a PU is susceptible to a potential interference from the CR. In a CRN, P_d is one of the important parameter in order to calculate the performance of the system. According to IEEE 802.22 WRAN standard, the value of P_d should be as maximum as possible under the constraint of probability of false alarm.

  Figure 7.5 shows the graph between P_d and SNR of the proposed scheme with other two existing schemes. It is found that our scheme yields better results and the detection performance is improved by 30.5% and 30% compared with the cyclostationary-based sensing method and adaptive SS at -10 dB SNR, respectively.

  Figure 7.6 shows that the proposed scheme has a minimum error rate compared with other two existing schemes, i.e., 0.1 at -6 dB SNR.

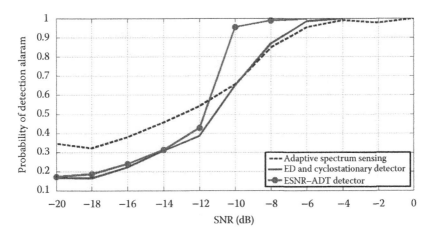

FIGURE 7.5
Probability of detection vs. SNR at $P_f = 0.1$, $N = 1000$, $\gamma = -6$ dB, and the QPSK modulation scheme with Rayleigh fading channel.

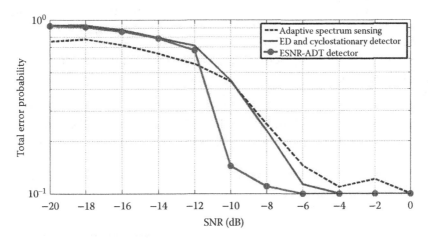

FIGURE 7.6
Total error probability vs. SNR at $P_f = 0.1$, $N = 1000$, $\gamma = -6$ dB, and the QPSK modulation scheme with Rayleigh fading channel.

Figure 7.7 depicts the receiver operating characteristics (ROC) curve. It shows the relationship between the false alarm and probability of detection throughout [25] of the SS method under several SNR values for the proposed scheme. At $P_f = 0.1$ and SNR = −10 dB, the detection probability is in the order of 0.9, which is an SS requirement of IEEE 802.22 [26,27].

The SS time defines the total time taken by a CR user to detect the PU signal. Suppose SS time is increased then the PU can utilize its spectrum in a better manner and the limit is decided that CR cannot interfere throughout that time. More PUs will be detected if SS is more, due to this the level of interference will be less. The SS time is directly related to the number of samples received by the CR user. More sensing time is dedicated to the PU signal detection, and less sensing time is available for transmissions, thereby degrading the CR throughput. This phenomenon is called the sensing-throughput trade-off [6] or sensing efficiency problem [7] in spread spectrum technique.

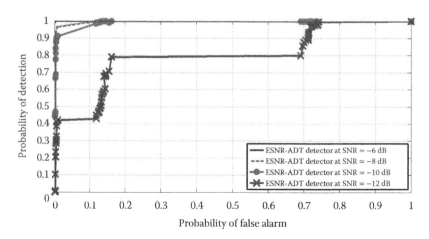

FIGURE 7.7
ROC curves for ESNR_ADT-based spectrum-sensing detector under different SNR values.

Figure 7.8 shows the graph of SS time versus SNR. The proposed scheme requires lesser sensing time than the existing schemes. It is observed that there is an inverse relationship between SS time and SNR. As SNR increases, the sensing time decreases. At −20 dB SNR, the proposed scheme requires approximately 48 ms while the existing schemes (cyclostationary-based sensing method and adaptive SS) require around 53.2 and 49.0 ms sensing time, respectively.

Figure 7.9 illustrates the detection probability (P_d) versus threshold value (λ) plots for different SNRs such as −6, −8, −10, and −12 dB. There is a relationship between the detection probability and threshold under different SNRs. It means, if the SNR increases, the detection probability also increases with respect to the threshold. The highest value of

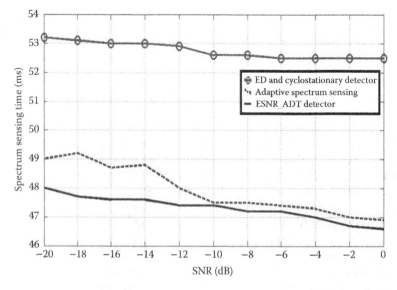

FIGURE 7.8
Spectrum-sensing time vs. SNR with $N = 1000$, $\gamma = -6$ dB, QPSK modulation scheme with Rayleigh fading channel.

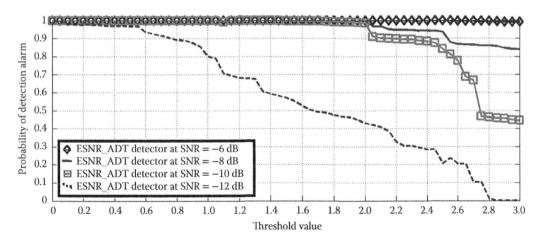

FIGURE 7.9
Probability of detection vs. threshold values at SNR = −6, −8, −10, and −12 dB, $N = 1000$, $\gamma = -6$ dB, and QPSK modulation scheme with Rayleigh fading channel.

probability of detection is around 1.0 throughout the range of threshold (λ) at −6 dB SNR. Analyzing Figure 7.9 shows that the proposed ESNR_ADT detector can detect the PU signal at −6 dB SNR with $N = 1000$ and $\lambda = 3.0$.

7.6 Collaborative Spectrum Sensing with Proposed ESNR_ADT Detector

Collaborative spectrum sensing (CSS) is used to mitigate the shadowing and fading problems to enhance the performance of both local and final sensing in a CRN [28–31]. All CRs use ESNR_ADT-based sensing technique to identify the signal. Once all CRs have declared the LS, they transmit their individual decisions in the binary form either 0 or 1 to the FC over error-free orthogonal channels to take a global decision. Error-free orthogonal channels show that the channel between CR and FC known as reporting channel is totally ideal, or noiseless, or error free. Suppose there are k numbers of CR users, all of them send their own LS F_i to a common FC as shown in Figure 7.10.

Finally, FC combines the binary bit decisions of all the CRs where each CR has a proposed scheme, i.e., two-stage detectors; further, it takes the final decision to declare the presence or absence of the PU spectrum as follows:

$$G = \sum_{i=1}^{k} F_i \qquad (7.46)$$

$$F_i = \begin{cases} 1, & \lambda_1 \leq X_i, \text{ or } \lambda_2 \leq Y_i \\ 0, & X_i < \lambda_1, \text{ or } Y_i < \lambda_2 \end{cases} \qquad (7.47)$$

In Equation 7.46, F_i is the LS of all the CR users, which combines and provides a global decision denoted by G. To take the global decision FC uses hard decision OR rule. The hard decision OR rule states that a signal is present only and only if any of the CRs sense a signal. It means if $F_i < 1$, then the signal is not detected and if F_i is greater or equal to 1, the signal is detected. The functional representation can be written as

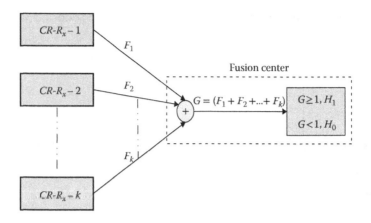

FIGURE 7.10
CSS technique using proposed ESNR_ADT scheme.

$$FC = \begin{cases} 0, & \sum_{i=1}^{k} F_i < 1 \\ 1, & \sum_{i=1}^{k} F_i \geq 1 \end{cases} \tag{7.48}$$

$$FC = \begin{cases} G < 1, & H_0 \\ G \geq 1, & H_1 \end{cases} \tag{7.49}$$

Equation 7.49 shows the output of FC in terms of G. Now, the performance of CSS-based ESNR_ADT detector in terms of probability of detection (P_D) and false alarm (P_F) can be calculated as

$$P_D = P_r\{G \geq 1 \mid H_1\} = P_r\left\{\sum_{i=1}^{k} F_i \geq 1 \mid H_1\right\} \tag{7.50}$$

$$P_D = 1 - \prod_{i=1}^{k}\left(1 - P_{D,i}^{ESNR\_ADT}\right) \tag{7.51}$$

Similarly, the false alarm (P_F) of the CSS-based ESNR_ADT detector can be computed as follows:

$$P_F = P_r\{G \geq 1 \mid H_0\} = P_r\left\{\sum_{i=1}^{k} F_i \geq 1 \mid H_0\right\} \tag{7.52}$$

$$P_F = 1 - \prod_{i=1}^{k}\left(1 - P_{F,i}^{ESNR\_ADT}\right) \tag{7.53}$$

$P_D^{ESNR\_ADT}$ is the probability of detection and $P_F^{ESNR\_ADT}$ is the false-alarm probability of individual CR users [32], computed using Equations 7.5 and 7.3, respectively.

Algorithm 2: CSS using proposed ESNR_ADT detector scheme

1. Given $\{F_1, F_2, F_3, ..., F_k\}$
2. Given $\{H_0, H_1\}$ as $\{0,1\}$
3. $G = F_1 + F_2 + F_3 + ... + F_k$
4. if $G \geq 1$

   FC = H_1;

   else

   FC = H_0;

   endif

7.7 Simulation Results and Analysis for CSS Using ESNR_ADT Detector

Figure 7.11 illustrates a graph between the probability of detection and SNR. We assume $P_f = 0.1$, samples $(N) = 1000$, and number of cooperative CRs $(k) = 3, 4, 5, 6, 7, 8, 9$, and 10. Analyzing Figure 7.11, we can say that the probability of detection increases as SNR increases. When there are three CR user, the probability of detection (P_d) is 0.9 at −11 dB SNR, while increasing the number of CR users (k), less SNR value is required to reach P_d at 0.9. As given that $k = 10$, −18.5 dB SNR (approximately) is required to achieve P_d at 0.9. The value of probability of detection, i.e., 0.9 is decided or approved by IEEE 802.22 [26,27] for SS.

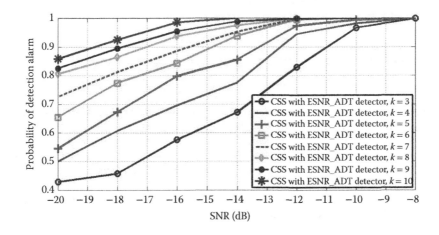

FIGURE 7.11

Probability of detection vs. SNR at $P_f = 0.1$, $N = 1000$, $\gamma = -6$ dB, $k = 3, 4, 5, 6, 7, 8, 9, 10$, and QPSK modulation scheme with Rayleigh fading channel.

7.8 Conclusion and Future Work

In this chapter, we presented a review study of various SS techniques. As we discussed earlier, there are various sensing techniques but three of them are mainly used, called matched filter, energy detection, and cyclostationary-based detection. Each of them has their own advantages and disadvantages. For instance, matched filter detection improves the SNR, but needs the PU's prior information. Energy detection does not require PU information, but degrades the performance at low SNR. Cyclostationary feature detection gives better results than both, but requires the PU information. We further discussed and explained the functions of CRNs and the challenges related to a CRN. Moreover, we have proposed a novel collaborative SS technique based on the estimated SNR with adaptive threshold in a CRN. This scheme improves the sensing time and overcomes the sensing failure problems. Numerical results indicate that in terms of detection, the proposed ESNR_ADT detection technique beats both the existing schemes (Adaptive spectrum sensing and ED and cyclostationary detector), by 30% and 30.5% at −10 dB SNR, respectively. It is also shown that the proposed scheme yields lesser sensing time than cyclostationary detection and adaptive SS scheme, by 5.2 ms and 1.0 ms at −20 dB SNR, respectively. We have further implemented the adaptive double-threshold with CSS scheme; it shows that at $P_f = 0.1$, 10 CR users ($k = 10$) are capable of sensing the PU licensed signal at −18.5 dB SNR. All results conclude that the proposed scheme exhibits better detection performance than the existing schemes. In future, we will try to further improve the proposed system quality in terms of detection.

Acknowledgments

We thank our parents for their support and motivation, for without their blessings and God's grace this chapter would not be possible. This work is dedicated to Anushka Gaur and Anshul Semwal, for their true and valuable love.

References

1. A. Bagwari, and B. Singh. Comparative performance evaluation of spectrum sensing techniques for cognitive radio networks. In *2012 Fourth IEEE International Conference on Computational Intelligence and Communication Networks (CICN-2012)*, pp. 98–105, 2012.
2. D. Cabric, S.M. Mishra, and R.W. Brodersen. Implementation issues in spectrum sensing for cognitive radios. In *Proceedings of the 2004 Asilomar Conference on Signals, Systems, and Computers*, vol. 1, pp. 772–776, 2004.
3. Y. Zeng, Y-C. Liang, A.T. Hoang, and R. Zhang. A review on spectrum sensing for cognitive radio: Challenges and solutions. *EURASIP Journal of Advanced Signal Processing*, 2010, 1–15, 2010.
4. C. Song, Y.D. Alemseged, H.N. Tran, G. Villardi, C. Sun, S. Filin, and H. Harada. Adaptive two thresholds based energy detection for cooperative spectrum sensing. In *Proceedings of the 2010 IEEE Consumer Communications and Networking Conference (CCNC)*, pp. 1–6, 2010.

5. R. Tandra, and A. Sahai. SNR walls for signal detection. *IEEE Journal of Selected Topic Signal Processing*, 2(1), 4–16, 2008.
6. Y.C. Liang, Y. Zeng, E. Peh, and A.T. Hoang. Sensing-throughput tradeoff for cognitive radio networks. *IEEE Transactions on Wireless Communications*, 7(4), 1326–1337, 2008.
7. W.Y. Lee, and I.F. Akyildiz. Optimal spectrum sensing framework for cognitive radio networks. *IEEE Transactions on Wireless Communications*, 7(10), 3845–3857, 2008.
8. W. Ejaz, N.U. Hasan, and H.S. Kim. SNR-based adaptive spectrum sensing for cognitive radio networks. *International Journal of Innovative Computing, Information and Control*, 8(9), 6095–6105, 2012.
9. I.F. Akildiz, B.F. Lo, and R. Balakrishan. Cooperative spectrum sensing in cognitive radio networks: A survey. *Physical Communication*, 4, 40–62, 2011.
10. Y. Hur, J. Park, W. Woo, K. Lim, C-H. Lee, H. Kim, and J. Laskar. A wideband analog multi-resolution spectrum sensing (MRSS) technique for cognitive radio (CR) systems. In *IEEE Proceedings of International Symposium on Circuits and Systems*, Island of Kos, pp.4090–4093, 2006.
11. L. Luo, N.M. Neihart, S. Roy, and D.J. Allstot. A two-stage sensing technique for dynamic spectrum access. *IEEE Transactions on Wireless Communications*, 8(6), 3028–3037, 2009.
12. S. Maleki, A. Pandharipande, and G. Leus. Two-stage spectrum sensing for cognitive radios. In *IEEE International Conference on Acoustic Speech and Signal Processing*, pp. 2946–2949, 2010.
13. W. Yue, B. Zheng, Q. Meng, and W. Yue. Combined energy detection and one-order cyclostationary feature detection techniques in cognitive radio systems. *The Journal of China Universities of Posts and Telecommunications*, 17(4), 18–25, 2010.
14. A. Fehske, J.D. Gaeddert, and J.H. Reed. A new approach to signal classification using spectral correlation and neural networks. In *Proceedings of IEEE DySPAN*, pp. 144–150, 2005.
15. Federal Communications Commission. Second Report and Order and Memorandum Opinion and Order, "Unlicensed operation in the TV broadcast bands," FCC 08-260, November 2008.
16. D. Cabric, A. Tkachenko, and R.W. Brodersen. Spectrum sensing measurements of pilot, energy, and collaborative detection. *IEEE MILCOM*, October 2007.
17. J. Lunden, V. Koivunen, A. Huttunen, and H.V. Poor. Spectrum sensing in cognitive radios based on multiple cyclic frequencies. In *IEEE Proceedings of Cognitive Radio Oriented Wireless Networks and Communications*, August 2007.
18. P.D. Sutton, K.E. Nolan, and L.E. Doyle. Cyclostationary signatures in practical cognitive radio applications. *IEEE Journal on Selected Areas in Communications*, 26(1), 13–24, 2008.
19. H. Urkowitz. Energy detection of unknown deterministic signals. In *Proceedings of IEEE*, 55(4), pp. 523–531, April 1967.
20. D. Chen, J. Li, and J. Ma. 2008. Cooperative spectrum sensing under noise uncertainty in cognitive radio. *Wireless Communications, Networking and Mobile Computing*, ISBN: 978-1-4244-2108-4, pp. 1–4, 2008.
21. M. López-Benítez, and F. Casadevall. Improved energy detection spectrum sensing for cognitive radio. *IET Communications*, 6(8), 785–796, 2012.
22. Z. Ling-ling, H. Jian-guo, and T. Cheng-kai. Novel energy detection scheme in cognitive radio. In *IEEE Conference on Signal Processing, Communications and Computing (ICSPCC)*, pp. 1–4, 2011.
23. A. Bagwari, and G.S. Tomar. Adaptive double-threshold based energy detector for spectrum sensing in cognitive radio networks. *International Journal of Electronics Letters* 1(1), 24–32, 2013.
24. C.H. Sun, W. Zhang, and K. Ben Letaief, Cooperative spectrum sensing for cognitive radios under bandwidth constraints. In *Proceedings of 2007 IEEE Wireless Communications and Networking Conference*, vols. 1–9, pp. 1–5, 2007.
25. T. Yucek, and H. Arslan. A survey of spectrum sensing algorithms for cognitive radio applications. *IEEE Communication Serveys and Toutorials*, 11(1), 116–130, 2009.
26. T. Do, and B.L. Mark. Improving Spectrum Sensing Performance by Exploiting Multiuser Diversity, Foundation of Cognitive Radio Systems, Prof. Samuel Cheng (Ed.), ISBN: 978- 953-51-0268-7, pp. 119–140, March 2012.
27. C. Cordeiro, K. Challapali, D. Birru, and S. Shankar, IEEE 802.22: The first worldwide wireless standard based on cognitive radios. In *Proceedings of DySPAN* 2005, November 2005.

28. W. Zhang, and K.B. Letaief. Cooperative spectrum sensing with transmit and relay diversity in cognitive radio networks. *IEEE Transactions Wireless Communications*, 7, 4761–4766, 2008.

29. G. Ganesan, and Y.G. Li. Cooperative spectrum sensing in cognitive radio networks. In *Proceedings of IEEE Symposium New Frontiers Dynamic Spectrum Access Networks (DySPAN'05)*, Baltimore, USA, pp. 137–143, November 2005.

30. S.M. Mishra, A. Sahai, and R. Brodersen. Cooperative sensing among cognitive radios. In *Conference Rec. IEEE International Conference on Communications*. (ICC'06), Turkey, vol. 4, pp. 1658–1663, June 2006.

31. K.B. Letaief, and W. Zhang. Cooperative communications for cognitive radio. In *Proceedings of the IEEE*, 97(5), 878–893, 2009.

32. J. Benko, Y.C. Cheong, and C. Cordeiro et al. 2006. A PHY/MAC Proposal for IEEE 802.22 WRAN Systems Part 1: The PHY. IEEE 802.22-06/0004r1, February 2006.

8

Collision of Counterfeit Detection on Spectrum Sensing for Cognitive Radio

Lailun Nahar and Fakir Mashuque Alamgir

CONTENTS

8.1 Introduction

At present, the formation of new radio access advances is constrained by the lack of an accessible radio range. These new advancements are turning out to be more transfer speed requesting because of their higher rate necessities. Cognitive radio (CR) is an encouraging innovation outfitted to take care of the range shortage issue, by resourcefully classifying the empty bits of the range and transmitting in them. However, the authorized or primary users (PUs) of the range are not influenced by this. This requires adjusting to the progressively changing range asset, finding out about the range inhabitance, settling on choices on the nature of the accessible range asset, including its normal length of time of utilization and likelihood of disturbance created by the PUs, among others. Hence, CR systems help to make productive utilization of the accessible range by utilizing groups, e.g., television telecasts frequencies <700 MHz that have been, as of late, checked for the CR operation. CR systems and range-detecting procedures are the characteristic approaches to permit these new innovations to be installed.

8.1.1 Cognitive Radio

CR is a versatile, crafty radio and system innovation that can naturally distinguish the accessible diverts in a remote range and change the broadcast parameters, empowering more interchanges to run simultaneously, and, furthermore, can enhance the radio working performance. Intellectual radio systems (called auxiliary systems, starting now and into the foreseeable future) will likewise need to coincide with the legacy ones which have the privilege to their range cut and along these lines cannot allow any obstruction.

8.1.2 History and Background Leading to CR

The idea of cognitive radio was initially proposed by Joseph Mitola III in a workshop at KTH (the Royal Institute of Technology in Stockholm) in 1998 and was presented in an article by Mitola and Gerald Q. Maguire, Jr. in 1999 [1]. It was a novel methodology in the remote correspondence field. The refinement plausibility in a software-defined radio (SDR) has now come to a level where every radio can possibly perform gainful assignments that help the clients, assist with the systems administration, and help minimize the unearthly clog. Radios are as of now showing a greater amount of these capacities in restricted ways. To bolster the innovations and administrative contemplations, three note-worthy applications, an SDR's ability to make it an intellectual radio, are given as follows:

- Range administration and improvements
- Interface with a wide assortment of systems and improvement of the system assets
- Interface with a human and providing an electromagnetic asset to help the mankind

Numerous advancements have collectively resulted in the range proficiency and psycho-logical radio innovations. These advances speak of a wide swath of commitments where-upon subjective innovations can be considered as an application on top of a fundamental SDR stage, executed to a great extent from computerized sign and universally useful gen-eral purpose processors (GPPs) made up of silicon. Most of the time, increased productiv-ity and other features added to refine the systems' administration of numerous radios to accomplish the end conduct, result in an added capacity and various benefits to the client.

These strings meet up to what we call today the intellectual radio period (Figure 8.1) [2]. Subjective radios are almost dependable applications that supersede an SDR, which is actu-alized to a great extent from the computerized sign processors and broadly useful proces-sors (GPPs) fabricated in silicon. By and large, the effectiveness and other shrewd backing to the client emerge by a complex system administration of numerous radios to accomplish the end conduct, which gives added ability and various advantages to the client.

8.1.3 Versatile Nature of CR

Conventional remote frameworks are normally assigned to work over a sure recurring band under a planned transmission arrangement and base, including physical (Phy) layer bal-ance/demodulation (modem), channel coder/decoder (codec), medium access control (MAC) conventions, and networking foundation, etc. Basically, legacy remote frameworks are unyielding, but the psychological radio is an adaptable remote correspondence framework.

Psychological radio is capable of a wide assortment of astute practices. It can screen the range and pick the frequencies that minimizes the impedance to existing correspondence

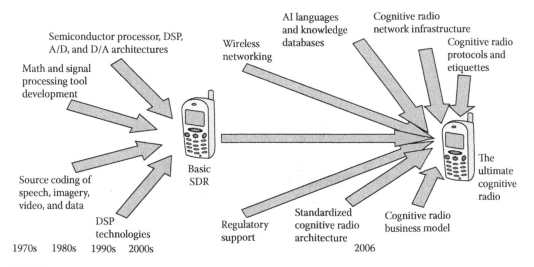

FIGURE 8.1
Technology timeline: SDR becomes the platform of choice for the cognitive radio. (From Fette, B., *Cognitive Radio Technology*, Academic Press, New York, 2009.)

movement. While doing so, it will take an arrangement of tenets that define what frequencies can be considered, what waveforms can be utilized, and what force levels can be utilized for the transmission, etc. It can also give rules for the entrance conventions by which range access is arranged with range permit holders (if any), and the decorum it must maintain with different clients of the range to guarantee that no client escapes the hub. Notwithstanding the range streamlining level, the psychological radio may be able to advance a waveform to one or more criteria. For instance, the radio may have the capacity to enhance the information rate, bundle achievement rate, administration cost, battery power minimization, or a combination of these criteria. The client does not see these levels of advanced channel examination and improvement with the exception of being the beneficiary of a brilliant administration.

The intellectual radio may additionally show practices that are more specifically evident to the client. These practices may include: (a) consciousness of geographical area, (b) familiarity with the nearby systems and their accessible administrations, (c) attention to the client and the client's biometric confirmation to accept financial exchanges, and (d) attention to the client and his/her organized destinations. The intellectual radio engineer must utilize the alerts to abstain from including the psychological usefulness that lessens the client's productivity. In the event that a client thinks about the radio as a phone and does not wish to get to different systems, the psychological radio engineer must give an outline that is well disposed to the client, convenient, and responsive, yet is not persistently connecting. On the off-chance that the radio's proprietor is a forced client, notwithstanding, the radio can be approached to look for various open doors, for example, access to different remote systems for information administrations, notification of the discriminating defining moments to help route, or a convenient financial data. The intellectual radio must offer usefulness that is convenient and valuable to its proprietor, not problematic. Not just that, some legacy frameworks are frightfully or transiently incompetent.

8.1.4 Need of the Flexible Wireless Communication System

It is normally believed that there is a shortage of frequencies that can be utilized for remote correspondences. This issue emerges from the extreme competition for utilization of range at frequencies <3 GHz. So, the wireless channels are scarce resources. From Figure 8.2,

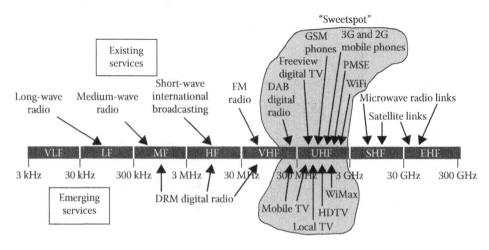

FIGURE 8.2
Frequency allocation for different purposes. DRM, digital radio mondiale. (From Wu, S.-H., *Phys. Commun.*, 2011.).

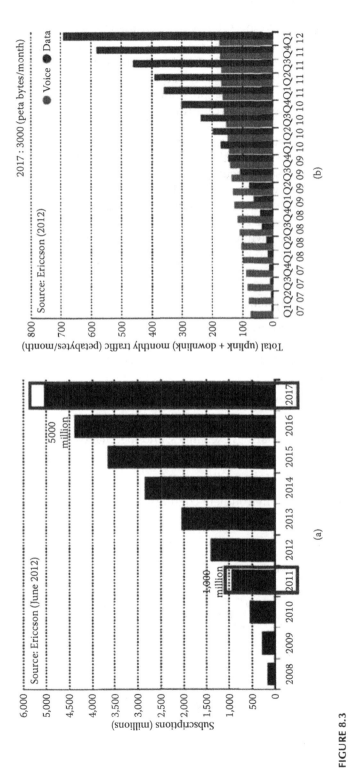

FIGURE 8.3

(a) Time vs. number of mobile users and (b) traffic vs. voice and data. (From *Wu, S.-H., Phys. Commun.,* 2011.)

3–300 kHz and 300 kHz to 300 MHz are allocated for the emergency services and digital radio, respectively [3].

The very high frequency 30–300 MHz is allotted for FM radio. Sweet spots for radio transmissions: 200 MHz to 3 GHz. TV, microwave ovens, mobile phones, Wi-Fi, Bluetooth, Zigbee, global positioning system (GPS), etc., all share these frequency ranges.

Figure 8.3a demonstrates that the quantity of the cell phones and the information movement in a portable system are growing exponentially, and the voice activity grows directly, whereby some legacy frameworks are frightfully or transiently wasteful, which is an enormous issue for a remote correspondence [3].

The graph in Figure 8.3b shows that the data traffic in mobile network increases exponentially along with the increase in the number of mobile devices and the voice traffic increases linearly, whereby some legacy systems are spectrally or temporally inefficient, which is a huge problem for wireless communication.

Not only the fleeting and geological variety in the range usage extended from 15% to 85%, but the range utilization also shifted in distinctive zones. Keeping in mind the end goal to use the range called "white spaces," the Federal Communications Commission (FCC) has issued a notice of proposed rule-making (NPRM-FCC 03-22) for progressing the CR innovation as a possibility to execute the arranged or sharp sharing (see Figure 8.4) [3].

8.1.5 Advantages of a CR System

There are many points of interest for the CR framework, which are given below:

- Reusage of unmoving frequencies in the white spaces
- Adaptive interchanges
- Powerful remote frameworks (system switches)
- Dynamic range access
- On-demand spectrum sharing, exchanges, and merchandising (see Figure 8.5) [3]

8.1.6 What Does It Take to Make a CR System?

- Spectrum and wireless environment cognition (radio power map)
- Spectrum sensing, user positioning, and radio activity monitoring

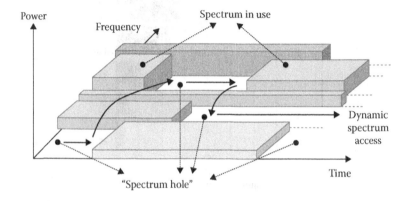

FIGURE 8.4
Concept of spectrum holes. (From Wu, S.-H., *Phys. Commun.*, 2011.)

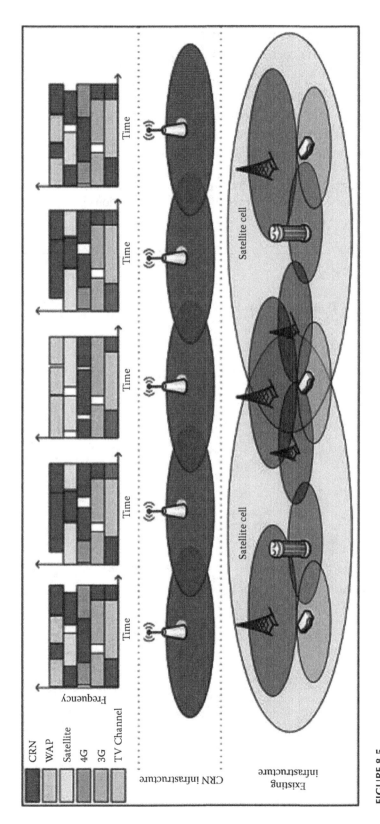

FIGURE 8.5
Spectrum sharing, exchanges, and merchandising. (From Wu, S.-H., *Phys. Commun.*, 2011.)

- System performance analysis and learning (cognitive multiple access)
- Spectrum allocation, power control, and interference management
- Interaction, cooperation, and decision making (dynamic spectrum access)
- Spectrum management, sharing, exchanges, and pricing
- Systems and network adaptation (reconfigurable radio and networks)
- SDR: reconfigurable Physical layer and MAC systems
- Software-defined network: heterogeneous networks

When there is any scarcity or unavailability of the frequency, CRs can share, exchange, or merchandise their frequency. Figure 8.6 shows some of these situations [3].

8.2 Features of CR

Frequency agility: Capacity of a radio to change its working recurrence to streamline the use under specific conditions.

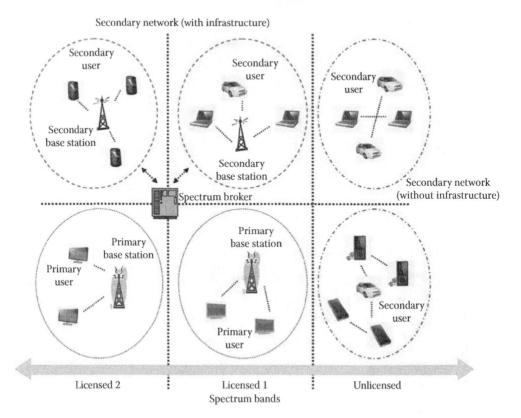

FIGURE 8.6
Spectrum bands. (From Wu, S.-H., *Phys. Commun.*, 2011.)

Dynamic frequency selection: Capacity to sense the signals from other adjacent transmitters with an end goal to pick an ideal working environment.

Location awareness: Capacity for a gadget to focus its area and the area of different transmitters. To begin with, it figures out if it is possible to transmit at all, and then chooses the proper working parameters, for example, the force and recurrence permitted in its area.

Negotiated use: CR can fuse a component that would empower the sharing of range under the terms of a prearranged assertion between a licensee and an outsider.

Adaptive modulation: Capacity to alter the transmission attributes and waveforms to endeavor chances to utilize the range.

Transmit power control: To allow transmission at full power limits when required, yet compel the transmitter energy to a lower level to permit more prominent sharing of the range when higher power operation is not required.

8.2.1 Interference Management and Spectrum Sensing

To share the spectrum with legacy systems, cognitive radio networks (CRNs) will have to follow some policies defined by the regulatory agencies [2]. These policies are based on the central idea where there are licensed PUs and unlicensed secondary users (SUs) which are allowed to use the spectrum as long as they do not disturb the communications of PUs. These policies deal with controlling the amount of interference that the SUs can incur to the PUs. Thus, the problem is interference management [2].

8.2.2 Receiver-Centric Interference Management

In the recipient-driven methodology [2] an obstruction limit at the collector is ascertained and used to focus the limitation on the transmitters' force around it. This impedance cutoff, called as obstruction temperature, is decided to be the most exceedingly terrible obstruction level that can be acknowledged without aggravating the recipient operation past its working point. In spite of the fact that this methodology obliges the information of the impedance to the furthest reach of all the recipients in an essential framework, such information relies on numerous variables, including individual areas, blurring circumstances, balances, coding plans, and administrations. Beneficiary-driven impedance administration procedures will not be tended to in this section as they have been as of late discounted by IEEE SCC41.

8.2.3 Transmitter-Centric Interference Management

In the transmitter-driven methodology, the center is moved to the wellspring of obstruction [2]. The transmitter does not know the impedance temperature, but during the process of detection, it tries to recognize a free data transmission. The detecting methodology permits the transmitter to group the channel status to choose whether it can transmit and with how much power. In real frameworks, since the transmitter does not know the recipients' area or their channel conditions, it cannot accumulate the amount of impedance these beneficiaries can endure. Subsequently, range detecting tackles the issue for the direst outcome imaginable, expecting solid impedance channels so the auxiliary framework transmits as soon as it detects an unfilled medium.

8.3 Spectrum-Sensing Smart Codec Design

8.3.1 Cognitive Cycle

An essential cognitive cycle starts with the radio scene investigation and distinguishing the range gaps, performing channel estimation for the channel limit, channel state, transmit force, transmit recurrence and issues in transmit force control and range administration. At the last, it sets up association with a fitting introductory handshake with the recipient.

Researchers have checked the calculation's productivity which designs the convolution encoder to create a lower bit error rate (BER) for expanded data transmission accessible, and therefore have tried the field-programmable gate array (FPGA) execution of the convolution encoder by utilizing a MATLAB® hardware description language (HDL) coder.

CR is a promising innovation to enhance the range application. The work examined in this chapter includes the rate receptive coder yielding the least BER for crisis administrations over psychological radio. The outcome checks the calculation's effectiveness which designs the convolution encoder to create a lower BER for expanded, accessible bandwidth. This can be promptly actualized in the SDR library. This has been tried by FPGA for the usage of the convolution encoder by utilizing MATLAB HDL coder. The coder yielded the FPGA actualized VHDL (VHSIC [very high speed integrated circuit] hardware description language) code as shown in previous studies [1] (see Figure 8.7) [1].

In this chapter, the idea of CR and the issue of a coder adaption to accessible transfer speed are challenged. Along these lines, the calculation is proposed in Smart Codec for the issue's arrangement, to legitimize its materialness by exhibiting the recreation, and the hardware execution results.

8.3.2 Types of CR

CR is categorized based on the arrangement of parameters considered in the settling transmission and gathering changes for authentic reasons. There are full CRs (Mitola radio) with every conceivable parameter detectable by a remote hub and spectrum-sensing CRs

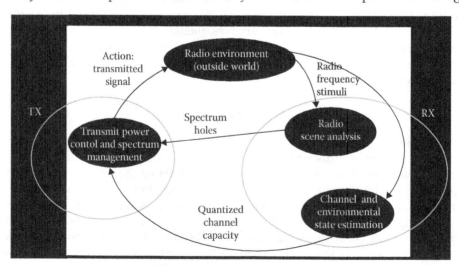

FIGURE 8.7
Cognitive cycle. (From Raut, R.D., and Kulat, K.D., *8th WSEAS International Conference ICO SSSE*, 17–19 October, 2009.)

considering just radio recurrence range. On the basis of range's accessibility, the CR can be divided into two classes: licensed band, for the authorized clients and unlicensed band, with access to unlicensed parts of the radio recurrence range.

8.3.3 Principle Functions of CR

1. *Range sensing:* This includes the essential transmitter identification. Psychological radios must have the capacity to figure out whether a sign from an essential transmitter is locally accessible. Coordinated filter discovery, energy identification, etc. are the systems used for the essential transmitter recognition. This technique is called cooperative location, which is used when data from different CR clients are consolidated for the essential client recognition.

2. *Range management:* Spectrum investigation and range choice are the vital assignments to be completed in the spectrum management.

3. *Range mobility:* This ought to guarantee a consistent operation and should trade the working frequencies as needed.

4. *Range sharing:* Spectrum booking technique deals with sharing the accessible range. The present work is for the range-detecting radios. When a transmission capacity is accessible and the accessible data transfer capacity is sufficiently wide, we have two choices:

   - To transmit mass information at a higher information rate, e.g., constant applications such as mobile services.
   - To transmit little parcels of information with high precision, needed in emergency services (time-bound crises data ought to deal with the information decrease to minimize the conceivable size in order to use the low information rates where the BER is low).

Present work concentrates on the second choice for enhancing the BER execution of the framework.

8.3.4 Displaying and Simulation of Spectrum-Sensing Smart Codec for CR

For displaying, the first thing was to set up a straightforward digital communication (DCOM) system model and after that test the encoder-decoder configuration utilizing MATLAB Simulink®. The next step is to test the usefulness of the codec in the DCOM system. After that a door-level model of encoder was readied, knowing that the MATLAB Simulink to the HDL converter backs just the behavioral-level squares. These strides were done to test the equipment execution probability of the codec. The entryway-level outline is given in Figure 8.8 [1].

In this model, the information bits are haphazardly produced to speak to the irregular discourse signals. The bit era recurrence additionally changes, considering the varieties in human discourse. Here, we are not worried about the sufficiency varieties. The model has been worked out for changing the frequencies of information and performs just as well over the entire determined scope of frequencies of data information. In this way, the model now comes to fruition with the accompanying three parameters as client characterized:

1. Information begin recurrence
2. Information end frequency
3. Perception time

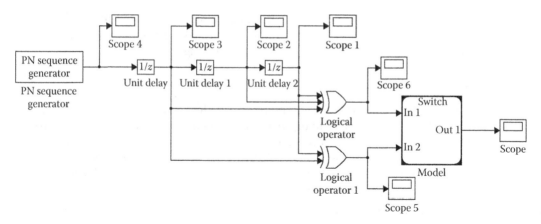

FIGURE 8.8

Gate-level design of the convolution encoder for Simulink® to HDL conversion. (From Raut, R.D., and Kulat, K.D., *8th WSEAS International Conference ICO SSSE*, 17–19 October, 2009.)

8.3.5 Result

The outcome is displayed as bits on the PC screen and the working frequencies are downsized to plot the charts (see Figure 8.9). The model works just as well at high frequencies and was tried a couple of times for test information at higher frequencies. The issue was that the reenactment time took hours because of the computational time needed in discovering to check the sum of the bits obtained from the info bit streams. The principal model was a basic, nonversatile, advanced, correspondence framework wherein the codec does not adjust to the accessible data transfer capacity. It was found that as the transfer speed builds, the BER increases, as evident from the diagram in Figure 8.9 [1].

The second model was readied with a calculation with adjustments to the expanding transmission capacity and using this transfer speed to make the information more secure, i.e., to reduce the BER. The chart in Figure 8.10 [1] demonstrates that the versatile codec

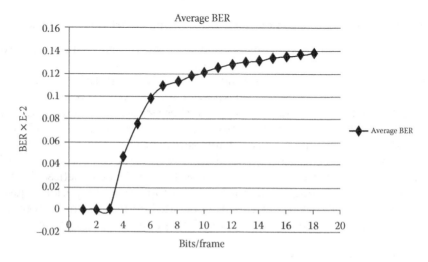

FIGURE 8.9

Bandwidth vs. bit error rate. (From Raut, R.D., and Kulat, K.D., *8th WSEAS International Conference ICO SSSE*, 17–19 October, 2009.)

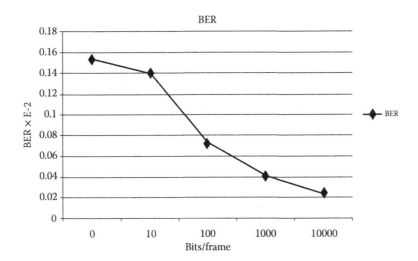

FIGURE 8.10
Bandwidth vs. BER. (From Raut, R.D., and Kulat, K.D., *8th WSEAS International Conference ICO SSSE*, 17–19 October, 2009.)

lessens the BER with an increment in the edge measure resulted from an increment in the transfer speed.

Cognitive users screen the range and are permitted to utilize it as long as they do not meddle with the authorized clients. We proposed a Smart Codec utilizing convolution codes wherein the codec faculties the range accessibility and changes the calculation for coding–decoding.

8.4 Overview of Spectrum Sensing for CR

Figure 8.10 displays the information combination rules for delicate and hard consolidating of helpful detecting, vitality proficiency of a few diverse detecting, and resting and sensor plans. Here, we can see that if the unearthly properties of the sign to be distinguished are known, and the sign has generally no usable components that can be effectively misused, then the separating-based indicators can be ideal. Likewise, it manages range detecting and remaking for the psychological radio. A range analyzer is utilized to copy a subjective radio for range detecting. The entire strategy of range detecting includes the detecting setup, instrument control, detecting capacity, and detecting situation, and the detecting result is introduced to the point of interest. The idea behind the hardware-based range detecting is to perform snappy and semi-persistent estimations. The time required for every estimation is around 80–110 ms. Three-dimensional ranges of CDMA sign, GSM signal, Wi-Fi sign, and digital TV (DTV) sign are discussed in [4].

8.4.1 Detecting Setup

Detecting setup comprises a PC/tablet, a range analyzer, and an omnidirectional reception apparatus. National Instruments (NI) LabVIEW-8.5 is installed on the PC to control the range analyzer and secure the detecting information. The PC and range analyzer are joined utilizing the general purpose interface bus (GPIB)-USB2 link. A spellbound,

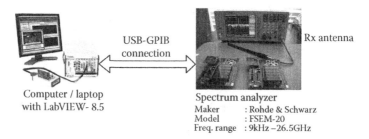

FIGURE 8.11
Setup diagram. (From Saini, A.S. et al., *2009 41st Southeastern Symposium on System Theory*, Tullahoma, TN, 2009.)

omnidirectional radio wire with 50 Ω unevenly feed impedance is utilized for every detecting situation (see Figure 8.11) [4].

8.4.2 Procedural Steps of Sensing the Spectrum

- Connect the range analyzer, PC/tablet, and accepting radio wire.

- Power on the range analyzer and physically set parameters, e.g., begin/stop recurrence, determination data transfer capacity, feature transmission capacity, lessening, breadth time, and so on.

- Open the Lab View square outline on the remote PC with NI LabView-8.5 introduced to it. Select the instrument GPIB port location from the menu list that shows the data instrument port choice box.

- Select the compass mode as single sweep showcase in set sweep mode alternative box. One scope is portrayed by three parameters range time, determination transmission capacity, and feature data transfer capacity. Where scope time is the time taken to finish its way from a given begin-recurrence to stop-recurrence amid one trigger.

- Select the fitting follow mode in set trace type alternative. A follow comprises 500 pixels on the level recurrence hub that implies the quantity of point for every estimation is 500. Choice of the follow mode relies upon our objective, i.e., what sort of information we require from the range analyzer.

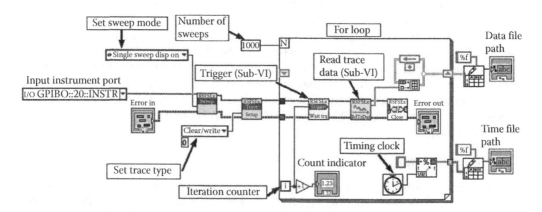

FIGURE 8.12
Sensing setup. (From Saini, A.S. et al., *2009 41st Southeastern Symposium on System Theory*, Tullahoma, TN, 2009.)

- Generally for a range analyzer, regularly specified follow modes are clear/write, average, max hold, and min hold. At that point a "For Loop" is presented in the following step and the usefulness appended to this For Loop (see Figure 8.12) [4].

8.4.3 Sensing Capability

The main advantage of our equipment-based spectrum sensing is that the semi-continuous measurements can be executed and the corresponding sensed data can be recorded automatically for online or off-line signal processing.

8.5 Implementation Issues in Spectrum Sensing for CR

This section introduces a new field of CRs with a special emphasis on one unique aspect of these radios—spectrum sensing. It is commonly believed that there is a spectrum scarcity of frequencies that can be economically used for wireless communications. This concern has arisen from the intense competition for the use of spectra at frequencies below 3 GHz. The FCC frequency allocation chart indicates the overlapping allocations over all of the frequency bands, which reinforces the scarcity mind-set. This section discusses about the sensing function and proposes a cross-layer approach for its implementation [5].

8.5.1 CR Front-End

Spectrum sensing is best addressed as a cross-layer design problem. CR sensitivity can be improved by enhancing the radio frequency (RF) front-end sensitivity, exploiting the digital signal processing gain for a specific PU signal and measurements (see Figure 8.13) [6].

There are two recurrence groups where the intellectual radios may work in future: 400–800 MHz (UHF TV groups) and 3–10 GHz. FCC has noticed that in the lower UHF groups each topographical region has a few unused 6 MHz wide TV channels. This recurrence band is especially engaging because of its good engendering properties for long-extended interchanges. The static TV channel allotments and timing prerequisites for range detecting are exceptionally casual. FCC support of UWB underlay systems in 3–10 GHz shows

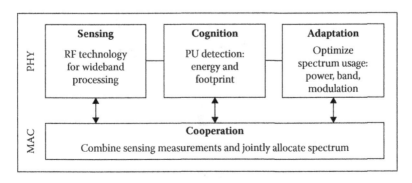

FIGURE 8.13
Cross-layer functionalities related to spectrum sensing. (From Axell, E., *Topics in Spectrum Sensing in Cognitive Radio*, Linköping University Electronic Press, Linkoping, 2009.)

that this recurrence extent can be opened for sharp utilization. Despite the working recurrence run, a wideband front-end could have construction modeling as portrayed in Figure 8.14 [5]. The wideband RF (Figure 8.15) sign displayed at the receiving wire of an intellectual radio incorporates the signals from close and broadly isolated transmitters, and from the transmitters working at generally distinctive force levels and channel data transfer capacities. Subsequently, the powerless signs can often be located in the vicinity of the extremely solid signs. In this way, there will be amazingly stringent necessities put on the linearity of the RF simple circuits and their capacity to work over wide data-transfer capacities. With a specific end goal to keep the prerequisites on the last simple to computerize an analog-to-digital (A/D) converter at a sensible level in a basically advanced structural planning, the front-end outline needs a tunable indent simple preparing square that would give a dynamic reach control.

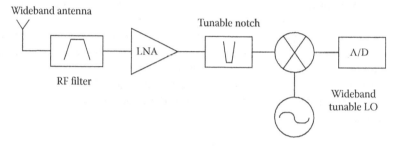

FIGURE 8.14
Wideband RF/analog front-end architecture for cognitive radio. (From Cabric, D. et al., *Proceedings the 38th Asilomar Conference on Signals, Systems, and Computers*, Pacific Grove, CA, 2004.)

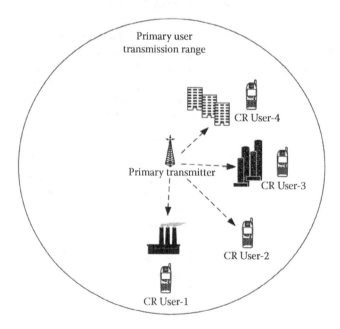

FIGURE 8.15
Noncooperative system. (From Armi, N. et al., *J. ICT Res. Appl.* 3, 109–122, 2009.)

8.5.2 Signal-Preparing Systems for Range Detecting

Focal points and impediments of three strategies that are utilized as a part of customary frameworks, i.e., coordinated channel, vitality indicator, and cyclostationary highlight identifier are discussed as follows:

Coordinated filter: An ideal route for distinguishing a sign is the coordinated channel. It boosts up the sign-to-commotion proportion. A coordinated channel adequately obliges the demodulation of an essential client signal.

Vitality detector: One method to improve the coordinated separating methodology is to perform a noncognizant recognition through vitality identification. This problematic method has been broadly utilized as a part of radiometry. A vitality locator can be actualized correspondingly to a range analyzer by averaging recurrence receptacles of the fast Fourier transform. Because of the unintelligent handling, the $O(1/SNR2)$ tests are obliged to meet a likelihood of identification imperative.

Cyclostationary feature detection: This can be utilized for recognition of an irregular sign with a specific regulation sort in a foundation of clamor and other balanced signs. Normal examination of stationary arbitrary signs depends on the auto-relationship capacity and force the otherworldly thickness. The cyclostationary signs display a connection among between generally isolated unearthly segments. Because of the excess brought about by the periodicity, spectral relationship capacity is likewise termed as cyclic range.

Helpful spectrum detecting: The execution of these methods is constrained due to the accepting sign quality which may be extremely debased because of multipath blurring and shadowing. In such a situation, helpful detecting may allay the issue of reducing, so as to recognize the likelihood of obstruction to an essential client. In helpful detecting, we depend on the variability of the sign quality in different areas. An extensive system of intellectual radios with detecting data traded among the neighbors would have a superior shot of distinguishing the essential client as opposed to individual detecting (see Table 8.1).

TABLE 8.1

Overview of Available Techniques for Spectrum Sensing

S. No.	Spectrum-Sensing Techniques	Advantages	Disadvantages
1.	Matched-filter detection	Best in Gaussian noise. Needs shorter sensing duration (less power consumption).	Obliges a former data on PU transmissions and additional equipment on hubs for synchronization with PU.
2.	Energy detection	Requires least amount of computational power of nodes.	Obliges longer detecting length of time (high power utilization). Exactness exceedingly relies upon the clamor-level varieties.
3.	Cyclostationary feature detection	Strongest to variety in the clamor levels.	Obliges a former learning about PU transmissions. Obliges high computational capacity on hubs.
4.	Cooperative sensing	Prescribed by FCC. Ensures that a foreordained obstruction to PU is not surpassed.	Obliges learning of area PU and forces a polyostensible figuring in the light of these areas.

Source: From Cabric, D. et al., *Proceedings the 38th Asilomar Conference on Signals, Systems, and Computers,* Pacific Grove, CA, 2004.

8.5.3 Advantages and Disadvantages

In this section we discuss the features and limitations of various sensing techniques. Table 8.1 shows the advantages and disadvantages of sensing techniques.

8.6 Relation with SDR

Programming characterized radio: It alludes utilizing of programming handling inside the radio framework or gadget to execute working.

- CR obliges an adaptable radio gadget. Programming characterized radios (SDRs) are the perfect stages for CR.
- Software-defined radio (SDR) will not be essential for CR, but rather exceedingly alluring.
- Software-characterized radio may conceivably carry out the occupation for the maximum translations of the CR.
- Even multiband and multimode radio gadgets can carry out the employment for some CR understandings.

8.7 Relation between Adaptive Radios

Versatile radio: Systems exhibiting an attention to its surroundings and capacity to respond naturally.

CR and versatile remote generally mean the same thing.

CR can incorporate the extra components past adjustment.

8.7.1 Cooperative Spectrum Sensing with AND Rule under AWGN

Cooperative spectrum sensing (CSS) can improve the spectrum sensing performance by introducing the spatial diversity in CRNs.

8.7.2 Combination of Soft and Hard

In agreeable discovery every sensor takes its own choice and transmits just its parallel number to the combination focus, then the combination focus consolidates the hard choice to one regular choice. Essentially, we can say that all the clients transmit their delicate choice to a combination focus, which consolidates the delicate qualities to one basic choice. On the off-chance there are M sensors and we wish to identify whether there is a sign present or not, then we need to separate between the accompanying two speculation tests:

$$H_0 : ym = Wm, \quad m = 0, \dots, M-1, \tag{8.1}$$

$$H_1 : ym = \dot{X}m + Wm, \quad m = 0, \dots, M-1, \tag{8.2}$$

where ym is the signal vector of length m which consists of a signal pulse noise. In Equation 8.2, Xm is the signal vector and Wm is the noise vector.

If the received signals at all sensors are independent, let $Z = (y^T_0, y^T_1, \dots, y^T_{M-1})^T$ then the log-likelihood ratio will be as follows:

$$Acoop \underline{\Delta} \log\left(\frac{P(Z|H_1)}{P(Z|H_0)}\right)$$

$$Acoop = \sum_{m=0}^{M-1} \log\left(\frac{P(ym|H_1)}{P(ym|H_0)}\right) \tag{8.3}$$

$$Acoop = \sum_{m=0}^{M-1} A(m) \tag{8.4}$$

where $A(m) \underline{\Delta} \log\left(\frac{P(ym|H_1)}{P(ym|H_0)}\right)$ is the log-likelihood ratio for the mth sensor. It means that if all the received signals are independent then the soft combining of the fusion rule is the sum of the log-likelihood ratios, which depends on the distribution of the signal to be detected [6,7].

8.7.3 Justification behind Selecting AND Rule

There are different rules for combining cooperative sensing such as AND, OR, and Voting rules. The OR rules decide the signal presence if any of the sensor reports a signal detection. So, for the OR rule the cooperative test decides on H_1, if

$$\sum_{m=0}^{M-1} A(m) \geq 1$$

Assume that the individual statistics $A(m)$ are quantized to one bit such that $A(m) = 0,1$ is the hard decision from the mth sensor. In this case when a signal is detected, it becomes 1; otherwise it becomes 0.

The voting rule decides that a signal is present if at least V of the M sensor or user has detected a signal for $1 \leq M$. Then the test decides H_1

$$\sum_{m=0}^{M-1} A(m) \geq V$$

where V is considered as $M/2$.

In AND rule, sensing results should be H_1, for deciding H_1, where H_1 is an alternate hypothesis that the observed band is occupied by a PU. If all sensors have detected a signal, then an AND rule decides that a signal is detected. So, here the cooperative test using the AND rule decides on H_1, if

$$\sum_{m=0}^{M-1} A(m) = M \qquad (8.5)$$

In this part, the AND principle has been considered for the range detection of the cooperative. It is expected to inspect the impact on the likelihood of discovery of the sign for the situation-shaped circumstance. If we select the OR principle here, we cannot legitimize the expanding's impact on the clients. In OR guidelines, it any of the sensor reports signal discovery then it chooses the sign recognition. Then again, in AND principle, if all sensors have recognized a sign, then a sign is distinguished. So for the best possible discovery of the sign and to figure out the impact, the AND standard is practical.

As shown in Figure 8.15 [8], the CR clients recognize the essential flag and choose whether the sign is available or not without anyone else's input. On the other hand, this system cannot identify the essential flag legitimately because of the blurring and shadowing. Figure 8.16 demonstrates the framework model of an agreeable sign recognition where the standout psychological radio client might distinguish the essential sign [9]. Here the clients are populated in the scope of essential transmitter. So it is normal that it can enhance the sign location likelihood [8]. From these figures, we can see that the helpful detecting is a powerful and alluring way to deal with numerous blurring, beneficiary's instability, and concealed primary problems.

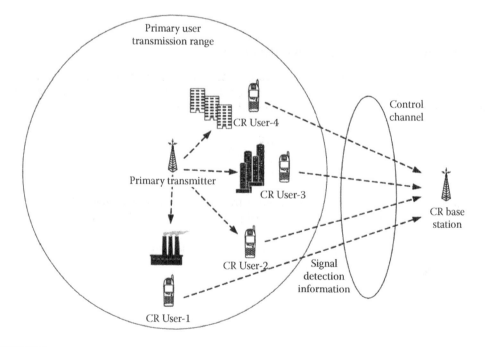

FIGURE 8.16

Cooperative system. (From Hugain, A.L., MS dissertation, University Libraries, Virginia Polytechnic Institute and State University, Blacksburg, VA, 2006.)

8.7.4 Calculation of AND Rule

In spectrum sensing, there are two types of errors, false alarm and misdetection. The probability of detection (P_d) and probability of false alarm (P_{fa}) are used for hard decision-based CSS for AND rules. We know that the P_d and P_{fa} depend on the threshold value, noise variance, and signal variance of the PU when the SNR value is large. We can calculate the (P_d) and (P_{fa}) by following formula:

$$P_d = Q\left(\frac{\sqrt{N}\left(\beta_{ED} - \left(\sigma^2 S + \sigma^2 n\right)\right)}{\sigma^2 S + \sigma^2 n}\right) \tag{8.6}$$

$$P_{fa} = Q\left(\frac{\sqrt{N}\left(\beta_{ED} - \sigma 2n\right)}{\sigma 2n}\right) \tag{8.7}$$

where σ^2_s is the PU signal variance, σ^2_n is the noise variance, and β_{ED} is the threshold value.

After calculating the P_d and P_{fa}, we can calculate the probability of false alarm and probability of detection of the CR for the M user for the AND rules.

$$C_d = 1 - \prod_1^n \left(1 - P_{d,k}\right) \tag{8.8}$$

$$C_d = 1 - \prod_1^n \left(1 - P_{fa,k}\right) \tag{8.9}$$

where n is the number of CR, and $P_{d,m}$ and $P_{fa,m}$ are the probabilities of detection and false alarm of the M users, respectively.

8.7.5 Additive White Gaussian Noise

Additive white Gaussian noise (AWGN) is a divert model in which the main disability is a direct option of the wideband or repetitive sound with a consistent otherworldly thickness, and a Gaussian dispersion of abundance. This model does not represent blurring, recurrence selectivity, impedance, nonlinearity, or dispersion [9].

In the AWGN environment, the detecting client determination plan is comparable to selecting the ideal number of helpful optional clients (SU) because of the considerable number of SUs having the same momentary identification for sign-to-clamor proportion (SNR) [9].

Figure 8.17 shows the average throughput versus the number of cooperative SUs under different reporting delays when $\gamma = -20$ dB [9]. It can be seen that the maximum average throughput might not be achieved when all the SUs within the CRN cooperate to sense the same PU channel.

The relative power of noise in an AWGN channel is typically described by quantities such as

- Signal-to-noise ratio (SNR) per sample: This is the actual input parameter to the AWGN function.

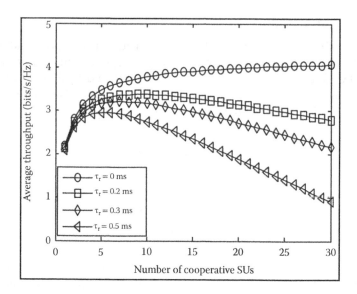

FIGURE 8.17
The average throughput vs. the number of cooperative users in the AWGN environment. (From Hugain, A.L., MS dissertation, University Libraries, Virginia Polytechnic Institute and State University, Blacksburg, VA, 2006.)

- Ratio of bit energy to noise power spectral density (EbNo): This quantity is used by the BER tool and performance evaluation functions in this toolbox.
- Ratio of symbol energy to noise power spectral density (EsNo).

8.8 Local Spectrum Sensing

To accomplish the precision and enhance the unwavering quality, helpful range detection is typically utilized. The expense of collaboration is overhead among the CR clients. This overhead can be diminished by enhancing the neighborhood range-detecting precision. We realized that an exact range-detecting procedure can decrease the likelihood of false alerts and misrecognition.

8.9 Probability of False Alarm and Probability of Misdetection

There are two types of errors in spectrum sensing: false alarm and misdetection. The probability that a signal will be detected when present is called the probability of detection. The probability of a noise fluctuation mistaken for a signal is called the probability of false alarm. Underutilization of the spectrum of the PUs and SUs can be determined by false alarm and misdetection.

8.10 Energy Efficiency

We know that as the number of cooperating users grows, the energy consumption of the CRN increases, but its performance generally saturates. Therefore, some techniques have been developed to improve the energy efficiency in CRNs. One simple technique to save energy is the on–off sensing or sleeping, where every CR will randomly turn off its sensing device with a probability of sleeping rate. Another technique is called censoring. In such a system a CR (m) will only send a sensing result if it is deemed informative, and flushes out the uninformative ones [10].

8.11 Proposed Framework for Cooperative Sensing

The framework of cooperative sensing consists of the PUs. In cooperating, the CR users include a fusion center (FC), all the elements of cooperative sensing, RF environment, including licensed and control channels, and an optional remote database [11].

Figure 8.18 outlines the structure of concentrated agreeable detecting from the physical layer point of view [10]. In this structure, a gathering of collaborating CR clients performs nearby detecting with an RF front-end and a neighborhood handling unit. The RF front-end can be designed for the information transmission in range detecting. Moreover, the RF front tends to incorporate the down-transformation of the RF signs and examines at the Nyquist rate by a simple-to-advanced converter analog

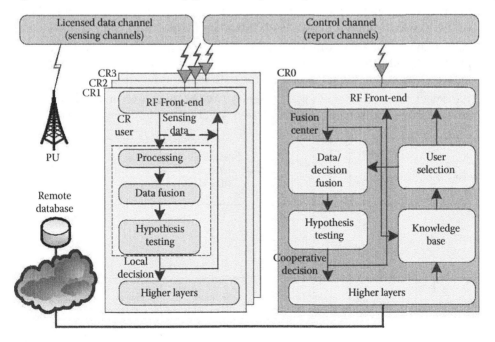

FIGURE 8.18
Framework of centralized cooperative sensing. (From Axell, E. et al., *Overview of Spectrum Sensing for Cognitive Radio*, Linköping University, Linköpings, 2005.)

to digital converter (ADC). The crude detecting information from the RF front-end can be straightforwardly sent to the FC, or be privately prepared for the nearby decision. To minimize the data transfer capacity prerequisite of the control channel, some nearby preparation is normally needed.

8.12 Work Flow

The cognitive cycle begins with the radio scene analysis and scanning for spectrum holes. Once the bandwidth is available, the transmitted frequency is decided. Thus, an M-file for bandwidth selection is written. The input signal is the digital data obtained from an analog source. We simulate the probability of false alarm and probability of misdetection for the CR user. We have been able to find out a way to reduce the miss-detection (see Figure 8.19).

8.13 Simulation Setup Process

1. At first we select the M-file as we have done in our simulation by MATLAB.

2. Then we declare the time bandwidth factor, number of cognitive users, path loss, and samples.

3. Next we calculate the probability of false alarm and SNR. For calculating the linear SNR, we considered the value of SNR to be 15 dB.

4. As we know that an accurate spectrum sensing technique can help to detect the probability of false alarms and misdetection more accurately, we calculated the local spectrum sensing for detecting the path loss and misdetection.

5. We detected the number of users under an AWGN environment. Under an AWGN environment, the sensing user selection scheme is equivalent to selecting the

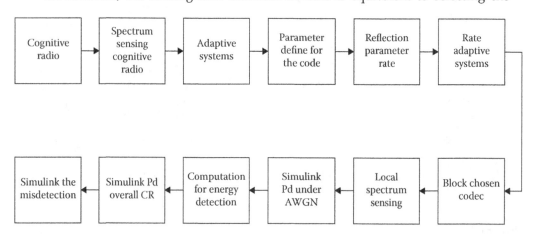

FIGURE 8.19
Projected system process.

optimal number of cooperative SUs due to all the SUs having the same instantaneous detection SNR.

6. To justify the effect of the cognitive user in the defined bandwidth, we increase the number of users.

7. Then we also change the time bandwidth factor for finding out the effect on our simulation.

8. Finally, we will be able to find out the effect of probability of false alarm and probability of detection.

8.14 Simulation Results

First we simulated the misdetection for the fixed bandwidth factor. Figure 8.19 shows the given SNR value as 15 dB and the time bandwidth factor as 1200. Here, with the increase of probability of false alarm initial probability of misdetection in a transmission way will also increase but will stop after some time and become a steady state.

When the energy consumption of the CRN increases, the performance generally saturates. We notice from Figure 8.20 that within the fixed time bandwidth factor, the probability of detection is also saturated with the consumption saturation.

In Figure 8.21, we have changed the time bandwidth factor from 1200 to 2000 for the same user and SNR value. We can distinguish that for the change of time and bandwidth

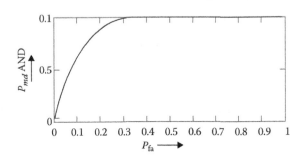

FIGURE 8.20
P_{fa} vs. P_{md} AND for bandwidth factor 1200.

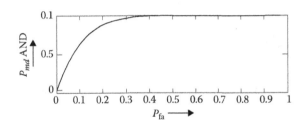

FIGURE 8.21
P_{fa} vs. P_{md} AND for bandwidth factor 2000.

factor, there is no effect on the probability of misdetection with the change of probability of false alarm.

When the noise power is only known to be contained within a bounded interval and the decision threshold is set to guarantee an upper bound on (P_{fa}) then achieving a desired (P_d) depends on a higher SNR value than a minimum level. Then (P_d) does not depend on time bandwidth factor.

In Figure 8.22, we observed the plot for the probability of misdetection of the user, against the probability of false alarm for the minimum number of users. The value of the probability of misdetection for a given value of probability of false alarm increases in a zigzag curve with the minimum number of users.

As we can observe from Figure 8.23 with the minimum number of users, the detection probability is not significant.

When we increase the number of cognitive users, we find that there is a change of probability of detection in the transmission way. In Figure 8.23, the probability of detection is plotted against the probability of false alarm for the increasing user numbers. Here we have kept the same time bandwidth factor to 1200, in order to examine the effect on the probability of detection in a busty case.

It does not increase after a certain time. It becomes saturated. It can be observed from the figure that increasing the number of users gives better performance of probability of detection than the minimum user. Here a group of cooperating CR users perform the local sensing with an RF front-end and a local processing unit. The CR users increase and the unused spectrum decreases within the RF environment. So the increased user detecting the unused spectrum and sharing it without harmful interference to other users gives a better performance of probability of detection. In Figure 8.24, we increase the number of users (CR users = 35). We observe that there is a significant plot for the probability of detection. It means that the detection has become more significant with the increasing number of users.

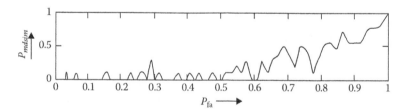

FIGURE 8.22

P_{fa} vs. P_{mdsim} for minimum CR user.

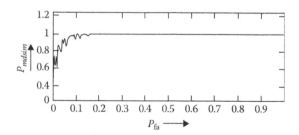

FIGURE 8.23

P_{fa} vs. P_{mdsim} after changing CR users to 20.

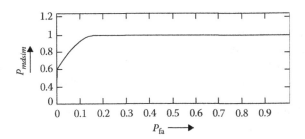

FIGURE 8.24
P_{fa} vs. P_{mdsim} after increasing the number of CR users to 35.

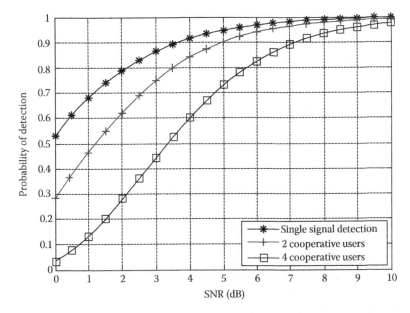

FIGURE 8.25
Probability of detection with change of SNR. (From Armi, N. et al., *J. ICT Res. Appl.*, 3, 109–122, 2009.)

Here, the cooperation among the cognitive users can increase the detection of probability for a given probability of false alarm. We can see in Figure 8.25 that with the increase of CR the probability of misdetection of users also increases. So the probability of detection for a given value of probability of false alarm has significantly achieved the optimal value of detection probability as the number of users increases.

8.15 Result Analysis

As we want to find out the significant impact on the probability of detection with the varying number of users, in this chapter the AND rule is being selected for cooperative sensing. Because we know that in the AND rule, if all the sensors or users have detected a signal, then a signal is considered detected. So, all the users have to use the spectrum. An accurate spectrum sensing technique can reduce the probability of false alarms and misdetection, and improves energy efficiency. These simulations are completed under an AWGN environment. In the AWGN environment, the sensing user selection scheme is equivalent to selecting the optimal number of cooperative SUs [11]. In the simulation part, we first checked if there was any effect of bandwidth factor on the misdetection probability. So we have changed the bandwidth parameter, keeping a higher SNR value. It can be distinguished that it does not affect the curve much. In both the cases (previous and new time-value factor) the probability of misdetection remains the same. The reason behind this is when the decision threshold is set to guarantee an upper bound on (P_f) then achieving a desired (P_d) depends on a higher SNR value. P_d does not depend on the time bandwidth factor. The false alarm affects the probability of misdetection. If the false alarm increases, then the probability of misdetection also increases. After that we have sorted out the effect of probability of detection against the probability of false alarm by varying the number of users and keeping a fixed SNR value of 15 dB. For the minimum user in a bound area the detection probability is not affected significantly. Though it increases, it shows a zigzag curve, which means sometimes the probability of misdetection decreases. But when we increase the user number of CRs, we achieve a significant value which increases with the probability of false alarm.

8.16 Comparison with the Real Life Implement

In this chapter, we have seen that the augmented number of users significantly increases the performance of the system. We also observed the plot for the probability of miss-detection against the probability of false alarm after varying the number of users (see Figure 8.25) [8].

Armi, Saad, and Arshad showed the probability of misdetection with varying SNR values, as shown in Figure 8.26. They also focused that OR rule is a more effective rule than the AND rule [8]. In this chapter, the probability of misdetection against the probability of false alarm is shown, after varying the number of users using the justified AND rule. As a result, we are able to determine the misdetection curve significantly.

Bansal and Mahajan [7] have built a code for spectrum sensing with the help of energy detection. But in this chapter, we have built the code for better detection of spectrum with the help of cooperative sensing. Reference [7] also shows that the number of PUs can be increased and how spectrum holes can be detected and the slot occupied in the absence of each PU. But in this chapter, we have increased the user within the range of the RF

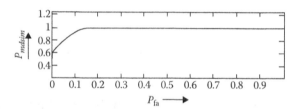

FIGURE 8.26
Probability of detection with varying user.

environment. Here we were able to show how CR can significantly detect the spectrum. This can help in the eigenvalue detection.

Hüseyin Arslan plotted a lower BER for the increased available bandwidth [12]. But in this chapter, we have achieved a higher (P_{dsim}) and (P_d).

8.17 Conclusion

In this part, we focused on the impact of likelihood of the mislocation and false alert in the wake of using so as to change the psychological client AND tenet. In an agreeable procedure, the AND standard is utilized to assess the framework execution by utilizing the likelihood of location (P_d) and SNR as metrics. We realize that helpful detection is a compelling and appealing way to deal with different blurring, beneficiary's vulnerability, and concealed essential issues. For vital productivity of the psychological radio systems, a few procedures have been created as of now. To minimize the transfer speed prerequisite of the control channel, some neighborhood handling is typically needed. So the exploration chipping away at subjective radio has been focused on the optional clients and none of the impact was brought on by these gadgets for the essential clients. The expense of participation is an overhead among the CR clients. This overhead can be decreased by enhancing the nearby range-detecting precision. We realized that an exact range-detecting procedure can lessen the likelihood of false alerts and misrecognition.

8.18 Negative Aspects

One of the major problems in the worst-case scenario is when when the CR users increase, the probability of detection becomes saturated in a certain value of probability of false alarm.

8.19 Future Work on CR

In this chapter, it has been demonstrated that as the cognitive client is expanded the likelihood of misidentification can also be fundamentally expanded. Identification of probability of misrecognition is vastly improved after taking the AND principle. It might likewise be seen that utilizing just a couple of clients helps us to acquire a superior location likelihood, in contrast with utilizing all the clients as a part of the system [13]. We might want to examine this matter and outline calculations as per which the clients must contemplate for the agreeable range detecting. It will be allowed that the intellectual radio innovation practically remotes systems administration that it will use to build up and to interface with any near by open unused radio range that encourages the client [12]. The blend of programming characterized radio and man-made brainpower will make new abilities for the business and military commercial center.

Acknowledgment

We express gratitude to our parents for their valuable guidance and motivation throughout our career.

References

1. Raut, Rajeshree D., and Kishore D. Kulat. 2009. Spectrum sensing smart codec design for cognitive radio. In *8th WSEAS International Conference ICO SSSE*. 17–19 October Genova, Italy. http://www.wseas.us/e-library/conferences/2009/genova/ICOSSSE/ICOSSSE-49.pdf. [Available online].
2. Fette, Bruce. 2009. *Cognitive Radio Technology*. New York: Academic Press. [Available online].
3. Wu, Sau-Hsuan. 2011. Cognitive radio systems and experiments. *Phys. Commun.* [Available online] http://140.113.144.123/CRLab/Unit%200-Introduction.pdf.
4. Saini, Amanpreet S., Zhen Hu, and Robert Qiu. 2009. Spectrum sensing and reconstruction for cognitive radio. In *2009 41st Southeastern Symposium on System Theory*, Tullahoma, TN. pp. 13–18. [Available online].
5. Cabric, Danijela, Shridhar Mubaraq Mishra, and Robert W. Brodersen. 2004. Implementation issues in spectrum sensing for cognitive radios. In *Proceedings the 38th Asilomar Conference on Signals, Systems, and Computers*. Pacific Grove, CA. pp. 772–776. [Available online].
6. Axell, Erikh. 2009. *Topics in Spectrum Sensing in Cognitive Radio*. Linköping: Linköping University Electronic Press. pp. 13–15. [Available online].
7. Bansal, Anugar, and Rita Mahajan. 2007. Building cognitive radio system using MATLAB. *Int. J. Electron. Comput. Sci. Eng.* 1: 1555–1560. [Available online].
8. Armi, N., N. Mohammad Saad, and Mohammad Arshad. 2009. Hard decision fusion based cooperative spectrum sensing in cognitive radio system. *J. ICT Res. Appl.* 3 (2): 109–122. [Available online].
9. Hugain, Akilah L. 2006. Antenna selection for public safety of cognitive radio. MS dissertation, University Libraries, Virginia Polytechnic Institute and State University, Blacksburg, VA. [Available online] https://theses.lib.vt.edu/theses/available/etd-05112006-143425/unrestricted/A_Hugine_Thesis.pdf.
10. Axell, Erik, Geert Leus, and Erik G. Larsson. 2005. *Overview of Spectrum Sensing for Cognitive Radio*. Linköping: Linköping University. [Available online] http://liu.diva-portal.org/smash/get/diva2:304989/FULLTEXT01.pdf.
11. Akyildiz, Ina F., and Brandon F. Lo. 2010. Cooperative spectrum sensing in cognitive radio networks: A survey. *J. Phys. Commun.* 4: 40–62. [Available online].
12. Arslan, Hüseyin. 2006. *Cognitive Radio, Software Defined Radio, and Adaptive Wireless Communication Systems*. Pearson Education. [Available online] www.springer.com/?SGID=0-102-1297-173694424-0.
13. Fette, Bruce, (ed.). 2006. *Cognitive Radio Technology*. Amsterdam, the Netherlands; Boston, MA: Newnes/Elsevier: [Available online] http://omidi.iut.ac.ir/SDR/2007/WebPages/07_CognitiveRadio/references/ebook/Fette%20B.A.(ed)%20Cognitive%20Radio%20Technology.pdf.

Part IV

Routing Algorithms and Layers in CRN

9

Physical Layer, Data Link Layer, Network Layer, Transport Layer, and Application Layer in Cognitive Radio Networks

M. N. Thippeswamy, A. Dinesh Prasanna, and F. Takawira

CONTENTS

9.1 Introduction

The scarcity of spectrum resources among unlicensed users is increasing day by day with the increasing number of spectrum band users. The Federal Communications Commission (FCC) responsible for the allocation of the spectrum bands has introduced the industrial, scientific, medical (ISM) bands for utilization by the unlicensed or secondary users (SUs). The scarcity of ISM bands has resulted in the need for spectral resources for the unprivileged users. Further studies have highlighted that in most of the cases, 50% of the spectrum bands allotted for the primary users (PUs) remain underutilized, thereby leading to a wastage of the spectral resources [1,2]. To carry out an efficient spectrum utilization, cognitive radios (CRs) are used which facilitate the effective reconfiguration to proficiently adapt to the surrounding environmental changes along with the cognitive capability. The initial configuration of the radio is done based on the spectrum-sensing techniques employed at the architectural level of the CR. Deployment of the CR requires a detailed knowledge of the layer-wise configuration to bring about the required functionality. The protocol stack of the CR is composed of five layers namely physical layer, data link layer, network layer, transport layer, and application layer. This type of layer-wise segregation of the functionalities and characteristics aids in the hierarchical addressing of the features of each layer, starting from the modulation schemes, coding techniques, and the sensing techniques that can affect the performance of the system. A complete overview of the layered architecture with the associated applications and limitations is discussed in Sections 9.2 through 9.6.

9.2 Architectural Overview of the CR

A CR otherwise called as the software-defined radio is designed with the main aim of reacting to the changes in the environment [3]. The functionalities of the CR starting from the spectrum sensing and spectrum decision require the initial sensing of the spectrum bands for the free spectral holes supported by the physical layer. The physical layer is to be customized with the respective interfaces to work in correspondence with the underlying application. The detected free spectral holes have to be cooperatively utilized among both the PUs and SUs, which require the dynamic accessibility feature to be performed by the cognitive node. The dynamic access control followed after the spectral-hole detection is the responsibility of the data link layer. In order to cope with the growing spectrum demands, the use of medium access control (MAC) protocol is necessary and therefore the MAC layer has become an integral part of the data link layer. Once the spectrum sensing is done, in the cognitive network followed by the dynamic access of the free spectral band, the CR has to next perform the naming and address mapping to identify the intended node in the network. It is very much obligatory to incorporate the configuration of the nodes according to the changes in the network. It also emphasizes the connection establishment and disconnection between the nodes. The cognitive architecture requires routing protocols which facilitate in the transmission of the data over the network in an efficient manner with minimal or no data loss. The routing protocols are made operable with the cognitive functionalities [4]. The operating frequency of the CR varies as the cognitive user has to be relocated from one spectrum band to another, based on the availability of the spectrum resources. With each change in the frequency, the CR has to be reconfigured to match the features such as the modulation scheme, dynamic spectrum access, and transmission power [5,6]. The transport layer brings these functionalities into effect thereby providing a platform for the dynamic frequency assortment. The data to be transmitted can be in the form of text, image, or multimedia which requires the quality of service (QoS) metrics for evaluating the performance of the system. The application layer deals with these quality-related issues based on the application underlying. The layer-wise protocol stack of a CR is represented in Figure 9.1 [7].

The working of the protocol stack with respect to the CR takes place with the implementation of an interface designed globally to interact with the environmental changes in a flexible manner. The designed radio interface is in continuous interaction with the radio environment through suitable application programming interfaces (APIs). The functionality of spectrum sensing is implemented using the sensing techniques and related control functions. The information so far collected is transmitted to the higher layers such that the radio reconfigurability characteristics are induced into the CR systems. The overview of an API-based architecture is done according to Le et al. [8] and is represented in Figure 9.2.

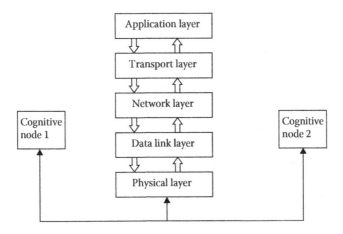

FIGURE 9.1
Protocol stack of cognitive radio node.

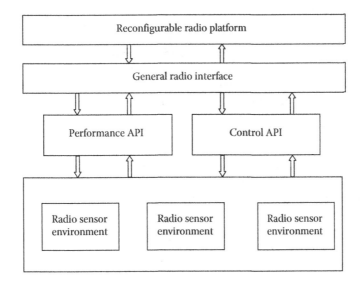

FIGURE 9.2
Interface level architecture of a cognitive radio. (From Le, B., *Building a Cognitive Radio: From Architecture Definition to Prototype Implementation,* PhD Dissertation, Virginia Polytechnic Institute and State University, Blacksburg, VA, 2007.)

9.3 Physical Layer

The physical layer, being the first layer, of the protocol architecture, is capable of handling the functionalities of modulation, channel sensing, and detection of the free spectral holes, and finally the coding methodologies. It is the lowermost layer of the protocol stack, performing the major tasks, and enables the implementation of cognitive capability in the cognitive radio network (CRN). The basic uncertainties caused during the sensing period on observation showcase that the probability of detection is achieved over a greater percentage. During the access period of the spectrum band, the observation carried out is regarding the probability of collision such that the PU activity does not interfere with the SU. The available spectral holes to be sensed can be of three different types, namely the black spaces, gray spaces, and white spaces. The black holes are the spectral holes which are interrupted by any form of interference caused by the unlicensed users. Gray spaces and white spaces are partial to any interference caused and hence can be used effectively by the SUs. The main issue that we come across during the sensing period is the interference that may occur due to the intervention of the PU in which case the sensing has to take place at the next available spectral hole. The important sensing techniques used currently can be classified broadly into three categories as discussed in Sections 9.3.1 through 9.3.3.

9.3.1 Noncooperative Sensing

Noncooperative sensing can be further classified into energy detection-based sensing, matched-filter detection-based sensing, and cyclostationary-feature detection–based sensing methods.

9.3.1.1 Energy Detection–Based Method

This method is followed to detect the presence of the PUs in the licensed spectrum bands. The energy required for detecting a PU is considered as the metric in this technique. It is a noncooperative sensing method which is the simplest method deployed for the detection of the PU. Energy detector is exclusively used to check the existence of the PU. In most of the cases the Neyman–Pearson (NP) lemma is used which states that the probability of detection (P_d) increases with the probability of false alarm (P_{fa}) [9–12]. This method is also advantageous as it does not require any prior information for the calculation for detecting the presence of a PU.

The block diagram for the energy detection method is shown in Figure 9.3 [13]. In Figure 9.3, the input signal, $x(t)$ is first passed through an ideal bandpass filter (BPF) with center frequency f_0 bandwidth, with transfer function as given by Equation 9.1:

$$H(f) = \begin{cases} \dfrac{2}{\sqrt{N_0}} & |f - f_0| \leq W \\ 0 & |f - f_0| > W \end{cases} \tag{9.1}$$

where N_0 is the one-sided noise power spectral density, which is convenient to compute the false alarm and detection probabilities using the related transfer function. After that the signal squared, and integrated in the observation interval T to produce a test statistic, V, is compared to a threshold, λ. The receiver makes a decision that the target signal has been detected if and only if the threshold is exceeded [14].

9.3.1.2 Matched-Filter Detection Method

The matched-filter method, also known as a coherent detector, uses the prior information of the waveforms associated with the PU such that the detection of the PU is done in a more accurate manner. This method aims at optimizing the output signal of the user to the corresponding noise ratio and which in turn is compared with the threshold that is preset [15]. The input signal $x(t)$ is made to convolve with the time shift version $h(t)$ of the predetermined signal $s(t)$. The obtained output Y is compared

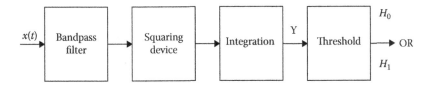

FIGURE 9.3
Working block diagram of an energy-detection method. (From Malik, S.A. et al., *Aust. J. Basic Appl. Sci.*, 4 (9), 4522–4531, 2010.)

with the threshold. The main drawback of this technique is that if the prior information obtained is not precise, the functioning of the matched filter is not up to the mark. The working block diagram of the matched-filter detector is represented in Figure 9.4 [16,17].

9.3.1.3 Cyclostationary-Feature Detection Method

To bring about the variation among the modulated signal and additive noise, the cyclostationary-feature detection is used. When the mean and autocorrelation of a signal are in the form of a periodic function then such a signal is called a cyclostationary signal. The features are extorted from and detection is performed on the input signal to check the presence of the PU. The main advantage of this detection method is that it can differentiate between the PU signal and the noise-causing signal such that the detection of the PU is carried out even at very low signal-to-noise ratio detection levels. The calculation of the mean of the signal involves very complex methodologies which makes this method of detection more beneficial. As the cognitive environment requires variation in the operating frequencies, the estimation of the correlation function in such a scenario is much difficult and time-consuming [18]. Different waveforms that serve as the input in this method are the sine wave carriers, digital spreading in a repeated manner, pulse trains, and the frequency-hopping sequences. The diagrammatic representation of the feature detector is as shown in Figure 9.5 [13].

9.3.2 Cooperative Spectrum-Sensing Method

The cooperative spectrum-sensing method is implemented in the CRN where the sensed information is cooperatively shared between the cognitive users for the detection of the presence of a PU. Ghasemi and Sousain [19] proposed the cooperative spectrum sensing for the first time to overcome the effects of shadowing, fading, hidden terminal problem, and noise uncertainty [20,21]. The use of common control channels (CCCs) for sharing the spectrum among multiple users has enabled the cooperative sensing technique to become effective over fading and shadowing. The cooperative sensing categories are described in the following sections.

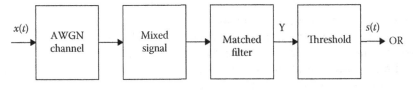

FIGURE 9.4
Block diagram of a matched-filter detector. (From Mohamad, M.H. and Sani, N.M., *Int. J. Eng. Technol.*, 13 (5), 2013.)

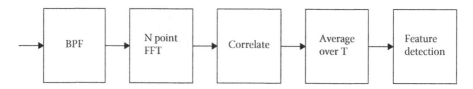

FIGURE 9.5
Block diagram of a cyclostationary-feature detector. BPF, bandpass filter; FFT, fast Fourier transform. (From Malik, S.A. et al., *Aust. J. Basic Appl. Sci.*, 4 (9), 4522–4531, 2010.)

9.3.2.1 Centralized Sensing

In a centralized sensing network, the cognitive nodes are connected to a centrally located cognitive controller. When any particular node collects any useful sensing information, it is forwarded to the central node which in turn coordinates with the activities in the CRN [22].

9.3.2.2 Distributed Sensing

In a distributed or decentralized sensing approach, we do not see the presence of a central controller node. Rather all the nodes are made responsible for the mitigation of the information in the overall network. Based on the information collected and gathered by all the nodes, the presence of the PU in the network is decided [23]. This sensing technique is much more useful compared to the centralized technique as it reduces the time required for the transmission of the collected signals to the central controller. It also reduces the initial cost required for the network deployment as it does not need a centralized infrastructure.

The main drawback of the cooperative sensing technique is that it often results in the increased data overheads at the central controller. As each node is individually made responsible for the collection of sensing data, the overall data collected is very large making the system less efficient [24,25].

9.3.3 Interference-Based Sensing

The third category is an interference-based detection which is a logical sensing technique where the presence of the signal of user A when it interferes with the signals of user B signifies that the signal A is present within the communicating range of signal B. It can be either a coherent or a noncoherent type of detection technique. In the coherent type of detection, the presence of the PU is estimated by comparing the received signal between the two users and this requires a predetermined knowledge about the PU signals [26]. Matched-filter detection is an example of the noncoherent detection method. Another level of categorization under this technique is based on the bandwidth where the sensing techniques can be carried out based on the narrowband or wideband detection approaches.

Apart from the spectrum-sensing functionalities, the physical layer is also responsible for the formation of an overall network connectivity. The network formed can be viewed as a circuit switching network, a packet switching network, or a virtual circuit switching. For a circuit switching network, there is a need for a dedicated communication link and the spectrum bands are reserved for the data transfer, and once the data is transferred the circuit link is broken and the reserved resources are de-allocated. A packet switching network involves the transmission of the data in the form of packets accompanied by the respective headers and trailers, and follows the dynamic allocation of the network resources. The packets received on the destination side are to be reordered in case they are received in a different order. A virtual switching network is a combination of both the packet switching and circuit switching networks deployed based on the requirement of the underlying application [27]. The modulation schemes followed at the physical layer are the time-division multiple access (TDMA), frequency-division multiple access (FDMA), code-division multiple access (CDMA), and the orthogonal frequency multiple access (OFDMA) along with the supporting standards such as Wi-Fi, WiMAX, WCDMA, CDMA, global system for mobile communication (GSM), and enhanced data for GSM evolution EDGE [28,29].

The attack associated with the physical layer is the primary-user emulation (PUE) attack where the SU poses as a PU, and interferes with the activity of the PU thereby hampering the efficiency of the network. The resources reserved for the PUs are forcefully captured by the SUs who behave as masked PUs. Upon the intervention of the PU, the SU has to switch back to another band making place for the PU. This type of attack mainly aims at increasing the utilization of the spectrum resources in the place of PU, or holding back the spectrum resources and not releasing them for the use of even the SU who were otherwise supposed to have the access to the spectral resources. To overcome this type of attack, it is the responsibility of the transmitting body to first confirm the identity of the user and check whether he is the PU or an imposter. The other attack is the objective function attack which is based on the calculation of the objective function by deducing the metrics used in the system. As the metrics change from one scenario to another, there is a need for the standardized use of metrics with their respective threshold values. Jamming of the spectral bands is another attack which results in prohibiting both the PUs and SUs from accessing the spectrum resulting in a denial of service (DoS). Jamming is often found in the physical layer and MAC layer. The types of jammer attacks include the constant jammer which sends the packets continuously irrespective of the MAC layer protocols; the deceptive jammer which sends the packets in a manner such that the other user remains only in the reception state; the random jammer which either acts as a constant jammer or a deceptive jammer; and the reactive jammer which upon sensing the communication in the channel starts with the continuous transmission of the message.

9.4 Data Link Layer

The data link layer in CRs is associated with bringing about the functionality of dynamic access of the spectrum based on the sensing information gathered by the sensing techniques of the physical layer. The SU has to first evaluate the availability of the spectrum band, its characteristics, and whether the channel is able to hold the coexistence between the PU and SU. The various criterion to be taken into account before selecting the spectrum band are as follows:

- The availability of spectrum band and its accessibility to the PU and SU separately, or together
- The access technology that follows either spectrum underlay or overlay mechanism
- The network criteria which can be either centralized where the cognitive controller is responsible for the overall network access, or distributed where each cognitive user is made responsible for the network performance
- The access behavior which can be either cooperative or noncooperative in nature

The MAC protocol is a policy followed by the data link layer for the coexistence of the PU and SU. A number of MAC protocols have been proposed so far to enhance the access utilities, which can be broadly classified into random access protocols, time-slotted protocols, and hybrid protocols. These protocols in turn follow a centralized or ad hoc architecture and can be divided based on the underlying architecture. The timing diagram of the MAC protocol is represented in Figure 9.6.

The random access protocols are generally based on the coexistence characteristics between the PU and SU, where the PUs are made to interact with the PU base station and the SUs are made to interact with a cognitive base station. The PUs follow the classic carrier sense medium access (CSMA) protocol for carrying out the data transmission activity in an infrastructure-based network [30]. The MAC protocols exclusively make use of the messages such as request-to-send and clear-to-send signals such that no interference is caused in the network while the PU is active. The sensing period here is τt. In the case of the cognitive users, this period is comparatively higher. Based on the distance between CR users and CR base station and the noise power, the base station decides the transmission parameters, namely the transmit power and data rate for the current transfer (the base station allows the SU to send the data). Only one packet is allowed to send in one round in order to minimize the risk of interference with the PUs. The problem with this is that the sensing time is longer. The dynamic open spectrum-sense sharing MAC protocol is mainly an ad hoc network-based protocol which introduces a new mechanism of using a busy tone when the spectrum band is busy in communication, all the other users are made to wait hearing the busy tone. But this method is less effective as it increases the number of messages to wait thereby increasing the overall load on the network.

The use of CCC in the network is necessary in case of many numbers of radio transceivers, for a single transceiver, or for the protocols which do not use the CCC. Distributed channel assignment is an extension of the IEEE 802.11 CSMA/CA protocol. It uses multiple transceivers with a dedicated out-of-band CCC for signaling. The protocol maintains the spectrum information and based on the information, data is transferred [31]. The disadvantage of this technique is that the use of separate CCCs results in the depletion of the spectrum resources.

Time-slotted protocols make use of the time division policies in order to facilitate the synchronization of the time between the users. The allotted time is divided basically into functioning the data channel and data transmission. The synchronized and time-slotted

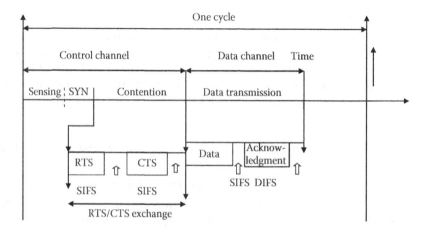

FIGURE 9.6
Timing diagram of a MAC protocol.

cognitive-MAC (C-MAC) protocol is proposed in [32] for distributed multichannel wireless networks. C-MAC operates over multiple channels and is able to effectively deal with the dynamics of resource availability due to PU, and mitigates the effects of the distributed quiet periods utilized for the PU signal detection. C-MAC includes two key concepts: one is the rendezvous channel (RC) and another is the backup channel (BC). RC is selected as the channel that can be used for the longest time throughout the network, without interruption among all other available choices. It is used for node coordination, PU detection, and multichannel resource reservation. The BC, determined by the out-of-band measurements, is used to immediately provide a choice of alternate spectrum bands in case of the appearance of a PU. The disadvantages are low scalability, prolonged spectrum switching, unclear issues on nonoverlapping of the BPs, and quiet periods. MAC protocols based on the channel-hopping strategies have also come into effect where both the sender and the receiver nodes are made to hop to a common channel, and the transmission of data occurs in this common channel rather than continued searching for the free spectral holes [33]. When such a method is followed the channel assignment between the pairs becomes easier than searching individually.

The issue associated with the MAC layer is the smaller back-off window attack (SBW) commonly seen in the distributed coordinated MAC protocols due to the backing off of a node for a random duration of time. But in case of a malicious node, we can observe that the back-off time does not increase thereby leading to a DoS attack [34]. As a solution to this, we can use a cumulative distribution function [35] to detect the nodes responsible for the SBW attack. The spectrum-sensing data falsification attack proposed in [36,37] occurs in case of a transmission of the false local sensing data over the network, thereby resulting in the incorrect spectrum decisions. The effect of this attack is more in case of a distributed network than in a centralized network. The solution for this attack is to obtain the total count of the sensing nodes which are busy at the moment, and compare this count with the threshold value. If the value of the count is greater than the threshold then the channel is said to be occupied. Yet another attack is the control channel saturation DoS attack found in a multihop CRN [38,39]. In case of a communication taking place among multiple users, all the users forward their MAC control frames during the negotiation phase, which results in the congestion as many users are forwarding the request at the same time. This may also result in attackers sending their MAC requests and thereby hindering the system performance. As a solution to this attack, the CR users are to be authenticated to hide their identity and display it only for the intended users.

9.5 Network Layer

Network layer is associated with the transmission of data which can be in the form of data packets or datagrams from a source node to the destination node. To establish a connection between the nodes in the network, the information about the free spectral bands is very much necessary along with the use of an effective MAC protocol to bring about an interference-free data transfer. The need for a suitable path is necessary to carry out the data transmission in a very effective manner. The routing in the network is carried out by using the routing protocols in the CRN. The network layer is also responsible for carrying the functionalities of naming and addressing where each operating host is given a unique domain name, and each node is assigned a unique IP address and a physical address.

The increase in the number of technologies using the unlicensed band, and the statistics provided by the FCC on the underutilization of the licensed bands [2] mainly led to the use of dynamic spectrum access to opportunistically use the licensed spectrum band. The mobility of the SUs has resulted in the need for close cooperation between the routing node and spectrum manager to make the routing node aware of the surrounding environment to take up a proper routing decision [40]. The unexpected presence of a PU at a location may lead to the path failures between the SUs, thereby increasing the need for rerouting the path. Abdelaziz and ElNainay [41] provided an insight into the challenges faced by routing in the CRNs compared to the multihop ad hoc networks where the cognitive networks are more prone to the effects of mobility of the nodes and their varying communication frequencies, and that the channel availability is based on the activity of the PU.

The routing protocols in the CRN can be broadly categorized based on their full-spectrum or local-spectrum knowledge. In case of the full-spectrum knowledge, a central entity maintains a map of the occupied spectrum in the network, and uses this detail to have knowledge about the efficient routes either by using the theoretical or mathematical tools. Some of the routing schemes which come under full-spectrum knowledge involve the routing through layered graphs [42], routing through colored graphs [43], and the routing and spectrum selection through conflict graphs [44]. In case of the local-spectrum knowledge, all the SUs have the information of the available spectrum along with the additional details about the frequency availability for communication. Some of the routing examples are minimum power routing [45], minimum delay-based routing [46], minimum throughput-based routing [47,48], geographic routing [49], and class-based routing [50].

The problem commonly found in the network layer is that the routing protocols often require transparency which is absent in most of the cases. The sink hole attack [51] is the most common attack found in the routing protocols where an attacker or a malicious node advertises itself with a best route and gains access to the data. This type of attack is very common in case of the infrastructure-based networks, where we see the presence of a central controller collecting the network-wide data. In case of the sink hole attack, the malicious node may pose as the central controller thereby collecting all the data. This type of attack is overcome by using geographic routing with a local communication system. Another type of attack is the hello flood attack where each node in the network is flooded by the hello messages forwarded by the attacker node. Here all the nodes follow a similar route to reach the destination node which is malicious and it is very difficult to identify this type of attack [51]. The use of session keys for authenticating the users is followed with the use of the symmetric keys. The session keys are used to verify the identity of the users. The use of the symmetric keys has made the system perform much faster.

9.6 Transport Layer

This layer is characterized to bring about a method to process the data delivery to effectively use the available scarce spectrum resources. It handles the congestion control mechanism of the system because with the detection of a free band all the interested nodes would come forward to transmit the data leading to an overload in the network. Not much work is carried out with respect to the transport layer and it is prone to many attacks, namely the lion attack which is the result of aftereffect of the PUE attack [52]. The occurrence of the PUE attack results in the handoff of the frequency by all the SUs for the utilization by the PU, but this is done without intimating the transmission control protocol (TCP) in the network layer. This finally results in very long timeouts ultimately followed by delay and packet loss [53]. This problem is taken care by implementing the physical, link, and transport layers into a collective cross layer. By doing so the TCP connections remain unchanged. The transport layer is also associated with a new technique called the layer preserving approach [54] with the introduction of two modules, namely the knowledge module and the cognitive module. We can see the presence of these modules at each layer of the protocol stack. The knowledge module contains data based on the application requirements with respect to each layer. The cognitive module contains the associated algorithms required at every layer. This type of modular approach helps in easier maintenance of the CN.

9.7 Application Layer

This layer is associated with the data production and extortion of the required features such that it can be transmitted to the destination sink. The additional functionalities provided by this layer are data dissemination, data aggregation, and data fusion [10]. The design and characteristics of this layer can be formulated based on the underlying service that the current application is used for. The applications can be of different types, namely the task-based applications, data-processing applications, and the workload-based applications.

9.8 Conclusion

The rising demand for the use of the CRs has resulted in the need for the development of the CR architecture and structure. In this regard, an introduction has been made to the layer-wise protocol stack of CR along with its respective functionalities. A layer-wise division is necessary as it simplifies the working of the CR by division of work among different layers. Physical layer being the lowermost layer performs the task of spectrum sensing which is the primary prerequisite of the CRN technology. This layer is also associated to perform the modulation of the data, coding of the data, detection of the PU, and much more. The data link layer is made in-charge to carry out the error check, fault tolerance, and to obtain a dynamic access to the spectrum through the MAC protocols. The network layer responsible for the transmission of data across the network aims at the development of a number of routing protocols to have a lossless data transmission in the network. The applicability of these three basic layers is much more compared to the transport layer and application layer. The deployment of the transport and application layers is done based on the underlying application rather than carrying out the predetermined functionalities as seen in the physical, data link, and network layers.

Acknowledgments

We thank our family and organizations for the immense support provided throughout the chapter.

References

1. Federal Communications Commission. 2003. *Facilitating Opportunities for Flexible, Efficient and Reliable Spectrum Use Employing Cognitive Radio Technologies*. Notice of proposed rulemaking and order, FCC 03–322. Washington, DC: Author.

2. Federal Communications Commission Spectrum Policy Task Force. 2002. *Report of the Spectrum Efficiency Working Group*. Washington, DC: Author.

3. Raychaudhuri, D., N. B. Mandayam, J. B. Evans, B. J. Ewy, and S. Seshan. 2006. CogNet—An architectural foundation for experimental cognitive radio networks within the future Internet. In *Proceedings of MobiArch '06*. pp. 1–4. ACM/IEEE.

4. Zhang, Q., A. B. J. Kokkeler, and G. J. M. Smit. 2006. A reconfigurable radio architecture for cognitive radio in emergency networks. In *Proceedings of 9th European Conference on Wireless Technology*, Manchester, UK.

5. Chen, K.-C., Y.-J. Peng, N. Prasad, Y.-C. Liang, and S. Sun. 2008. Cognitive radio network architecture: Part I—General structure. In *Proceedings of the ACM International Conference on Ubiquitous Information Management and Communication*, Seoul, Korea.

6. Mitola, J., and G. Q. Maguire. 1999. Cognitive radios: Making software radios more personal. *IEEE Personal Communication* 6 (4): 13–18.

7. Pescosolido, L. 2013. *Basics of Cognitive Radio Networks with Examples of CR-Oriented Protocol Design*. Rome, Italy: Sapienza University.

8. Le, B. 2007. *Building a Cognitive Radio: From Architecture Definition to Prototype Implementation*. PhD Dissertation. Virginia Polytechnic Institute and State University, Blacksburg, VA.

9. Mercedes, D., M. Plataa, A. Gabrie, and A. Reatig. 2012. Evaluation of energy detection for spectrum sensing based on the dynamic selection of detection-threshold. International Meeting of Electrical Engineering Research (ENIINVIE-2012). *Procedia Engineering* 35: 135–143. doi: 10.1016/j.proeng.2012.04.174

10. Akyildiz, I. F., W.-Y. Lee, M. C. Vuran, and S. Mohanty. 2006. NeXt generation/dynamic spectrum access/cognitive radio wireless networks: A survey. *Computer Networks* 50 (13): 2127–2159. doi:10.1016/j.comnet.2006.05.001

11. Akyildiz, I. F., B. F. Lo, and R. Balakrishnan. 2011. Cooperative spectrum sensing in cognitive radio networks: A survey. *Physical Communication* 4 (1): 40–62. doi:10.1016/j.phycom.2011.12.003

12. Ziafat, S., W. Ejaz, and H. Jamal. 2011. Spectrum sensing techniques for cognitive radio networks: Performance analysis. In *2011 IEEE MTT-S International Microwave Workshop Series on Intelligent Radio for Future Personal Terminals*, Daejeon. pp. 1–4. doi:10.1109/IMWS2.2011.6027191

13. Malik, S. A., M. A. Shah, A. Dar, A. Haq, A. U. Khan, and T. Javed. 2010. Comparative analysis of primary transmitter detection based spectrum sensing techniques in cognitive radio systems. *Australian Journal of Basic and Applied Sciences* 4 (9): 4522–4531.

14. Ma, J., G. Y. Li, and B. H. Juang. 2009. Signal processing in cognitive radio. *Proceedings of the IEEE* 97 (5): 805–823.

15. Ziafat, S., W. Ejaz, and H. Jamal. 2011. Spectrum sensing techniques for cognitive radio networks: Performance analysis. In *Intelligent Radio for Future Personal Terminals (IMWS-IRFPT), 2011 IEEE MTT-S International Microwave Workshop Series on*, Daejeon. pp. 1–4. IEEE.

16. Sahai, A., N. Hoven, and R. Tandra. 2004. Some fundamental limits in cognitive radio. In *Proceedings of the Allerton Conference on Communication, Control, and Computing*, Monticello, IL. Extract.

17. Mohamad, M. H., and N. M. Sani. 2013. Energy detection technique in cognitive radio system. *International Journal of Engineering and Technology* 13 (5): 69–73.

18. Cabric, D., S. M. Mishra, and R. W. Brodersen. 2004. Implementation issues in spectrum sensing for cognitive radios. In *Proceedings of the 38th Asilomar Conference on Signals, Systems and Computers*, vol. 1, Pacific Grove, CA. pp. 772–776.

19. Ghasemi, A., and E. S. Sousa. 2005. Collaborative spectrum sensing for opportunistic access in fading environments. In *First IEEE International Symposium on New Frontiers in Dynamic Spectrum Access Networks*, Baltimore, MD. pp. 131–136. doi:10.1109/DYSPAN.2005.1542627
20. Unnikrishnan, J., and V. Veeravalli. 2008. Cooperative sensing for primary detection in cognitive radio. *IEEE Journal on Selected Areas in Signal Processing* 2 (1): 18–27.
21. Chen, Y., Q. Zhao, and A. Swami. 2009. Distributed spectrum sensing and access in cognitive radio networks with energy constraint. *IEEE Transactions on Signal Processing* 57 (2): 783–797.
22. Di Renzo, M., L. Imbriglio, F. Graziosi, and F. Santucci. 2009. Distributed data fusion over correlated log-normal sensing and reporting channels: Application to cognitive radio networks. *IEEE Transactions on Wireless Communications* 8 (12): 5813–5821.
23. Noorshams, N., M. Malboubi, and A. Bahai. 2010. Centralized and decentralized cooperative spectrum sensing in cognitive radio networks: A novel approach. In *2010 IEEE 11th International Workshop on Signal Processing Advances in Wireless Communications (SPAWC)*, Marrakech. pp. 1–5. doi:10.1109/SPAWC.2010.5670998
24. Zeng, Y., Y. C. Liang, A. T. Hoang, and R. Zhang. 2010. A review on spectrum sensing for cognitive radio: Challenges and solutions. *EURASIP Journal on Advances in Signal Processing* 2010: 1–15.
25. Wang, B. and K. J. Ray Liu. 2011. Advances in cognitive radio networks: A survey. *IEEE Journal of Selected topics in Signal Processing* 5 (1): 5–23.
26. Garhwal, A., and P. P. Bhattacharya. 2012. A survey on dynamic spectrum access techniques for cognitive radio. *International Journal of Next-Generation Networks* 3 (4): 15–32.
27. Wiglynski, A. M., M. Nekovee, and Y. T. Hou. 2010. *Cognitive Radio Communication Networks.* Burlington, MA, USA: Elsevier, ISBN 978-0-12-374715-0.
28. Zhao, L., Sh. Chen, and X. Gan. 2011. From reconfigurable SDR to cognitive femto-cell: A practical platform. In *2011 International Conference on Wireless Communications and Signal Processing (WCSP)*, Nanjing. pp. 1–6. IEEE, doi:10.1109/WCSP.2011.6096754
29. Liu, D., A. Nilsson, E. Tell, Di Wu, and J. Eilert. 2010. Bridging dream and reality: Programmable baseband processors for software-defined radio. *IEEE Communications Magazine* 47 (9): 134–140. doi:10.1109/MCOM.2009.5277467
30. Lien, S.-Y., C.-C. Tseng, and K.-C. Chen. 2008. Carrier sensing based multiple access protocols for cognitive radio networks. In *Proceedings of IEEE International Conference on Communications*, Beijing. pp. 3208–3214.
31. Pawelczak, P., R. Venkatesha Prasad, L. Xia, and I. G. M. M. Niemegeers. 2005. Cognitive radio emergency networks—Requirements and design. In *Proceedings of the IEEE Dynamic Spectrum Access Networks*, Baltimore, MD. pp. 601–606.
32. Cordeiro, C., K. Challapali. 2007. C-MAC: A cognitive MAC protocol for multichannel wireless networks. In *IEEE Proceedings of DySPAN'07*, Dublin, Ireland.
33. Kamruzzaman, S. M., E. Kim, D. G. Jeong, and W. S. Jeon. 2012. Energy-aware routing protocol for cognitive radio ad hoc networks. *IET Communications* 6 (14): 2159–2168.
34. Bian, K., and J. M. Park. 2006. MAC-layer misbehaviors in multi-hop cognitive radio networks. In *Proceedings of the 2006 US-Korea Conference on Science, Technology and Entrepreneurship*, Teaneck, NJ. pp. 65–73.
35. Wang, W., Y. Sun, H. Li, and Z. Han. 2010. Cross-layer attack and defense in cognitive radio networks. In *Proceedings of the IEEE Global Telecommunications Conference*, Miami, FL.
36. Karlof, C., and D. Wagner. 2003. Secure routing in wireless sensor networks: Attacks and countermeasures. In *Proceedings of the 1st IEEE International Workshop on Sensor Network Protocols and Applications*, Berkeley, CA, USA. pp. 113–127.
37. Mathur, C., and K. Subbalakshmi. 2007. Security issues in cognitive radio networks. *Cognitive Networks: Towards Self-Aware Networks*. New York, NY: Wiley. pp. 284–293.
38. Zhu, L., and H. Zhou. 2008. Two types of attacks against cognitive radio network MAC protocols. In *International Conference on Computer Science and Software Engineering*, Vol. 4, Wuhan, China. pp. 1110–1113.

39. Bian, K., and J.-M. Park. 2006. MAC-layer misbehaviors in multi-hop cognitive radio networks. In *2006 US-Korea Conference on Science, Technology, and Entrepreneurship (UKC2006)*, Teaneck, NJ.

40. Cesana, M., F. Cuomo, and E. Ekici. 2011. Routing in cognitive radio networks: Challenges and solutions. *Ad Hoc Networks (Elsevier)* 9: 228–248.

41. Abdelaziz, S., and M. ElNainay. 2012. *Survey of Routing Protocols in Cognitive Radio Networks.* USA: Elsevier. pp. 1–20. http://wrc-ejust.org/crn/images/Surveys/RPCRNs.pdf

42. Xin, C., B. Xie, and C.-C. Shen. 2005. A novel layered graph model for topology formation and routing in dynamic spectrum access networks. In *First IEEE International Symposium on New Frontiers in Dynamic Spectrum Access Networks, DySPAN*, Baltimore, MD. pp. 308–317. doi:10.1109/DYSPAN.2005.1542647

43. Zhou, X., L. Lin, J. Wang, and X. Zhang. 2009. Cross-layer routing design in cognitive radio networks by colored multigraph model. *Wireless Personal Communications* 49 (1): 123–131. doi:10.1007/s11277-008-9561-7

44. Wang, Q., and H. Zheng. 2006. Route and spectrum selection in dynamic spectrum networks. In *3rd IEEE Consumer Communications and Networking Conference, CCNC 2006*, Las Vegas, NV, USA, Vol. 1., pp. 625–629.

45. Pyo, C. W., and M. Hasegawa. 2007. Minimum weight routing based on a common link control radio for cognitive wireless ad hoc networks. In *Proceedings of the International Conference on Wireless Communications and Mobile Computing*, Shanghai, China. pp. 399–404.

46. Ma, H., L. Zheng, X. Ma, and Y. Iuo. 2008. Spectrum aware routing for multi-hop cognitive radio networks with a single transceiver. In *Proceedings of the 3rd International Conference on Cognitive Radio Oriented Wireless Networks and Communications*, Singapore. pp. 1–6.

47. Pefkianakis, I., S. Wong, and S. Lu. 2008. SAMER: Spectrum aware mesh routing in cognitive radio networks. In *Proceedings of the 3rd IEEE Symposium on New Frontiers in Dynamic Spectrum Access Networks*, Chicago, IL. pp. 1–5.

48. Ding, L., T. Melodia, S. Batalama, and M. J. Medley. 2009. ROSA: Distributed joint routing and dynamic spectrum allocation in cognitive radio ad hoc networks. In *Proceedings of the 12th ACM International Conference on Modeling, Analysis and Simulation of Wireless and Mobile Systems*, Tenerife, Spain. pp. 13–20.

49. Xie, M., W. Zhang, and K.-K. Wong. 2010. A geometric approach to improve spectrum efficiency for cognitive relay networks. *IEEE Transactions on Wireless Communications* 9 (1): 268–281.

50. How, K. C., M. Ma, and Y. Qin. 2010. An opportunistic service differentiation routing protocol for cognitive radio networks. In *Proceedings of the IEEE Global Telecommunications Conference*, Miami, FL.

51. Karlof, C., and D. Wagner. 2003. Secure routing in wireless networks: Attacks and countermeasures, *Ad Hoc Networks* 1: 293–315.

52. León, O., J. Hernandez-Serrano, and M. Soriano. 2009. A new cross-layer attack to TCP in cognitive radio networks. In *Proceedings of the 2nd International Workshop on Cross Layer Design (IWCLD '09)*, Palma, Spain. pp. 1–5.

53. Hernandez-Serrano, J., O. León, and M. Soriano. 2011. Modeling the lion attack in cognitive radio networks. *EURASIP Journal on Wireless Communications and Networking* 2011:242304, 10 pp.

54. Sarkar, D., and H. Narayan. 2010. Transport layer protocols for cognitive networks. *Proceedings of the IEEE INFOCOM Workshops*, San Diego, CA.

10

Delay Models for Epidemic-Like Routing in Multihop Secondary Networks

Pin-Yu Chen, Shin-Ming Cheng, Weng Chon Ao,
Hui-Yu Hsu, and Kwang-Cheng Chen

CONTENTS

10.1 Introduction

Recently, the idea of proposing secondary systems (SSs) coexisting with the primary (licensed) systems (PSs) has received dramatic attention as it holds a tremendous promise for increasing the utilization of the scarce radio spectrum. The unlicensed secondary users (SUs) sense the surrounding environment and adapt their operations around those of the licensed primary users (PUs) to opportunistically exploit the available resources while limiting their interference to the PUs. Typical examples include the cognitive radio network (CRN) and machine-to-machine communication networks, among others. In interweave paradigm [1], the SUs seek and exploit the temporary spectrum opportunities without causing any interference to the PUs. To further improve the spectrum usage, the SUs are allowed to concurrently transmit with the PUs in an underlay paradigm as long as sufficient operation of PUs is ensured.

In an ad hoc environment with one channel and slotted ALOHA medium access control (MAC) protocol, access probability control is an instinctive solution for the spectrum access adaptation in the underlay paradigm. In particular, each SU virtually tosses a coin independently with its access probability and transmits if it gets heads. By adjusting the access probability, the subset of SUs acting as interferers could be controlled to prevent violating PUs outage constraint, i.e., outage probability relative to a signal-to-interference-noise-ratio (SINR) threshold. However, the random access for opportunistic transmission at the SU introduces an unpreventable medium access delay. In addition, the unreliable links among the SUs introduce a potential retransmission delay due to an unsuccessful reception at the secondary receiver. To concatenate the SUs as a secondary network, quality of service (QoS) provisioning for end-to-end packet transmissions is a must. However, the mentioned delays challenge conventional path-determined, single-path routing toward QoS guarantee in the secondary networks [2,3].

To tackle the aforementioned challenges, the well-known opportunistic routing without a preestablished path is considered as an appropriate choice [4,5]. To further decrease the delivery delay or increase the reliability for an end-to-end transmission, a multipath routing scheme enabling the transmissions through multiple routes is intuitively feasible [6], which is referred as diverse routing [7]. Motivated by the phenomenon that the transportation of diseases resembles the data dissemination dynamics in the communication networks, we focus on a multipath flooding-based routing scheme named epidemic-like routing, aiming at exploiting the advantages of path diversity. Initially, epidemic routing is proposed in partially connected networks where every node carries and forwards the information to the encountered nodes. Without losing the generality, we use the term epidemic routing and epidemic-like routing interchangeably since the epidemic model is also suitable for evaluating the performance of flooding-based routing protocols [8].

We assume that the node locations are a realization of the homogeneous Poisson process to statistically study the end-to-end delay of the multipath routing schemes [9,10]. By applying stochastic geometry, we could derive the maximum number of the successful transmission the network can support, while simultaneously meeting the outage constraints at the PU and SU. Under this framework, the medium access and retransmission delays of various routing schemes can be unified in a tractable manner. In particular, we use the stochastic geometry to investigate the data delivery dynamics in the multihop secondary networks via epidemic-like routing schemes. In contrast to routing in the traditional wireless ad hoc networks, our model incorporates the effects of channel awareness and interference on medium access and retransmission delays for the secondary networks. The simulation results verify the validability of our model in the sense that the complicated data delivery dynamics can be characterized by our proposed model, and therefore the model serves as a powerful tool for studying the epidemic-like routing in the secondary networks.

Rest of the chapter is organized as follows: we survey the related works in Section 10.2. In Section 10.3, we describe the preliminaries including the epidemic model and epidemic-like routing. Section 10.4 presents the network model for the following analysis. Section 10.5 studies the performance of epidemic-like routing. The comparisons of the proposed model and the simulation results are discussed in Section 10.6. In Section 10.7, we describe the simulation flowchart for epidemic-like routing in the secondary networks. Finally, Section 10.8 concludes this chapter.

10.2 Related Works

This section surveys the existing routing designs in the secondary networks (primarily in CRNs) as well as the delay modeling of routing schemes in the traditional ad hoc networks. Figure 10.1 illustrates the main operations of the current single and multipath routing

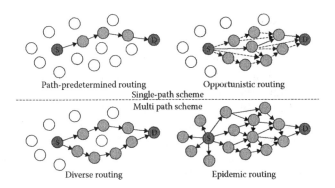

FIGURE 10.1
Taxonomy of the routing schemes in secondary networks. Solid arrows stand for the actual routes and dash arrows for the potential routes. It is straightforward that the destination has more chances to receive the packet via multiple paths, and epidemic-like routing inherently produces a large buffer occupancy due to its spreading nature.

schemes that could be adopted in the secondary networks and the details are described in Sections 10.2.1 through 10.2.4.

10.2.1 Path-Predetermined Routing

In a secondary network, spectrum availability mainly depends on the PU behavior and shall be considered as a performance metric in the route computation. A probabilistic metric is proposed in [11] to stochastically capture the PU behaviors. A path is determined based on predicting the available duration of the secondary links according to the awareness of PUs in [12] whereas [13] chooses a path with the highest connectivity evaluated by exploiting the PU activity. Cross-layer designs combining the resource allocation, power control, and routing are proposed in [14] to select a path with guaranteed bit-error rate and bound power consumption. A cluster model is applied in [15] to reduce the routing overhead when a common control channel is nonexistent.

10.2.2 Opportunistic Routing

To reduce the possible retransmissions, the next relay is selected at each hop for each packet according to the local actual network performance in the opportunistic routing [4]. Moreover, each packet can take advantage of those long but low-quality transmission links to reduce the hop count to its destination. However, how to design a feasible algorithm and evaluate its performance in a secondary network remains an open issue. Previous researches [16] proposed an opportunistic routing algorithm in CRN considering the highly dynamic link availability features.

10.2.3 Diverse Routing

To adapt to the dynamic environment in a secondary network, replicated packets carried by disjoint paths can be utilized to improve the end-to-end reliability. The idea was realized by Wang et al. [17] who proposed a workable algorithm and Chang et al. [6] further evaluated the end-to-end reliability using an analytical model. In addition, coding techniques such as network coding [18] and path-time virtual multiple-input multiple-output (MIMO) coding [19] have been proposed for the diverse routing.

10.2.4 Epidemic-Like Routing

Epidemic routing has been regarded as one practical way to achieve routing in the intermittently connected mobile ad hoc networks (ICMAHNs) or delay tolerant networks [20,21]. Despite the fact that the epidemic-like routing relaxes the necessity of routing table maintenance and route discovery, the inevitable overhead of the heavy buffer occupancy shall be mitigated. A unified probabilistic forwarding scheme, including two-hop forwarding and conventional epidemic routing as a special case, is proposed for ICMAHNs [22].

Regarding analytical models for studying the end-to-end features (such as capacity and delay) of routing schemes in the ad hoc networks, we concentrate on the works based on stochastic geometry since a tractable closed-form solution is provided. Xu and Wang [9] proposed a model to analyze the upper bound of end-to-end delay on a route in a traditional ad hoc network, while only Vaze [23] investigated the complicated throughput-delay-reliability tradeoffs in such networks. Jacquet et al. [24] further studied the delay and routing selection in the opportunistic routing. The extended work [10] investigated the transmission capacity in the diverse routing. However, all the mentioned literatures only consider the role of intrasystem interference on the outage constraint of a node. When considering a secondary network consisting of both the intrasystem as well as intersystem interferences among SUs and PUs, things become more complicated. In a previous work [25], Ao et al. developed and explored a framework to model the complicated characteristics and relationship among connectivity, interference, and latency in a secondary network. Base on the framework, we further analyze the end-to-end delay of the multipath and single-path routing schemes in a secondary network. Table 10.1 summarizes the existing literatures investigating the routing algorithm or analysis in the conventional ad hoc network or the multihop secondary network.

In contrast to all the mentioned efforts, the novelty of this chapter exists in the following aspects:

- We propose a delay model for epidemic-like routing in the secondary networks. The model incorporates the medium access and retransmission delay of the secondary networks and is able to estimate the system buffer occupancy and probability of packet delivery.

- The proposed model can be used to predetermine the global timeout value such that the system occupancy can be maximally reduced provided the probability of packet delivery is guaranteed.

- We establish a flowchart for simulating the epidemic-like routing in the secondary networks. The codes will be made available to the public in the near future.

TABLE 10.1

A Summary of Routing Algorithms and Analytical Models in Ad Hoc and Secondary Networks

		Single-Path Scheme		Multipath Scheme	
		Path-Predetermined	Opportunistic	Diverse	Epidemic
Ad hoc	Algorithm	AODV, DSR		[7]	
	Analytical	[9]	[24]		[22,26–28]
Secondary	Algorithm	[12,13]	[16]	[6,17–19]	

10.3 Preliminaries

To realize the routing merits in the secondary networks, especially epidemic-like routing, we introduce some fundamental concepts related to the performance modeling in epidemic-like routing, since it serves as a natural reference to other multipath routing schemes.

10.3.1 Susceptible Infected–Recovered Model and Global Timeout Scheme

Inspired from epidemiology, data dissemination in communication networks has been surprisingly found to resemble the transportation of epidemics [29,30]. Similar to the conventional susceptible-infected-recovered (SIR) model, a noninformed (i.e., susceptible) node receives a packet and keeps it in the buffer as if the node is infected, and later on the infected node discards the packet when the packet is either outdated or is successfully delivered to the destination. The latter case is as if the node is immune to the virus (an infected node recovers from the disease forever). The interactive dynamics of the compartmental model can be characterized by ordinary differential equations [29], where $I(t) + S(t) + R(t) = M + 1$ is the total population with M relaying nodes (including the source node) and one destination node. $I(t)$, $S(t)$, and $R(t)$ are the infected, susceptible, and recovered subpopulations, respectively.

In [31], several novel ideas stemmed from the biological phenomenon are proposed to delete the unnecessary packets to mitigate the resource consumption for epidemic-like data dissemination. Among all mechanisms, the VACCINE recovery scheme is one of the most vigorous mechanisms to efficiently save the buffer occupancy with the aid of "anti-packet" spreading. Once the destination receives the packet, it transmits the anti-packet to all neighboring nodes so that the nodes carrying the replicated data can discard the packet, and those that have not received the packet will not store it in the buffer. Moreover, a global time-to-live (TTL) value is determined at the source and passed down to all the replicated packets. After the TTL expires, all nodes delete both packets and anti-packets from their buffers.

10.3.2 Flooding-Based Epidemic Routing

A profound framework for evaluating the performance of epidemic-like broadcast protocols in the wireless sensor networks has been rigorously analyzed in [8]. The data dissemination resembles the stretch of a ripple which is generated from the source node, and the information propagation speed is shown to be $I(t) / I(t)$. Let β be the average number of neighbors. Due to spatial propagation, only half of the neighbors of an infected node are effectively susceptible [32]. With the global timeout duration T and VACCINE recovery scheme, the data dissemination dynamics can be characterized by [33]

$$\begin{cases} \dfrac{dI(t)}{dt} = \varphi(t)\dfrac{\beta}{2}c\sqrt{I(t)}\dfrac{M - I(t) - R(t)}{M} - \mu(t)\dfrac{\beta}{2}c\sqrt{R(t) + P(t)}\dfrac{I(t)}{M}, \\[2ex] \dfrac{dR(t)}{dt} = \mu(t)\dfrac{\beta}{2}c\sqrt{R(t) + P(t)}\dfrac{I(t)}{M} + \mu(t)\dfrac{\beta}{2}c\sqrt{R(t) + P(t)}\dfrac{M - I(t) - R(t)}{M}, \\[2ex] \dfrac{dP(t)}{dt} = \mu(t)\dfrac{\beta}{2}\dfrac{I(t)}{M}(1 - P(t)), \quad \text{for } t \leq T, \\[2ex] I(t) = 0 \text{ and } R(t) = 0, \quad \text{for } t > T, \end{cases} \tag{10.1}$$

where $\varphi(t)$ is the infection rate function of delivery delay, $\mu(t)$ is the recovery rate function of delivery delay, β is the average number of neighbors, $c = 2\sqrt{\beta+1}$ and $P(t)$ is the cumulative density function (CDF) of delivery delay.

For $t \leq T$, as proved in [8], the dissemination dynamics of both the packet and anti-packet can be regarded as an infection circular strip stretching out from the source node at the beginning, and a recovery circular strip stems when the destination node receives the packet. For $t > T$, both the packets and anti-packets are deleted from the network, thus both the infected and the recovered subpopulation are zero.

Remark 1. To the best of authors' knowledge, the performance evaluation of the epidemic-like routing in a secondary network remains an open issue since the coexistence of PUs and SUs is beyond the scope of traditional epidemic routing. A more general performance modeling is discussed in Section 10.5.

10.4 System Model

We consider a network model where a secondary network coexists with a PS as illustrated in Figure 10.2. Each SU is transparent to PUs and attempts to optimize the end-to-end delay while guaranteeing the receiver sensitivity of PU. The spatial distributions of the primary transmitters (PTs) and SUs are assumed to follow the homogeneous Poisson point processes (PPPs) with densities λ_{PT} and λ_{SU}, respectively. Each PT has the transmission power P_{PT} and a dedicated primary receiver (PR) located at a fixed distance r_{PT} with an arbitrary direction. The spatial distribution of PRs also forms a homogeneous PPP with the same density λ_{PT} correlated with that of the PTs. The interference measured by a typical PR located at the origin is representative of the interference seen by the other PRs due to the stationary characteristics of PPP [34]. The following two lemmas characterize the permissible active density of the SUs regarding outage constraint of PR sensitivity and deployment of the avoidance region, which further distinguish the secondary network from other networking paradigms.

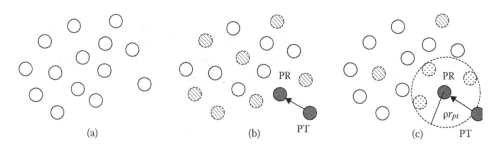

FIGURE 10.2
System model of a secondary network. (a) Absence of PS. The network topology is similar to the traditional wireless ad hoc networks. (b) Outage constraint of PS. Slashed nodes are deactivated according to the active probability $\tilde{p}$. (c) Avoidance region. Dotted nodes are deactivated since they are in the vicinity of primary receiver, while other slashed nodes are deactivated according to the active probability $\hat{p}$.

10.4.1 Outage Constraint of PR Sensitivity

To mitigate the interference to PRs, the SUs exploit slotted ALOHA as the distributed spectrum access protocol. As shown in Figure 10.2b, each SU tosses a coin independently in each time slot and accesses the spectrum with head probability $\tilde{p}$, where $\tilde{p}$ is the parameter of independent and identically distributed Bernoulli random variables, $B_i(\tilde{p})$.

Lemma 10.1. To avoid interference from SUs violating the outage constraint at a PR,

the permissible active density of SUs is $\tilde{\lambda}_{SU} = \left(\dfrac{-\ln 1 - \varepsilon_{PR} - \dfrac{\eta_{PR}}{P_{PT} r_{PT}^{-\alpha}} N}{r_{PT}^2 \eta_{PR}^\delta K_\alpha} - \lambda_{PT} \right) \left(\dfrac{P_{PT}}{P_{SU}} \right)^\delta$, and the

active probability is $\tilde{p} = \dfrac{\bar{\lambda}_{SU}}{\lambda_{SU}}$.

Proof. Let $\Phi_{PT} = \{X_i\}$ ($\Phi_{SU} = \{Y_i\}$) denote the locations of the PTs (SUs). The receiver sensitivity of a PR is maintained when only $\tilde{p}$ portion of SUs are allowed to transmit. This subset of SUs, denoted as $\Phi_{SU}(\tilde{p}) = \{Y_i : B_i(\tilde{p}) = 1\}$ with density $\tilde{\lambda}_{SU} = \tilde{p}\lambda_{SU}$, is obtained by independent thinning of Φ_{SU} with probability $\tilde{p}$. We have the outage constraint as follows:

$$\mathbb{P}\left(\frac{\mathcal{G}_{PT} P_{PT} r_{PT}^{-\alpha}}{N + I_{SU} + I_{PT}} \geq \eta_{PR} \right) = 1 - \varepsilon_{PR} \tag{10.2}$$

where ε_{PR} is the maximum outage probability imposed on PR, $\mathcal{G}_{PT}$ is the channel power gain of the desired link and is supposed to be exponentially distributed with unit mean (i.e., slow flat Rayleigh fading channel), α is the path-loss exponent, η_{PR} is the SINR threshold of PR, N is the noise-power level, $I_{SU} = \sum_{Y_i \in \Phi_{SU}(\tilde{p})} \mathcal{G}_{Y_i} P_{SU} \|Y_i\|^{-\alpha}$ is the interference from SUs to a typical PR, and $I_{PT} = \sum_{Y_i \in \Phi_{SU}(\tilde{p})} \mathcal{G}_{X_i} P_{PT} \|X_i\|^{-\alpha}$ is the interference from other PTs. $\| \ \|$ denotes the distance to the origin, P_{SU} is the transmission power of SU and the channel power gain $\mathcal{G}_{X_i}$ and $\mathcal{G}_{Y_i}$ of the interfering links are also exponentially distributed with the unit mean. The left hand side of Equation 10.2 can be evaluated as [25]

$$\mathbb{P}\left[\mathcal{G}_{PT} \geq \frac{\eta_{PR}}{P_{PT} r_{pT}^{-\alpha}} (N + I_{SU} + I_{PT}) \right]$$

$$= \exp\left(-\frac{\eta_{PR}}{P_{PT} r_{pT}^{-\alpha}} N \right) \mathbb{E}\left[\exp\left(-\frac{\eta_{PR}}{P_{PT} r_{pT}^{-\alpha}} I_{SU} \right) \right] \mathbb{E}\left[\exp\left(-\frac{\eta_{PR}}{P_{PT} r_{pT}^{-\alpha}} I_{PT} \right) \right] \tag{10.3}$$

$$= \exp\left(-\frac{\eta_{PR}}{P_{PT} r_{pT}^{-\alpha}} N \right) \exp\left\{ -\left(\tilde{\lambda}_{SU} (\frac{P_{SU}}{P_{PT}})^\delta + \lambda_{PT} \right) r_{PT}^2 \eta_{PR}^\delta K_\alpha \right\},$$

and Equations 10.2 and 10.3, when $\dfrac{-\ln\left(1-\varepsilon_{PR}\right)-\dfrac{\eta_{PR}}{P_{PT}r_{pT}^{-\alpha}}N}{r_{PT}^2\eta_{PR}^{\delta}K_{\alpha}}\geq\lambda_{PT}$ we obtain the permissible active density as follows:

$$
\tilde{\lambda}_{SU}=\left(\dfrac{-\ln\left(1-\varepsilon_{PR}\right)-\dfrac{\eta_{PR}}{P_{PT}r_{pT}^{-\alpha}}N}{r_{PT}^2\eta_{PR}^{\delta}K_{\alpha}}-\lambda_{PT}\right)\left(\dfrac{P_{PT}}{P_{SU}}\right)^{\delta}\Delta\sigma P_{SU}^{-\delta}
\tag{10.4}
$$

where $K_{alpha}=\dfrac{2\pi^2}{\alpha\sin 2\pi/\alpha}$ and $\delta=2/\alpha$.

Furthermore, if a PT does not impose interference on other PRs (e.g., the code division multiple access [CDMA] is exploited), additional SUs are allowed to be activated due to looser outage constraint.

Corollary 10.1. Additional $\lambda_{PT}\left(\dfrac{P_{PT}}{P_{SU}}\right)^{\delta}$ density of the SUs are activated when $I_{PT}=0$.

Proof. This is a direct result of Equation 10.4 when λ_{PT} is set to be 0.

10.4.2 Avoidance Region

If an SU is in the vicinity of a PR, deactivation of the SU (instead of following slotted ALOHA with certain access probability) may increase the overall permissible active density while maintaining the same receiver sensitivity of the PR as illustrated in Figure 10.2c. With the capability of dynamic spectrum access, an SU is deactivated when it is located within the radius $\rho\gamma_{PT}$ of a PR, where ρ is a reasonably small nonnegative value named the avoidance region radius coefficient. In other words, each PR has an SU-avoidance region with a radius $\rho\gamma_{PT}$, and the permissible active density of the SUs increases following the next lemma [25].

Lemma 10.2. The permissible active density of SUs satisfying the outage constraint of PR sensitivity is enhanced from $\tilde{\lambda}_{SU}$ to $\bar{\lambda}_{SU}\geq\tilde{\lambda}_{SU}$, and $\bar{\lambda}_{SU}=\tilde{\lambda}_{SU}\dfrac{\pi/2}{\pi/2-\tan^{-1}\left(\sqrt{\dfrac{P_{PT}}{\eta_{PR}P_{SU}}}\rho^2\right)}$

when $\alpha=4$.

Proof. If an SU is deactivated when it is located within the radius ρ of a PR and has an SU-avoidance region with a radius ρ, the probability of an SU located in $\mathcal{B}(PR;\rho)$ is $1-\exp(-\lambda PT\pi\rho^2)$, where the notation $\mathcal{B}(x;r)$ represents the circle of radius r centered at x. The interference from SUs at a typical PR located at origin becomes

$$
I'_{SU}=\sum_{Y_i\in\Phi^{\hat{p}}_{SU}\setminus\mathcal{B}(0;\rho)}G_{Y_i}P_{SU}\left\|Y_i\right\|^{-\alpha}1_{Y_i\notin\mathcal{B}(PR;\rho)}.
\tag{10.5}
$$

Also, we have the moment generating function of I'_{SU} as given by

$$
\mathbb{E}\left[\exp(-tI'_{SU})\right]=\exp\left(-2\pi\hat{\lambda}_{ST}\exp-\lambda_{PT}\pi\rho^2\int_{\rho}^{\infty}\dfrac{x}{1+\dfrac{x^{\alpha}}{tP_{SU}}}dx\right).
\tag{10.6}
$$

Substituting $t=\dfrac{\eta_{PR}}{P_{PT}r_{pT}^{-\alpha}}$ and $\alpha=4$ in Equation 10.6, we have

$$\mathbb{E}\left[\exp\left(-\frac{\eta_{PR}}{P_{PT}r_{PT}^{-\alpha}}I'_{SU}\right)\right] = \exp\left\{-\hat{\lambda}_{ST}\exp\left(-\lambda_{PT}\pi\rho^2\right)r_{PT}^2\left(\frac{\eta_{PR}P_{SU}}{P_{PT}}\right)^{\frac{1}{2}}\right.$$

$$\left.\left[\frac{\pi}{2} - \pi\tan^{-1}\left(\sqrt{\frac{P_{PT}}{\eta_{PR}P_{SU}}\frac{\rho^2}{r_{PT}^2}}\right)\right]\right\} \tag{10.7}$$

Compared with the case without an avoidance region, i.e., $\rho = 0$ or Equation 10.4 with $\alpha = 4$, $K_4 = \pi^2/2$, we have

$$\frac{-\hat{\lambda}_{ST}\exp\left(-\lambda_{PT}\pi\rho^2\right)}{\tilde{\lambda}_{SU}} = \frac{\pi^2/2}{\pi^2/2 - \tan^{-1}\left(\sqrt{\frac{P_{PT}}{\eta_{PR}P_{SU}}\frac{\rho^2}{r_{PT}^2}}\right)} \geq 1 \tag{10.8}$$

10.5 Epidemic-Like Routing Model in Multihop Secondary Networks

Taking into account the active density of SUs for satisfying the outage constraints of the PSs, we incorporate the concept of avoidance region in Section 10.4.2 to formulate the performance of an epidemic-like routing, including the traditional wireless ad hoc networks as a special case. In addition, the advantage of relaxing the need for route discovery renders the epidemic-like routing a suitable scheme for the secondary network, since the end-to-end path information may not be available to all SUs owing to the spectrum uncertainties.

Proposition 1. For epidemic-like routing with a global time-out duration T and VACCINE scheme deployed by avoidance region, the data dissemination dynamics can be characterized by

$$\begin{cases} \dfrac{dI(t)}{dt} = \psi(t)\dfrac{\beta}{2}\widehat{pc}\sqrt{I(t)}\dfrac{M-I(t)-R(t)}{M} - \mu(t)\dfrac{\beta}{2}\widehat{pc}\sqrt{R(t)+P(t)}\dfrac{I(t)}{M}, \\[2mm] \dfrac{dR(t)}{dt} = \mu(t)\dfrac{\beta}{2}\widehat{pc}\sqrt{R(t)+P(t)}\dfrac{I(t)}{M} + \mu(t)\dfrac{\beta}{2}\widehat{pc}\sqrt{R(t)+P(t)}\dfrac{M-I(t)-R(t)}{M}, \\[2mm] \dfrac{dP(t)}{dt} = \psi(t)\dfrac{\beta}{2}\hat{p}\dfrac{I(t)}{M}\left(1-P(t)\right), \text{ for } t \leq T, \\[2mm] I(t) = 0 \text{ and } R(t) = 0, \text{ for } t > T, \end{cases} \tag{10.9}$$

where $\hat{p} = \dfrac{\hat{\lambda}_{SU}}{SU}$ is the active probability of an SU, β is the average number of neighbors per

SU, $c = 2\sqrt{\beta+1}$, $\psi(t) = \mu(t) = e^{-\beta\hat{p}\left(\frac{I(t)+R(t)+P(t)}{M}\right)T_F}$, and T_F is the frame time.

Proof. Compared to the flooding-based epidemic routing in Equation 10.1, the propagation of packets and anti-packets is further affected by the active probability $\hat{p}$ in the secondary networks. Assuming the traffic of an SU and its neighboring nodes follows a Poisson process with arrival rate $g = \beta\hat{p}$ packets per unit time, the infection rate is the collision-free probability given by

$$\psi(t) = e^{-g\left(\frac{I(t)+R(t)+P(t)}{M}\right)T_F} = e^{-\beta\hat{p}\left(\frac{I(t)+R(t)+P(t)}{M}\right)T_F} \tag{10.10}$$

since the interference from neighboring SUs is regarded as contentions for an SU. The same argument applies to $\mu(t)$. In addition, suppose there is a circular region with a sufficiently large radius R_c, the number of SUs in the region is $M+1 = \lambda_{SU}\pi R_c^2$, and the average number of neighbors of an SU (i.e., the SUs who successfully receive the packet) can be computed as

$$\beta = \lambda_{SU}\int_0^{R_c}\mathbb{P}\left(\frac{\mathcal{G}_{SU}P_{SU}r^{-\alpha}}{I_{PT}+N} \geq \eta_{SU}\right)2\pi r\,dr$$

$$\beta \overset{R_c \to \infty}{=} \lambda_{SU}\int_0^\infty\exp\left\{-\frac{\eta_{SU}N}{P_{SU}}r^\alpha - \lambda_{PT}\left(\frac{P_{PT}}{P_{SU}}\right)^\delta\eta_{SU}^\delta K_\alpha r^2\right\}2\pi r\,dr. \tag{10.11}$$

From [35, Section 2.33], $\beta = k_5 P_{SU}^{1/2}$ when $\alpha = 4$, where

$$k_5 = \frac{\lambda_{SU}\pi}{2}\sqrt{\frac{\pi}{\eta_{SU}N}}\exp\left\{\frac{\lambda_{PT}^2 P_{PT}\pi^4}{16N}\right\}erfc\left(\frac{\lambda_{PT}P_{PT}^{\frac{1}{2}}\pi^2}{4N^{\frac{1}{2}}}\right) \tag{10.12}$$

and $erfc(x) = \frac{2}{\sqrt{\pi}}\int_x^\infty e^{-t^2}dt$ is the complementary error function.

Note that the flooding-based epidemic routing model in Equation 10.1 is a degenerate case of our model when $\hat{p} = 1$. Moreover, we can obtain the average buffer occupancy per SU as $Q = \int_0^T I(t)dt$ by Little's formula [33]. Note that there is clearly a tradeoff between the TTL value and average buffer occupancy. With Lemma 10.1, Lemma 10.2, and Equation 10.11, we then derive $\beta\hat{p}$, the average number of active neighbors per SU.

Corollary 10.2. The effective average number of the neighbors in a secondary network is

$$\beta\hat{p} = \sigma k_5\pi\left\{2\lambda_{SU}\left[\frac{\pi}{2} - \tan^{-1}\left(\sqrt{\frac{P_{PT}}{\eta_{PR}P_{SU}}}\rho^2\right)\right]\right\}^{-1}, \quad \text{when } \alpha = 4.$$

Proof. By Proposition $1 = k_5 P_{SU}^{\frac{1}{2}}$, when $\alpha = 4$, and by Lemma 10.2 $\hat{p} = \frac{\hat{\lambda}_{SU}}{\lambda_{SU}}$. Hence we obtain the corollary. Note that β shall be larger than some threshold β_{th} to prevent the network from disconnecting, which mainly depends on the channel fading and path loss, and is numerically analyzed in [36], e.g., $\beta_{th} = 4.52$ when there is no fading effect. Moreover, Q is a function of P_{SU} (or β) and T since it is the integer of the infected subpopulation up to time T. To minimize Q, we formulate the optimization problem as follows:

Minimize

$$Q(P_{SU}, T)$$

Subject to

$$P_{SU} \geq f^{-1}(\beta_{th}), \quad P(T) \geq 1 - \varepsilon_T, \tag{10.13}$$

where $\beta = f(P_{SU})$ from Equation 10.11. The lower bound of P_{SU} is to meet the condition that $\beta > \beta_{th}$ to prevent the network from disconnecting, and the CDF of delivery delay up to T is constrained with the maximum delay outage probability ε_T. From Corollary 10.2, $\beta \tilde{p}$ is a monotonically decreasing function of P_{SU}, decreasing P_{SU} induces a lower delivery delay due to increment of the active SUs and henceforth lower T and Q. When $\alpha = 4$, we have $\beta = k_5(P_{SU})^{\frac{1}{2}} \geq \beta_{th}$ and the optimal transmission power of SU becomes $P_{SU}^* = \left(\dfrac{\beta_{th}}{k_5}\right)^2$. In addition, it is trivial that the k_5 optimal global timeout value T^* satisfies $P(T^*) = 1 - \varepsilon_T$ since Q is an increasing function in T.

10.6 Performance Evaluation

This section evaluates the epidemic-like routing in a secondary network by implementing the stochastic geometry, medium access control, and interference in the simulation environment. Detailed descriptions of the simulation process are discussed in Section 10.7. Following [25], the system parameters are set to be $N = 10^{-9}$ mW, $\lambda_{PT} = \dfrac{10^{-5} \text{ PUs}}{m^2}$, $\lambda_{SU} = \dfrac{10^{-3} \text{ SUs}}{m^2}$, $P_{PT} = 0.3$ mW, $P_{SU} = 0.1$ mW, $\eta_{PR} = 3$, $\eta_{SU} = 3$, $\alpha = 4$, $r_{PT} = 15$ m, $\varepsilon_{PR} = 0.05$, $\varepsilon_{SU} = 0.1$, $\rho = 2$, and $T_F = 1$ s on a 800 m × 800 m square field. The simulation results are the ensemble averages of 10,000 simulations by C++. All differential equations in Proposition 1 are approximated by difference equations.

The minimized TTL value of the epidemic-like routing with respect to delay outage probability is shown in Figure 10.3. It is obvious that the delay outage probability decreases

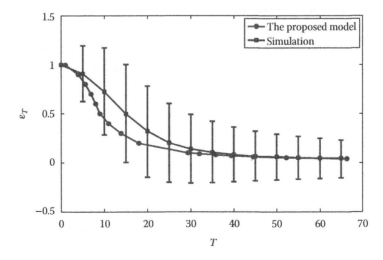

FIGURE 10.3
Minimized TTL value of an epidemic-like routing with respect to delay outage probability. Error bars represent the standard deviation of 10,000 simulations.

as the TTL value increases. The proposed model well matches the simulation results when $\varepsilon_T \leq 0.2$, which is of practical importance since most of the routing protocols have delay outage constraints within this regime. Note that for a small TTL value, although the proposed model tends to overestimate the probability of the data delivery, it is still within 1 standard deviation of the ensemble mean.

Figure 10.4 shows the minimized TTL value of the epidemic-like routing with respect to the average buffer occupancy. The proposed model is shown to have the same tendency with respect to the simulation results. The discrepancy of the proposed model and the simulation results can be explained by the fact that the average buffer occupancy Q is the cumulation of the infected population up to time T as discussed in Section 10.5. The proposed model can be used to assess the tendency of buffer occupancy for analyzing the tradeoffs between the delay outage probability and buffer occupancy. As shown in Figure 10.5, the buffer occupancy increases exponentially fast as we decrease the delay

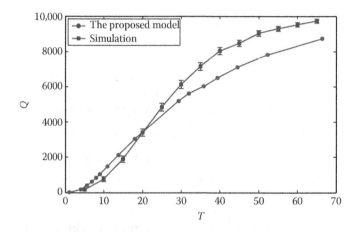

FIGURE 10.4
Minimized TTL value of the epidemic-like routing with respect to average buffer occupancy. Error bars represent the standard deviation of 10,000 simulations.

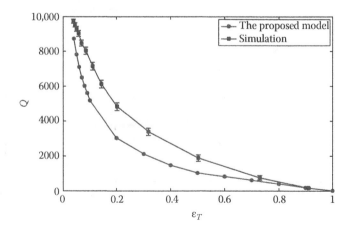

FIGURE 10.5
Minimized average buffer occupancy with respect to delay outage probability. Error bars represent the standard deviation of 10,000 simulations.

outage probability, which is demonstrated by both the proposed model and the simulation results. This suggests that to achieve a low delay outage probability in a secondary network, one would anticipate a large buffer occupancy.

10.7 Simulation Flowchart

In this section, we describe the flowchart for simulating epidemic-like routing in the secondary networks. The codes will be made available to public in the near future. The flowchart of the simulation process is summarized in Figure 10.6. We initialize the system by setting up the environmental parameters including random node deployment, wireless fading channel, transmission power, and so on. We randomly pick a node as the initially infected one and the destination one. The global timeout value is predetermined.

If the current time is smaller than the global timeout value, each infected node has a timing clock for transmission, which is associated with the medium access probability (i.e., the active SU density). The nodes that received the packet (i.e., the SINR is above a certain value) are regarded as newly infected nodes. If the destination node received the packet, the anti-packets are propagated following the same procedure, and therefore some nodes will turn into the recovered state. All infected and recovered nodes keep on transmitting until the global timer goes off.

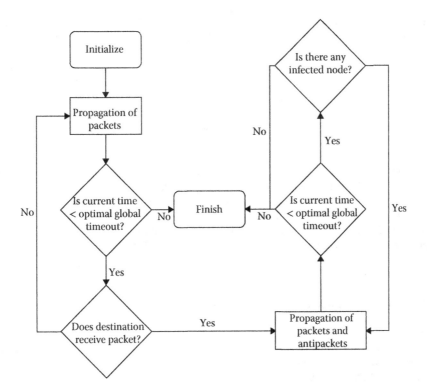

FIGURE 10.6
Flowchart of the simulation process.

10.8 Conclusion

In this chapter, we proposed the delay models for epidemic-like routing in the secondary networks that incorporate the influences of PR sensitivity, dynamic spectrum access, and power control of SUs. The proposed model successfully characterizes the complicated data delivery dynamics in the secondary networks and serves as a powerful tool for studying the tradeoffs among delay outage probability, global timeout value, and buffer occupancy in the secondary networks. Therefore, this chapter offers new avenues toward routing design and delay analysis in the secondary networks.

References

1. S. A. Goldsmith, I. Jafar, C. Marí, and S. Srinivasa. Breaking spectrum gridlock with cognitive radios: An information theoretic perspective. *Proc. IEEE*, 97(5):894–914, May 2009.
2. Y.-C. Liang, K.-C. Chen, G. Y. Li, and P. Mahonen. Cognitive radio networking and communications: An overview. *IEEE Trans. Veh. Technol.*, 60(7):3386–3407, Sept. 2011.
3. M. Youssef, M. Ibrahim, M. Abdelatif, L. Chen, and A. Vasilakos. Routing metrics of cognitive radio networks: A survey. *IEEE Commun. Surv. Tuts.*, 16(1):92–109, First Quarter 2014.
4. H. Khalife, N. Malouch, and S. Fdida. Multihop cognitive radio networks: To route or not to route. *IEEE Netw.*, 23(4):20–25, July/Aug. 2009.
5. K.-C. Chen, B. K. Cetin, Y.-C. Peng, N. Prasad, J. Wang, and S. Lee. Routing for cognitive radio networks consisting of opportunistic links. *Wiley Wireless Commun. Mobile Comput.*, 10(4):451–466, Apr. 2010.
6. H.-B. Chang, S.-M. Cheng, S.-Y. Lien, and K.-C. Chen. Statistical delay control of opportunistic links in cognitive radio networks. In *Proc. IEEE PIMRC '10*, pp. 2248–2252, Sept. 2010.
7. Q. She, X. Huang, and J. P. Jue. How reliable can two-path protection be? *IEEE/ACM Trans. Netw.*, 18(3):922–933, June 2010.
8. P. De, Y. Liu, and S. K. Das. An epidemic theoretic framework for vulnerability analysis of broadcast protocols in wireless sensor networks. *IEEE Trans. Mobile Comput.*, 8(3):413–425, Mar. 2009.
9. Y. Xu and W. Wang. The limit of information propagation speed in large-scale multihop wireless networks. *IEEE/ACM Trans. Netw.*, 19(1):209–222, Jan. 2011.
10. Y. Chen and J. G. Andrews. An upper bound on multi-hop transmission capacity with dynamic multipath routing. *IEEE Trans. Inf. Theory*, 58(6):3751–3765, June 2012.
11. H. Khalife, S. Ahuja, N. Malouch, and M. Krunz. Probabilistic path selection in opportunistic cognitive radio networks. In *Proceedings of the IEEE GLOBECOM '08*, New Orleans, LA, Dec. 2008.
12. Q. Guan, F. R. Yu, S. Jiang, and G. Wei. Prediction-based topology control and routing in cognitive radio mobile ad hoc networks. *IEEE Trans. Veh. Technol.*, 59(9):4443–4452, Nov. 2010.
13. Abbagnale and F. Cuomo. Gymkhana: A connectivity-based routing scheme for cognitive radio ad hoc networks. In *Proceedings of the IEEE INFOCOM '10 Workshops*, San Diego, CA, Mar. 2010.
14. L. Ding, T. Melodia, S. N. Batalama, J. D. Matyjas, and M. J. Medley. Cross-layer routing and dynamic spectrum allocation in cognitive radio ad hoc networks. *IEEE Trans. Veh. Technol.*, 59(4):1969–1979, May 2010.

15. X.-L. Huang, G. Wang, F. Hu, and S. Kumar. Stability-capacity-adaptive routing for high-mobility multihop cognitive radio networks. *IEEE Trans. Veh. Technol.*, 60(6):2714–2729, July 2011.

16. S.-C. Lin and K.-C. Chen. Spectrum aware opportunistic routing in cognitive radio networks. In *Proceedings of the IEEE GLOBECOM '10*, Miami, FL, Dec. 2010.

17. X. Wang, T. Kwon, and Y. Choi. A multipath routing and spectrum access (MRSA) framework for cognitive radio systems in multi-radio mesh networks. In *Proceedings of the CoRoNet '09*, Las Vegas, NV, p. 55–60, Sept. 2009.

18. P.-Y. Chen, W. C. Ao, and K.-C. Chen. Rate-delay enhanced multipath transmission scheme via network coding in multihop networks. *IEEE Commun. Lett.*, 16(3):281–283, Mar. 2012.

19. I.-W. Lai, C.-H. Lee, and K.-C. Chen. A virtual MIMO path-time code for cognitive ad hoc networks. *IçEEE Commun. Lett.*, 17(1):4–7, 2013.

20. H. Huang, D. Zeng, S. Guo, H. Yao, and T. Miyazaki. Stochastic analysis on epidemic dissemination of lifetime-controlled messages in DTNs. In *Proceedings of IWCMC '13*, Cagliari, Sardinia, Italy, pp. 1578–1583, July 2013.

21. Q. Wang and Q. Wang. Restricted epidemic routing in multi-community delay tolerant networks. *IEEE Trans. Mobile Comput.*, 14(8):1686–1697, Nov. 2014.

22. T. Matsuda and T. Takine. (p,q)-Epidemic routing for sparsely populated mobile ad hoc networks. *IEEE J. Sel. Areas Commun.*, 26(5):783–793, June 2008.

23. R. Vaze. Throughput-delay-reliability tradeoff with ARQ in wireless ad hoc networks. *IEEE Trans. Wireless Commun.*, 10(7):2142–2149, July 2011.

24. P. Jacquet, B. Mans, P. Muhlethaler, and G. Rodolakis. Opportunistic routing in wireless ad hoc networks: Upper bounds for the packet propagation speed. *IEEE J. Sel. Areas Commun.*, 27(7):1192–1202, Sept. 2009.

25. W. C. Ao, S.-M. Cheng, and K.-C. Chen. Phase transition diagram for underlay heterogeneous cognitive radio networks. In *Proceedings of the IEEE GLOBECOM '10*, Miami, FL, Dec. 2010.

26. A. Jindal and K. Psounis. Contention-aware performance analysis of mobility-assisted routing. *IEEE Trans. Mobile Comput.*, 8(2):145–161, Feb. 2009.

27. M. Marathe and A. K. S. Vullikanti. Computational epidemiology. *Commun. ACM*, 56(7):88–96, July 2013.

28. S. De Abreu and R. M. Salles. Modeling message diffusion in epidemical DTN. *Ad Hoc Networks*, 16:197–209, 2014.

29. D. J. Daley and J. Gani. *Epidemic Modelling: An Introduction*. UK: Cambridge University Press, 2001.

30. P.-Y. Chen and K.-C. Chen. Information epidemics in complex networks with opportunistic links and dynamic topology. In *Proceedings of the IEEE GLOBECOM '10*, Miami, FL, Dec. 2010.

31. Z. J. Haas and T. Small. A new networking model for biological applications of ad hoc sensor networks. *IEEE/ACM Trans. Netw.*, 14(1):27–40, Feb. 2006.

32,. S.-M. Cheng, W. C. Ao, P.-Y. Chen, and K.-C. Chen. On modeling malware propagation in generalized social networks. *IEEE Commun. Lett.*, 15(1):25–27, Jan. 2011.

33. X. Zhang, G. Negli, J. Kurose, and D. Towsley. Performance modeling of epidemic routing. *Comput. Netw.*, 51(8):2867–2891, July 2007.

34. J. Kingman. *Point Processes*. Oxford, UK: Clarendon Press, 1993.

35. S. Gradshteyn, I. M. Ryzhik, A. Jerey, and D. Zwillinger. *Table of Integrals, Series, and Products*, Daniel Zwillinger (ed.), 6th Edition. San Diego, CA, USA: Elsevier, 2014.

36. R. Hekmat and P. V. Mieghem. Connectivity in wireless ad-hoc networks with a log-normal radio model. *Mob. Netw. Appl.*, 11:351–360, June 2006.

Part V

Challenges in Cognitive Radio Networks/Energy Utilization in Cognitive Radio Networks

11

Discrete Resource Allocation in Cooperative Cognitive Radio Networks

Lucas Sampaio, Fábio Renan Durand, and Taufik Abrão

CONTENTS

11.1 Introduction

Fast expansion of multimedia service and continuous growth of wireless data transfer in the last decade along with the spectrum scarcity skyrocketed the spectrum license prices across the world. For instance, in 2013 AT&T spent $1.9 billion to buy 39 regulated spectrum licenses [1].

The concept of cognitive radio networks (CRNs) arises as an alternative to the licensed spectrum paradigm. CRN operates simultaneously with another network cell, denominated as the primary cell, sharing the same spectrum band. The users of the primary cell transmit over the licensed spectrum bands and are herein denominated as the primary users (PUs). The cognitive radio users who use the spectrum bands in an opportunistic fashion are denominated as the secondary users (SUs).

Both PUs and SUs may or may not coexist in the same geographical area, i.e., the primary cell and CRN are usually either partially or fully overlapped. In both the configurations, the SUs access the spectrum in two different modes, namely overlay and underlay, both are opportunistic spectrum access modes. In the overlay mode, the SU transmits over a PU channel that is not busy. In the underlay mode, the SU transmits over a busy PU channel subjected to a power density spectral mask.

Therefore, spectrum allocation and power control are the fundamental aspects of CRNs since optimizing both may lead to energy efficiency (EE) and spectral efficiency (SE) improvements, while simultaneously satisfying the necessary power density spectral masks for underlay mode. Moreover, to further explore the diversity dimensions, cooperative communications can be used in the CRN aiming to improve its performance.

In this chapter, we present a discrete resource allocation scheme for CRNs with delay tolerance and statistical quality of service (QoS).

11.1.1 Related Work and Contributions

Since it is seen as a promising technology for the fifth generation of mobile telecommunications which will be able to reduce the spectrum scarcity problem as well as cheapen the cost for telecommunications around the world, CRNs have been the subject of study for many researchers around the globe in the last decade.

First proposed by Mitola and Maguire [2], cognitive radio technology is mainly explored in two different frontiers: (1) to identify the spectrum holes, i.e., bands and subbands that are not being used in a specific geographic area and (2) how to use the available resources (spectrum and energy) in an optimized way to maximize the EE, SE, and social fairness, etc.

This chapter mainly focuses on the resource allocation with an emphasis on cross-layer optimization along with a plain overview of the work done in this area. For instance, in [3], a framework for the cognitive radio–assisted cooperation scheme for downlink transmissions in orthogonal frequency division multiple access (OFDMA)–based networks is proposed. Subcarrier allocation as well as power allocation algorithms are designed based on Lagrange dual decomposition method, and simulations show a performance increase compared to noncooperative and time-sharing cooperative schemes. In [4], the concept of effective capacity (EC) is used in a cognitive radio scenario along with the spectrum-sensing employed technique to create a power allocation scheme. The optimization problem is solved through the Lagrange multipliers method.

Akin and Gursoy [5] investigated the performance of different transmission schemes in CRNs with the statistical QoS provisioning—channel sensing parameters, throughput, and QoS constraints, on both underlay and overlay transmission modes, analyzed to determine their impact in the overall system performance. Shen et al. [6] presented algorithms that maximize the throughput in the cooperative sensing cognitive radios and also proved that the optimization problem inherent to the transmission scheme can be converted into a convex optimization problem and thus can be solved using robust techniques.

To propose a new resource allocation scheme, this chapter solves the spectrum allocation and power control problems for OFDMA-based relay-assisted CRNs by two different PUs or primary cells; broadcasting cells, such as television broadcast, emergency broadcast services, and radio stations; and dynamic cells, such as Wi-Fi access points (routers), GSM, 3G, and 4G networks. Also, to be deployable the proposed resource allocation algorithm is a deterministic discrete algorithm. The numerical results presented herein show the system parameters impact as well as the resource allocation scheme's overall performance.

11.1.2 Cognitive Radio Systems

Consider an OFDMA cooperative system with a CRN geographically overlapped with a PU cell (PUC) and a broadcast service area (BSA). The spectrum is composed of continuous transmissions in predefined bandwidths (BSA) and dynamic transmissions which may occur in different spectrum bands at different times. In terms of commercial scenarios, the first kind of PUC is equivalent to broadcasting services in urban areas such as television channels, radio stations, and other regulated bands that bear almost nonstop transmissions. On the other hand, a different mobile communication technology can be considered as an example for dynamic transmissions, since the allocated bands and subbands change with time.

In both the scenarios, each cognitive radio may transmit using three different types of channels: N_d dedicated channels, which are only used by the CRN; unused regulated channels (overlay mode), e.g., a television channel whose owner does not broadcast in some area; and used regulated channels, in which the cognitive radio transmission may not surpass a predetermined interference level on the PU signal (underlay mode), e.g., Wi-Fi, 3G, and 4G networks.

Hence, we first introduce the array $\phi = [\phi_1, \phi_2, \dots, \phi_{N_c}] = \{0,1\}^{N_c}$, where N_c is the number of cognitive radio channels. Note that ϕ is a binary variable, hence $\phi_n = 1$ means the nth channel is busy, i.e., it is being used by the PU, and $\phi_n = 0$ characterizes that the cognitive radio channel is available for the SU transmissions as illustrated in Figure 11.1.

The proposed scenario is presented in Figure 11.2, in which three different services are present in the same environment: a regulated broadcast service, a primary-cell base

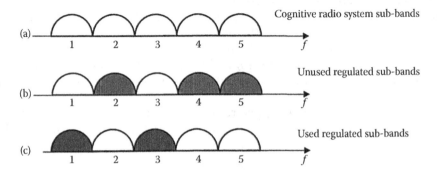

FIGURE 11.1

(a) Example of five sub-bands used in a cognitive radio network (CRN). (b) The colored sub-bands are unused, i.e., $\phi_2 = \phi_4 = \phi_5 = 0$; therefore overlay mode is used in those sub-bands. (c) The colored sub-bands are used by primary users, i.e., $\phi_1 = \phi_3 = 0$; therefore underlay mode has to be used on those sub-bands.

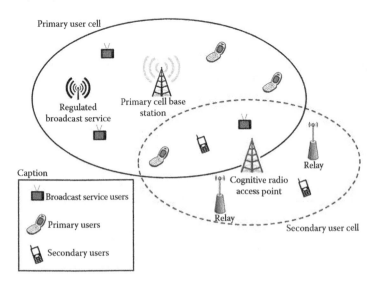

FIGURE 11.2

CRN and primary cell configuration.

station, and a relay-assisted CRN. The broadcast service operates constantly such that the values of ϕ for that service channel are always constant. The primary cell service, on the other hand, operates dynamically such that the users in that network may stop using the service or become active at a certain time slot. Therefore, the transition between busy and channel-free states of the PUC can be modeled as a Markovian process and each channel has a probability of changing the states during the spectrum-sensing phase. Finally, the relay-assisted CRN operates using a reserved spectrum as well as opportunistically transmitting over the spectrum dedicated to other two services. Besides, in the CRN, the transmission may occur with or without the assistance of relays such that the CRN access point (AP) is responsible for resource allocation and thus defines how to communicate with each SU.

Therefore, after probing the spectrum and defining which channels are available for underlay and overlay transmission modes, the CRN AP separates the spectrum into sub-bands or subcarriers which are then allocated to the users based on factors, such as maximum transmission rate, EE, and social fairness.

Herein the subcarrier allocation is represented through the α, β, and γ (hyper)matrices for which each $\alpha_{k,n} \in \{0,1\}$ represents the subcarrier assignment of user k and subchannel n using the direct link between the AP and SU; $\beta_{r,n} \in \{0,1\}$ is the subcarrier assignment between the AP and relay station (RS) r, and $\gamma_{r,k,n_1,n_2} \in \{0,1\}$ is the subcarrier allocation between the rth RS and the kth cognitive radio user using the channel n_1 on the first hop and channel n_2 on the second hop.

Figure 11.3 illustrates the probing (spectrum sensing) and transmission phases, with the allocated spectrum and transmission power, for a scenario with broadcast, PU, and SU services in the overlay and underlay modes. Power spectrum density for both the broadcast and primary cell services is shown in Figure 11.3a. The white spaces (or spectrum holes)

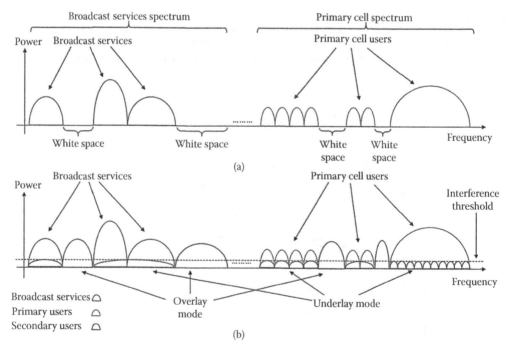

FIGURE 11.3
CRN scenario configuration.

are identified as unused bands/sub-bands. Transmission phase of the CRN is presented in the form of power spectral density of three different services (Figure 11.3b). This phase occurs once the subcarrier and power allocation procedures are performed on the CRN AP. As stated earlier, these procedures are of paramount importance to achieve the optimization goals such as the maximum EE and SE.

Since this scenario considers a relay-assisted CRN, it is important to reconsider the three different transmission modes used in direct transmission, half-duplex relay-assisted transmission, and full-duplex relay-assisted transmission. Direct transmission provides a direct communication between the CRN AP and SU. Half- and full-duplex relay-assisted transmissions refer to the relay-assisted transmission modes in which the transmission can occur using either only one channel for both AP-RS hop and RS-SU hop (half-duplex) or different channels for each hop. Therefore, the number of bits that can be transmitted depend directly on the transmission mode.

11.2 System Model

Consider the downlink of a relay-assisted CRN such that $N = N_d + N_c$ is the number of available subchannels. There are K users in the system and R RSs. The direct mode transmission has a superior bound of the number of bits transmitted per unit of bandwidth, given by Shannon–Hartley theorem:

$$b_{k,n}^D = \log_2\left(1 + \frac{p_{k,n}}{N_0 B}\frac{h_{k,n}}{(d_k)^\lambda \Gamma}\right) \tag{11.1}$$

where k and n are the SU and subcarrier indexers, respectively; $p_{k,n}$ is the transmission power; $h_{k,n}$ is channel power gain between AP and kth SU on subchannel n; Γ is signal-to-noise ratio (SNR) gap; N_0 is the noise power spectral density; B in the subchannel bandwidth; d_k is the distance between the AP and the kth SU; and λ is the path-loss exponent.

For the multilevel quadrature amplitude modulation (M-QAM) with gray coding, the SNR gap is bounded according to [7]

$$\Gamma \geq \frac{1}{3}\left(Q^{-1}\left[\frac{Pe}{4}\right]\right)^4 \tag{11.2}$$

where Pe is the bit error probability and the Q function is defined as follows:

$$Q(x) = \frac{1}{\sqrt{2\pi}}\int_x^\infty e^{-t^2/2}\,dt \tag{11.3}$$

For a nonsquare M-QAM, the SNR gap is the strict inequality of Equation 11.2. For simplicity's sake, we assume that the SNR gap is equivalent for both square and nonsquare M-QAMs, and is computed through the equality in Equation 11.2.

The half-duplex transmission scheme is limited by the time-sharing factor $S \in (0,1)$ and the lowest SNR. Considering that the cognitive radio user receives both the direct path signal and the relayed one, and that maximum ratio combining is implemented at the user receiver, the upper bound for the number of bits transmitted by a unit of bandwidth is given as follows:

$$b_{r,k,n}^{H} = \frac{1}{2} \min \left\{ \log_2 \left(1 + \frac{p_{r,n}}{N_0 B} \frac{z_{r,n}}{(d_r)^{\lambda} \Gamma} \right), \log_2 \left(1 + \frac{p_{r,n} h_{k,n}}{(d_k)^{\lambda} \Gamma N_0 B} + \frac{p_{r,k,n} g_{r,k,n}}{(d_{r,k})^{\lambda} \Gamma N_0 B} \right) \right\} \quad (11.4)$$

where n is the subcarrier indexer, $p_{k,n}$ is the transmission power, $h_{k,n}$ is the direct path complex channel gain between the AP and the SU, $z_{r,n}$ is the channel power gain between the AP and the rth RS, $p_{r,k,n}$ is the transmission power between the RS r and SU k, $g_{r,k,n}$ is the channel power gain between the rth RS and the kth user, d_k is the distance between the AP and the kth SU, d_r is the distance between the AP and the rth RS, and $d_{r,k}$ is the distance between the RS r and the kth SU.

Similarly, the full-duplex transmission scheme is limited only by the lowest SNR; therefore, the upper bound of bits transmitted per bandwidth unit is equivalent of the half-duplex mode with $S = 1$, i.e.,

$$b_{r,k,n_1,n_2}^{F} = \min \left\{ \log_2 \left(1 + \frac{p_{r,n_1}}{N_0 B} \frac{z_{r,n_1}}{(d_r)^{\lambda} \Gamma} \right), \log_2 \left(1 + \frac{p_{r,n_1} h_{k,n_1}}{(d_k)^{\lambda} \Gamma N_0 B} + \frac{p_{r,k,n_2} g_{r,k,n_2}}{(d_{r,k})^{\lambda} \Gamma N_0 B} \right) \right\} \quad (11.5)$$

where $n_1 \neq n_2$, n_1 and n_2 are the first and second hop channels, respectively.

11.2.1 Effective Capacity in OFDMA Relay-Assisted CRNs

The concept of EC was first proposed by Wu and Negi [8] and is associated to queuing models in the data-link layer for delay sensitive communications. The EC mathematical model can be compared with a first-in first-out buffering system which is employed to match the input rate (arrival process) in the link control layer to the output rate (service process) in the physical layer. Its existence prevents data loss, since any delayed traffic is stored in the buffer until it can be transmitted.

Assuming that the arrival and service processes are stationary, then for a given time t, the QoS exponent θ, which represents the decay rate of the tail distribution of the queue length $Q(t)$, satisfies [9]

$$\lim_{q \to \infty} \frac{\ln \left(\Pr \left(Q(t) \geq q \right) \right)}{q} = -\theta \quad (11.6)$$

i.e., the probability of the queue length exceeding a certain threshold q decays exponentially fast as the threshold q increases. As a consequence, given a large tolerable stationary queue length q_{max}, the following approximation is valid for the buffer violation probability [9]:

$$\Pr \left(Q(t) \geq q_{max} \right) \approx e^{-q_{max} \theta} \quad (11.7)$$

Therefore, a small value of $\theta > 0$ implies a slower decay rate which means the system delay constraints are less restrictive. On the other hand, a larger θ means the decay rate is faster and therefore the system delay requirements are too restrictive. Particularly, when $\theta \to 0$ the system can tolerate a delay of arbitrary size, and when $\theta \to \infty$ the system cannot tolerate any delay. Similarly, when the communication link experiences an observable delay D and considering that the maximum tolerable delay is $d_{\max}$ the following approximation holds [8]

$$\Pr\left(D \geq d_{\max}\right) \approx e^{-\theta\, \tilde{r} d_{\max}} \leq \epsilon \tag{11.8}$$

where $\tilde{r}$ is the arrival process rate (in bits per second) and ϵ is the delay bound violation probability. The QoS exponent for a given user can be determined as follows:

$$\theta \geq \frac{-\log(\epsilon)}{\tilde{r} d_{\max}} \left[\frac{1}{\text{bits}}\right] \tag{11.9}$$

When the delay bound is the main QoS metric it is possible to derive the following QoS metric:

$$\theta_D = \theta r = \frac{-\log(\epsilon)}{d_{\max}} \tag{11.10}$$

Hence, EC can be interpreted as the maximum and constant supported rate given a maximum delay bound and it is the probability of violation. As discussed in [8–14], EC for the OFDM channels can be described as follows:

$$C = -\frac{1}{\theta} \ln\left(\mathbb{E}\left[e^{-\theta T B \log_2(1+\text{SNR})}\right]\right) \tag{11.11}$$

where $\mathbb{E}[\cdot]$ is the mathematical expectation operator, T is the transmission period, B is the channel bandwidth, and SNR is the signal-to-noise power ratio. Equation 11.11 can be extended to find the EC in terms of supported bits/s per unit of bandwidth (bits/s/Hz). Hence, for the kth user on the nth subchannel of a CRN, the direct channel transmission EC can be defined as follows:

$$C_{k,n} = -\frac{1}{\theta_k} \ln\left(\mathbb{E}\left[\mathcal{I}_{k,n}\right]\right) \tag{11.12}$$

where

$$\mathcal{I}_{k,n} = \exp\left(-\theta_k \log_2\left(1 + \frac{p_{k,n}}{N_0 B} \frac{h_{k,n}}{\left(d_k\right)^\lambda \Gamma}\right)\right) \tag{11.13}$$

To simplify the notation, consider the following definitions:

$$P_{k,n} = \frac{p_{k,n}}{\left(d_k\right)^\lambda \Gamma N_0 B} \tag{11.14}$$

$$P_{r,n} = \frac{p_{r,n}}{\left(d_r\right)^\lambda \Gamma N_0 B} \tag{11.15}$$

$$P_{r,k,n} = \frac{p_{r,k,n}}{\left(d_{r,k}\right)^\lambda \Gamma N_0 B} \tag{11.16}$$

For non-line of sight (NLOS) channels, for which the channel power gain assumes an exponential distribution, the random variable $\omega_{k,n} = P_{k,n} h_{k,n}$ is an exponentially distributed random variable with $P_{k,n}$ mean and probability density function $f(\omega_{k,n}) = (1 / P_{k,n})e^{-(1/P_{k,n})\omega_{k,n}}$ the EC can be computed as follows:

$$\mathbb{E}[\mathcal{I}_{k,n}] = \int_0^\infty \exp\left(-\theta_k \log_2\left(1 + \omega_{k,n}\right)\right) \ f\left(\omega_{k,n}\right) \ \mathrm{d}\omega_{k,n} \tag{11.17}$$

$$\mathbb{E}[\mathcal{I}_{k,n}] = \int_0^\infty \exp\left(-\theta_k \log_2\left(1 + \omega_{k,n}\right)\right) \ \frac{1}{P_{k,n}} e^{-\frac{1}{P_{k,n}}\omega_{k,n}} \mathrm{d}\omega_{k,n} \tag{11.18}$$

$$\mathbb{E}[\mathcal{I}_{k,n}] = \left(\frac{1}{P_{k,n}}\right)\exp\left(\frac{1}{P_{k,n}}\right)E_{A_k}\left[\frac{1}{P_{k,n}}\right] \tag{11.19}$$

where $A_k = \dfrac{\theta_k}{\ln(2)}$ and $E_A[x] = \int_1^\infty e^{-xt} t^{-A}\mathrm{d}t$. Hence EC for direct transmission considering NLOS channels is as follows:

$$C_{k,n}^D = -\frac{1}{\theta_k}\ln\left(\left(\frac{1}{P_{k,n}}\right)\exp\left(\frac{1}{P_{k,n}}\right)E_{A_k}\left[\frac{1}{P_{k,n}}\right]\right) \tag{11.20}$$

Figure 11.4 illustrates the differences between continuous and discrete ECs as well as the results considering $\Gamma > 0$.

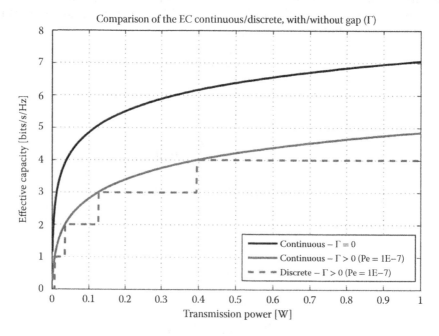

FIGURE 11.4
Effective capacity and transmission power for $\theta = 1, d = 1$ km, $\lambda = 4, N_0 = 4\times10^{-21}$ W/Hz, and $B = 100$ kHz.

The relay assisted transmission has its EC capped by the lowest EC link, i.e., EC is either AP-to-relay EC or the relay-to-mobile terminal EC. Considering NLOS channels, the AP-to-relay EC expression is similar to the direct link EC:

$$C_{r,n} = -\frac{1}{\theta_k} \ln\left(\left(\frac{1}{P_{r,n}}\right)\exp\left(\frac{1}{P_{r,n}}\right)E_{A_k}\left[\frac{1}{P_{r,n}}\right]\right)$$

(11.21)

EC of the link between the relay r and kth user is given as follows:

$$C_{r,k,n} = -\frac{1}{\theta_k}\ln\left(\mathbb{E}[\mathcal{I}_{r,k,n}]\right)$$

(11.22)

where

$$\mathcal{I}_{r,k,n} = \exp\left(-\theta_k \log_2\left(1 + P_{r,n}h_{k,n} + P_{r,k,n_2}g_{r,k,n_2}\right)\right)$$

(11.23)

We must first analyze the behavior of the random variables $z_{k,n}$ and $g_{r,k,n}$. Considering that both the channels experience NLOS fading, the random variables are exponentially distributed. The analysis is fulfilled by the following definition:

$$\begin{aligned}\delta_1 &= P_{r,n}\,h_{k,n}\\ \delta_2 &= P_{r,k,n}\,g_{r,k,n}\end{aligned}$$

(11.24)

Since $h_{k,n}$ and $g_{r,k,n}$ have unit mean, the probability density functions for δ_1 and δ_2 are as follows:

$$f_1(\delta_1) = \begin{cases} a_1 e^{-a_1\delta_1}, & \delta_1 \geq 0 \\ 0, & \delta_1 < 0 \end{cases}$$

$$f_2(\delta_2) = \begin{cases} a_2 e^{-a_2\delta_2}, & \delta_2 \geq 0 \\ 0, & \delta_2 < 0 \end{cases}$$

(11.25)

where $a_1 = \dfrac{(d_r)^\lambda \Gamma N_0 B}{p_{r,n}}$ and $a_2 = \dfrac{(d_{r,k})^\lambda \Gamma N_0 B}{p_{r,k,n}}$. The probability density function of $\delta = \delta_1 + \delta_2$ is equivalent to the convolution of both probability density functions given that δ_1 and δ_2 are independent process. Therefore,

$$(f_1 * f_2)(\delta) = \int_{-\infty}^{+\infty} f(\delta - \delta_2)g(\delta_2)\,d\delta_2$$

(11.26)

$$(f_1 * f_2)(\delta) = \int_{0}^{\delta} f(\delta - \delta_2)g(\delta_2)\,d\delta_2$$

(11.27)

$$(f_1 * f_2)(\delta) = \int_{0}^{\delta} a_1 e^{a_1(\delta - \delta_2)}a_2 e^{a_2\delta_2}\,d\delta_2$$

(11.28)

$$f(\delta) = \begin{cases} -\dfrac{a_1 a_2}{a_1 - a_2}\left(e^{-a_1\delta} - e^{-a_2\delta}\right), & a_1 \neq a_2 \\ (a_1)^2\,\delta\,e^{-a_1\delta}, & a_1 = a_2 \end{cases}$$

(11.29)

The probability density function $f(\delta)$ can now be used to find an analytical expression for the EC of the relay-assisted channel. Hence,

$$\mathbb{E}[\mathcal{I}_{k,n}] = \int_0^\infty \exp(-\theta_k \log_2(1+\delta))\ f(\delta)\ d\delta \tag{11.30}$$

$$\mathbb{E}[\mathcal{I}_{k,n}] = \begin{cases} \int_0^\infty e^{(-\theta_k \log_2(1+\delta))} \left(-\dfrac{a_1 a_2}{a_1 - a_2} \left(e^{-a_1\delta} - e^{-a_2\delta} \right) \right) d\delta \\[4mm] \int_0^\infty e^{(-\theta_k \log_2(1+\delta))} \left((a_1)^2\ \delta\ e^{-a_1\delta} \right) d\delta \end{cases} \tag{11.31}$$

$$\mathbb{E}[\mathcal{I}_{k,n}] = \begin{cases} \left(-\dfrac{a_1 a_2}{a_1 - a_2} \left(e^{-a_1} E_{A_k}[a_1] - e^{-a_2} E_{A_k}[a_2] \right) \right), & a_1 \neq a_2 \\[4mm] -\dfrac{(a_1)^2}{\theta_k - \ln(2)} \left(\ln(2) - e^{a_1} E_{A_k-1}[a_1] (\ln(2)(a_1-1)+\theta_k) \right), & a_1 = a_2 \end{cases} \tag{11.32}$$

Therefore, EC for the link between the relay and cognitive radio user in NLOS channels is given as follows:

$$C_{r,k,n} = \begin{cases} -\dfrac{1}{\theta_k} \ln \left(-\dfrac{a_1 a_2}{a_1 - a_2} \left(e^{-a_1} E_{A_k}[a_1] - e^{-a_2} E_{A_k}[a_2] \right) \right) & a_1 \neq a_2 \\[4mm] -\dfrac{1}{\theta_k} \ln \left(-\dfrac{(a_1)^2}{\theta_k - \ln(2)} \left(\ln(2) - e^{a_1} E_{A_k-1}[a_1] (\ln(2)(a_1-1)+\theta_k) \right) \right) & a_1 = a_2 \end{cases} \tag{11.33}$$

The EC of the relay-assisted communication channel is limited by the lower of the two effective capacities, i.e., it is either limited by AP-to-relay EC or relay-to-cognitive user EC. Also, the limitation depends on whether the system operates in full- or half-duplex. For half-duplex configuration, EC for NLOS channels is given as follows:

$$C_{r,k,n}^H = S \min\{C_{r,n}, C_{r,k,n}\} \tag{11.34}$$

If $a_1 \neq a_2$,

$$C_{r,k,n}^H = S \min \begin{cases} -\dfrac{1}{\theta_k} \ln (a_1 \exp(a_1) E_{A_k}[a_1]), \\[4mm] -\dfrac{1}{\theta_k} \ln \left(-\dfrac{a_1 a_2}{a_1 - a_2} \left(e^{-a_1} E_{A_k}[a_1] - e^{-a_2} E_{A_k}[a_2] \right) \right) \end{cases} \tag{11.35}$$

else,

$$C_{r,k,n}^H = S \min \begin{cases} -\dfrac{1}{\theta_k} \ln (a_1 \exp(a_1) E_{A_k}[a_1]), \\[4mm] -\dfrac{1}{\theta_k} \ln \left(-\dfrac{(a_1)^2}{\theta_k - \ln(2)} \left(\ln(2) - e^{a_1} E_{A_k-1}[a_1] (\ln(2)(a_1-1)+\theta_k) \right) \right) \end{cases} \tag{11.36}$$

Full-duplex EC is seen as a particular case of the half-duplex EC in which $S=1$. Also, AP-RS channel and RS-SU channel must be different, i.e.,

$$C_{r,k,n_1,n_2}^F = \min\{C_{r,n_1}, C_{r,k,n_2}\} \tag{11.37}$$

If $a_1 \neq a_2$,

$$C_{r,k,n_1,n_2}^F = \min \left\{ \begin{array}{l} -\dfrac{1}{\theta_k} \ln \left(a_1 \exp(a_1) E_{A_k}[a_1] \right), \\[4mm] -\dfrac{1}{\theta_k} \ln \left(-\dfrac{a_1 a_2}{a_1 - a_2} \left(e^{-a_1} E_{A_k}[a_1] - e^{-a_2} E_{A_k}[a_2] \right) \right) \end{array} \right\}$$ (11.38)

else,

$$C_{r,k,n_1,n_2}^F = \min \left\{ \begin{array}{l} -\dfrac{1}{\theta_k} \ln \left(a_1 \exp(a_1) E_{A_k}[a_1] \right), \\[4mm] -\dfrac{1}{\theta_k} \ln \left(-\dfrac{(a_1)^2}{\theta_k - \ln(2)} \left(\ln(2) - e^{a_1} E_{A_k - 1}[a_1] \left(\ln(2)(a_1 - 1) + \theta_k \right) \right) \right) \end{array} \right\}$$ (11.39)

where $a_1 = \dfrac{(d_r)^\lambda \Gamma N_0 B}{p_{r,n_1}}$ and $a_2 = \dfrac{(d_{r,k})^\lambda \Gamma N_0 B}{p_{r,k,n_2}}$.

11.3 Resource Allocation Problems in Relay-Assisted CRNs

To maximize the CRN EC, the following optimization problem can be posed through considering the individual effective capacities for each user in the system as well as for each subcarrier:

$$\text{maximize} \quad \sum_{k=1}^{K} \sum_{n=1}^{N} \alpha_{k,n} C_{k,n}^D + \sum_{r=1}^{R} \sum_{k=1}^{K} \sum_{n=1}^{N} \beta_{r,k,n} C_{r,k,n}^H + \sum_{r=1}^{R} \sum_{k=1}^{K} \sum_{n_1=1}^{N} \sum_{n_2=1}^{N} \gamma_{r,k,n_1,n_2} C_{r,k,n_1,n_2}^F$$

$$\text{s.t.} \quad (C.1) \sum_{n=1}^{N} \alpha_{k,n} C_{k,n}^D + \sum_{r=1}^{R} \sum_{n=1}^{N} \beta_{r,k,n} C_{r,k,n}^H + \sum_{r=1}^{R} \sum_{n_1=1}^{N} \sum_{n_2=1}^{N} \gamma_{r,k,n_1,n_2} C_{r,k,n_1,n_2}^F \geq C_{k,\min}, \quad \forall k$$

$$(C.2) \sum_{k=1}^{K} \alpha_{k,n} + \sum_{r=1}^{R} \sum_{k=1}^{K} \beta_{r,k,n} + \sum_{r=1}^{R} \sum_{n_1=1}^{N} \sum_{n_1=1}^{N} (\gamma_{r,k,n,n_1} + \gamma_{r,k,n_1,n}) \leq 1, \quad \forall n$$

$$(C.3) \sum_{k=1}^{K} \sum_{n=1}^{N} \alpha_{k,n} p_{k,n} + \sum_{r=1}^{R} \sum_{k=1}^{K} \sum_{n=1}^{N} \beta_{r,k,n} p_{r,n} + \sum_{r=1}^{R} \sum_{k=1}^{K} \sum_{n_1=1}^{N} \sum_{n_2=1}^{N} \gamma_{r,k,n_1,n_2} p_{r,n_1} \leq P_{\max}^{AP} \qquad (11.40)$$

$$(C.4) \sum_{r=1}^{R} \sum_{k=1}^{K} \sum_{n=1}^{N} \beta_{r,k,n} p_{r,k,n} + \sum_{r=1}^{R} \sum_{k=1}^{K} \sum_{n_1=1}^{N} \sum_{n_2=1}^{N} \gamma_{r,k,n_1,n_2} p_{r,k,n_2} \leq P_{\max}^{RS}$$

$$(C.5) \alpha_{k,n} \phi_n p_{k,n} + \beta_{r,k,n} \phi_n p_{r,n} + \beta_{r,k,n} \phi_n p_{r,k,n} \leq P_{th}^{\max}, \quad \forall r,k,n$$

$$(C.6) \gamma_{r,k,n_1,n_2} \phi_{n_1} p_{r,n_1} \leq P_{th}^{\max}, \quad \forall r,k,n_1,n_2$$

$$(C.7) \gamma_{r,k,n_1,n_2} \phi_{n_2} p_{r,k,n_2} \leq P_{th}^{\max}, \quad \forall r,k,n_1,n_2$$

$$(C.8) \phi_n, \alpha_{k,n}, \beta_{r,k,n}, \gamma_{r,k,n_1,n_2} \in \{0,1\} \quad \forall r,k,n,n_1,n_2$$

$$(C.9) p_{k,n}, p_{r,n}, p_{r,k,n} \geq 0 \quad \forall r,k,n$$

where (C.1) is the minimum EC condition ($C_{k,\min}$); (C.2) makes sure that only one user is transmitting on the nth channel; (C.3) is the maximum transmission power constraint at the AP ($P_{\max}^{AP}$); (C.4) is the maximum transmission power constraint at the RS ($P_{\max}^{RS}$); (C.5)–(C.7) are the maximum transmission power constraints in the underlay transmission mode ($P_{th}^{\max}$); (C.8) is the binary variables constraint; and (C.9) is the nonnegativeness power constraint.

Optimization problem is a mixed integer optimization problem, since the spectrum allocation variables are binary and the transmission power is nonnegative real-valued. The transmission power used in the current telecommunication systems does not assume continuous values. Since fractions of bits cannot be transmitted on a communication channel, the transmission power may also be considered discrete. Thus, the optimization problem can be seen as an integer programming problem.

The continuous relaxation can be considered as an upper bound for the original problem and is often solved using convex optimization techniques due to its concave programming.

EC maximization problem in relay-assisted CRNs is solved using a divide-and-conquer bit-loading algorithm, described in the following section.

11.3.1 Discrete Resource Allocation Algorithm

The following factors are considered to solve the optimization problem in a discrete domain:

- If (C.1) is too restrictive, the problem becomes a simple power control in which a minimum EC must be reached for each user. Note also that the problem may or may not have a solution.

- If (C.1) is inexistent, i.e., $C_{k,\min} = 0$ for all users, then the user with the lowest combination of QoS exponent and path loss will transmit in all available subcarriers.

- For any cooperative transmission, if the ECs on both the hops are different then power allocation is inefficient.

Therefore, the optimization problem can be first solved for the overlay mode channels and later for the underlay mode channels. Hence, the first subproblem that must be solved is the relay selection problem. Since the EC metric does not consider instantaneous channel state information, it is reasonable to establish the cooperative links based on the distance between AP-SU (d_k), AP-RS (d_r), and RS-SU ($d_{r,k}$). Then, the direct path is selected when the following condition is satisfied:

$$p_k < p_r + p_{r,k} \tag{11.41}$$

where p_k is the transmission power to achieve 1 bit/s/Hz through the direct channel, and p_r and $p_{r,k}$ are the transmission powers needed to achieve 1 bit/s/Hz on the first hop (AP-RS) and the second hop (RS-SU), respectively. Table 11.1 provides parameter values of the effect of path loss and relay positioning.

Figure 11.5 shows the transmission power for the direct transmission as well as full-duplex relay-assisted modes for different path-loss exponents considering the binary phase shift keying (BPSK) modulation. It is noteworthy that the best relay positioning configuration is where the first and second hops are equidistant, i.e., the distance between AP and RS is equal to the distance between RS and SU.

Although this approach offers a substantial reduction in the transmission power, the full-duplex transmission mode uses twice the spectrum band compared with the direct or half-duplex transmissions; hence, the SE in the channels allocated to full-duplex transmission

TABLE 11.1

Simulation Parameter Values to Determine
the Effect of Path Loss and Relay Positioning

K	1 User
N	1 Subcarrier
RS	1 Relay station
θ	1
Pe	10^{-7}
d_k	$\in \{0.4, 2\}$ km
d_r	$(0, d_k)$ km
$d_{r,k}$	$1 - d_r$

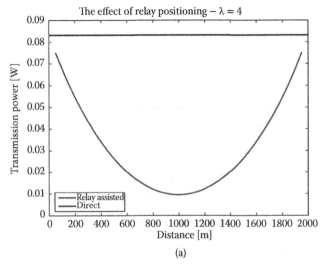

(a)

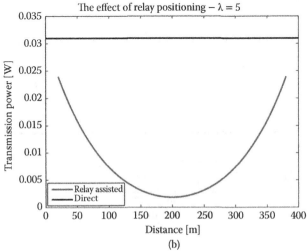

(b)

FIGURE 11.5
Relay positioning for different path-loss exponents: (a) $\lambda = 4$, $d_k = 2$ km, and (b) $\lambda = 5$, $d_k = 0.4$ km.

mode are halved. To keep up with the direct transmission SE and transmission rate, the relay-assisted communication must transmit twice the data carried out over a direct channel. Figure 11.6 shows the total transmission power for the direct and relay-assisted modes with the BPSK modulation (a) and 4-QAM (b). Simulation parameters are given in Table 11.1.

In Figure 11.6, relay positioning is even more important when a cooperative scenario with the same SE and transmission rate of a noncooperative one is considered. Since increase in the transmission power with transmission rate is nonlinear, cooperative

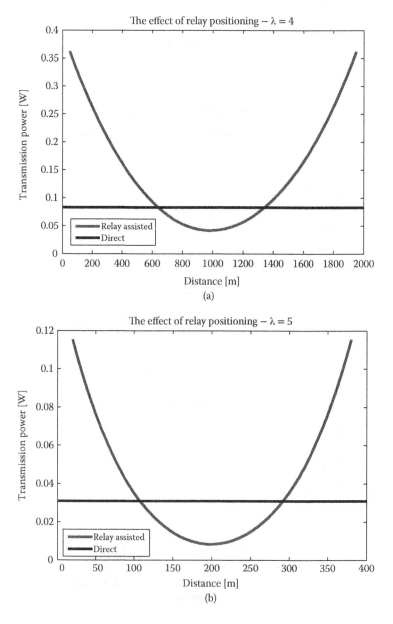

FIGURE 11.6
Relay positioning for different path-loss exponents considering the same spectral efficiency and transmission rate: (a) $\lambda = 4$, $d_k = 2$ km, and (b) $\lambda = 5$, $d_k = 0.4$ km.

communication for a few modulations uses more power to sustain the SE and transmission rate compared with a noncooperative communication scheme. Since this is not the focus of this chapter, we consider a cooperative scenario where the SE and system throughput are not necessarily the same as a noncooperative communication.

11.3.1.1 Power Control and Effective Capacity Maximization Routine

Once the relay selection is achieved, the algorithm must solve the second subproblem which is an equivalent form of power control and subcarrier assignment problem in the relay-assisted OFDMA-based networks. It is represented in the main optimization problem by the constraint (C.1). The classic power control and subcarrier assignment problem for an OFDMA-based relay-assisted CRN is given as follows:

$$\sum_{k=1}^{K}\sum_{n=1}^{N}\alpha_{k,n}C_{k,n}^{D} + \sum_{r=1}^{R}\sum_{k=1}^{K}\sum_{n=1}^{N}\beta_{r,k,n}C_{r,k,n}^{H} + \sum_{r=1}^{R}\sum_{k=1}^{K}\sum_{n_1=1}^{N}\sum_{n_2=1}^{N}\gamma_{r,k,n_1,n_2}C_{r,k,n_1,n_2}^{F} = C_{k,\min}, \quad \forall k$$

$$\text{s.t. (C.1)} \sum_{k=1}^{K}\alpha_{k,n} + \sum_{r=1}^{R}\sum_{k=1}^{K}\beta_{r,k,n} + \sum_{r=1}^{R}\sum_{n=1}^{N}\sum_{n_1=1}^{N}(\gamma_{r,k,n,n_1} + \gamma_{r,k,n_1,n}) \le 1, \quad \forall n$$

$$\text{(C.2)} \sum_{k=1}^{K}\sum_{n=1}^{N}\alpha_{k,n}p_{k,n} + \sum_{r=1}^{R}\sum_{k=1}^{K}\sum_{n=1}^{N}\beta_{r,k,n}\,p_{r,n} + \sum_{r=1}^{R}\sum_{k=1}^{K}\sum_{n_1=1}^{N}\sum_{n_2=1}^{N}\gamma_{r,k,n_1,n_2}p_{r,n_1} \le P_{\max}^{AP}$$

$$\text{(C.3)} \sum_{r=1}^{R}\sum_{k=1}^{K}\sum_{n=1}^{N}\beta_{r,k,n}\,p_{r,k,n} + \sum_{r=1}^{R}\sum_{k=1}^{K}\sum_{n_1=1}^{N}\sum_{n_2=1}^{N}\gamma_{r,k,n_1,n_2}p_{r,k,n_2} \le P_{\max}^{RS}$$

$$\text{(C.4)}\alpha_{k,n}\phi_n p_{k,n} + \beta_{r,k,n}\phi_n p_{r,n} + \beta_{r,k,n}\phi_n p_{r,k,n} \le P_{th}^{\max}, \quad \forall r,k,n$$

$$\text{(C.5)}\gamma_{r,k,n_1,n_2}\phi_{n_1} p_{r,n_1} \le P_{th}^{\max}, \quad \forall r,k,n_1,n_2$$

$$\text{(C.6)}\gamma_{r,k,n_1,n_2}\phi_{n_2} p_{r,k,n_2} \le P_{th}^{\max}, \quad \forall r,k,n_1,n_2$$

$$\text{(C.7)}\phi_n, \alpha_{k,n}, \beta_{r,k,n}, \gamma_{r,k,n_1,n_2} \in \{0,1\} \quad \forall r,k,n,n_1,n_2$$

$$\text{(C.8)}p_{k,n}, p_{r,n}, p_{r,k,n} \ge 0 \quad \forall r,k,n$$

(11.42)

The aforementioned optimization problem may also be solved as a convex optimization problem. However, due to the nature of the solution proposed here, the classical power control and subcarrier assignment will be solved through bit loading which increases the modulation scheme with the lowest energy cost at each iteration. Power allocation that grants b bits/s/Hz at each iteration can be determined by the Newton–Raphson method with an adaptive step size used to find the root of the following equation:

$$C_n - b_n = 0 \tag{11.43}$$

where C_n is the EC of the nth subcarrier given by equations, and according to the transmission mode related to that subchannel; and b_n is the number of bits allocated to the nth subcarrier. The pseudocode for the bit-loading algorithm is presented in Algorithm 1.

Once the power control and subcarrier assignment is complete, a new bit-loading algorithm takes place to keep allocating the power and subchannels until the maximum transmission power constraints are saturated, i.e., until any further bit allocation results in one (or both) of the following inequalities:

$$\sum_{k=1}^{K}\sum_{n=1}^{N}\alpha_{k,n}p_{k,n} + \sum_{r=1}^{R}\sum_{k=1}^{K}\sum_{n=1}^{N}\beta_{r,k,n}p_{r,n} + \sum_{r=1}^{R}\sum_{k=1}^{K}\sum_{n_1=1}^{N}\sum_{n_2=1}^{N}\gamma_{r,k,n_1,n_2}p_{r,n_1} > P_{max}^{AP} \tag{11.44}$$

and,

$$\sum_{k=1}^{K}\sum_{r=1}^{R}\sum_{n=1}^{N}\beta_{r,k,n}p_{r,k,n} + \sum_{k=1}^{K}\sum_{r=1}^{R}\sum_{n_2=1}^{N}\sum_{n_1=1}^{N}\gamma_{r,k,n_1,n_2}p_{r,k,n_2} > P_{max}^{RS} \tag{11.45}$$

The second bit-loading algorithm is presented in Algorithm 2.

11.3.1.2 Alternative Approach

To evaluate the proposed algorithm performance in terms of the total transmission power and achieved EC, a second approach is presented here. It consists of two main steps: the first one gives the same amount of subcarriers for each user in the system; therefore, when N is not a multiple of K, the remaining subcarriers are randomly allocated. The second

---

Algorithm 1 Bit-Loading Algorithm for Power Control and Subcarrier Assignment

---

Input: d_k, d_r, $d_{r,k}$, θ_k $\forall k, r$

Output: $p_{k,n}$, $p_{r,n}$, p_{r,k,n_1,n_2}, $\alpha_{k,n}$, $\beta_{r,k,n}$, γ_{r,k,n_1,n_2};

    $b_n = 0$, for all n;

   repeat

        Find the power that satisfies (43) for each user, channel and transmission mode with $b = b + 1$;

        Choose the user k, channel n and transmission mode whose transmission power increment is the lowest
one and the minimum effective capacity for that user has not yet been achieved;

        if $b_n = 0$ **then**

            Allocate the nth channel to the choosen user;

            Set $\alpha_{k,n}$, $\beta_{r,k,n}$, and γ_{r,k,n_1,n_2} according to transmission mode chosen;

        end if

        $b_n = b_n + 1$;

        if (C.4)—(C. 6) in (42) are not satisfied for the some channel **then**

            if $b_n = 1$ **then**

                Discard user and relay for that channel;

            else

                $b_n = b_n - 1$;

                Recalculate the allocated power for the new b;

            end if

        end if

   until (42) is solved

Algorithm 2 Bit-Loading Algorithm for Effective Capacity Maximization

---

Input: $d_k, d_r, d_{r,k}, \theta_k, b \; \forall k, r$

Output: $p_{k,n}, p_{r,n}, p_{r,k,n_1,n_2}, \alpha_{k,n}, \beta_{r,k,n}, \gamma_{r,k,n_1,n_2}$;

    $b_n = 0$, for all n;

    repeat

        Calculate (45) for each user, channel and transmission mode with $b = b + 1$;

        Choose the user k, channel n and transmission mode whose transmission power increment is the lowest one;

        if $b_n = 0$ **then**

            Allocate the nth channel to the choosen user;

            Set $\alpha_{k,n}, \beta_{r,k,n}$, and γ_{r,k,n_1,n_2} according to transmission mode chosen;

        end if

        $b_n = b_n + 1$;

        if (C.5)—(C. 7) in (42) are not satisfied for the some channel **then**

            if $b_n = 0$ **then**

                Discard user and relay for that channel;

            else

                $b = b - 1$;

                Recalculate the allocated power for the new b and skip the bit loading process on that channel;

            end if

        end if

    until (44) or (45) are satisfied

---

step sets the transmission power of the occupied cognitive channels to the threshold P_{th}^{max} and the remaining power is equally distributed over the dedicated and cognitive channels operating in the overlay mode.

11.4 Numerical Results

To evaluate the algorithm performance, simulations were conducted using MATLAB® Platform. The system simulation parameter values for the first scenario are presented in Table 11.2.

Figure 11.7 shows the geographical disposition of the SUs, RSs, and AP for scenario 1 with two SUs receiving information from the AP through relay-assisted communication. Evidently, user 1 is in the cell border, while user 2 is relatively close to the top right RS; hence, communicating with user 2 is easier (more power efficient) than user 1. Figures 11.8 and 11.9 show the proposed scheme performance in the first scenario (See Table 11.2) considering both cooperative and noncooperative communications.

Figure 11.8 shows the transmission power and EC evolution throughout the proposed algorithm iterations. For the proposed algorithm, there is a great increase in EC, as well as in transmission power, on the first iteration due to the subcarrier allocation procedure. The algorithm presents a final EC of 8.2 megabits per second (Mbps). On the other

TABLE 11.2

Simulation Parameter Values for the First Scenario

No. of users	$K = 2$
No. of dedicated channels	$N_d = 8$
No. of cognitive channels	$N_c = 8$
No. of subcarriers	$N = 16$
QoS exponent	$\theta_k = 0.5$ for all $k = 1, \ldots, K$
Bit-error-rate tolerance	$Pe = 10^{-3}$
Noise power spectral density	$N_0 = 4 \times 10^{-21}$
Subcarrier bandwidth	$B = 100$ kHz
No. of underlay mode subchannels	40% of N_c
Path-loss exponent	$\lambda = 4$
Maximum transmission power at AP	$P_{max}^{AP} = 2$ W
Maximum transmission power at each RS	$P_{max}^{RS} = 2$ W
Threshold transmission power for underlay channels	$P_{th}^{max} = 5$ mW
Minimum effective capacity	$C_{k,min} = 128$ Kbps, $k = 1, \ldots, K$

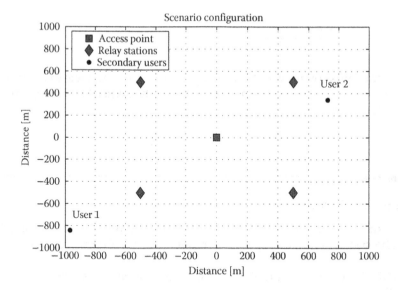

FIGURE 11.7
Secondary users, relay stations, and access-point geographic positioning in scenario 1.

hand, the noncooperative scheme achieves 7.6 Mbps and the alternative algorithm only 6.8 Mbps.

In Figure 11.9, we observe different power allocations for the two SUs in scenario 1 and how both the users achieve effective capacities greater than minimum one. It is also noteworthy how the border cell user 1 EC degrades without the cooperative

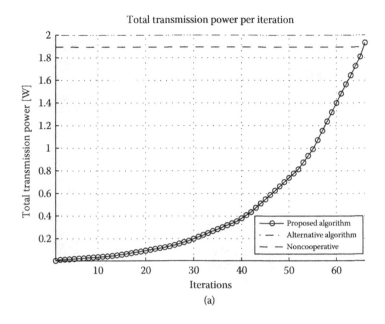

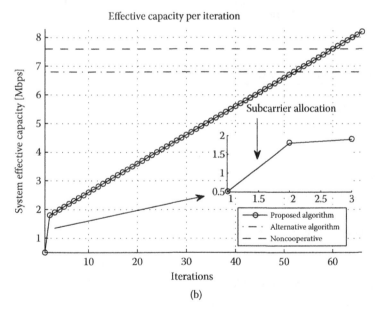

FIGURE 11.8
Total transmission power (a) and effective capacity (b) per iteration for scenario 1.

communication. The alternative algorithm loses in performance terms for both approaches since it is mainly in the subcarrier allocation policy instead of the power allocation routine.

To further analyze the proposed algorithm, Table 11.3 provides the simulation parameter values.

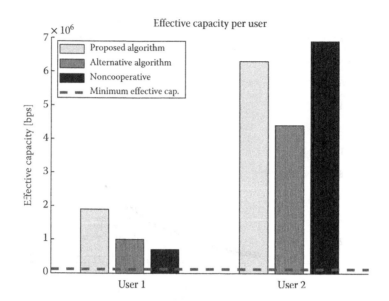

FIGURE 11.9

Effective capacity per user for scenario 1 using three different approaches: the proposed algorithm, the alternative algorithm, and the proposed algorithm without relay assistance.

TABLE 11.3

Simulation Parameter Values to Analyze the Proposed Algorithm

No. of users	$K = 3$
No. of dedicated channels	$N_d = 8$
No. of cognitive channels	$N_c = 8$
No. of subcarriers	$N = 16$
QoS exponent	$\theta_k = 0.5$ for all $k = 1, \ldots, K$
Bit-error-rate tolerance	$Pe = 10^{-3}$
Noise power spectral density	$N_0 = 4 \times 10^{-21}$
Subcarrier bandwidth	$B = 100$ kHz
No. of underlay mode subchannels	40% of N_c
Path-loss exponent	$\lambda = 4$
Maximum transmission power at AP	$P_{max}^{AP} = 2$ W
Maximum transmission power at each RS	$P_{max}^{RS} = 2$ W
Threshold transmission power for underlay channels	$P_{th}^{max} = 50$ mW
Minimum effective capacity	$C_{k,min} = 128$ Kbps for all $k = 1, \ldots, K$

Figure 11.10 shows the proposed algorithm evolution throughout the iterations as well as the other two approaches' performances, in terms of both the total transmission power and EC. One may observe that the proposed approach performance gets even more perceptive with the increase in system loading: the proposed algorithm now achieves 8.6 Mbps while the noncooperative scheme and the alternative algorithm achieve 6.8 and 5.2 Mbps, respectively.

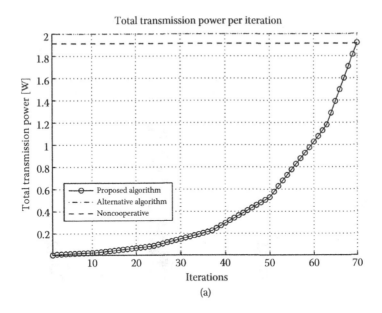

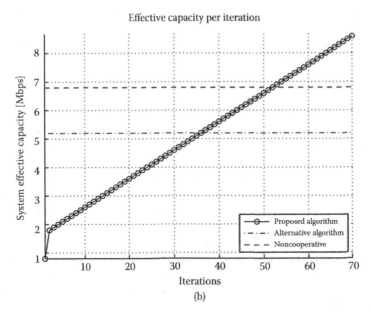

FIGURE 11.10
Total transmission power (a) and effective capacity and (b) per iteration.

In Figure 11.11, the EC of each user is presented for each of the three different approaches: the proposed algorithm, the alternative algorithm, and the noncooperative scheme. In the first scenario, most of the differences in results are related to the subcarrier allocation policies. The results for this scenario magnify the conclusion since the only approach where user 1 has the greatest EC occurs when the alternative algorithm is used.

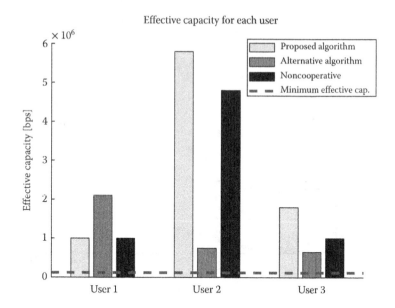

FIGURE 11.11
Effective capacity per user for scenario 2 using three different approaches: the proposed algorithm, the alternative algorithm, and the proposed algorithm without relay assistance.

11.5 Conclusions

In this chapter, we modeled and presented a discrete solution for the EC maximization optimization problem in cooperative cognitive OFDMA-based networks.

The impacts of cooperative communication were briefly analyzed in terms of the transmission power, transmission rate, and/or SE reduction. We also presented the simulation results to determine the best relay positioning between the SU and the AP.

Through simulations, the proposed algorithm is shown to outperform both the alternative approach and the noncooperative scenario, although further statistical analysis must be conducted to confirm the preliminary conclusions.

Future work includes analyzing the proposed approach in more realistic scenarios and the continuous relaxation version of the problem to present an upper bound for the problem solution (compared with discrete versions). Heuristics and convex optimization techniques are to be applied to solve the resource allocation problem in cooperative cognitive OFDMA-based networks.

References

1. Chen, B.X. (2013). AT&T Will Buy Some Verizon Spectrum for $1.9 Billion [Online]. Available at http://bits.blogs.nytimes.com/2013/01/25/att-will-buy-some-verizon-spectrum-for-1-9-billion/Œ_r=0
2. Mitola, J. and Maguire, G.Q. (1999). Cognitive radio: Making software radios more personal. *IEEE Personal Communications*, 6 (4): 13–18.

3. Cao, Y., Jiang, T., Wang, C. and Zhang, L. (2012). Crac: Cognitive radio assisted cooperation for downlink transmissions in OFDMA-based cellular networks. *IEEE Journal on Selected Areas in Communications*, 30 (9): 1614–1622.
4. Hammouda, M., Akin, S. and Peissig, J. (2014). Effective capacity in cognitive radio broadcast channels. *IEEE Global Communications Conference (Globecom 2014)*, Austin, TX.
5. Akin, S. and Gursoy, M. (2010). Effective capacity analysis of cognitive radio channels for quality of service provisioning. *IEEE Transactions on Wireless Communications*, 9 (11): 3354–3364.
6. Shen, J., Jiang, T., Liu, S. and Zhang, Z. (2009). Maximum channel throughput via cooperative spectrum sensing in cognitive radio networks. *IEEE Transactions on Wireless Communications*, 8 (10): 5166–5175.
7. Cioffi, J.M. (2015). A Multicarrier Primer [Online]. Available at http://web.stanford.edu/group /cioffi/documents/multicarrier.pdf. [Accessed 6 September 2015].
8. Wu, D. and Negi, R. (2003). Effective capacity: A wireless link model for support of quality of service. *IEEE Transactions on Wireless Communications*, 2 (4): 630–643.
9. Chang, C.-S. (1994). Stability, queue length, and delay of deterministic and stochastic queueing networks. *IEEE Transactions on Automatic Control*, 39 (5): 913–931.
10. Chang, C.-S. and Thomas, J.A. (1995). Effective bandwidth in high-speed digital networks. *IEEE Journal on Selected Areas of Communications*, 13 (6): 1091–1100.
11. Chang, C.-S. (2000). *Performance Guarantees in Communication Networks*. London, UK: Springer.
12. Ahn, S., Wang, H., Han, S. and Hong, D. (2010). The effect of multiplexing users in QoS provisioning scheduling. *IEEE Transactions on Vehicular Technology*, 59 (5): 2575–2581.
13. Qiao, D., Gursoy, M.C. and Velipasalar, S. (2009). The impact of QoS constraints on the energy efficiency of fixed-rate wireless transmissions. *IEEE Transactions on Wireless Communications*, 8 (12): 5957–5969.
14. Abrão, T., Sampaio, L., Yang, S. et al. (2016). Energy efficient OFDMA networks maintaining statistical QoS guarantees for delay-sensitive traffic. *IEEE Access*, 4: 774–791. doi: 10.1109/ ACCESS.2016.2530688

12

Interference Alignment in MIMO Cognitive Radio Networks

Manish Mandloi, Vimal Bhatia, and Robin Singh Bhadoria

CONTENTS

12.1 Introduction

With a rapid growth in the number of users, the demand for a higher throughput in wireless communication systems is also increased, which in turn requires an excessive use of the available spectrum. Scarcity of the available spectrum has become a big issue today as it is significantly underutilized due to the fixed spectrum licensing policies (Federal Communications Commission [FCC], 2005). With this motivation, the concept of cognitive radio (CR) has been proposed as a promising approach for efficient utilization of the available spectrum (Haykin, 2005; Kolodzy, 2005). CR relies on the fact that some frequency bands of the primary (licensed) users (PUs) are unoccupied or partially occupied most of the times. These unoccupied bands are called as white spaces. The main idea behind the cognitive radio network (CRN) is that a set of unlicensed devices called cognitive or secondary users (SUs) are allowed to use the white spaces without degrading the quality of service (QoS) of the PUs. Besides the availability of white spaces, SUs are allowed to send their information with power comparable to the noise level of the primary user (PU), in order to be considered as noise. The spectral efficiency of CRNs depends on the availability of white spaces in the primary network. The coexistence of PUs and SUs with the same radio resources results in an interference-intensive environment. Various techniques on interference management in CRNs are available in the literature based on the transmit precoding and transmit beam-forming in Wang et al. (2008), Yamaguchi (2004), and Phan et al. (2009).

Currently, multiple-input multiple-output (MIMO) systems are getting increased attention because of their capability to achieve higher capacity (Foschini and Gans, 1998). MIMO systems are well known for providing a higher multiplexing and diversity gain compared with the other systems which are equipped with single antennas. There are several challenges resisting the practical implementation of the MIMO systems which include modulation schemes, MIMO precoding, and symbol-vector detection. However, our major concern in this chapter is the precoding and postcoding in such systems. Under transmit power constraints in a MIMO link, if the channel state information (CSI) is known at the transmitter as well as at the receiver end, a famous algorithm called the water-filling algorithm can be used to allocate the power in the singular modes of channel matrix. Water-filling in singular modes is a spectral efficient way of power allocation with the limited power available at the transmitter. More recently, the focus is on the systems with a large number of antennas known as the large-MIMO systems (Chockalingam and Rajan, 2013). In this chapter, we consider that each user is equipped with multiple antennas and hence the channel between any two users will be a MIMO channel.

In a dense network scenario, occurrence of white space might be a rare event and thus no additional spectral efficiency could be achieved. Some extra tools are required to use the available resources more efficiently. Interference alignment (IA), a recently proposed interference-management technique, is an effective way to mitigate the interference and achieve the maximum degrees of freedom (DoF) in the wireless interference channels (Cadambe and Jafar, 2008; Maddah-Ali et al., 2008; Ghasemi et al., 2010). In IA, all the transmitters chose their precoder in a way that the undesired signal at each receiver is aligned in a single subspace and the desired signal is aligned in a separate subspace. The receiver linearly transforms the received signal in the subspace orthogonal to the subspace which contains only the interference signal. In dense CRNs, interference limits the system throughput, and hence, IA proves to be a better candidate to extract an additional spectral efficiency. The idea of IA in CRNs is based on the fact that, often, under power limitations, when the PU tries to maximize its rate using power allocation on singular modes of its channel, some of the singular modes are left unused or vacant. SUs can utilize these vacant modes by aligning their transmission along these modes without affecting the PU's performance (Perlaza et al., 2008, 2010; Amir et al., 2011). Using IA in CRNs, the SUs design their precoders in such a way that they do not cause any interference at the primary receiver. Furthermore, the postcoders at the secondary receivers are designed to suppress the interference received from the primary transmitter. In this chapter, we first discuss the basic IA technique in the multiuser (MU) MIMO networks, and then move on to IA in CRNs. We provide the proper design methods for pre- and postcoders in primary and secondary networks. We discuss IA in CRN with a PU and an SU, where the PU maximizes its transmission rate under power constraint and the SU utilizes the vacant singular modes. Further, we consider the case when there are MUs present in the secondary network.

12.2 Interference Management in CRNs

CR is a promising technique which allows the MUs to coexist with the licensed user. However, the interference in CRNs is a main issue which occurs due to the coexistence of PUs and SUs in a single network, sharing the same radio resources. A proper interference-management technique is thus required to control the interference in such networks. The presence of interference in the CRN slightly depends on the type of spectrum sharing models considered to achieve the spectral efficiency. In this section, we will briefly discuss the types of spectrum sharing techniques available in the literature (Kolodzy, 2005; Goldsmith et al., 2009). We will also discuss a metric used to measure or control the amount of interference generated at the primary receiver due to the secondary transmission.

12.2.1 Types of Spectrum Sharing in CR

There are mainly three different models of cognitive spectrum sharing which cognitive users follow based on the network-side information to utilize the licensed resources of the PUs (Kolodzy, 2005; Goldsmith et al., 2009). These models are classified as underlay spectrum sharing (USS), overlay spectrum sharing (OSS), and interweave spectrum sharing (ISS), respectively. Each model uses different strategies to access the licensed spectrum with minimum possible interference to the PU.

12.2.1.1 Underlay Spectrum Sharing

The USS model is based on the fact that the interference caused by the SUs at the primary receiver must be below a predefined threshold. In this setting, the SUs are assumed to have the knowledge about the interference they cause to the primary receiver. With this knowledge, SUs adaptively change their transmission power to maintain the interference below a predefined threshold value. These transmission restrictions imposed on the SUs limit their communication range. This model is mostly used when the occurrence of the spectrum holes is rare, such as in a dense network scenario.

12.2.1.2 Overlay Spectrum Sharing

In this model, cognitive users are aware of the codebook and message of a noncognitive user. With the help of this knowledge, cognitive users decode their own information from the received signal. The noncognitive user's information can be used to cancel/mitigate the interference caused by the cognitive user. However, decodability of the noncognitive users' information limits the transmission of the cognitive user. Although it sounds less practical, in such models it is assumed that the noncognitive users' information is known at the cognitive receiver prior to its own transmission.

12.2.1.3 Interweave Spectrum Sharing

This model is based on the concept of opportunistic spectrum access which was originally the motivation behind the CR systems. In interweave spectrum sharing, the vacant spectrum holes are being utilized by the cognitive users. While using the spectrum, the cognitive devices continuously keep track of it and stop their transmission whenever a PU is detected. In this type of spectrum sharing, no interference is caused to the PUs, but the presence of a spectrum hole is required for the secondary transmission to begin. This model could not be used in a dense network scenario where the occurrence of a spectrum hole is a rare event.

12.2.2 Interference Temperature

Interference temperature in the CRNs is a new metric to measure the amount of interference caused by secondary transmissions at the primary receiver (Haykin, 2005). It signifies the interference-tolerance capability of the primary receiver in the presence of an SU. Interference temperature limits the transmission power of the SU such that the QoS of the PU remains in the reliable region. In other words, an SU is allowed to use a frequency band as long as its transmission does not exceed the interference temperature limits. The underlay model of spectrum sharing highly requires such a metric at the primary receiver to limit the secondary transmission beyond the tolerance limit. There are several definitions available in the literature to compute this metric which depend on the geographical location of the users and their channel conditions. For more details on various definitions of the interference temperature, readers are referred to articles by Brown (2005) and Hong et al. (2008, 2009).

12.3 Basics of IA

Interference can be defined as a disturbance in communication between the desired pair of users. When the MUs coexist in the same network, sharing the same resources, interference is generated at all the receivers due to unwanted transmissions. Interference in MU wireless communication is a bottleneck to achieve a higher throughput gain. With an increasing number of users, interference in the network increases, and hence, the proper control of interference is highly required to achieve the maximum DoF. In wireless communications, DoF is defined as the ratio of the achieved sum capacity (C_{sum}) and the logarithm of total transmit power (P_t) at a high power level which can be given as

$$\text{DoF} = \lim_{P_t \to \infty} \frac{C_{sum}}{\log_2 P_t}$$

The DoF can also be defined as the number of interference-free signaling streams available for transmission. Proper alignment and cancellation of interference is thus required in an MU network to achieve the interference-free signaling streams. Solution to this is the pioneering work by Cadambe and Jafar (2008) on IA in the MU systems. Although there are several traditional interference avoidance schemes available in the literature, IA outperforms all in terms of DoFs. In this section, first, we discuss some of the traditional interference avoidance schemes and then provide a brief overview on IA in MU-MIMO networks.

12.3.1 Traditional Interference Avoidance Schemes

In wireless interference channels, a simple and effective way to avoid the weak interference is treating the interference as noise (TIN) at each receiver with modified statistical parameters such as variance and mean. More often, when the number of users grows, the interference power level increases and thus it cannot be treated as noise. However, recently several articles by Geng et al. (2015), Shang et al. (2009), and Annapureddy and Veeravalli (2009) focus on the optimality of TIN in the wireless interference channels. In some scenarios, when the interference power is strong compared with the signal power, the interfering signal can be decoded and cancelled from the received signal. The processed signal will then be free from the interference given the interfering signal is decoded correctly. In such situations, the decodability of interfering signal limits the achievable rate of other users, and hence is not a proper candidate for achieving higher throughput gains when the interference level is moderate.

Other methods used for interference avoidance are based on the orthogonalization of the available dimension, such as time or frequency. These schemes are known as time-division multiple access (TDMA) or frequency-division multiple access (FDMA) for sharing the available resources (Rappaport, 1996). In TDMA, the entire time slot is shared among the users in such a way that at a particular time only one user will occupy the entire frequency band. Per-user throughput in TDMA is inversely proportional to the number of users. This results in a number of user-dependent throughputs in TDMA. Similarly, in FDMA, the entire frequency band is divided into sub-bands and each sub-band is dedicated to a single user. This divides the entire bandwidth among the available users. In both these interference avoidance schemes (i.e., TDMA/FDMA), overall DoFs are divided equally among the users. In these schemes, when the number of users is high, the achievable DoF per user will be much less.

12.3.2 System Model

We consider a K-user pair MIMO system where each transmitter j is equipped with M_j transmit antennas, and each receiver j is equipped with N_j receiver antennas for $j = 1$, 2, ..., K, as shown in Figure 12.1. Let H_{ij} be $N_i \times M_j$ MIMO Rayleigh-faded channel matrix from jth transmitter to the ith receiver. The received vector at kth receiver is given by the following equation:

$$Y_k = \sum_{j=1}^{K} H_{kj} X_j + N_k \qquad (12.1)$$

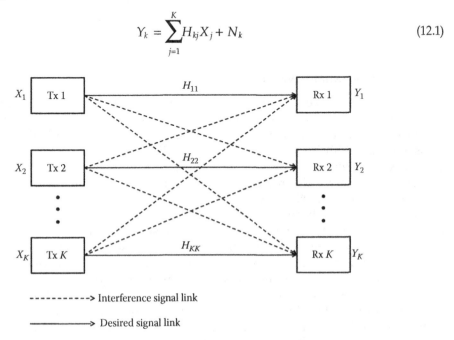

FIGURE 12.1
K-User MIMO interference channel.

$$Y_k = H_{kk}X_k + \sum_{\substack{j=1 \\ j \neq k}}^{K} H_{kj}X_j + N_k \tag{12.2}$$

where X_j is $M_j \times 1$ dimensional vector transmitted from the jth transmitter and N_k is the additive white Gaussian noise (AWGN) vector at the kth receiver, where each element is independent and identically distributed with zero mean and unit variance. We consider the global knowledge of channel state information (CSI) at each user (both transmitter and receiver). Let the transmit power at transmitter k assumed to be $E\left[X_k^2\right] = P_k$. In Equation 11.2, the first term denotes the desired signal from the desired transmitter and the second term corresponds to the interfering signal from the remaining $(K - 1)$ undesired transmitters.

We also consider a reciprocal channel as in Gomadam et al. (2008) for the K-user pair MIMO channel defined previously, where the roles of transmitters and receivers are interchanged. The assumption of such networks simplifies the iterative processing wherein both the transmitter and receiver jointly design the pre- and postcoders. The system equation in the reciprocal network is defined as follows:

$$\bar{Y}_k = \bar{H}_{kk}\bar{X}_k + \sum_{\substack{j=1 \\ j \neq k}}^{K} \bar{H}_{kj}\bar{X}_j + \bar{N}_k \tag{12.3}$$

where $\bar{Y}_k$ is the received vector at the kth receiver and $\bar{X}_k$ is the transmitted vector in the reciprocal network of the original system. The channel matrix in the reciprocal network is assumed to be $\bar{H}_{ij} = H_{ji}^{H}$. The transmit power in the reciprocal networks is assumed to be $E\left[\bar{X}_k^2\right] = \bar{P}_k$.

12.3.3 IA in MU-MIMO Networks

In this section, we give a brief overview of IA in MU-MIMO networks. IA is a promising technique to mitigate the effect of interference and achieve maximum DoF in the wireless interference channels (Cadambe and Jafar, 2008; Maddah-Ali et al., 2008; Ghasemi et al., 2010). The basic idea of IA is to align the transmission in such a way that the overall interference at the receiver falls in a single subspace called as interference subspace (IS) and the desired signal will lie in a distinct subspace called as desired subspace (DS). IS and DS are two separate subspaces which lie in a common subspace called the received subspace. The desired signal can be decoded without any interference by projecting the received signal onto the subspace orthogonal to the IS. Proper designs of pre- and postcoding matrices, at the transmitter and receiver end respectively, are required to achieve the alignment and cancellation of interference. Firstly, the precoding matrices to align the transmission are chosen jointly by all the transmitters so that at the receiver end, the interference caused by the undesired transmitters spans the same subspace. Let V_j be $M_j \times d_j$ precoder used for precoding the $d_j \times 1$ information symbol vector S_j at the jth transmitter, where d_j is the DoF required by the jth user. The transmit vector at the jth transmitter is given by $X_j = V_j \times S_j$. The received vector at the ith receiver can then be written as follows:

$$Y_i = H_{ii}V_iS_i + \sum_{\substack{j=1, \\ j \neq i}}^{K} H_{ij}V_jS_j + N_i \tag{12.4}$$

Precoders V_j for $j = 1, 2, ..., K$ are chosen based on the criteria given as follows:

$$\text{span}(H_{i1}V_1) = \text{span}(H_{i2}V_2) = \text{span}(H_{i3}V_3) = \cdots = \text{span}(H_{iK}V_K) \neq \text{span}(H_{ii}V_i)$$

where $i = 1, 2, 3, ..., K$. The above condition ensures that the overall interference at the ith receiver will span a single subspace. Once the precoders are designed, the postcoders are also designed at the receivers to project the received subspace onto a subspace which is orthogonal to IS in order to decode the signal free from interference. At the kth receiver, we process the received signal Y_k by using the precoder U_k^H as follows:

$$\tilde{Y}_k = U_k^H Y_k = U_k^H H_{kk} V_k S_k + \sum_{\substack{j=1, \\ j \neq k}}^{K} U_k^H H_{kj} V_j S_j + U_k^H Z_k \tag{12.5}$$

Thus, the design of postcoders at the receiver should satisfy following IA conditions to suppress the received interference from the undesired transmitters:

$$U_i^H H_{ij} V_j = 0, \quad \forall j = 1, 2, 3, ..., K, j \neq i$$

and

$$\text{rank}(U_i^H H_{ii} V_i) = d_i \ \forall \ i = 1, 2, ..., K$$

To satisfy the above IA conditions, the columns of U_i must be orthogonal to the columns of the matrix which are given by

$$I_i = \left[H_{i1}V_1, H_{i2}V_2, \cdots, H_{i(i-1)}V_{i-1}, H_{i(i+1)}V_{i+1}, \cdots, H_{iK}V_K \right]^H$$

which means that the columns of U_i must lie in the null-space of the matrix I_i. In the K-user scenario, through IA each user can achieve half of the total available DoFs in the system which is quite high compared with the traditional techniques, such as TDMA/FDMA and TIN. For a K-user interference channel with random time-varying coefficients, the sum capacity characterized in Cadambe and Jafar (2008) and Gomadam et al. (2008) is

$$C_{\text{sum}}(\text{SNR}) = \frac{K}{2} \log(\text{SNR}) + O(\log(\text{SNR})) \tag{12.6}$$

where SNR is defined as the signal-to-noise ratio and is equal to the total transmit power with the noise power of each user normalized to 1. Equation 12.6 shows that the capacity per user is 1/2 with an extra factor which depends on the logarithm of SNR, i.e., $O(\log(\text{SNR}))$ and is negligible at high SNR values. This means that through IA, each user achieves half the DoFs which could have been fully achieved in the absence of interferers. The feasibility of an IA depends highly on the suitable choice of pre- and postcoders which depends on the number of users, number of antennas at each user, and the DoF required by each user. For a brief overview on IA and its feasibility conditions, readers are recommended to refer to Jafar (2011). Several algorithms to achieve the IA are available in the literature (Peters and Heath, 2011; Santamaria et al., 2010; Kumar and Xue, 2010; Mohapatra et al., 2011; Nagarajan and Ramamurthi, 2010; Yu and Sung, 2010; Peters and Heath, 2009; Zhang et al., 2012; Nourani et al., 2009; Ganesan et al., 2011). In this chapter, we follow the iterative algorithm proposed by Gomadam et al. (2008) to align the interference in MU-MIMO networks. In Gomadam et al. (2008), the total leakage interference due to all undesired transmitters at each receiver is reduced iteratively. Under feasible conditions, the algorithm converges and results in a perfect alignment of interference. The steps followed in the IA algorithm in Gomadam et al. (2008) are given as follows:

Step 1: Choose arbitrary precoding and postcoding matrices at each user, respectively, i.e., $\{V_i\}_{i=1}^{K}$ and $\{U_i\}_{i=1}^{K}$.

Step 2: Compute the interference covariance matrix at each receiver i as

$$Q_i = \sum_{\substack{j=1, \\ j \neq i}}^{K} \frac{P_j}{d_j} \left(H_{ij} V_j V_j^H H_{ij}^H \right) \ \forall \ i = 1, 2, \ldots, K. \tag{12.7}$$

Step 3: Choose the postcoding matrix U_i at each receiver using the interference covariance matrix as

$$U_i = \varnothing_d [Q_i] \ \forall \ i = 1, 2, \ldots, K$$

where $\varnothing_d[A]$ denotes the d smallest eigenvectors of the matrix $\mathbf{A}$.

Step 4: Reverse the channel (i.e., the reciprocal network) and compute the interference covariance matrix in the reciprocal network using the postcoding matrices found in *Step 3* as

$$\bar{Q}_i = \sum_{\substack{j=1, \\ j \neq i}}^{K} \frac{\bar{P}_j}{d_j} \left(\bar{H}_{ij} \bar{V}_j \bar{V}_j^H \bar{H}_{ij}^H \right) \ \forall \ i = 1, 2, \ldots, K \tag{12.8}$$

where $\bar{V}_i = U_i$ in the reciprocal network.

Step 5: Choose the postcoding matrices in the reciprocal networks as

$$\bar{U}_i = \varnothing_d \left[\bar{Q}_i \right] \ \forall \ i = 1, 2, \ldots, K$$

where $V_i = \bar{U}_i$ is the precoding matrix at each transmitter.

Step 6: Reverse the direction of the transmission and repeat *Step 2* to *Step 5* till convergence.

Finally, a set of all the pre and potcoding matrices will be computed. Feasibility conditions and solvability of IA in MU-MIMO networks can be referred from Yetis et al. (2010). For further details on IA in MU-MIMO networks, we recommend readers to please go through several other IA algorithms proposed in Peters and Heath (2009, 2011), Santamaria et al. (2010), Kumar and Xue, (2010), Mohapatra et al. (2011), Nagarajan and Ramamurthi (2010), Yu and Sung, (2010), Zhang et al. (2012), Nourani et al. (2009), and Ganesan et al. (2011).

12.4 IA in MIMO CRNs

In CRNs, the main task of the SUs is to share the resources available with PUs in such a way that the SUs do not degrade the QoS of the PU. In Section 12.2.1, we discussed some of the spectrum sharing mechanisms in CRNs to manage the interference properly. However, in a dense network scenario, there may not be any white spaces available in the primary, and hence, the SUs will not be allowed to transmit their information. In such cases, the PUs allow a certain range of interference from the secondary transmitter which is called interference temperature as discussed in Section 12.2.2. In the absence of white spaces, some additional tools are required to achieve the spectral efficiency in CRNs. IA has been successfully applied in CRNs to achieve the additional spectrum efficiency under power constraints at the primary transmitter (Perlaza et al., 2008, 2010; Amir et al., 2011).

12.4.1 System Model

In this setup, we consider a CRN where there is a single point-to-point (P2P) MIMO link for a PU which coexists with another P2P-MIMO link of SU as shown in Figure 12.2. Let H_{PP}, H_{SS} be the direct channel links for the PUs and SUs, respectively. H_{PS} and H_{SP} denote the interference link from the secondary transmitter to primary receiver and from the primary transmitter to the secondary receiver, respectively. We assume that the PU is unaware of the presence of the SU, and thus it does not participate in IA. Signal alignment and interference suppression is done at the secondary transmitter and receiver, respectively. Furthermore, we also assume that the PU uses V_P and U_P as precoder and postcoder matrix to achieve the maximum throughput on the direct link H_{PP}.

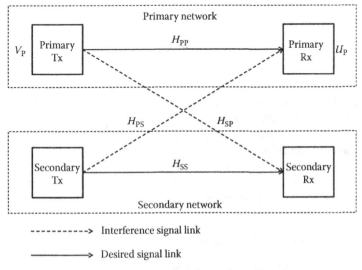

FIGURE 12.2
A MIMO cognitive radio network with a single primary and single secondary user pair.

12.4.2 Signal Alignment in Primary Network

In a P2P-MIMO link, under power constraints, the throughput can be maximized by using the well-known water-filling algorithm for power allocation (Tse and Vishwanath, 2005). In this algorithm, most of the transmit power is allocated to the singular modes with higher singular value of the channel matrix. With the help of water-filling over the singular modes of the channel matrix, the precoder and postcoder are designed in the primary network in such a way that the PUs throughput can be maximized. The singular value decomposition (SVD) of a primary MIMO channel matrix H_{PP} is given by

$$H_{PP} = U_0 \Lambda_0 V_0^H \tag{12.9}$$

where Λ_0 is an $M_P \times M_P$ dimensional diagonal matrix whose diagonal entries are nonnegative singular values of the channel matrix arranged in a descending order. The columns of U_0 and V_0 contain the left and the right singular vectors of the channel matrix H_{PP}, respectively. The columns of precoder (V_P) and postcoder (U_P) are chosen such that they maximize the primary rate given by

$$\max_{\text{trace}(P_0) \le P_{\max}} \log_2 \left| I_M + \frac{1}{\sigma} H_{PP} V_P P_0 V_P^H H_{PP}^H \right| \tag{12.10}$$

where σ is the per antenna noise variance of AWGN noise at the primary receiver. The optimal solution to the optimization problem in Equation 12.10 is given by the classical water-filling algorithm. The optimal power allocation matrix is a diagonal matrix with its diagonal elements given as follows:

$$P_o(i,i) = \left[\beta - \frac{\sigma^2}{\lambda_i^2} \right]^+ \forall \ i = 1, 2, \ldots, M \tag{12.11}$$

where $[a]^+$ denotes the maximum of $(0, a)$ and β is the Lagrangian multiplier which can be determined by using the following criteria:

$$\sum_{i=1}^{M} P_0(i,i) = P_{\max} \tag{12.12}$$

Often, after power allocation in the primary link's singular modes, some of the modes are left vacant. These vacant modes can then be utilized by SUs without affecting the QoS of PUs. Let us assume that power allocation (PA) allocates d_0 singular modes out of available M modes. In other words, the primary transmitter aligns its transmission in the subspace spanned by the first d_0 column vectors of the matrix V_P and in a similar way, the receiver aligns its reception in the subspace spanned by the first d_0 column vectors of matrix U_P. Thus, the number of vacant modes will be $M-d_0$. Secondary transmitters can use $M-d_0$ modes only for transmitting their information to their corresponding receivers.

12.4.3 Signal and IA in Secondary Network

In CRN, since the PU is unaware of the presence of SU, the SU transmission should be in a way that it does not affect the QoS of the PU. IA in CRN is a powerful interference mitigation technique which ensures that the transmission from the SU does not provide any interference to the primary receiver. It also empowers the secondary receiver with sufficient tools to suppress the interference it receives from the primary transmitter. Let us assume that the secondary transmitter precodes the transmit signal S_{St} using the precoder matrix G_S. The transmit signal from the secondary transmitter can be written as $X_S = G_S S_{St}$. At the primary receiver, the received signal can be written as follows:

$$Y_P = \underbrace{H_{PP}V_P S_{Pt}}_{\text{desired signal}} + \underbrace{H_{PS}G_S S_{St}}_{\text{interference signal}} + N_P \tag{12.13}$$

where N_P is the AWGN noise at the primary receiver. The primary receiver then filters the received signal by using postcoding matrix U_P given as follows:

$$\tilde{Y}_P = U_P^H Y_P = U_P^H H_{PP}V_P S_{Pt} + U_P^H H_{PS}G_S S_{St} + U_P^H N_P \tag{12.14}$$

The secondary transmitter chooses the precoder in such a way that the interference due to its transmission shrinks to zero at the primary receiver, i.e.,

$$U_P^H H_{PS}G_S = 0$$

Thus, the columns of G_S are chosen from the null-space of the matrix $U_P^H H_{PS}$. This selection of G_S results in the zero interference at the primary receiver and hence no degradation in QoS for the primary is caused. The received signal Y_S at the secondary receiver is given by

$$Y_S = H_{SP}V_P S_{Pt} + H_{SS}G_S S_{St} + N_S \tag{12.15}$$

The secondary receiver uses the postcoding matrix B_S in order to suppress the interference from the primary transmitter as follows:

$$\tilde{Y}_S = B_S^H Y_S = B_S^H H_{SP}V_P S_{Pt} + B_S^H H_{SS}G_S S_{St} + B_S^H N_S \tag{12.16}$$

To completely remove the interference from a PU, the columns of the postcoder B_S are chosen from the null-space of the matrix $(H_{SP}V_P)^H$, i.e., $B_S^H H_{SP}V_P = 0$. After processing the received signal, it can be rewritten as

$$\tilde{Y}_S = B_S^H H_{SS}G_S S_{St} + B_S^H N_S \tag{12.17}$$

From $\tilde{Y}_S$ the secondary receiver will extract the interference-free signal, transmitted by the corresponding transmitter in the interference-rich channel.

12.4.4 IA in CRNs with Multiple SUs

In Section 12.4.3, IA in CRNs is discussed for secondary networks with a single SU. However, in this section, we will discuss the IA in CRNs when a single primary P2P-MIMO link coexists with multiple SUs. In such a scenario, the interference at the primary receiver will be present from the multiple secondary transmitters. Also, the interference at secondary receivers will be due to primary as well as secondary transmitters.

Let us consider K SUs coexisting with a PU denoted by "0" as shown in Figure 12.3. We denote the channel between ith receiver and the jth transmitter as H_{ij} for $i = 0, 1, 2, ..., K$ and $j = 0, 1, 2, ..., K$. To start with, the PU allocates the total available transmission power

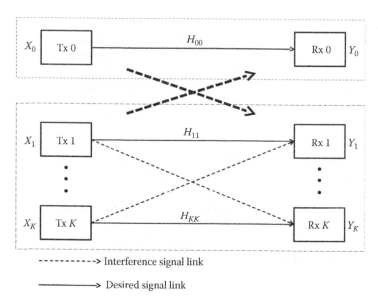

FIGURE 12.3
MU-MIMO secondary network with a single P2P-MIMO primary link.

on to the strong singular modes of the primary link H_{00} using the water-filling algorithm (as discussed in Section 12.4.2). Each SU then aligns its transmission and reception in the following two stages.

Stage 1: IA at SUs to avoid the interference to and from the PU

In this stage, the interferences caused by the secondary transmitters at the primary receiver and that at the secondary receivers due to the primary transmission are aligned. Each secondary transmitter designs the precoding G_i and the postcoding matrix B_i for $i = 1, 2, ..., K$, respectively, by using the method similar to one discussed in Section 12.4.3. This selection of G_i and B_i results in two separate networks (primary and secondary) coexisting without any interference between them. However, in a secondary network the interference at each secondary receiver will be present because of the presence of multiple SUs.

Stage 2: IA in secondary network

From stage 1, the interference caused to and from the PU is completely removed. However, in secondary networks, the interference will be present due to the MUs in the same network. In this stage, the SUs will modify their precoders and postcoders in such a way that the interference from the undesired users can also be cancelled. The received signal at the ith receiver can be written as follows:

$$Y_i = H_{ii}\hat{V}_i S_i + \sum_{\substack{j=1, \\ j \neq i}}^{K} H_{ij}\hat{V}_j S_j + N_i \tag{12.18}$$

where $\hat{V}_i = G_j V_j$ is the modified precoder at the ith transmitter. Equation 12.18 can be rewritten as follows:

$$Y_i = H_{ii} G_i V_i S_i + \sum_{\substack{j=1, \\ j \neq i}}^{K} H_{ij} G_j V_j S_j + N_i \tag{12.19}$$

The receiver then processes the received signal using the postcoding matrix as given as follows:

$$\tilde{Y}_i = \hat{U}_i^H Y_i = \hat{U}_i^H H_{ii} V_i S_i + \sum_{\substack{j=1, \\ j \neq i}}^{K} \hat{U}_i^H H_{ij} V_j S_j + \hat{U}_i^H N_i \tag{12.20}$$

where $\hat{U}_i = B_i U_i$ is the postcoding matrix at the ith receiver. The processed signal is expanded as follows:

$$\tilde{Y}_i = \hat{U}_i^H Y_i = U_i^H B_i^H H_{ii} V_i S_i + \sum_{\substack{j=1, \\ j \neq i}}^{K} U_i^H B_i^H H_{ij} V_j S_j + \tilde{N}_i \tag{12.21}$$

From Equation 12.21, the problem now reduces to finding suitable matrices V_i and U_i at each SU, i.e., $i = 1, 2, \ldots, K$. To solve this problem, we consider an equivalent system equation as follows:

$$\tilde{Y}_i = U_i^H \bar{H}_{ii} S_i + \sum_{\substack{j=1, \\ j \neq i}}^{K} U_i^H \bar{H}_{ij} S_j + \tilde{N}_i \tag{12.22}$$

where $\bar{H}_{ij} = B_i^H H_{ij} G_j$ is the equivalent channel matrix between the ith receiver and the jth transmitter in the new system which consists of SUs only. It can be noticed that the primary and secondary networks are separated in two different networks using the same radio resources, by proper design of G_i and B_i in stage 1. The problem of IA in the secondary network can be solved using the iterative algorithm (discussed in Section 12.3.3, i.e., the case of MU-MIMO network) with the equivalent channel matrix. The feasibility of IA depends on the number of users in the secondary network, the number of antennas at each user in primary as well as secondary network, and the total DoF required by the PU. A brief overview on feasibility conditions on IA can be found in Perlaza et al. (2008) and Amir et al. (2011). Several other articles on IA in CRNs such as Yang et al. (2013), Zhou and Thompson (2008), Rezai and Tadaion (2014), Koo and Park (2012), Chen et al. (2012), Lee et al. (2011), and Abdelhamid et al. (2012) discuss IA in CRNs with different techniques. In Koo and Park (2012), user cooperation–based IA in CRN is discussed where the PU cooperates with the SUs in designing the precoders (as discussed in Section 12.4.5), i.e., the primary receiver has the capability to suppress the interference caused by the secondary transmitters. This results in additional gain in the secondary throughput.

12.4.5 IA in CRNs with Primary Users' Cooperation

In this section, we briefly discuss the IA in CRNs when the primary receiver cooperates with the SUs in aligning the interference and signal in corresponding subspaces, which was discussed originally in Koo and Park (2012). Rather than aligning the signal in the direction of singular modes, the primary receiver participates in interference suppression which helps in increasing the data rate for SUs. This can be thought of as a compromise between IA with and without cognitive users. The achievable rate of the PU does not degrade much as long as the interference from the SUs does not spill out of the used singular modes into the modes used by the PU. The only change in this procedure lies in the design of the primary receivers' postcoding matrix. The primary receiver chooses its postcoding matrix from the smallest eigenvectors of the interference covariance matrix from the secondary transmitters. For completeness we present the procedure followed as in Koo and Park (2012).

Step 1: Precoder design at the primary transmitter using the SVD of primary channel matrix and choosing the precoder V_P at primary transmitter from the eigenvectors corresponding to the d largest eigenvalues of the matrix $(H_{00}^H H_{00})$, or by using the water-filling algorithm.

Step 2: Secondary receivers choose their postcoders by aligning their receiver in the direction of the unused singular modes.

Step 3: Secondary transmitters initialize their precoders arbitrarily.

Step 4: Based on the received interference covariance matrix, the primary receiver updates its postcoding matrix in the direction of the minimum eigenvalues.

Step 5: Secondary receivers update their postcoding matrices in a similar manner as in Section 12.4.3.

Step 6: Similarly, the secondary transmitters now update their transmission direction.

Step 7: *Steps 4* to *6* are repeated till convergence.

12.5 Conclusions

In this chapter, we discussed the IA in MIMO CRNs for achieving the additional spectral efficiency in a dense network scenario under the transmit power constraint at the PU. IA is a promising candidate through which maximum DoFs can be achieved in the wireless interference channel. The design of precoders and postcoders in CRNs with single and multiple SUs coexisting with a single PU is discussed. PU, under power constraint, allocates its power to the strong singular modes of the direct channel. The unused singular modes are then used by the SUs for their transmission without causing any interference at the primary receiver. It can also be viewed as opportunistic IA in CRNs, in the sense that the SUs actively search for the singular modes left vacant by the PU.

Acknowledgments

We thank our parents, IIT Indore, and the editors of the book for their support and motivation.

References

Abdelhamid, B., Elsabrouty, M., and Elramly, S. (2012). Novel interference alignment in multi-secondary users cognitive radio system. *2012 IEEE Symp. on Computers and Commun. (ISCC)*, 785–789.

Amir, M., El-Keyi, A., and Nafie, M. (2011). Constrained interference alignment and spatial degrees of freedom of MIMO cognitive networks. *IEEE Trans. Inf. Theory*, 57(5), 2994–3004.

Annapureddy, V. S., and Veeravalli, V. V. (2009). Gaussian interference networks: Sum capacity in the low-interference regime and new outer bounds on the capacity region. *IEEE Trans. Inf. Theory*, 55(7), 3032–3050.

Brown, T. X. (2005). An analysis of unlicensed device operation in licensed broadcast service bands. In *Proceedings of the IEEE DySPAN' 05*, Baltimore, USA, 11–29.

Cadambe., V. R., and Jafar, S. A. (2008). Interference alignment and degrees of freedom of K-user interference channel. *IEEE Trans. Inf. Theory*, 54(8), 3425–3441.

Chen, G., Xiang, Z., Xu, C., and Tao, M. (2012). On degrees of freedom of cognitive networks with user cooperation. *IEEE Wire. Commun. Lett.*, 1(6), 617–620.

Chockalingam, A., and Rajan, B. S. (2013). *Large MIMO Systems*. Cambridge: Cambridge University Press.

Federal Communications Commission (FCC). (2005). Facilitating opportunities for flexible, efficient, and reliable spectrum use employing cognitive radio technologies. FCC ET Docket No. 03-108.

Foschini, G. J., and Gans, M. J. (1998). On limits of wireless communications in a fading environment when using multiple antennas. *Wire. Pers. Commun.*, 6(3), 311–335.

Ganesan, R. S., Weber, T., and Klein, A. (2011). Interference alignment in multi-user two way relay networks. In *2011 IEEE 73rd Vehicular Technology Conference (VTC Spring)*, Yokohama, 1–5.

Geng, C., Naderializadeh, N., Avestimehr, A. S., and Jafar, S. A. (2015). On optimality of treating interference as noise. *IEEE Trans. Inf. Theory*, 61(4), 1753–1767.

Ghasemi, A., Motahari, A. S., and Khandani, A. K. (2010). Interference alignment for the K user MIMO interference channel. In *Proceedings of the IEEE International Symposium on Information Theory (ISIT)*, Austin, TX, 360–364.

Goldsmith, A., Jafar, S. A., Maric, I., and Srinivasa, S. (2009). Breaking spectrum gridlock with cognitive radios: An information theoretic perspective. *Proc. IEEE*, 97(5), 894–914.

Gomadam, K., Cadambe, V. R., and Jafar, S. A. (2008). Approaching the capacity of wireless networks through distributed interference alignment. In *Global Telecommunications Conference, 2008. IEEE GLOBECOM 2008. IEEE*, New Orleans, LO, 1–6.

Haykin, S. (2005). Cognitive radio: Brain-empowered wireless communications. *IEEE J. Sel. Areas Commun.*, 23(2), 201–220.

Hong, X, Chen, Z, Wang, C. X, Vorobyov, S. A., and Thompson, J. S. (2009). Cognitive radio networks. *IEEE Veh. Technol. Mag.*, 4(4), 76–84.

Hong, X., Wang, C. X., and Thompson, J. (2008). Interference modelling of cognitive radio networks. In *Proceedings of the IEEE VTC' 08 Spring*, Singapore, 1851–1855.

Jafar, S. A. (2011). Interference alignment: A new look at signal dimensions in communication networks. *Future Trend Commun. Inf. Theory*, 7(1), 1–136.

Kolodzy, P. J. (2005). Cognitive radio fundamentals. *SDR Forum*, Singapore.

Koo, B., and Park, D. (2012). Interference alignment with cooperative primary receiver in cognitive networks. *IEEE Commun. Lett.*, 16(7), 1072–1075.

Kumar, K. R., and Xue, F. (2010). An iterative algorithm for joint signal and interference alignment. In *Proceedings of the IEEE International Symposium on Information Theory (ISIT)*, Austin, TX, 2293–2297.

Lee, K. J., Sung, H., and Lee, I. (2011). Linear precoder designs for cognitive radio mutliuser MIMO downlink systems. *(ICC), 2011 IEEE International Conference on Communications*, Kyoto, 1–5.

Maddah-Ali, M. A., Motahari, A. S., and Khandani, A. K. (2008). Communication over MIMO X channels: Interference alignment, decomposition, and performance analysis. *IEEE Trans. Inf. Theory,* 54(8), 3457–3470.

Mohapatra, P., Nissar, K. E., and Murthy, C. R. (2011). Interference alignment algorithm for the *K* user constant MIMO interference channel. *IEEE Trans. Signal Proc.,* 59(11), 5499–5508.

Nagarajan, V., and Ramamurthi, B. (2010). Distributed cooperative precoder selection for interference alignment. *IEEE Trans. Veh. Technol.,* 59(9), 4368–4376.

Nourani, B., Motahari, S. A., and Khandani, A. K. (2009). Relay-aided interference alignment for the quasi-static X channel. *IEEE International Symposium on Information Theory, 2009. ISIT 2009.* Seoul, 1764–1768.

Perlaza, S. M., Debbah, M., Lausaulce, S., and Chaufray, J. M. (2008). Opportunistic interference alignment in MIMO interference channels In *IEEE 19th International Symposium on Personal, Indoor and Mobile Radio Communications, 2008. PIMRC 2008.* 1–5.

Perlaza, S. M., Fawaz, N., Lausaulce, S., and Debbah, M. (2010). From spectrum pooling to space pooling: Opportunistic interference alignment in MIMO cognitive networks. *IEEE Trans. Signal Proc.,* 58(7), 3728–3741.

Peters, S. W., and Heath Jr., R. W. (2009). Interference alignment via alternating minimization. In *ICASSP 2009. IEEE Intern. Conf. on Acoustics, Speech and Signal Proceedings 2009,* Taipei, 2445–2448.

Peters, S. W., and Heath Jr., R. W. (2011). Cooperative algorithms for MIMO interference alignment. *IEEE Trans. Veh. Technol.,* 60(1), 206–218.

Phan, T. K., Vorobyov, S. A., Sidiropolous, N. D., and Tellambura, C. (2009). Spectrum sharing in wireless networks via QoS-aware secondary multicast beamforming. *IEEE Trans. Signal Proc.,* 57(6), 2323–2335.

Rappaport, T. S. (1996). *Wireless Communications: Principles and Practice.* Englewood Cliffs, NJ: Prentice-Hall.

Rezai, F., and Tadaion, A. (2014). Interference alignment in cognitive radio networks. *IET Commun.,* 8(10), 1769–1777.

Santamaria, I., Gonzalez, O., Heath Jr., R. W., and Peters, S. W. (2010). Maximum sum-rate interference alignment algorithms for MIMO channels. *2010 IEEE Glob. Telecommun. Conf. (GLOBECOM 2010),* Miami, FL, 1–6.

Shang, X., Kramer, G., and Chen, B. (2009). A new outer bound and the noisy-interference sum-rate capacity for Gaussian interference channels. *IEEE Trans. Inf. Theory,* 55(2), 689–699.

Tse, D. N. C., and Vishwanath, P. (2005). *Fundamentals of Wireless Communications.* Cambridge: Cambridge University Press.

Wang, C. X., Chen, H. H., Hong, X., and Guizani, M. (2008). Cognitive radio network management: Tuning in to real-time conditions. *IEEE Veh. Tech. Mag.,* 3(1), 28–35.

Yamaguchi, H. (2004). Active interference cancellation technique for MB-OFDM cognitive radio. In *Proceedings of the 34th European Microwave Conference,* Amsterdam, the Netherlands, 1105–1108.

Yang, H. J., Shin, W. Y., Jung, B. C., and Paulraj, A. (2013). Opportunistic interference alignment for MIMO Interfering multiple-access channels. *IEEE Trans. Wire. Commun.,* 12(5), 2180–2192.

Yetis, C. M., Gou, T., Jafar, S. A., and Kayran, A. H. (2010). On feasibility of interference alignment in MIMO interference networks. *IEEE Trans. Signal Proc.,* 58(9), 4771–4782.

Yu, H., and Sung, Y. (2010). Least squares approach to joint beam design for interference alignment in multiuser multi-input multi-output interference channels. *IEEE Trans. Signal Proc.,* 58(9), 4960–4966.

Zhang, L., Song, L., Zhang, Z., Lei, M., and Jiao, B. (2012). Interference alignment with differential feedback. *IEEE Trans. Veh. Tech.,* 61(6), 2878–2883.

Zhou, J., and Thompson, J. S. (2008). Linear precoding for the downlink of multiple input single output coexisting wireless systems. *IET Commun. (Special Issue on Cognitive Access),* 2(6), 742–752.

Part VI

Applications of Cognitive Radio Networks

13

Cognitive Radio for Mobile Ad Hoc Networks and Wireless Sensor Networks: Applications, Open Research Issues, and Research Directions

Rinki Sharma

CONTENTS

13.1 Introduction

As communication on the move has become popular, research interest in wireless network technologies has increased with the goal of providing efficient and reliable communication over wireless. While the data traffic exchanged over the wireless medium is expected to grow in future, the limitation of the available electromagnetic spectrum is a challenge. Cognitive radio technology (CRT) tries to overcome this challenge. This chapter discusses the significance and applications of CRT in mobile ad hoc networks (MANETs) and wireless sensor networks (WSNs). The issues and challenges of using CRT in ad hoc and sensor networks are discussed. This chapter also discusses the ongoing research in this area and presents future research directions along with the available standards and ongoing standardization activities. To carry out an experimental research in this domain, researchers must be made aware of the available tools and test beds. This chapter presents a survey and discussion about the capabilities of available tools and test beds.

13.2 Introduction to CRT

As the trend of communication on the move has become popular, research interest in wireless communication and related technologies has increased with the goal of achieving efficient and reliable communication over wireless. While data exchanged over the wireless medium is expected to grow in the future, the limitation of the available electromagnetic spectrum is a challenge. CRT tries to overcome this challenge through dynamic spectrum access (DSA), allowing efficient and flexible access to the available frequency spectrum [1].

CRT was introduced by Dr. Joseph Mitola III in 1999, and was defined as follows [1]:

The term *cognitive radio* (CR) identifies the point at which the wireless personal digital assistants and related networks are sufficiently computationally intelligent about the radio resources and related computer-to-computer communications to

1. Detect the user communications needs as a function of use context
2. Provide the radio resources and wireless services most appropriate to those needs

CRT is based on software-defined radio (SDR) and allows intelligent spectrum sensing, management, and access to facilitate efficient and reliable wireless communication among nodes supporting the CRT. SDR is a communication system in which the transmission parameters can be reconfigured, such as different bands of operating frequency, transmission power, and modulation. Through dynamic configuration of their operating parameters accomplished with CRT nodes, SDRs are capable of determining the vacant frequency bands and using these bands for an opportunistic exchange of data, thus improving the utilization of the limited available spectrum.

A node supporting the CRT is capable of sensing the radio spectrum to detect the unused frequency bands (also known as white spaces or spectrum holes) for data communication, thus enhancing the utilization of the available frequency spectrum.

13.3 Significance of CRT in Ad Hoc and Sensor Networks

Wireless ad hoc and sensor networks operate in dynamically changing environments caused mainly due to node mobility, interference from neighbor nodes, and transition of nodes between operational and nonoperational modes. For efficient and reliable communication in such networks, the CRT plays a potential role. This section discusses the role of CRT in wireless ad hoc and sensor network.

MANETs: These are the temporary networks formed among neighboring mobile nodes located within communication range of each other, which communicate without the support of any infrastructure. Due to the mobility of nodes, interference among neighboring nodes may vary constantly and will be higher in the regions where they are densely placed, and lower in the sparsely placed regions. Provision for dynamic spectrum access (DSA) can help in mitigation of interference among the nodes in a MANET, thus enhancing the performance and efficiency of the network. To achieve this, compatibility between CRT and MANETs becomes essential. As the communication environment in MANETs is highly dynamic due to the node mobility, the CRT would enable a node to sense the changes in its surroundings and adapt accordingly by using an appropriate frequency spectrum to avoid interference with the neighboring nodes. Apart from a simple exchange of data between two nodes within communication range, MANETs are also used in critical applications such as emergency and rescue operations, soldier ad hoc networks for defense and military communication, and health care. Such applications require low-latency and reliable communication, which can be achieved through the DSA.

Vehicular ad hoc networks (VANETs): These are a type of MANET wherein the mobile nodes are the vehicles. Technologies such as intelligent transportation systems use VANETs to achieve the inter-vehicle communication for applications such as collision avoidance assistance, cornering speed control, adaptive cruise control, obstacle avoidance assistance, and adaptive frontal lightning, to name a few. These are the critical applications for which the communication among the participating nodes should take place in real time (without, or with the least possible, delays) and without corruption. In such applications, the DSA can help through available alternate frequency bands which are less crowded, as it can drastically reduce the delays due to reduced contention and corruption of packets because of interference.

WSNs: These are used in the applications such as structural health monitoring (SHM), to sense the leakage of radiations in nuclear power plants, soil moisture control (agriculture), body area networks (health care), and industrial and home automation. Sensor nodes are placed in the remote locations to sense different parameters. WSNs are expected to have longer lifetimes so that the sensor nodes do not need to be recharged/replaced often. Hence, energy efficiency becomes an essential requirement for these networks. For this, sensor nodes maintain low-duty cycle, and transit between sleep and wake-up modes, and are configured to operate with a low transmission power to achieve an energy-efficient communication. In order to ensure reliable communication, the sensor nodes are placed densely and need to share the available wireless medium for communication.

MANETs (based on IEEE 802.11 standard) and WSNs (based on Zigbee) operate in industrial, scientific, and medical (ISM) bands as these bands are license exempted. However, because of this, the ISM bands are crowded as devices using various technologies such as Wi-Fi and Bluetooth also operate in these bands. Due to this, the communication carried out in these bands is prone to interference and corruption. Corrupted packets also need to be retransmitted, leading to a higher energy consumption at the communicating nodes. For the MANET and WSN nodes, which operate with a limited battery power, energy efficiency is very important. High energy consumption of the nodes due to corruption and retransmission of the packets can reduce the network lifetime. Densely deployed MANETs and WSNs lead to higher instances of contention among the sensor nodes trying to access the shared wireless medium. This can cause delays in transmission of information over the network, leading to an inefficient communication.

Therefore, to attain a reliable and efficient communication over these networks, it is essential that the communicating nodes are made capable of using the unutilized spectrum (white spaces or spectrum holes) by using CRT. Some of the advantages of using the CRT for MANETs and WSNs are listed as follows:

1. *Dynamic spectrum access:* The data exchanged over the unlicensed ISM bands is prone to interference and corruption which is not suitable for MANET and WSN

applications that require low-latency and reliable communication. Leasing a dedicated frequency band for such applications (to avoid interference and corruption) increases the deployment and operational costs of the network. Use of CRT allows a dynamic access to the available spectrum holes or white spaces, thus avoiding the interference-prone bands for reliable data transmission.

2. *Energy-efficient communication through reduced packet corruption*: Communication over interference prone ISM bands leads to the corruption of the packets. Such corrupted packets may need to be retransmitted which increases the power consumption at the transmitting nodes. The nodes, particularly in MANETs and WSNs, rely on a limited battery power for communication. Therefore, the energy efficiency becomes crucial for such nodes. With energy efficiency being essential for the operation of MANETs and WSNs, CRT helps the nodes to avoid the crowded and interference-prone bands. Energy-efficient communication increases the lifetimes of MANETs and WSNs.

3. *Power-efficient communication*: Signal deterioration due to path loss is less at lower frequencies compared to higher frequencies of the electromagnetic spectrum. With the help of a DSA, nodes equipped with CRT can select lower frequencies of operation thus achieving longer transmission range and reduced energy consumption. This reduces the number of nodes required to cover a particular region. Such power-efficient communication increases the lifetimes of the MANET and WSN.

4. *Reduced latency through reduced contention*: Currently, all the nodes in a MANET or WSN are configured to operate on a particular frequency band. This increases the contention among the nodes in the network to access the shared frequency band, leading to delays in medium access. Using CRT will allow more options for the accessible spectrum, thus achieving reduced contention. Dynamic access to frequency bands also allows reduced contention among nodes, thus making the network capable of handling the low-latency communication.

5. *Coexistence of overlapping networks*: Dynamic spectrum management through CRT can allow coexistence of overlapping networks in space, thus achieving enhanced utilization of available resources, and increasing the performance of the concerned networks.

6. *Operation under different spectrum regulations*: Different countries/regions have different regulations regarding the usage of the spectrum. Making the nodes equipped with CRT allows them to operate under varying spectrum regulations.

7. *Security*: It is easy to hack/sniff data in a wireless network or jam a wireless network, if all the nodes operate over a single frequency. However, if the nodes change their frequency of operation constantly, it becomes difficult to perform such attacks. With DSA, nodes can change their frequency of operation thus avoiding the hacking or jamming attacks.

13.4 Challenges and Open Research Issues in Implementation of CRT in MANETs and WSNs

MANETs and WSNs comprise both the stationary and mobile nodes that rely on limited battery power. The radio environment in these networks changes constantly due to node mobility, making the implementation of CRT a challenge. Also, the nodes need to constantly scan the radio environment to check the availability of the spectrum, or may need to switch the spectrum to vacate it for the licensed user, or to avoid interference with other nodes. Carrying out these operations leads to increase in energy consumption of the nodes with limited battery power. This section presents and discusses various challenges and open research issues in the implementation of CRT in MANETs and WSNs.

13.4.1 Duration of Spectrum Sensing

The longer the duration of spectrum sensing, the more accurate will be the result, thus reducing the chances of corruption of signals due to interference between the secondary user (SU) and primary user (PU). However, the duration of spectrum sensing has a direct impact on end-to-end delay, which further impacts the quality of service (QoS) of the network. Until a spectrum is available, the nodes need to put the entire traffic on hold, leading to a delay in data communication. In case the PU wants the spectrum being used by the SU back, the SU will need to suspend the ongoing communication, vacate the spectrum, and look for another vacant channel to resume the communication. This can lead to an increased end-to-end delay and a degraded QoS.

13.4.2 Energy Efficiency

Energy efficiency is a major challenge, and a key design factor in the CRT-based wireless networks. Factors such as modulation and coding schemes to achieve the required data rates, required transmission power and receiver sensitivity, frequency of transmission, and spectrum mobility (ability of SU to change or switch between different spectrum holes, so as to avoid interference with PU) directly affect the used battery power and lifetime of the node. Hence, it is essential to choose these design parameters by taking energy efficiency requirements of the nodes into consideration.

13.4.3 Operating Frequency Aware Spectrum Sharing

In the CRT, multiple nodes can dynamically access the available spectrum, which is shared among these nodes. A node can use a portion of the spectrum that is not being used by any other node at that instant. Before using a portion of the spectrum for data communication, a node needs to be aware of the radio environment in its vicinity and also check for the presence of interference in that spectrum due to neighboring communication. Also, since multiple nodes try to access the shared spectrum, there needs to be some coordination among these nodes to ensure a proper operation. If the PU wants to use the spectrum, then the SU needs to switch to another vacant portion of the spectrum to continue communication. Therefore, it is observed that in cognitive radio networks (CRNs), the communicating nodes need to change their frequency of operation quite often.

As the frequency of operation increases, the communication range of the node decreases provided its transmission power remains the same. Therefore, with the capability of DSA, if a node changes its operating frequency, its communication range is bound to change, leading to a change in the number of its neighboring nodes and the resulting prospective interferers. This also varies the degree of contention among nodes to access the network. Therefore, it is required to design and develop the operating frequency aware spectrum-sharing mechanisms that can adapt to the changes in the frequency of operation and the neighboring radio environment.

13.4.4 Location Awareness

In a CRN much of the decision regarding spectrum access depends on a node's proximity to its neighbors. It decides the probability of interference between nodes operating in a particular frequency band. If nodes are aware of their proximity to other nodes based on the interference range and coverage, then they can use this information to determine the spectrum utilization, spectrum access, and probability of interference. In case of MANETs, and certain WSNs, applications, where participating nodes are mobile, the radio environment changes constantly over time and space. Therefore, the devices need to be conscious about the changing locations of neighboring nodes affecting the radio environment surrounding the node. Location awareness of the neighbor nodes, and using this information to make appropriate spectrum utilization and access decisions, brings in new challenges and is an open research issue.

13.4.5 Reconfigurability

It is known that the CRT-enabled devices are capable of operating at different frequencies according to the changing radio environment. However, in addition to the capability of operating at different frequencies, these devices should also be capable of reconfiguring modulation techniques and transmission power. Based on the type of application, the required data rate can be decided. For applications that demand low-latency, high data rate is more important than the error rate, and modulation techniques that provide a high data rate [such as M-ary quadrature amplitude modulation (M-QAM)] should be used. For applications that give more importance to reliability and correctness of the data, a low error rate is the required. For such applications, modulation techniques that provide a low bit error rate can be used, e.g., binary phase shift keying or quadrature phase shift keying.

Similarly, transmission power should be reconfigured to reduce the interference among neighbor nodes while avoiding the link outage. Reducing the transmission power of the transmitting node such that the transmitted signal is strong enough to reach the destination/source would help in mitigating the interference with other nodes.

13.5 Research Directions

The challenges and open research issues were explained and discussed in Section 13.4. This section presents the ongoing research activities and some of the solutions available in the literature to overcome these challenges.

13.5.1 Spectrum Sensing

Spectrum sensing is a primary task for MANET and WSN nodes supporting the CRT. For this, the nodes need to constantly sense the spectrum for the presence of spectrum holes. Spectrum sensing in MANETs and WSNs can be carried out in two ways: (1) distributed spectrum sensing and (2) centralized spectrum sensing.

In distributed spectrum sensing, all nodes in the network sense the spectrum for the presence of white spaces or spectrum holes. Therefore, each node must be capable of sensing the complete channel and identifying the spectrum holes.

However, the nodes forming MANETs or WSNs have limited battery power which is further drained by distributed spectrum sensing leading to reduced lifetime of the node and the network comprising such nodes. Particularly in WSNs, the network consists of both fully functional devices (FFDs) and reduced functional devices (RFDs). The RFDs have limited battery and processing power. Therefore, distributed spectrum sensing is difficult to realize in MANETs and WSNs.

In centralized spectrum sensing, the task of spectrum sensing is carried out by a designated single node, for example, the cluster head in MANETs, the network coordinator (which is an FFD) in WSNs and a roadside unit in VANETs. In this method, the designated single node can sense the spectrum for presence of the spectrum holes and broadcast it to other nodes in the network. For reliable delivery of this information to all the nodes in the network, certain intermediate nodes (such as FFD/routers) retransmit or forward the information received from the designated single node to other nodes in the network.

In addition, the PU can transmit beacons to indicate the availability or unavailability of the spectrum. Information in these beacons can be used by the SU to determine the presence or absence of spectrum.

The range of spectrum sensing frequencies could be fixed or variable. In the fixed range, the nodes need to sense the spectrum only over a specific range of frequencies and their physical layer components are designed accordingly. In case of variable range, the sensing frequency range varies adaptively based on change in the conditions of the surrounding environment (e.g., increased interference) or application requirements (e.g., voice/video transmission that requires a dedicated channel without interference). There should be a limit on the spectrum sensing duration after which the node should abort the transmission. This would save the node from sensing the spectrum relentlessly and wasting its energy.

Spectrum sensing can also be categorized as proactive and reactive. In proactive spectrum sensing, the node can sense the spectrum constantly, even in the absence of data traffic to be exchanged over the network. While this method of spectrum sensing involves higher energy consumption, it would allow the nodes to maintain a list of available spectrum, thus reducing the average end-to-end delay of communication due to the time spent in spectrum sensing when the data is ready to be transmitted. This method provides a trade-off of low latency for increased energy consumption. In case of reactive spectrum sensing, the node starts sensing the spectrum only when it has the data to be transmitted. This method is energy efficient, but the time taken for spectrum sensing can increase the end-to-end delay.

For energy-efficient spectrum sensing with lower end-to-end delay, the centralized scheme with proactive spectrum sensing can be used, wherein a designated single node (such as cluster head in MANETs, network coordinator in WSNs, and roadside unit in VANETs) can sense the spectrum proactively and broadcast the availability of the spectrum to other nodes in the network. Interested nodes can use this broadcasted information to select the appropriate spectrum for communication.

13.5.2 Energy Efficiency

For nodes using the CRT, a significant amount of energy gets consumed in spectrum sensing and spectrum switching [2]. For nodes in MANETs and WSNs, which run on limited battery power, energy efficiency is critical to keep the network functional. Two most common methods to achieve the energy efficiency in MANETs and WSNs are transmission power control and transition to sleep mode when the nodes are not participating in communication.

Apart from saving the energy, controlling the transmission power such that it is just sufficient for the signal to reach the designated receiver also helps in mitigating the interference among neighbor nodes. When idle, nodes can transit to sleep mode for energy conservation. Bdira and Ibnkahla [3] have developed a cognition algorithm which uses information about the channel condition to adaptively configure sleep time and modulation scheme of the sensor nodes. The authors have demonstrated that using the cognition-based information on channel condition to select an appropriate modulation technique and scheduling sleep time of the nodes enhances energy efficiency of the nodes, thus increasing the overall network lifetime.

13.5.3 Spectrum Sharing

Numerous spectrum-sharing techniques in MANETs and WSNs have been proposed and studied in the literature out of which two major techniques called centralized sharing and distributed sharing are discussed here. In centralized spectrum sharing, a designated node (called a cluster head or network coordinator) controls the allocation of the spectrum and its access. This designated node can create a spectrum allocation map (with information such as allocated spectrum, vacant spectrum, frequency of vacant spectrum, and history of the vacant spectrum) [4], and guide other nodes in the network to select the appropriate spectrum for usage. In the distributed spectrum-sharing technique, every individual node is responsible for spectrum sharing. For this, the node needs to maintain information about its surrounding radio environment and follow local or global policies (based on the design of its spectrum-sharing algorithm) to make appropriate decisions on the spectrum access and sharing.

The distributed spectrum-sharing technique can be further classified into cooperative spectrum sharing and noncooperative spectrum sharing. In the cooperative spectrum sharing, every node shares the information it possess regarding its neighbor radio environment with other nodes in the network. Based on the radio environment information maintained by the node itself and that available from other nodes, the spectrum access and sharing decision is made. Due to exchange of information among the nodes, cooperative spectrum-sharing technique leads to high overheads in the network and energy consumption.

In the noncooperative spectrum-sharing technique (also known as selfish spectrum-sharing), nodes do not share any information regarding their neighboring radio environment with each other. Every node makes the decision regarding spectrum sharing and access based on its own information. In this technique, the network overhead and energy consumed at the nodes are low compared to that in cooperative spectrum sharing.

13.5.4 Location and Topology Awareness

In the CRNs, the ability of a node to reuse the available spectrum dynamically depends on the probability of interference based on the proximity among nodes, their communication, and interference ranges. Network topology awareness along with the knowledge of spectrum allocation can help a node to compute the probability of interference with neighboring nodes over a particular frequency spectrum. It also provides information about the network connectivity and node distribution. Nodes supported with a global positioning system functionality can determine their location and share it with their neighbor nodes. Nodes can also maintain and share their neighbor tables, which can be used to compute the network connectivity and density. Such location and topology information can be maintained by nodes in a manner similar to the radio environment maps, based on which a node can estimate the spectrum usage while making decisions regarding spectrum access, sharing, and switching. Location information-based CRN architectures are discussed in [5–8]. Models developed in the literature help in statistical estimation of location distribution which can be used to estimate characteristics of the network. This information can be used to depict the spectrum occupation while making decisions regarding spectrum allocation and reuse.

13.5.5 Reconfigurability

A CRT-enabled node is capable of scanning the spectrum for its availability and select the appropriate frequency band for operation. Being reconfigurable, its radio can be dynamically programmed based on the characteristics of the frequency of operation and neighboring radio environment. The CR hardware can be programmed to communicate over a range of frequencies. One such hardware design of the CR transceiver is presented in [9]. The main components of this transceiver are the RF front-end and baseband processing unit. The RF front-end comprises an amplifier, mixer, and analog-to-digital converter, while the baseband processing unit comprises a modulator/demodulator and encoder/decoder. All these components can be reconfigured through a control bus.

In CRNs, the RF antenna of a transceiver should be capable of scanning and detecting signals over a wide range of frequencies. Therefore, it should be designed in such a way that it is capable of detecting even a weak signal from its radio environment, and make appropriate decisions regarding spectrum availability and its access. The RF antenna of a node using CRT should also be designed to be capable of receiving signals from the transmitters operating at different frequencies, locations, power levels, and modulations. However, as pointed out in [10,11] designing such a transceiver is a challenge since it requires analog-to-digital convertor of multi-GHz speed with high resolution.

RF front-end for CR-enabled nodes can also be designed using multiple antennas that can receive the signals selectively from particular nodes. Beam-formed antennas can be used to take the advantages achieved through directivity of antennas such as increased communication range and reduced interference, as discussed in [12,13].

13.6 Standardization Activities

For compatibility and interoperability between devices based on CRT, it is essential to standardize the use of SDR in the CRNs. This would require coordination among the research groups in academia, industry, and other organizations working in this area. For this, the IEEE Standards Coordinating Committee 41 (SCC41) is established to form related standards for the next-generation radio and spectrum management involving different working groups (WGs), namely IEEE 1900.x, where "x" represents one of the WGs. This section explains the scope of each WG in brief [14].

IEEE 1900.1: Definitions and concepts for DSA—this WG is responsible for preparing technically precise definition for the terms related to CR and developing the glossary for the same. This standard also describes relation between the terms and concepts related to CR.

IEEE 1900.2: Recommended practice for analysis of in-band and adjacent band interference and coexistence between the radio systems: An important goal of CR is the efficient usage of the available wireless spectrum. As different nodes try to access the available spectrum, interference analysis becomes crucial for the appropriate deployment of the network and usage of the available spectrum. IEEE 1900.2 WG established a standard platform where disputing parties can resolve their concerns regarding coexistence and interference.

IEEE 1900.3: Recommended practice for conformance evaluation of SDR software modules: This WG is concerned with the conformance of software components in the SDR-based wireless devices. It allows the coexistence and compliance of the software part in SDR devices.

IEEE 1900.4: Architectural building blocks enabling network-device distributed decision making for optimized radio resource usage in heterogeneous wireless access networks—this

WG deals with the coexistence of the heterogeneous air interface in CRNs. It allows simultaneous use of various heterogeneous wireless technologies to be used over a CR device. The IEEE 1900.4 WG comprises two sub-groups, namely IEEE 1900.4a and IEEE 1900.4.1.

IEEE 1900.4a: Architectural building blocks enabling network-device distributed decision making for optimized radio resource usage in heterogeneous wireless access networks. Amendment: The aim of this WG is to develop a standard for the architecture and interfaces for dynamic spectrums access networks in the white space frequency bands. This would allow the efficient usage of white spaces.

IEEE 1900.4.1: Interfaces and protocols enabling distributed decision making for optimized radio resource usage in heterogeneous wireless networks: The IEEE 1900.4.1 is concerned with the development of standards for interfaces and protocols to enable the distributed decision making for the optimized radio resource usage in the heterogeneous wireless networks. It also provides context information for the decision-making process.

IEEE 1900.5: Policy language requirements and system architectures for DSA systems: This WG develops the policy language and architectures for interoperable and vendor independent control of the CR functionality. It works toward standardizing the essential features of policy language which can be bound to various policy architectures developed for the CR devices to be used in DSA applications.

IEEE 1900.6: Spectrum sensing interfaces and data structures for DSA and other advanced radio communication systems: Started in July 2008, this WG works toward developing the standard for information exchange among the spectrum sensors and their clients, for radio communication. Based on this standard, the exchange of information can take place in a technology-independent way, thus maintaining the scalability of the network and compatibility among the participating devices.

IEEE 1900.7: Radio interface for white space DSA radio systems supporting fixed and mobile operation: This WG aims to develop a standard for the physical layer and medium access control (MAC) layer specifications to enable the communication over white spaces.

13.7 The IEEE 802.22 Standard for Wireless Regional Area Networks

To overcome the scarcity of the spectrum and to support communication based on the CRT, the IEEE 802.22 standard was developed for wireless regional area networks (WRANs) technology. The devices based on this standard carry out the communication over the unused TV spectrum. Such devices use the CRT to avoid interference with the incumbent services. The IEEE 802.22 standard specifies the air interface including the physical and MAC layer specifications for point-to-multipoint communication. This standard is developed to support the communication among fixed and mobile nodes over VHF/UHF TV broadcast frequency bands between 54 and 862 MHz. The MAC and Phy layers of a WRAN are designed to support nodes as far as 100 km with traffic scheduling in appropriate RF signal propagation conditions and up to a distance of 30 km without traffic scheduling. Apart from supporting the CRT to avoid interference with the incumbent services, this standard also comprises techniques that support geolocation capability, spectrum sensing, spectrum management, and provision to access the database of the incumbent services [15].

13.8 Existing Architectures, Tools, and Test Beds

For efficient utilization of the limited radio spectrum, the Defense Advanced Research Projects Agency (DARPA) started the neXt Generation (XG) program with the goal of attaining DSA through CRT. The research community has been working toward developing an architecture to support the CR-based systems. Some of the most widely used architectures are presented in this section.

A CR approach for the usage of virtual unlicensed spectrum (CORVUS) architecture is presented in [16]. In this architecture, the operations of local spectrum sensing, detecting the PU, and allocation of the spectrum are implemented in a coordinated manner through a secondary-user group (SUG). Every user in an SUG accesses an available spectrum pool and uses the control channel to exchange the spectrum-sensing information among each other. The CORVUS test bed [17] has been used to evaluate the physical and link layer performance of the developed architecture. Willkomm et al. [18] presented a reliable link maintenance protocol based on CORVUS.

To support the temporal and spatial DSA for vehicular environments, the DRiVE/ OverDRiVE projects are developed. The European dynamic radio for IP services in vehicular environments (DRiVE) [19] was developed for heterogeneous wireless access. DRiVE was further extended to support the multicast data transmission in the vehicular environment, and was named as OverDRiVE (over dynamic radio networks in vehicular environments) [20].

An orthogonal frequency division multiplexing (OFDM)–based CRN called OCRA is presented in [21]. This architecture is developed to support the OFDM-based spectrum management in the heterogeneous networks. The OCRA network also supports the usage of noncontiguous, multispectrum communication for an enhanced network throughput.

Dynamic intelligent management of spectrum for ubiquitous mobile network (DIMSUMnet) is presented in [22]. This architecture implements the statistically multiplexed access (SMA) to the spectrum in the coordinated access band (CAB) for fair and efficient utilization of the spectrum. In this architecture, a spectrum broker permanently owns the CAB, and leases it on demand.

The Nautilus project proposes a distributed and scalable coordination framework for the open spectrum ad hoc networks [23]. In this framework, centralized control is not used for operation. This framework allows the nodes to decide their spectrum requirements individually, and negotiate the spectrum access within the self-organized groups.

GNU (GNU in Not Unix) radio is widely used for implementation of the CR designs. It is an open source software toolkit which can be used for building and deploying the SDRs [24]. Being open source, the GNU radio project provides a library of signal processing blocks and their complete source codes.

The CR test bed developed at Berkley Wireless Research Center (BWRC) comprises a Berkley emulation engine (BEE2) and several CR front-ends [25]. The BEE2 is a multi–field-programmable gate array (FPGA) emulation engine capable of connecting to 18 radio front-ends. This is used to experiment with various sensing schemes and PU identification techniques.

A complementary metal–oxide–semiconductor (CMOS)–based CR platform is developed by Motorola. It is capable of operating at channel frequencies of 10 MHz to 4GHz with channel bandwidths varying from 8 kHz to 20 MHz. The platform can be configured to receive and transmit the wireless signals of both experimental and standard wireless protocols through flexible programming of its radio frequency integrated circuit (IC).

Cavalcanti et al. [26] implemented a conceptual design of CR-based WSNs in OPNET's (Optimum Network) Zigbee/802.15.4 library and compared its performance with original Zigbee/802.15.4 implementation.

A CRN simulation platform is developed with an open source network simulator OMNeT++ (Objective Modular Network Testbed in C++) and a MiXiM (the MiXedsIMulator) framework [27]. The developed simulator allows the configuration of parameters such as number of SUs and PUs, spectrum sensing based on energy detection, mobility models, propagation channel models, network topologies, and medium access models to study the behavior of simulated CRNs [27].

Iris is a set of libraries which can be used to develop the SDRs [28,29]. The running radio can be reconfigured in Iris through a configuration file for achieving the CR functionality.

References

1. Mitola III, J. (2000). Cognitive Radio. Doctoral dissertation. Royal Institute of Technology, Sweden.
2. Yilmaz, H. B., Eryigit, S. and Tugcu, T. (2015). Cooperative spectrum sensing. In *Cognitive Radio and Networking for Heterogeneous Wireless Networks*. Switzerland: Springer International Publishing, pp. 67–107.
3. Bdira, E. and Ibnkahla, M. (2009). Performance modelling of cognitive wireless sensor networks applied to environmental protection. In *Proceedings of the IEEE Globecom*, Honolulu, HI.
4. Zhao, Y., Le, B. and Reed, J. H. (2006). Network support—The radio environment map. In *Cognitive Radio Technology*, 2nd ed. Amsterdam, The Netherlands: Elsevier.
5. Celebi, H. and Arslan, H. (2007). Utilization of location information in cognitive wireless networks. *IEEE Wireless Commun.*, 14: 6–13.
6. Karr, A. F. (1991). *Point Processes and Their Statistical Inference*, 2nd ed. New York, NY: Marcel Dekker.
7. Stoyan, D., Kendall, W. S. and Mecke, J. (1995). Stochastic geometry and its applications. New York, NY: John Wiley & Sons.
8. Riihijärvi, J., Mähönen, P., Wellens, M. and Gordziel, M. (2008). Characterization and modelling of spectrum for dynamic spectrum access with spatial statistics and random fields. In *Personal, Indoor and Mobile Radio Communications, 2008. PIMRC 2008. IEEE 19th International Symposium on IEEE*, Cannes, pp. 1–6.
9. Jondral, F. K. (2005). Software-defined radio: Basics and evolution to cognitive radio. *EURASIP J. Wireless Commun. Netw.*, 3: 275–283.
10. Cabric, D. (2008). Addressing feasibility of cognitive radios. *Signal Process. Mag. IEEE*, 25 (6): 85–93.
11. Han, C., Wang, J., Yang, Y. and Li, S. (2008). Addressing the control channel design problem: OFDM-based transform domain communication system in cognitive radio. *Comput. Netw.*, 52 (4): 795–815.
12. Sharma, R., Kadambi, G., Vershinin, Y. A. and Mukundan, K. N. (2014). A survey of MAC layer protocols to avoid deafness in wireless networks using directional antenna. In *Handbook of Research on Progressive Trends in Wireless Communications and Networking*. Edited by M. A. Matin. Vol. 1. Hershey: IGI Global, pp. 479–517.
13. Lei, Z. and Shellhammer, S. J. (2009). IEEE 802.22: The first cognitive radio wireless regional area network standard. *IEEE Commun. Mag.*, 47 (1): 130–138.

14. Murroni, M., Prasad, R. V., Marques, P. et al. (2011). IEEE 1900.6: Spectrum sensing interfaces and data structures for dynamic spectrum access and other advanced radio communication systems standard: Technical aspects and future outlook. *Commun. Mag. IEEE*, 49 (12): 118–127.

15. IEEE 802.22 Working Group. (2011). IEEE standard for information technology—Telecommunications and information exchange between systems wireless regional area networks-specific requirements: Cognitive wireless RAN medium access control (MAC) and physical layer (PHY) specifications: Policies and procedures for operation in the TV bands. *IEEE*, pp. 1–672.

16. Čabrić, D., Mishra, S. M., Willkomm, D. et al. (2005). A cognitive radio approach for usage of virtual unlicensed spectrum. In *Proceedings of 14th IST Mobile Wireless Communications Summit*, pp. 1–4.

17. Mishra, S. M., Čabrić, D., Chang, C. et al. (2005). A real time cognitive radio testbed for physical and link layer experiments. In *New Frontiers in Dynamic Spectrum Access Networks. DySPAN 2005. First IEEE International Symposium on IEEE*, Baltimore, MD, USA, pp. 562–567.

18. Willkomm, D., Gross, J. and Wolisz, A. (2005). Reliable link maintenance in cognitive radio systems. In *New Frontiers in Dynamic Spectrum Access Networks, 2005. DySPAN 2005. First IEEE International Symposium on IEEE*, Baltimore, MD, USA, pp. 371–378.

19. Xu, L., Tönjes, R., Paila, T. et al. (2000). DRiVE-ing to the internet: Dynamic radio for IP services in vehicular environments. In *Local Computer Networks, Proceedings. 25th Annual IEEE Conference on IEEE*, Tampa, FL, pp. 281–289.

20. Leaves, P., Moessner, K., Tafazolli, R. et al. (2004). Dynamic spectrum allocation in composite reconfigurable wireless networks. *Commun. Mag. IEEE*, 42 (5): 72–81.

21. Akyildiz, I. F. and Li, Y. (2006). OCRA: OFDM-based cognitive radio networks. Broadband and Wireless Networking Laboratory Technical Report.

22. Buddhikot, M. M., Kolodzy, P., Miller, S. et al. (2005). DIMSUMnet: New directions in wireless networking using coordinated dynamic spectrum. In *World of Wireless Mobile and Multimedia Networks, WoWMoM 2005. Sixth IEEE International Symposium on IEEE*, Taormina - Giardini Naxos, Italy, pp. 78–85.

23. Nautilus project [Online]. Available at: https://www.cs.ucsb.edu/~htzheng/cognitive/nautilus.html (accessed on 27 May 2016).

24. GNU radio. Available at: http://gnuradio.org/ (accessed on 27 May 2016).

25. Chang, C., Wawrzynek, J. and Brodersen, R. W. (2005). BEE2: A high-end reconfigurable computing system. *IEEE Des. Test Comput.*, 2: 114–125.

26. Cavalcanti, D., Das, S., Wang, J. and Challapali, K. (2008). Cognitive radio based wireless sensor networks. In *Computer Communications and Networks, 2008. ICCCN '08. Proceedings of 17th International Conference on IEEE*, pp. 1–6.

27. Caso, G., De Nardis, L. and Holland, O. (2015). Simulation of cognitive radio networks in OMNeT++. In *Cognitive Radio and Networking for Heterogeneous Wireless Networks*. Switzerland: Springer International Publishing, pp. 291–313.

28. Sutton, P., Lotze, J., Lahlou, H. et al. (2010). Iris: an architecture for cognitive radio networking testbeds. *Commun. Mag. IEEE*, 48(9): 114–122

29. Doyle, L. E., Sutton, P. D., Nolan, K. E. et al. (2010, April). Experiences from the Iris testbed in dynamic spectrum access and cognitive radio experimentation. In *2010 IEEE Symposium on New Frontiers in Dynamic Spectrum*, pp. 1–8.

14

Analysis for Cognitive Radio Sensor Network Architecture and Its Role in Dynamic Spectrum Management

Rachit Jain, Animesh Kumar Jha, Robin Singh Bhadoria, and K. V. Arya

CONTENTS

14.1 Introduction

The cognitive radio (CR) communication system is capable of collecting the information about its location, radio-frequency spectrums, and the present environment, so that it can decide and execute the predefined objectives. In the case of spectrum utilization, the high priority licensed users are called primary users whereas the unlicensed users are termed as the secondary users who can also use the spectrum. CR is the most emerging issue in the wireless communications where a wireless node senses its environment including the spectrum holes. The cognitive radio networks (CRNs) establish the communication in an opportunistic manner by isolating the licensed users. The major difficulties faced by a CRN include the efficient detection of spectrum holes and the interference with the network utilized by the primary users [1].

The sensor networks aided CR technology proves to be efficient as it provides a mechanism of sensor network utilization for the licensed and unlicensed users simultaneously. The concept of sensor network aided CR technology can be understood with the help of Figure 14.1.

Wireless senor networks (WSNs) utilize the spectrum to know the primary user consumption and hence, provide information of the availability of the spectrum holes which can be utilized by the users of secondary networks. Therefore, the users of secondary networks can transfer and share the information without causing any transmission impairment to the primary network. It is evident from Figure 14.1 that the three components,

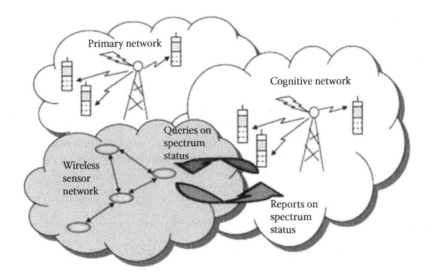

FIGURE 14.1
Sensor network-aided cognitive radio.

i.e., primary network, cognitive network, and WSN stay in coexistence with each other all the time and share a lot of activities in common.

CR is also called as the *direct spectrum access* and represents a new generation communication where the spectrum is utilized effectively. It is like a radio which communicates as per the environment in which it is operating.

It is different from the classic wireless network and is capable of sensing the spectrum availability and accordingly reconfigures the spectrum dynamically. It allows the secondary user to sense and use the available spectrum when the primary user is not using it, and vacate it when the primary user returns. CR is also equipped with the capability of determining the empty or less noisy spectrum and hence, to get a better overall performance if the unoccupied spectrum channels are utilized properly.

Limitation of WSNs can be removed with the help of CR technique, which is an improved and advanced version of the classical wireless communication system. CR technique is developed by removing the limitations of previously available techniques by suitable planning and learning. For spectrum utilization, the CR techniques start interfacing with the wireless sensors and consequently result in the effective utilization of idle or vacant channels [2,3].

Primary users can utilize the spectrum anytime but secondary users can utilize it only when it is not used by the primary users. To improve the efficiency of WSNs, the sensor nodes need to be equipped with the CR technology. The modified CR technology-enabled wireless sensor node must possess the following qualities:

- Trustable environment access
- Sensing the surroundings
- Transmission control
- Spectrum sensing
- Spectrum sharing
- Channel prediction

- Reconfiguration capability
- Fairness
- Secure routing

CR provides multiple accesses to many unlicensed users to use the licensed channels, which improves the efficiency of communications in the WSN. When CR technology and wireless sensors are combined together, a new platform is available to researchers and experts. This gives an opportunity to develop the new applications and programs that overcome the loopholes of the existing WSN. These provisions would increase the transmission range in order to enhance the efficiency of the system [1,4].

14.2 Architectural Paradigm for Cognitive Radio Sensor Networks

It is possible to render a WSN with the capability of the CR as well as dynamic spectrum management, thereby arising a new sensor network paradigm, known as the cognitive radio sensor networks (CRSNs). Commonly, CRSNs are the series of scattered and dispersed type of networks having wireless sensors. These sensors sense the predefined activities and transmit the related information to the neighboring nodes. In addition to the conventional sensing activities, CRSN nodes also sense the availability of the spectrum and update the neighboring cognitive sensors [5,6].

The architecture of CRSNs is explained in [2,7,8], where the information and data is shared and transferred through multiple hops. A representative architecture of a CRSN is shown in Figure 14.2. A wireless sensor node senses the present environment whereas the CRSN nodes have an inbuilt capability of sensing the spectrum as well. The sink controls the formation of groups, how the spectrum is allocated, and how the route is given as per the topology structure.

The CRSN nodes would finally transmit the sensed information to the sink which controls the information of groups, spectrum allocations, and its associated routing information based on the available topology. CRSN nodes together create a sensor field with some special nodes having high power sources termed as actors (full functional devices). The job of an actor is similar to the broker which at times bargains for the spectrum as well as coordinates the channel assignment task. The actors are a part of the network topology and are capable of having effective communication with the sink. The sink consists of a number of cognitive transmitters and receivers with limitless power resulting in receiving and transmitting the multiple information concurrently.

The approved primary users occupy and use the certified band whereas the secondary users try to use the certified band for communication during the absence of primary users. CRSN is a dispersed group of networks using wireless CR sensor nodes that share the sensed information with all the available channels. In the current scenario, the available wireless network seems to be crowed and overloaded which provides good opportunity for design and implementation of the CRSN's architecture.

The hardware architecture of a CRSN node consists of following four components as shown in Figure 14.2:

- Sensing unit
- Processing unit

- Transceiver unit
- Power unit

For some special applications, the CRSN nodes may be upgraded to have the localization and mobilization units along with the already built CR transmitter and receiver [9]. However, CRSN nodes also have limitations such as limited communication capabilities and small memory space. CR units are capable of adapting the communication parameters such as modulation and carrier frequency through the sensor nodes. Like a conventional wireless sensor node, the battery could be critical resources in the CRSN sensor node as well (Figure 14.3).

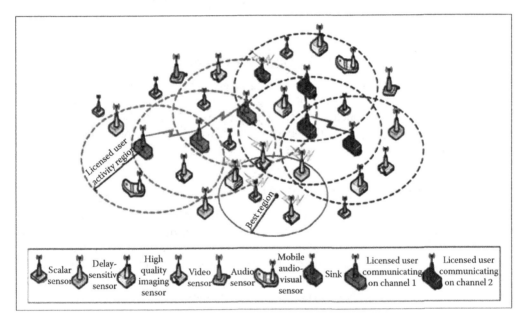

FIGURE 14.2
Architecture of a CRSN. (Courtesy of Prakash, P. et al., Issues in realization of cognitive radio sensor networks, *International Journal of Control and Automation*, 7(1), 141–152, 2014.)

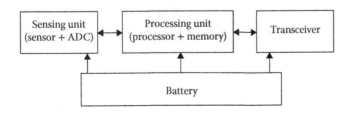

FIGURE 14.3
CRSN hardware structure. (Courtesy of Abolarinwa, J.A. et al., Cognitive radio-based wireless sensor networks as next generation sensor network: Concept, problems and prospects, *Journal of Emerging Trends in Computing and Information Sciences*, 4(8), 2013.)

14.3 Potential Application Areas of CRSNs

14.3.1 Indoor Sensing Application

Several indoor applications, such as telemedicine, home monitoring, and factory automation usually need an implemented network of sensor nodes covering a small area. Actor nodes can also be a part of the deployment in certain cases involving industrial operation automation, smart buildings, etc. The concern in such applications lies with the unlicensed bands that are usually crowded, and the best example is the industrial scientific and medical bands. Therefore, many challenges such as packet loss, collisions, and congestion affect the performance of the traditional sensor networks significantly. The opportunistic spectrum access of CRSNs may help to mitigate these challenges and prove to be beneficial in case of the crowded spectrum [4,10].

14.3.2 Multiclass Heterogeneous Sensing Applications

Multiple sensor networks with distinct sensing objectives help a few applications to coexist over a common area. The variety of data gathered from the multiple sensor networks is considered to arrive at a conclusive decision. Similarly, different sensor nodes deployed over the same area may help a single sensor network to sample the event signal over multiple dimensions including the scalar measurements.

14.3.3 Real-Time Surveillance Applications

Some applications such as target detection and tracking, which fall under a real-time surveillance queue, require minimum channel access and communication delay. The conventional WSN with a fixed spectrum allocation may fail to achieve this objective, especially if the operating spectrum band is crowded. For the efficient real-time surveillance applications, this is accomplished by a CRSN in which sensor nodes maintain minimum access to the available channels to control the communication delay.

14.3.4 Multimedia Applications

The multimedia applications require high bandwidth, reliable communication, and timing which is not so easy in the classic sensor nodes due to their limitations and restrictions. CRSN sensor nodes are free to exchange the communication channel dynamically as required by the environment. Hence, the CRSN provides improved performance in multimedia communications with the proper utilization of the spectrum. For example, during hop-by-hop packets transmission in a CRSN, every node tries to use the high frequencies and maximum data rate to achieve the high bandwidth required for the multimedia applications.

14.3.5 Health Care

In health care, the medical condition of a remote patient could be monitored by implanting the specific wireless sensor node on the body of the person and hence body sensors are gaining popularity. In many remote areas of the developing countries (e.g., Nepal and India) wireless body area network (BAN) is getting implemented in the health care systems. In 2011, BAN was approved by the Institute of Electrical and Electronics Engineers

(IEEE) 802.15 standard Task Group 6. These types of health services are best for the distant areas where hospitals and health specialists are not readily available. The timely availability of information regarding health is very important in monitoring the patients' condition in the remote areas. The classic sensor networks are not capable of meeting such requirements due to the delayed transmission caused by spectrum, power, etc. Therefore, the CR wearable body sensors provide a better solution to improve the health services [11,12].

14.3.6 Transportation and Vehicular Networks

Wireless access vehicular environments governed by the IEEE 1609.4 standard are very useful to provide the communications among multiple vehicles due to the availability of multichannel operations. However, unavailability of sufficient spectrum in the conventional sensor networks creates a bottleneck in addressing the issue related to the required spectrum. An attempt (though not up to the mark) to provide the safety on highways is being made by using the CR WSNs [13,14].

14.3.7 Underwater Sensor Application

The underwater performance of a classic wireless network is highly affected by the movement of waves, fishes, and ships in the sea. Therefore, CRSNs which choose the spectrum dynamically may provide better results as these sensors collect a lot of scientific data regarding underwater surveillance, pollution monitoring, etc.

14.3.8 Agriculture Application

Sensors are used to collect the information such as soil condition, plant development, and requirement of fertilizer and water. These can be properly controlled by using a CRSN which provides great results in the field of agriculture [15,16].

14.4 Dynamic Spectrum Management in CRSNs

To regulate the dynamic spectrum access, an effective spectrum-management framework is deployed. Some of the research issues and major challenges for dynamic spectrum management in CRSNs are well described in [10,16–20].

14.4.1 Spectrum Sensing

One of the most important functions of CRSN that differentiates it from the conventional WSN is the "spectrum sensing." The nodes operate on spectrum bands hence, a spectrum usage mechanism needs to be defined before the transmission. Some of the spectrum sensing strategies are described below:

14.4.1.1 Matched Filter

Matched-filter-based detection is used when the primary user transmission characteristics are accessible. CRSN nodes would need extra electronic equipment for every primary user. It will increase the value and complexity for low-end sensors.

14.4.1.2 Energy Detection

In the energy detection method, the CRNS nodes require an easier spectrum-sensing technique, so that a precise performance level is achieved by reducing the energy consumption. Moreover, performance of this technique depends on the power-level variations and hence, it is difficult to identify a small increments in the detection energy. The possible cause could be the additional activities on part of the primary user or increase in noise.

14.4.1.3 Feature Detection

In this method, the carrier frequency and cyclic prefixes must be well known. This method is more appropriate for the special CRSN cases where the network has big processor power.

14.4.1.4 Interference Temperature

This technique needs the CRSN nodes to grasp the locations of the primary user for interference measuring. Moreover, it is going to be too computationally intense for the low-end sensors.

14.4.2 Types of Spectrum Sensing

14.4.2.1 Parallel and Sequential

In parallel sensing, N number of channels are sensed in parallel whereas in sequential sensing channels are sensed one by one.

14.4.2.2 Proactive and Reactive

In the proactive approach, the CRSN node senses the spectrum on a regular basis without caring about the immediate need of data transmission, while in the case of the reactive approach, the spectrum is only sensed upon the availability of the data to be transmitted.

14.4.2.3 Local and Cooperative

In local sensing, the CRSN node senses the spectrum individually to make a decision on the channel selection based on the busy or idle state, whereas in cooperative sensing, the decision of channel selection is made by considering the requirement of the neighboring nodes.

14.4.2.4 Centralized and Distributed

In the centralized approach, a central device collects all the information and then makes a decision, while in distributed, each CR decides for itself.

14.4.2.5 Synchronous and Asynchronous

In synchronous mode, all the CRSN nodes use the similar sensing techniques and single timeline to sense the channel whereas in the asynchronous mode, each CRSN node does it independently.

14.4.2.6 In-Band and Out-of-Band

An in-band approach collects the information about already transmitting channels while an out-of-band approach only worries about the nontransmitting channels.

A pictorial representation of commonly used spectrum-sensing techniques is shown in Figure 14.4.

14.4.3 Spectrum Decision

Akyildiz et al. [20] and Mercier et al. [21] have described that the CRSN analyzes the data collected by the sensors to make a decision regarding the channel selection and transmission parameters. However, in their spectrum-decision method the consumption of power and need for additional memory (if required) have not been considered.

In the conventional WSN, the access of channels as per individual spectrum decision increases the chances of collision. Moreover, if the multiple nodes run identical algorithms or rule to tackle the collision, they may try to switch over to other available channels which may lead to a collision in the new channel too. The availability of multiple channels in a CRSN would address the above mentioned collision problem effectively, but many channels may remain unused. Therefore, a suitable strategy needs to be adapted for proper spectrum-utilization decision to enhance the efficiency of overall system.

Some of the research objectives regarding the spectrum-decision technique are as follows.

14.4.3.1 Spectrum-Decision Parameters

The decision on crucial parameters is very important as the computation of signal-to-noise ratio (SNR) and data rate is simple, but the determination of various errors and delay associated with the links is a difficult task.

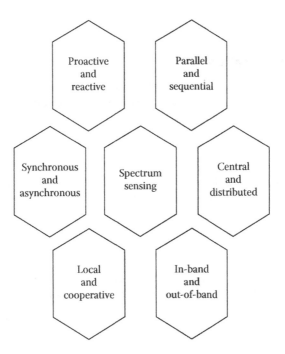

FIGURE 14.4
Types of spectrum sensing.

14.4.3.2 Handling Heterogeneity

New decision methods are required for the heterogeneous networks as they have different types of sensor nodes and channel parameters, and hence, for proper coordination in the heterogeneous networks smart decisions are deployed.

14.4.3.3 Distribution Using Control Data

In conventional multichannel networks, a common control channel is used to provide the proper coordination among various spectrum techniques to share the control data whereas in CRSNs there is no dedicated control channel.

14.4.4 Spectrum Handoff

Handoff is the technique in which channels are switched from a poor signaling site to the new channel site having strong signaling power. In a spectrum handoff, the CRSN node contains all the data and information regarding the primary user.

The primary user does its activities at regular intervals of time with the help of spectrum-sensing techniques. If the channels' condition is aggravated to degrade the communication performance, the CRSN nodes automatically would switch to the new channels for better performance and the process is referred to as spectrum handoff.

In a CRSN, to perform the spectrum handoff, the nearby idle channel must be identified to swap. However, identification in swapping of channels may result in delays, degraded performance, and wastage of resources. Therefore new methods are required to be developed to overcome the loss occurred due to the spectrum handoff.

14.5 CRSN Communication

Communication is a key parameter in establishing a connection between the two nodes. In reference to layered architecture, the description of functionality associated with each layer is given below:

14.5.1 Physical Layer

It is an interface between the data link and the physical wireless medium, additionally accountable for the spectrum sensing and transmission of parameters as per the spectrum decisions.

14.5.2 Data Link Layer

This layer is accountable for frames reception between the sensors and for reliable transmission. The error control and medium access control is also carried out here.

14.5.3 Network Layer

Proper routing, wireless networking, such as ad hoc and multi-hop, are considered properly in this layer.

14.5.4 Transport Layer

In this layer congestion control and proper end-to-end delivery of the control packets are taken into account.

14.5.5 Application Layer

This layer enables the information associated to the sensor node, generates it, and enhances the deficient field of information into it. Finally, communicates it to the corresponding sink. Proper scanning of the network is done by WSN and hence, it knows the presence of the spectrum holes which affect the secondary network. Related information provided to the secondary network has the knowledge of loopholes of the network and it starts communicating without any harmful interference to the primary network [22,23].

14.6 Challenges and Issues in CRSNs

Some challenges and issues related to the development of CRSN are well explained by authors of [24–27]. The details of these challenges along with the possible solutions to overcome them are discussed in this section.

14.6.1 False Alarm/Misdetection Probability

The parameters associated with the availability of the primary users on the channel are detection, false alarm, and misdetection probabilities. The detection probability tells about the right detection of the absence of the primary user, while misdetection probability indicates that the CRSN is unable to detect the primary user on the channel. The false alarm probability tells about the failure of the CRSN to determine the absence of the primary user.

The misdetection and false alarm may restrict the entry of the secondary user consequently violating the very objective of the CRSN as one will lead to the interference with the primary user and the other will create the underutilization of the spectrum. Other issues associated with the misdetection and false alarm probabilities are frequent channel switching and long waiting delay which leads to overall performance degradations. However, the misdetection and false alarm probabilities have been studied extensively in reference to the IEEE 802.22 and CR ad hoc networks but a detailed study needs to be carried out for proper estimation of these parameters in reference to CRSNs.

14.6.2 CRSN Hardware

CRSN hardware structure is shown in Figure 14.5 and it consists of six major units as depicted below:

- Sensing unit
- Processing and storage unit
- CR unit
- Miscellaneous unit
- Transceiver unit
- Power unit

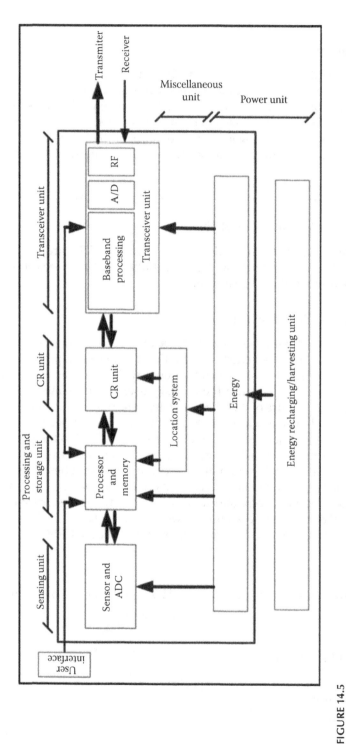

FIGURE 14.5

CRSN hardware structure. (Courtesy of Joshi, G.P. et al., Cognitive radio wireless sensor networks: applications, challenges and research trends, *Sensors*, 13, 11196–11228, 2013.)

The sensing unit has sensors along with an analog-to-digital convertor. This converts the signal into digital form and sends it to the processing unit. The processed signal goes to the CR unit where it is recognized in terms of its carrier frequency, modulation, and transmission power. Joshi et al. [2] showed that artificial intelligence techniques could be used for an effective recognition of the signals. After that it goes to the transmission unit, where it is transmitted to next unit.

14.6.3 Topology Changes

Topology refers to the physical layout of the network which affects the network lifetime. CRSNs use similar topologies as used in classical WSNs. However, it has been observed that the self-configuring topology is more effective than the static topology. Like the conventional WSN, a CRSN also faces the problem of hardware failure due to energy reduction. The topologies commonly used in CRSNs are the same as used in the conventional WSN but change more frequently. The following topologies as suggested by [5] are common in a CRSN:

- Mobile CRSNs
- Ad hoc CRSNs
- Heterogeneous CRSNs
- Hierarchical CRSNs
- Clustered CRSNs

It has been observed that the routes having a lower number of hops of longer hop-distance are more energy consuming than the routes with more hops of shorter hop-distances [28].

14.6.4 Fault Tolerance

CRSNs need to be developed in a way so that it takes care of establishing the paths in the presence of node or link failure. The faults could occur any time due to malfunction of the software or natural disasters. Therefore, the CRSN should be designed to tackle the failure-related issues. De Souza et al. [29] presented the survey on fault tolerance in a conventional WSN and identified that the commonly occurring faults are network fault, node fault, and sink fault, etc. Therefore, the challenging issue of fault tolerance cannot be ignored in CRSNs also. The protocol designed for the CR should provide the provision for fault tolerance so that the overall performance of networks is not affected by the occurrence of fault in the system.

14.6.5 Clustering

In the large networks, in order to reduce the energy consumption and communication overheads the concept of cluster can be used in routing. Different types of clustering used in CRSNs are given as follows:

- Dynamic
- Static
- Homogeneous
- Heterogeneous

14.6.6 Selection of Channel

Selection of channel is done considering the primary user's behavior as the secondary user must leave the channel on arrival of the primary user. Therefore, no formal understanding could be built between the primary and secondary users. To avoid interference with the primary user, channel-selection algorithms should be developed intelligently by keeping the channel-utilization pattern of the primary user in mind.

14.6.7 Scalability

CRSN must be designed looking into the scalability issues for future expansion as many nodes may be added to the network based on the instantaneous requirement. Hence, intelligent algorithms must be implemented in the original design.

14.6.8 Consumption of Power

Nodes in CRSN have limited power which is consumed for the following activities:

- Transmission and reception of packets
- Route discovery
- Spectrum sensing
- Data processing
- Multiple antennas to monitor activities
- Channel negotiation

Power consumption is a vital issue in designing the conventional WSN, while in CRSN also it is a main factor needed to be considered as it affects the network lifetime.

14.6.9 Quality of Service

To ensure the quality of service (QoS), various parameters are taken into considerations such as delay, bandwidth, reliability, jitter, residual power, and memory requirement. As the arrival of the primary user in the channel is unpredictable, the misdetection may hamper the QoS [30].

14.6.10 Security

CR sensors can be easily attacked and the information can be stolen. Therefore, security must be provided to save the CRSN from threats. Joshi et al. [31] identified the following issues related to CRSN securities:

- Insertion of false data
- Modification of data
- Usage of common channels
- Unacceptable interference
- Access to private data
- Usage of idle channels to secondary users

Generally, different attacks affect different layers of the network. The details of some popular attacks are discussed as follows.

14.6.10.1 Routing Layer Attack

In the routing layer attack, the routine path is altered or a wrong route is provided which results in a delayed or a wrong destination delivery of packets [32,33]. Three types of attacks responsible for such behaviour are given below.

14.6.10.1.1 Sybil Attack

In this attack, multiple identities of different nodes could be done by a single node (malicious node) which results in same packets delivered to multiple locations. This could create the problem of congestion or network jamming, leading to a wastage of power and energy.

14.6.10.1.2 Wormhole Attack

This attack creates a fake node that could flush the wrong route information to other nodes existing in the network. It consumes the network energy and creates the fake or empty packets that results in overheads or congestion of the network.

14.6.10.1.3 Sinkhole Attack

In this attack, the intruder broadcasts the false information about the shortest path giving the intuition of the efficient path to an intermediate node. However, this efficient path is misleading and a packet sent through this path either gets lost or goes to the longest/congested route resulting in an infinite delay.

14.6.10.2 MAC Layer Attack

Attacks under this category include transmitting the unwanted packets or frames repeatedly to the already congested routes. This would consume more battery power, occupy channels' bandwidth, and result in annoying operation behaviour. It could finally lead to denial of service (DoS) attack on the media access control (MAC) layer.

14.6.10.3 Physical Layer Attack

This attack mainly focuses on jamming the network that may lead to broadcasting the radio signals over wireless channels. This interferes with the CR sensors' operations in the physical layer. This may result in a DoS attack on the physical layer. Another attack possible in this category is tempering and damaging the sensing unit of the CRSN node.

14.6.11 Sensing Techniques

Joshi et al. [2] and Yuan et al. [34] well defined the sensing techniques in which the unused spectrum is properly used by the CRSN node. Improper sensing of the spectrum done by the secondary users may lead to interference and hence if the secondary users detect the channel with good accuracy the chances of interference automatically decreases. Sensing techniques are divided into two:

1. Signal processing techniques
2. Cooperative sensing

14.6.11.1 Signal Processing Techniques

14.6.11.1.1 Matched-Filter Detection

In this technique, a demodulation of primary user signals is done, which is then received by the CRSN nodes at both the physical and MAC layers. This involves the order of modulation and its type, bandwidth used, operating frequency, and packet format. The advantage of using this method is that it incurs a short time. It decreases the SNR and number of signal samples required. A major drawback with this technique is that it consumes more battery power and runs process with high complexity. It also requires better knowledge of the target users.

14.6.11.1.2 Energy Detection

This technique is quite famous for its simplicity. It senses the energy of the signal which does not depend on the previous information of the primary users. But its accuracy is poor, hence it is not used for the detection of spectrum signals that have low SNR. This detection technique is not capable of distinguishing the primary users from secondary users.

14.6.11.1.3 Cyclostationary Detection

In this detection, the modulated signals are synchronized with a sinusoidal carrier wave, cyclic prefix pulse signals, and hopping sequences. Therefore, it gives an improved performance in the regions where SNR is low. This detection method is complex and unable of high-speed sensing, but signal categorization is good.

14.6.11.2 Cooperative Sensing

Radio communication over wireless channels has some serious negative aspects such as penetration of signal, scattering, and multipath fading that could also affect the CRSN node judgements. These nodes could not sense several channels at the same time and have various hardware restrictions. Hence cooperation and sharing of information improves the overall performance. This method could be categorized as follows.

14.6.11.2.1 Centralized Cooperative Spectrum Technique

In this technique, every CRSN node does the spectrum sensing, locally and individually, which decides whether a primary user signal is absent or present on a specific channel. After taking the decision, the sensor node sends this information to a centralized hub which acts as a data collector, cluster head, or server. Finally, this centralized hub decides the presence of a primary user on particular channel. Therefore, at any instance if the CRSN node would like to transmit the data, it must request the central hub to determine presence or absence of a primary user on a particular channel.

14.6.11.2.2 Decentralized Cooperative Spectrum Sensing

In this technique, there is no concept of centralized hub and hence, it works in a decentralized approach. The CRSN node responds to the immediate data collector of its cluster which acts as cluster head. This cluster head also involves intercluster communication. It performs the local spectrum sensing at its own cluster and informs the other CRSN nodes about the spectrum decision. Cluster heads thus share the information with their nearby clusters. Hence, all the clusters have updated information of their adjacent clusters. This would require a spectrum information table which is necessary for the proper cooperation in handling the memory and large calculations overhead in this technique.

14.6.11.2.3 *Hybrid Cooperative Spectrum Sensing*

This technique uses the best of the previously defined techniques and hence, both centralized and decentralized techniques are present in the hybrid spectrum-sensing technique. The CRSN node transmits the data in a decentralized manner whereas the central hub could request the cluster head to share the channel information if required. This technique is costly and complex as it requires an extra hardware setup for spectrum sensing which could be an exigent issue for hardware constraint in CRSNs. Even though, cooperative sensing has several advantages over noncooperative sensing it has problems in establishing a CRSN.

14.7 Conclusion

In almost every situation, the overall performance of a CRN increases. CRSN improves the quality of communication, sharing of information and proper utilization, accessibility of spectrum, and elasticity in the channel as per the situation. Also numerous channels are available to sort the issues created in the congested, overloaded communications in the classic networks. Hence, it gives more efficient results in terms of spectrum utilization and less interference which is the basic requirement of a large and cost-effective network. Many researches are going on in this field to establish more economic, secured, trustworthy, and flexible networks for the benefits of the users, and to create a smart CRSN node more and more flexible applications, algorithms as per demand, simplified hardware, and user-friendly software should be developed.

References

1. Tragos, E., Zeadally, S., Fragkiadakis, A. and Siris, V. (2013). Spectrum assignment in cognitive radio networks: A comprehensive survey. *IEEE Communication Survey and Tutorial*, 15: 1108–1135.
2. Joshi, G.P., Nam, S.Y. and Kim, S.W. (2013). Cognitive radio wireless sensor networks: Applications, challenges and research trends. *Sensors*, 13: 11196–11228. http://www.mdpi.com/journal/sensors/s130911196
3. Jin, Z.L., Kim, B.S., Guan, D.H., and Cho, J.S. (2013). A probabilistic routing protocol based on priori information for cognitive radio sensor networks. *Applied Mechanics and Materials*, 303: 210–214.
4. Sengupta, S., Subbalakshmi, K.P. (2013). Open research issues in multi-hop cognitive radio networks. *IEEE Communication Magazine*, 51: 168–176.
5. Akan, O.B., Karli, O.B. and Ergul, O. (2009). Cognitive radio sensor networks. *IEEE Networks*, 23: 34–40.
6. Ariananda, D.D., Lakshmanan, M.K. and Nikookar, H. (2009). A survey on spectrum sensing techniques for cognitive radio. In *Proceedings of the Second International Workshop on Cognitive Radio and Advanced Spectrum Management (CogART 2009)*, May, Aalborg, Denmark, pp. 74–79.
7. Masonta, M., Mzyece, M. and Ntlatlapa, N. (2013). Spectrum decision in cognitive radio networks: A survey. *IEEE Communication Survey and Tutorial*, 15: 1088–1107.

8. Wang, Y., Yuehong, L., Yuan, F. and Yang, J. (2013). A cooperative spectrum sensing scheme based on trust and fuzzy logic for cognitive radio sensor networks. *International Journal of Computer Science*, 10: 275–279.

9. Oto, M.C., Akan, O.B. (2012). Energy-efficient packet size optimization for cognitive radio sensor networks. *IEEE Transaction Wireless Communication*, 11: 1544–1553.

10. Oey, C.H., Christian, I. and Moh, S. (2012). Energy- and cognitive-radio-aware routing in cognitive radio sensor networks. *International Journal Distributed Senor Network*, 636723: 1–11.

11. Lang, W., Zhu, Y. and Li, H. (2012). Security architecture for energy-efficient wireless cognitive sensor network. In *Proceedings of the IEEE Cyber Technology in Automation, Control, and Intelligent Systems (CYBER 2012)*, May, Thailand, pp. 12–16.

12. Park, S., Heo, J., Kim, B., et al. (2012). Optimal mode selection for cognitive radio sensor networks with RF energy harvesting. In *Proceedings of the IEEE 23rd Personal Indoor and Mobile Radio Communications (PIMRC 2012)*, 9–12 September, Sydney, Australia, pp. 2155–2159.

13. Aalamifar, F., Vijay, G., Abedi Khoozani, P. and Ibnkahla, M. (2011). Cognitive wireless sensor networks for highway safety. In *Proceedings of the First ACM International Symposium on Design and Analysis of Intelligent Vehicular Networks and Applications (DIVANet '11)*, October–November, FL, USA, pp. 55–60.

14. Feng, S. and Zhao, D. (2010). Supporting real-time CBR traffic in a cognitive radio sensor network. In *Proceedings of the IEEE Wireless Communications and Networking Conference (WCNC)*, April, Sydney, Australia, pp. 1–6.

15. Jamal, A., Tham, C.K. and Wong, W.C. (2012). Event detection and channel allocation in cognitive radio sensor networks. In *Proceedings of the IEEE International Conference on Communication Systems (ICCS 2012)*, 21–23 November 2012, Singapore, pp. 157–161.

16. Wu, C., Ohzahata, S. and Kato, T. (2012). Dynamic channel assignment and routing for cognitive sensor networks. In *Proceedings of the International Symposium on Wireless Communication Systems (ISWCS 2012)*, Paris, France, pp. 86–90.

17. Joshi, G.P. and Kim, S.W. (2011). Mitigating the control channel bottleneck problem in dense cognitive radio networks. *International Journal of Physical Sciences*, 6: 4832–4837.

18. Hu, Z., Sun, Y., Ji, Y. (2011). A dynamic spectrum access strategy based on real-time usability in cognitive radio sensor networks. In *Proceedings of the Seventh International Conference on Mobile Ad-Hoc and Sensor Networks (MSN 2011)*, 16–18 December, Beijing, China, pp. 318–322.

19. Zhang, T. and Yu, X. (2010). Spectrum sharing in cognitive radio using game theory—A survey. In *Proceedings of the Sixth International Conference on Wireless Communications Networking and Mobile Computing (WiCOM)*, September, Chengdu, China, pp. 1–5.

20. Akyildiz, I.F., Lee, W.Y., Vuran, M.C. and Mohanty, S. (2008). A survey on spectrum management in cognitive radio networks. *IEEE Communication Magazine*, 46: 40–48.

21. Mercier, B., Fodor, V., Thobaben, R. and Skoglund, M. (2008). Sensor networks for cognitive radio: Theory and system design. In *Proceedings of the ICT Mobile and Wireless Communications Summit (ICT '08, Stockholm, Sweden)*.

22. Li, X., Wang, D., McNair, J. and Chen, J. (2011). Residual energy aware channel assignment in cognitive radio sensor networks. In *Proceedings of the IEEE Wireless Communications and Networking Conference (WCNC 2011)*, March, Cancun, Mexico, pp. 398–403.

23. Han, J.A., Jeon, W.S. and Jeong, D.G. (2011). Energy-efficient channel management scheme for cognitive radio sensor networks. *IEEE Transaction Vehicular Technology*, 60: 1905–1910.

24. Zhang, H., Zhang, Z., Chen, X. and Yin, R. (2011). Energy efficient joint source and channel sensing in cognitive radio sensor networks. In *Proceedings of the IEEE International Conference on Communications (ICC 2011)*, June, Kyoto, Japan, pp. 1–6.

25. Vijay, G., Ben Ali Bdira, E. and Ibnkahla, M. (2011). Cognition in wireless sensor networks: A perspective. *IEEE Sensor Journal*, 11: 582–592.

26. Liang, Z., Feng, S., Zhao, D. and Shen, X.S. (2011). Delay performance analysis for supporting real-time traffic in a cognitive radio sensor network. *IEEE Transaction Wireless Communication*, 10: 325–335.

27. Jia, J.G., He, Z.W., Kuang, J.M. and Wang, H.F. (2010). Analysis of key technologies for cognitive radio based wireless sensor networks. In *Proceedings of the IEEE 6th International Conference on Wireless Communications Networking and Mobile Computing (WiCOM '10)*, September, Chengdu, China, pp. 1–5.

28. Cayirci, E. and Rong, C. (2008). *Security in Wireless Ad Hoc and Sensor Networks*. Chichester, UK: John Wiley & Sons Ltd.

29. De Souza, L.M.S., Vogt, H. and Beigl, M. (2007). *A Survey on Fault Tolerance in Wireless Sensor Networks*. Karlsruhe, Germany: Interner Bericht, Fakultät für Informatik, Universität Karlsruhe.

30. Liang, Z. and Zhao, D. (2010). Quality of service performance of a cognitive radio sensor network. In *Proceedings of the IEEE International Conference on Communications (ICC)*, May, Cape Town, South Africa, pp. 1–5.

31. Joshi, G.P., Kim, S.W. and Kim B.S. (2009). An efficient MAC protocol for improving the network throughput for cognitive radio networks. In *Proceedings of the Third International Conference on Next Generation Mobile Applications, Services and Technologies (NGMAST '09)*, September, Cardiff, UK, pp. 271–275.

32. Cavalcanti, D., Das, S., Jianfeng, W. and Challapali, K. (2008). Cognitive radio based wireless sensor networks. In *Proceeding of the IEEE 17th International Conference on Computer Communications and Networks*, August, St. Thomas U.S. Virgin Islands, pp. 1–6.

33. Fitzek, F.H.P. and Katz, M.D. (2006). *Cooperation in Wireless Networks: Principles and Applications*. Berlin: Springer.

34. Yuan, W., Leung, H., Chen, S. and Cheng, W. (2011). A distributed sensor selection mechanism for cooperative spectrum sensing. *IEEE Transaction on Signal Processing*, 59: 6033–6044.

15

Business Valuation and Cost-Capacity Modeling of the Cognitive Radio Enabled Beyond 4G- and 5G-Based Wireless Heterogeneous Networks

Vladimir Nikolikj and Toni Janevski

CONTENTS

15.1 Introduction

The emerging mobile broadband (MBB) wireless and mobile network architectures tend to become more heterogeneous with macro base station (MaBS), micro base station (MiBS), pico base station (PBS), and femtocell base station (FBS) sites, complemented by particular wireless local area networks (WLAN or Wi-Fi), access points (APs), and enabled with various radio access technologies (RATs). The term *broadband wireless heterogeneous network* (HetNet) denotes a radio access network (RAN) supporting a mix of RATs granting access to the same mobile device (MD). Also, the HetNet refers to a RAN based on "hierarchically different cell structures" when a particular RAT is served by various types of base station (BS)/AP sites. With this regard, it becomes evident that the mobile paradigm intensively moves from the mobile network operator (MNO)–driven approach implemented beyond 3G RATs, such as the universal mobile telecommunications system (UMTS)/high-speed packet access (HSPA) (third generation partnership project [3GPP] release 6/7), mobile WiMax 1.5 (Institute of Electrical and Electronics Engineers [IEEE] 802.16-2009), and cellular systems for the fourth generation (4G) long-term evolution (LTE) RAT (3GPP release 8/9) out of the International Telecommunication Union (ITU) IMT-2000 specifications [1], toward the user-driven or service-centric approach supported beyond 4G RATs which are (according to the ITU IMT-advanced umbrella [2]) LTE-advanced or "LTE-A" (3GPP LTE Release 10 and beyond) [3] and wireless MAN-advanced or "Mobile WiMax System Release 2.0" (WiMax 2.0) (IEEE Std 802.16-2012) [4].

Nevertheless, even the RATs for the near future are designed to exploit the frequencies from the restricted microwave spectrum that is deficient to satisfy the exponentially increasing capacities and user data-rate demands. One of the most recognized advanced radio systems that enables the use of the existing resources more effectively is the cognitive radio system (CRS) (IEEE Std 802.22-2011) [5]. The CRS is aware of its environment and makes decisions considering the performance of the whole radio system and is able to sense its environment and perform accordingly, and shows remarkable potential for increasing the spectral efficiency in the wireless systems. Thus, it is expected that the CRS will gain significant importance from the future HetNets aiming to provide higher and guaranteed user data rates.

Also, due to further need to compensate for the lack of spectrum, recent researches extensively pay attention to the achievements of the millimeter wave (mmW) cellular systems, relying on the vast available spectrum bandwidth in the range of 28–300 GHz band. In the past few years, the researches [6–14] through empirical findings delivered substantial methodologies for the novel mmW-based cellular systems, expected to be one of the foundations for the fifth generation (or 5G). Accordingly, the carrier frequencies in the 28, 38, and 73 GHz bands with channel bandwidth up to 1.0 GHz can be used at steerable directional horn antennas implemented in the BS and MDs. It is expected that with the further RAT improvements and using carrier aggregation, the peak data rate of 5G mmW-based systems will be multiple of tens of giga-bits per second (Gbps), and the user data rates will be around 1.0 Gbps. Also, from the high consideration is the mmW WLAN deployment based on the IEEE 802.11ad standard which enables up to 7.0 Mbps per cell. Despite the standardization of 5G by 3GPP and ITU, due to the great potential of mmW communications, according to Niu et al. [6] multiple international organizations have emerged for the standardization, such as IEEE 802.15.3 Task Group 3c (TG3c) [15] and IEEE 802.11ad standardization task group [16]. To address the overall techno-economic challenges, it should be considered that the recent researches [17,18] are seriously addressing the backhaul challenge by proposing a novel cost-effective, fiber-based backhaul infrastructure, which leverages the existing point-to-point (PTP) passive optical network (PON)-based fiber-to-the-node access network solutions.

These extraordinary performances and challenges beyond 4G and mmW 5G systems, preferably supported with CRS, were our object to evaluate their capabilities from a techno-economic perspective, to be a ground for the future mobile data services. Hence, in this chapter we present a comparative cost-capacity modeling of several emerging HetNet deployments and determine their costs of production and earnings before interest and taxes (EBIT) margins. In that regard, we perform a broad network dimensioning that is applied to the residential dense-urban environment demanding the high data volumes (a few hundred times the mobile/wireless traffic of the typical private data users). Furthermore, in the cases of the capacity overprovisioning, we evaluate the manners to guarantee the quality of service (QoS) (guaranteed user data rates) for a chosen number of subscribers. Consequently, we consider a method for the advanced dynamic sharing of the radio resources between the MNOs supporting CRS and considering different levels of service probability.

15.2 Literature Review

The basis for our techno-economic modeling can be found in the comprehensive contributions [19–32]. All of these publications treat several approaches to respond to a particular traffic demand cost-efficiently via the expansion strategies for different HetNet deployments with a mix of RATs, or a mix of BS/AP classes. The cost-capacity comparisons of the PBS, MiBS, and MaBS sites equipped with wideband code division multiple access (WCDMA) and HSPA RATs including IEEE 802.11a and IEEE 802.11n Wi-Fi APs, are delivered in [19–22]. LTE (Release 8), and HSPA equipped MaBS and FBS sites are widely treated in [23,24]. Markendahl and Mäkitalo [23] consider the construction of a business center with inside-deployed FBS sites and outside-deployed MaBS sites to provide the indoor coverage. These authors also cover the issue of wall attenuation calculated based on the legacy propagation models, such as Okumura-Hata, which could be mitigated with denser BS layouts placed outside. Further techno-economic assessment of MaBS and FBS sites supporting the HSPA/LTE RATs is covered in [25–28]. Elasticity evaluation of the capital expenditures (CAPEX) covering different modifications of the involved cost, capacity, and coverage unit items is delivered in [19,29]. Cost-capacity analysis with site reuse is originally covered in [23], with a remark that this reference does not consider detailed deployment scenarios based on the factual area per building floor in square meters, but only the overall area of 1 km^2 with the coverage and user-oriented approach.

Furthermore, all of the previous studies consider only either a typical PTP or traditional PON-based backhaul architectures for the RAN as in [31,32]. Even more, many of the findings in all the previously mentioned articles deal with the microwave spectrum, up to 2.6 GHz [19,30] bands and with per single carrier channel bandwidth of 5, 15, and maximum 20 MHz [19,23,24]. Finally, all of these contributions assess the profit margins and cost-effectiveness of the HetNets with very low data demand targets and relatively insignificant data rates per single user, compared to beyond 2020 estimates, for instance given as target in [33]. With regard to CRSs [5], the literature review shows no particular reference covering its impact on the business alongside the technical benefits coming with the dynamic access to the available spectral opportunities, in order to adopt the operations of the network, such as support interoperability, decrease interference, and increase throughputs [34–37].

15.3 Research Methodology

15.3.1 Description of the Research Method

The research method consists of *network dimensioning*, *cost modeling*, and *profitability modeling*. Based on the combination of the achievable capacity, related to the available spectrum and spectral efficiency of a particular RAT, together with the coverage performances of various BS/AP classes, we obtain an outcome of the network dimensioning the total number of BS/AP sites to be constructed to satisfy the desired data demand of the users. Then, we proceed with the cost modeling using the network dimensioning results as the inputs, which are further multiplied with the unit costs of particular type of BS/AP class. Finally, we conduct the profitability modeling, based on the production cost, CAPEX annualization, average revenue per user, and an assumption of the overall operational expenditures. The result is the gained profit margin for the MNO [38].

15.3.2 Reliability of the Research Method

To identify if the obtained cost-capacity and profitability findings in this chapter are consistent, we describe the approach used for the reliability assessment of the used research methodology in this section. For that purpose, related to the network dimensioning, we perform a check to make sure that the resulting coverage of particular type of BS/AP class is satisfactory for the targeted user's average data rates. The way to do so is to assure that the requirement on average user data rates (obtained by conversion of the considered levels of user demand into bps) could be satisfied even at the cell borders. The widely accepted parameter for determining the data rate conditions at the cell border is called the *cell-edge user throughput* defined as the 5% point of the cumulative distribution function of the user throughput normalized with the overall cell bandwidth and measured in (bps/Hz) [39]. Consequently, the confidence in our case is reached through ensuring a guarantee that the coverage is adequate for the targeted data rates at the cell borders. For doing this, first we dimension the capacity of the cell of a particular BS/AP based on the *average cell spectral efficiency* (bps/Hz/cell)) for every particular RAT in accordance to the standardized or empirically obtained values. Then, for the single snapshot of the uniformly distributed users within the considered area, based on the targeted average capacity of the analyzed area (e.g., in Gbps/km^2), we obtain the quantity of BS/AP sites needed to accept the user demand, and thus we yield the range or the concrete BS/AP.

Further, based on the standardized or empirical values for the *cell-edge spectral efficiency* related to the particular RAT performances obtained for certain coverage range and bandwidth size, we calculate the cell-edge user data rate and compare its value with the targeted average user data rate. The condition to accept certain HetNet layout with a particular density of BS/APs in the area (or the condition to accept the range of every cell) is that the cell-edge user data rate is identical or higher than the average user data rate of interest. In that case, we conclude that the coverage is sufficient for the data rates of interest and we consider the obtained results as relevant. Otherwise, the cell range should be further decreased until the coverage becomes sufficient, or until the link budget would be *good enough* for the purpose to provide the realistic desired data rates even at the cell borders. The consequence of the range decrease is the decrease of the sizes of the cells which at the end delivers a higher density of BSs/APs to be deployed.

15.4 HetNet Dimensioning

We perform dimensioning in the super-densely populated urban city area comprising the indoor and outdoor environment of 1.0 km^2 with population of 400,000 citizens. In accordance with the test case "dense urban information society" introduced in [33], we define the *residential evaluation scenario*. We consider a market with three MNOs with 33% subscriber share.

The penetration of the users accessing the broadband internet via mobile infrastructure is 75%, by what the density is 100,000 users/km^2/MNO. The monthly average usage of the smartphone, tablets, and laptops will rise up to 2.7, 12.2, and 6.9 GB, respectively, by 2018 [40]. Additionally, it is predicted that beyond 2020 communication networks need to satisfy 500 GB/user/month in the "dense urban information society" [33]. Being the main consideration of the network deployment, we assume that 90% of the monthly traffic is in download, or 450 GB/user, what we denote as high usage and three times lower monthly volume or with 150 GB/user denoted as low demand. Also, we assume that a residential user will generate 80% of the traffic indoors [41]. Assuming this share, we yield for the high-demand case, a 360 GB/user to be served indoors and 90 GB/user outdoors. In case of the low demand, the adequate outdoor/indoor share will be 30/120 GB/user.

We represent the generated traffic/capacity over a given area as a function of the MBB population density per MNO ρ (or in our case 100,000 users/km^2) as follows [31]:

$$G(t) = \rho \times 1024 \times 8 \frac{1}{3600} \frac{1}{f_{dh}} \frac{1}{n_d} \tau(t) \sum_k D_k s_k \ (\text{Gbps/km}^2) \tag{15.1}$$

where D_k is the average data demand per month in GB for terminal k (i.e., s_{pc}, s_{tablet}, $s_{s.phone}$), $\tau(t)$ stands for a typical daily traffic variation in terms of the percentage of number of active users for a given time t, f_{dh} stands for the busy hours during a day (time during a day with the most traffic [29]), and n_d stands for the days with user activity during the month. According to [33], we consider that the usage will be spread throughout the 9 h a day (11.11% busy hour ratio) or $f_{dh} = 9$ across 30 days of a month or $n_d = 30$. Further, in combination with the forecasted values, using Equation 15.1 it is possible to calculate the peak area traffic demand at the busy hour as G (Gbps/km^2) = $\max_t(G(t))$ under the assumption that all of the subscribers are active during the busy/peak hour (i.e., $\tau_{max} = 100\%$), for the purpose of maximizing the probable cost-capacity estimates of an MNO. Consequently, Table 15.1 summarizes the area capacity values and the average user data rates for each of the considered levels of user demand.

Regarding the backhaul access services, we consider a typical PTP and PON-based infrastructure, according to [31,32], where the traffic is aggregated by 48 ports gigabit Ethernet switch (GES) per floor, connected via optical fiber of $n \times 1$ Gbps to the optical network unit (ONU). The cells inside a building are connected to a GES with $n \times$ fast Ethernet connections. The ONU is connected to the optical line terminal (OLT) via $n \times 10$ Gbps optical links SFP+. The OLT is composed of 4×10 gigabit-capable passive optical network GPON ports, each supporting up to 32 users connected via the ONU.

Also, according to [17], we assume that a part of the future RAN backhaul will be build based on the intermediate aggregation nodes enabled with the wave division multiplexing (WDM) backhaul infrastructure with 10G wavelengths from the central office to the BS sites having active remote nodes (ARNs) that consist of an Ethernet switch with 3 racks $\times$ 40 Gbps (or total 120 Gbps), where each rack has four ports with 10G capacity. Traffic is aggregated at the ARN which is also designed to offer statistically multiplexed bandwidth and to support 1.0 Gbps per user, based on the enabled high-speed statistical multiplexing features. Also, we assume provisioning of the 10 Gbps bandwidth pipes to the buildings. Additionally, as proposed in [18], we assume that such backhaul architecture owns

TABLE 15.1

Capacities of the Dense Urban Area (Tbps/km^2)

Residential Scenario—Environment	Intensity	GB/User/Month	Mbps/User	Tbps/km^2
Outdoor	Low	30	0.25	0.024
Outdoor	High	90	0.76	0.083
Indoor	Low	120	1.01	0.099
Indoor	High	360	3.03	0.34

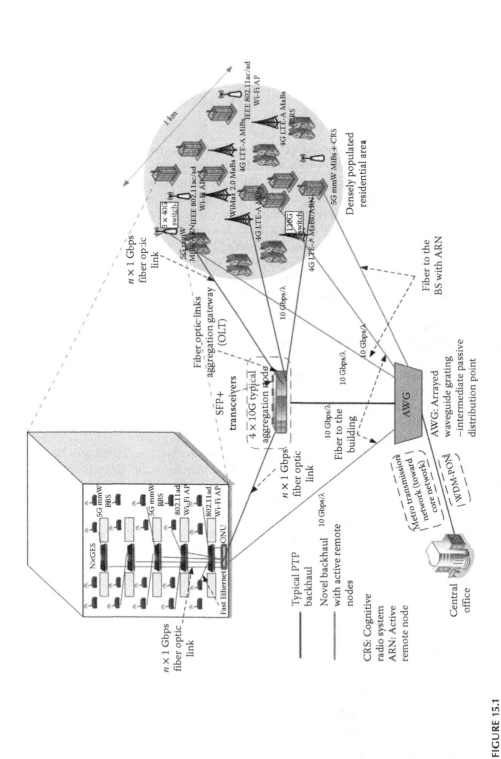

FIGURE 15.1

HetNet-based RAN architecture for the analyzed residential area consists of radio access part with >4G and 5G BS/AP sites, cognitive radio, and transmission part of combined PTP and novel high-speed aggregation backhaul network with ARNs.

the capabilities of the novel intelligent mobile backhaul RAN architecture which evolves the standalone ring-based Ethernet PON by simply collocating (overlying) the small cells and the MaBS with the ONUs, while capitalizing on existing fibered (available fiber backhaul over dark fibers) and powered ONUs. Finally, Figure 15.1 illustrates the HetNet-based RAN architecture according to the analysis discussed earlier.

15.5 Coverage and Capacity Assessment

We model the site coverage as $A = \pi r^2$ (km^2), where the site range is r (km). In this chapter, we consider 4G LTE-A MaBSs/MiBS and WiMax 2.0 MaBS sites with three sectors and up to three carriers of 20 MHz. Also, we assume that the three sectors and carrier aggregation of up to three carriers will be supported by 5G mmW MiBS, PBS, and FBS sites. Further, we assume Wi-Fi APs to be provided with single cell and omnidirectional antenna.

As outlined in [23], the range of the cell in urban area moves from 0.6 km at 2.6 GHz to 1.4 km at 900 MHz (considering the system parameters from [42]). For the urban dense area, according to [23,24] 0.57 km range is considered for the MaBS. We assume 0.25 km cell range for the 4G LTE-A MaBS sites and 0.1 km cell range for the MiBS sites equipped with 4G LTE-A and 5G mmW RATs in line with the 3GPP urban micro (UMi) model [43]. Literature [7–10] also considers a 0.1 km range for three sector 5G mmW MiBS sites. In line with [12,19,22], for the 5G mmW PBS we consider a 0.02 km range. According to [26], the network system capacity, T_{syst}, can be calculated based on the following equation:

$$T_{syst} = WN_{site}N_{cell}S_{eff} \tag{15.2}$$

where W is the size of the available spectrum bandwidth in MHz, N_{site} is the quantity of BS/AP sites, N_{cell} is the quantity of cells, and S_{eff} is the *average cell spectral efficiency* in bps/Hz/cell.

The average cell spectral efficiency for LTE-A is 4.2 and 3.8 bps/Hz/cell for the microcellular and base coverage urban environments and the respective cell-edge spectral efficiencies are equal to 0.15 and 0.10 for the frequency division duplex (FDD) urban micro (UMi) and FDD urban macro (UMa) channel models (20 MHz carrier) [39].

As we elaborated earlier, an additional increase of the areal spectral efficiencies could be achieved with an introduction of the CRS functionality. In line with [34], Figure 15.2 depicts how the unique features of a CRS conceptually interact with the radio environment within the cognition cycle that is continually run by the cognitive radio to observe the spectral opportunities, create plans to adapt, decide, and act to explore the best opportunities. According to [38], the maximum spectral efficiency gain due to the CRS is significant and in the range of 60%. For simplicity reasons, we assume the application of CRS only in the case of 4G LTE-A MaBs, by what we assess its impact on the cost-capacity performances in comparison to the deployment without CRS being implemented.

Regarding the deployments with the WiMax 2.0, in line with [44], with the use of (4×2) MIMO, we consider the average downlink spectral efficiency of 3.2 bps/Hz and the cell-edge user throughput of 0.09 bps/Hz. The IEEE 802.16 m standard enables the aggregation of few 20 MHz channels and could support the peak data rates >1.0 Gbps. According to [45], the performance target should be met for the cell ranges up to 5 km for the rural areas. In this chapter concerning urban scenario, we consider the WiMaXMaBS cell radius of 500 m applicable in urban areas.

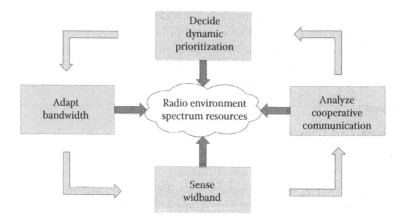

FIGURE 15.2
Cognitive cycle in the functional architecture of cognitive radio. (With kind permission from Springer Science+Business Media: *Cognitive Radio Networks from Theory to Practice*, Khattab, A. et al. (eds).)

TABLE 15.2

RAT-Specific Parameters for BS/AP Classes Placed Outside within Residential Area

RAT Factors	WiMax 2.0 MaBS	4G LTE-A MaBS	4G LTE-A MaBS (CRS)	4G LTE-A MiBS	4G LTE-A MiBS (CRS)	5G mmW MiBS	Wi-Fi IEEE 802.11ac AP
Range (km)	0.5	0.25	0.25	0.10	0.10	0.10	0.10
Coverage (km²)	0.79	0.2	0.2	0.03	0.03	0.03	0.003
Sectors	3	3	3	3	3	3	1
Carriers	1	1	1	1	1	1	1
Bandwidth (MHz) [1]	20	20	20	20	20	500	80
Carrier (GHz)	0.45	2.6	2.6	2.6	2.6	28	28
Average cell Spectral efficiency (SE) (bps/Hz)	3.2	3.8	6.08	4.2	6.72	3.38	16.25
Average cell capacity (Mbps)	64	76	121.6	76	134.4	1690	1300
Average site capacity (Mbps)	192	228	365	252	403.2	5070	1300
Cell-edge SE (bps/Hz)	0.09	0.10	0.16	0.15	0.24	0.105	16.25
Cell-edge data rate (Mbps)	1.8	2.0	3.2	3.0	4.8	52.28	1300

Further, [7] and [10] provide simulation-based analysis to estimate the capacity increases of candidate outdoor mmW cellular systems in the urban area. Thus, the following free-space loss model equation presented in [12] is most closely representing the channel models from [9] obtained empirically for the 0.1 km distance between the BS and MD:

$$PL_{FS,dB} = 112.4 + 20 \log_{10}(f_c) + 20 \log_{10}(d) \tag{15.3}$$

where f_c is the carrier frequency in GHz, and d is the distance in km.

Based on the empirical results of [7–10], for the mmW bands Table 15.2 contains the average and the cell-edge spectral efficiencies for 28 and 73 GHz carrier frequencies. Related to the channel sizes, for the 5G mmW system, we consider the 50–50 uplink (UL)–downlink (DL) time division duplex split of the 1 GHz bandwidth (or 500 MHz chunk in DL) [7,10,12]. Regarding the bandwidth of the 4G LTE-A RAT, we assume bandwidth chunks of up to 20 MHz.

The data rates of users served Wi-Fi cannot be higher than 50%–60% of the physical layer nominal bit rates [46]. IEEE 802.11ac Aps operate in the 5 GHz band with 80 MHz and can provide up to 1.3 Gbps at 30 m distance [47]. We assume that the average cell capacities at the distances of 30 m (IEEE 802.11ac) will be also available at the cell edges for the single users. Table 15.2 depicts all the previously elaborated RAT-specific parameters of various BS/AP classes.

15.6 Modeling of the Cost Structure and Profitability

We evaluate the site construction, radio, and backhaul transmission equipment as the CAPEX items of BS and electric power, O&M, site rent, and backhaul transmission rent as operating expenditures (OPEX) items of BS. The cost structure modeling is based on the approach introduced in [19,25]. The total network cost comprising radio access network (C_{RAN})–related costs, business-driven ($C_{BUS/COM}$) costs, and costs for spectrum license (C_{SPEC}) normalized per unit area (A_{SYS}) can be presented as follows:

$$C_{TOT} = C_{RAN} + C_{BUS/COM} + \frac{C_{SPEC}}{A_{SYS}} \left[\frac{cost}{area} \right] \tag{15.4}$$

In this chapter, we eliminate the spectrum and business expenditure as sunk cost. We consider the present values of the RAN-related cost or the total accumulated net present value (NPV (C_{TOT})) of the network represents the sum of the yearly cost as annualized CAPEX and OPEX, which are discounted by 12.5% (equal to the level of weighted average cost of capital (WACC) [13]) for the network life cycle of $K = 10$ years, or

$$\text{NPV } (C_{TOT}) = \text{NPV (OPEX)} + \text{NPV (Ann.CAPEX)} \tag{15.5}$$

$$\text{NPV(OPEX)} = \sum_{i=0}^{K-1} \frac{\text{OPEX}^{(i)}}{(1 + \text{WACC})^i} \tag{15.6}$$

$$\text{OPEX}^{(i)} = \sum_j N_j^{(i)} c_j^{\text{OPEX}} (1 + p_j^{\text{OPEX}})^{i-1} \tag{15.7}$$

$$\text{NPV(Ann.CAPEX)} = \sum_{i=0}^{K-1} \frac{\text{Ann.CAPEX}^{(i)}}{(1+\text{WACC})^i} \tag{15.8}$$

$$\text{Ann.CAPEX}^{(i)} = \sum_j I_j^{(i)} \cdot \gamma \tag{15.9}$$

$$I_j^{(i)} = \sum_j M_j^{(i)} c_j^{\text{CAPEX}} (1 + p_j^{\text{CAPEX}})^{i-1} \tag{15.10}$$

$$\gamma = \frac{\text{WACC}(1+\text{WACC})^n}{(1+\text{WACC})^n - 1} \tag{15.11}$$

where Ann.CAPEX represents the annualized CAPEX, $I_j^{(i)}$ represents the investment in asset type "j" ∈ {equipment of a particular BS or AP class, transmission links, backhaul equipment...} in year "i," and γ the parameter which is annualizing the present value of the capital investments with the discount rate again equal to WACC with "n" annualization periods in years. The other symbols used have the following meaning: $N_j^{(i)}$, operated equipment of kind "j" in year "i"; $M_j^{(i)}$, number of purchased equipment of kind "j" in year "i"; c_j^{CAPEX} and c_j^{OPEX} are the associated per unit CAPEX and OPEX, respectively, for the equipment type "j" in the initial year; and p_j^{CAPEX} and p_j^{OPEX} denote the respective yearly price trends.

The cost calculation in this chapter is based on the depicted RAN architecture in Figure 15.1. Table 15.3 consists of the CAPEX and OPEX estimates for the Greenfield BS/AP classes equipped with various RATs as well as the net present value of the total discounted cost for 10 years.

The findings related to the cost items (CAPEX and OPEX) for 4G LTE-A MaBS, 4G LTE-A MiBS, 5G mmW MiBS sites, and IEEE 802.11ac Wi-Fi AP sites are elaborated in details in our contribution [48] which is based on the cost items inputs from [11,19,23,24,27,49–51]. Additionally, here we add elaborations related to the MaBS site equipped with a WiMax RAT

TABLE 15.3

Cost Item Assumptions (Deployment with Three Carriers and Three Cells per Sector)

				OPEX		Cost NPV	
BS/AP Class/RAT		CAPEX		Radio Equipment	Transmission	Site	Transmission
4G LTE-A/WiMax 2.0 MaBS	30.0	30.0	30.0	15.0	10.0	9.0	277
4G LTE-A MiBS	15.0	30.0	10.0	15.0	5.0	2.5	180
5G mmW MiBS	8.0	30.0	8.0	15.0	5.0	2.5	171
5G mmW PBS	6.0	10.0	2.5	5.0	0.0	1.5	54
5G mmW FBS	4.0	7.0	1.5	4.0	0.0	1.0	40
WLAN 802.11 ac/ad AP	2.5	5.0	1.0	3.0	0.0	0.5	28

and novel backbone architecture to be used for the 5G architectures. Thus, according to [52], the CAPEX for the three-sector WiMaxMaBS site moves from 22.0 k€ to 37.0 k€, depending if the compact or distributed type of BS site is used. By this, we consider the average price of 30.0 k€ for three-sector WiMaxMaBS. Furthermore, in line with [18] the cost of the optimal EPON-based solution saves more than 50% of deployment cost in comparison to that of the typical PTP case because it ensures that the core of the network equipment is used more productively. Also, according to [17], the novel backhaul architecture offers good value for its performance, providing more than 10 times more bandwidth compared to what the cost per Mbps offered to the user is, around five times lower. Finally, Figure 15.3 depicts the total discounted cost structure of the considered HetNet deployments clustered by radio equipment, site build-out, and maintenance- and transmission-related expenditures.

Related to the profitability modeling, we use the methodology developed in [28] and further detailed in [24]. The calculation of the production cost per GB and its relation to the entire cost which includes overall OPEX and the annualized CAPEX per GB (in line with [33] calculated based on Equation 15.9), together with the revenues is the essence of this methodology. The depreciation period we assume to be 20 years for sites and 5 years for the radio equipment. The discounted rate we assume to be again equal to WACC, or 12.5%. Also, we consider the earnings before interest, taxes, depreciation and amortization (EBITDA) margin to be 55% based on the assumption that overall OPEX of the MNO business is 45%.

The total production cost per GB (Pr.COST (GB)) is given by the following equation:

$$Pr.COST(GB) = Ann.CAPEX(GB) + Ov.OPEX(GB) \qquad (15.12)$$

By considering the revenue per GB in €, we are able to calculate the EBIT margin as follows:

$$EBIT_{MARGIN}(\%) = Pr.COST(GB) / REVENUE(GB) \qquad (15.13)$$

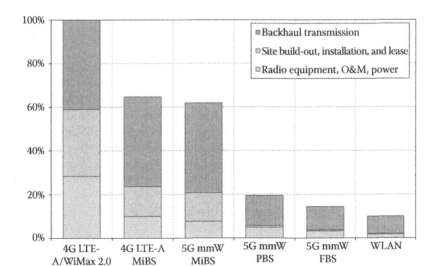

FIGURE 15.3
Resulting cost structure of considered BS/AP classes discounted in comparison to 4G LTE-A/ WiMaxMaBScosts.

15.7 Results for the Cost-Capacity and Profitability Analysis

For the sake of simplicity we only consider the infrastructure expenditures in the next sub-sections. The total CAPEX needed for a particular HetNet deployment can be calculated as multiplication of the number of BS/AP sites ($N_{BS/AP}$) needed to satisfy the demand of particular area and the CAPEX items ($C_{BS/AP}$) of that sites, or as follows:

$$\text{CAPEX}_{\text{HetNet}} \approx C_{BS/AP} N_{BS/AP} \tag{15.14}$$

15.7.1 HetNet with Sole RAT Deployment

Related to the realization of the outdoor-to-indoor coverage with 5G mmW MiBS to compensate for the wall attenuation of 42.0 dB, based on Equation 15.3, we yield an additional $4000 \times$ 5G mmW MiBS site. Table 15.4 depicts the CAPEX and the number of sites needed to respond to the desired demand/capacity with particular RATs utilized independently. The lowest CAPEX occurs with the 5G mmW MiBS deployment in the case of outdoor demand fulfillment (up to 1.5 M€ in case of new sites and 1.1 M€ for the reused sites). In this case the cost for satisfying the high- and low-demand levels is the same since a same number of $32 \times$ 5G mmW MiBS sites should be deployed to fulfill the coverage of the area under consideration. As this is a coverage-driven deployment, a capacity overprovisioning is achieved with 158 Gbps/km². As the CAPEX needed to satisfy even low-demand levels in the outdoor environment moves from 6.1 to 10.0 M€ with new MaBS sites with and without CRS, respectively, the relational selection for the outdoor deployments are exactly with the 5G mmW MiBS sites.

WiMax 2.0 has the highest cost-efficiency due to its lower spectral efficiency compared with the 4G LTE-A. Consequently, we further focus on the 4G LTE-A deployment, since with the use of the CRS technique its cost decreases to comparable levels with the 5G mmW MiBS and IEEE 802.11ac Wi-Fi APs, e.g., around 2.7 M€ in the case of low demand. With only 3.0 M€, Wi-Fi IEEE 802.11ac AP shows a substantially low level of CAPEX, but also in this case the capacity overprovisioning is evident with the tremendous 449 Gbps/km² due to the coverage limitations of Wi-Fi APs.

Clearly, the most cost-inefficient deployment is brought in the case when the 5G mmW MiBS placed outside is intended to be used for the indoor coverage. The reason for this is that the carrier frequencies in the mmW band are inefficient to penetrate the walls of buildings and suffer from high attenuation. The indoor coverage could be satisfied in the most cost-efficient manner with the deployment of 4G LTE-A at MiBS sites (the microwave frequencies own much higher wall penetration capabilities), when the CAPEX are around 30.0 M€ with the use of new sites for the high-demand level.

Figure 15.4 depicts the profit margins of an MNO achieved with the analyzed HetNets deployed with the sole RAT deployment.

We assume a basis for the profit margin calculation to be an average monthly revenue per low-demand user—average revenue per user (ARPU) of 20.0€ and per high-demand user 30.0€ [28]. A significant margin increase can be witnessed with the implementation of the CRS functionality. Thus, in the case of 4G LTE-A MiBS deployments the gain is higher by 10% in the case of site reuse and high indoor demand, and around 20% in case of new sites. A CRS implemented to 4G LTE-A MiBS brings the EBIT margin to 48%. Regarding outdoor coverage, the positive profit margin is experienced at all deployments, macro deployments with the highest value in the case of site reuse with the 4G LTE-A MaBS deployment,

TABLE 15.4

CAPEX Needed to Satisfy Low- and High-Residential Demands

HetNet with Single RAT	Environment	Demand	BS/AP Type	Number of Sites	CAPEX (M€)	Capacity (Gbps/ km²)
WiMaX 2.0 (1 × 20 MHz)	Outdoor	Low	MaBS new	132	11.9	24.7
			MaBS reuse	132	5.3	24.7
		High	MaBS new	438	39.4	82.3
			MaBS reuse	438	17.5	82.3
	Outdoor	Low	MaBS new	111	10.0	24.7
			MaBS reuse	111	4.4	24.7
		High	MaBS new	369	33.2	82.3
4G LTE-A (1 × 20 MHz)			MaBS reuse	369	14.8	82.3
	Indoor	Low	MiBS new	392	21.6	98.8
			MiBS reuse	392	13.7	98.8
		High	MiBS new	1338	73.6	329.2
			MiBS reuse	1338	46.8	329.2
	Outdoor	Low	MaBS new	68	6.1	24.7
			MaBS reuse	68	2.7	24.7
4G LTE-A with cognitive radio system (1 × 20 MHz)		High	MaBS new	232	20.9	82.3
			MaBS reuse	232	9.3	82.3
	Indoor	Low	MiBS new	250	13.8	98.8
			MiBS reuse	250	8.8	98.8
		High	MiBS new	836	46.0	329.2
			MiBS reuse	836	29.3	329.2
	Outdoor	Low	MiBS new	32	1.5	158.4
			MiBS reuse	32	1.1	158.4
		High	MiBS new	32	1.5	158.4
5G mmW (1 × 500 MHz)			MiBS reuse	32	1.1	158.4
	Indoor	Low	MiBS new	4000	184	19,800
			MiBS reuse	4000	136	19,800
		High	MiBS new	4000	184	19,800
			MiBS reuse	4000	136	19,800
Wi-Fi IEEE 802.11ac (1 × 80 MHz)	Outdoor	Low	AP new	354	3.0	449.4
		High	AP new	354	3.0	449.4

and CRS (45% for the outdoor low demand and 31% for the outdoor high-demand level), followed by the regular 4G LTE-A MaBS deployment with 16.3% and WiMax 2.0 MaBS deployment with 9.1% in the case of high-demand level and site reuse. Nevertheless, it can be seen that the profit margins are negative when the outdoor high-demand level is satisfied with the Greenfield sites, with close to zero value only for the MaBS deployment with the LTE-A supporting the CRS functionality.

Being the most appropriate outdoor deployment with the highest cost efficiency, as expected, the 5G mmW MiBS sites bring the highest profitability of around 50% in the case of low- and the high-demand levels (see Table 15.4). Also, the IEEE 802.11ac Wi-Fi APs bring a more than satisfactory profit margin of 43%–47% for low to high demand. Thus, these two small cells deployments for the outdoor coverage could be treated as substantially profitable solutions.

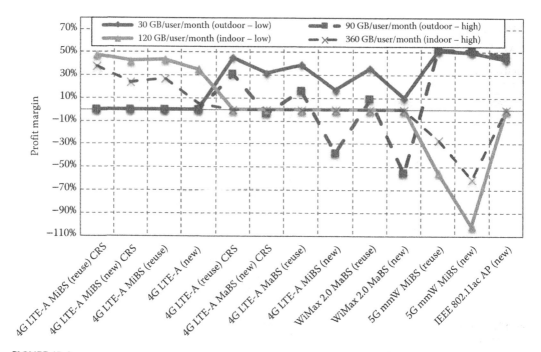

FIGURE 15.4
Achieved EBIT margins by MNO.

Still, if MNO chooses to deploy outside 5G mmW MiBS sites for the indoor coverage, it will face a highly negative margin. In case of low-indoor demand, the negative margin moves from around −60% and up to −95% for the case of site reuse and new sites, respectively. The negative values are lower in the case of the high-indoor demand level and 5G mmW MiBS deployment due to the higher revenue assumed (from −30% and up to −60% for the case of site reuse and new sites, respectively).

15.7.2 HetNet Deployed with Mix of RATs

The following deployment scenarios with a mix of RATs are considered:

- 5G mmW MiBS and 4G LTE-A MaBS
- 5G mmW MiBS and 4G LTE-A MaBS with CRS
- IEEE 802.11ac Wi-Fi APs and 4G LTE-A MaBS
- IEEE 802.11ac Wi-Fi APs and 4G LTE-A MaBS with CRS
- IEEE 802.11ac Wi-Fi APs and 5G mmW MiBS

We dimension each of the considered mixed of RATs in a manner that after the initial 100 Gbps/km² are covered with the BSs with cells with a higher range order, small cells are added. The target is to evaluate which of the mixed capacity expansion strategies provides the lowest CAPEX. CAPEX dependencies from the user density per km² are plotted in Figure 15.5. Thus, a couple of conclusions can be drawn. For instance, if we compare the CAPEX curve for the stand-alone 4G LTE-A MaBS deployment with the mix deployment of 4G LTE-A MaBS and IEEE 802.11ac Wi-Fi APs it is evident that the mixed RAT solution becomes more cost efficient for densities >450,000 user/km². Further, for the densities up

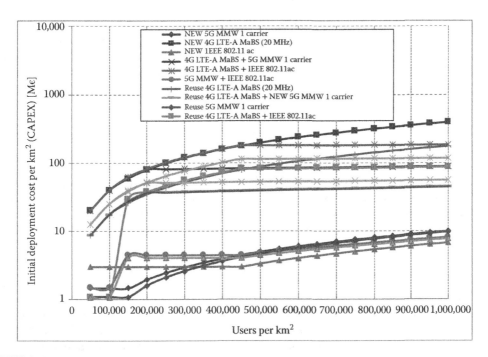

FIGURE 15.5
CAPEX (in M€) as a function of number of user per km² (logarithmic scale).

to 150,000 users/km², the most cost-efficient solution is the deployment combining the 4G LTE-A MaBS reused sites and IEEE 802.11ac Wi-Fi APs.

Also, it is worth mentioning that the most cost-efficient deployment between the mix-RAT solutions is the deployment considering 4G LTE-A MaBS site reuse complemented with the 5G mmW MiBS sites (one carrier) in the hot spots.

Finally, it is clear that for the user density >350,000 user/km², the most cost-efficient overall solution is the sole deployment with the IEEE 802.11ac Wi-Fi APs which could be of particular interest for the MNOs market challengers which lack the previously deployed macro layer.

15.8 Use of Cognitive Radio for Guaranteeing QoS for Capacity Overprovisioning

We analyze the case of serving the users generating low indoor demand with 4G LTE-A MiBS with the CRS already deployed to satisfy the high-indoor demand. In such a case, based on the previous analysis, a 134.4 cell capacity could be achieved, by what 329 Gbps/km² area capacity will be overprovisioned, if we compare with the needed 98.8 Gbps/km². We consider 3.03 Mbps as the guaranteed user data rate which corresponds to 1.0 Erlang or 1 channel of traffic (total number of channels are 44). Consequently, the average data rate obtained by residential indoor low-demand environment of approximately 1.0 Mbps/user parallels to a traffic load of 0.3 Erlang (the average data rate of 1.01 Mbps can be ensured to 43 users).

Based on the tele-traffic theory, we could determine the number of users receiving the 3.03 Mbps data rate which is guaranteed with certain outage/blocking probability, i.e., the value of the average data rate achieved with the high-demand level.

The final goal is to apply CRSs with a dynamical prioritization to cooperating MNOs by how much they will increase the capacity and provide a guaranteed QoS to the users seeking the premium services. Hence, for a certain loss probability (E_{loss}) and given number of available channels per cells C, we calculate with the Erlang loss formula [53], the offered traffic flow O in Erlang, and by that the average channel utilization will be given as

$$\eta = \frac{O}{C} \tag{15.15}$$

We calculate the number of the "best-effort" users N_{best} as ratio between the number of available channels per cells C, and the best effort user data rate in Erlang. Finally, the number of users that could be served with a guaranteed data rate of 3.03 Mbps, N_{guar}, with particular service probability (SP = 1 − E_{loss}) can be presented as follows:

$$N_{guar} = N_{best} \frac{O_{E_{loss}}}{C} \tag{15.16}$$

The capacity of a wireless channel weakens with more firm requirements on blocking probability. Consequently, Figure 15.6 depicts the number of served users with the guaranteed data rate of 3.03 Mbps as a function of available channels C per cell with different outage probabilities $E_{loss} \in \{0.02, 0.05, 0.10, 0.20\}$. It can be seen that with 80%, 90%, 95%, and 98% of probability 50, 42, 38, and 34 users, respectively, can obtain a constant data rate of 3.03 Mbps.

In line with [54], this approach could be used as an advanced method of *radio resource sharing* between MNOs that aim to share the radio resources or jointly use a single carrier for the purpose of lowering the investment costs as compared to the case when each MNO uses a dedicated carrier. Therefore, permanent share of the cell capacity can be kept for each MNO and without doubling the carriers. So, with two MNOs equally sharing the capacity with $C_1 = C_2 = C/2 = 7.0$ channels (equally sized shares) the total capacity is reduced with 14%, 11%, 9%, and 6% in case of 2%, 5%, 10%, and 20% of loss probability, respectively.

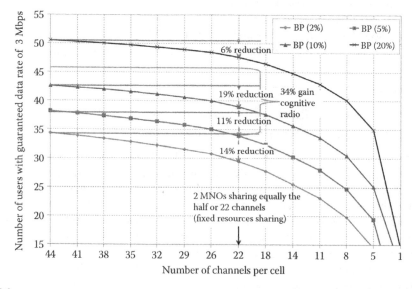

FIGURE 15.6
Number of users with a guaranteed QoS when served by 4G LTE-A MiBS, with indicated capacity gain due to dynamical prioritization with cognitive radio functionality.

To avoid this fixed sharing solution that minimizes the capacity of the system, or at the end could jeopardize the cost efficiency, we further consider an implementation of the CRS to enable dynamical prioritization of the MNO's radio resource shares based on their current load. We assume that such a CRS is implemented with the dynamical prioritization "method with nonpreemptive priority queuing in admission control," a method that was originally introduced in [54] and whose analytics we briefly describe next.

We consider standard Poisson traffic model according to which the overall traffic O_i of MNO_i is represented as follows:

$$O_i = \lambda_i T \tag{15.17}$$

where λ_i is the average arrival rate of the new connections for MNO_i and T is the average occupation of a connection. The overall traffic in our case can be given by $O = O_1 + O_2$. Each MNO has guaranteed access to a total number of $C_1 = C_2 = C/2$ cell channels. Further, the guarantee level of each MNO, G_i, is defined as follows:

$$G_i = C_i / A_i \tag{15.18}$$

so that MNOs with a traffic A_i, below the threshold of minimum capacity C_i, obtain a higher level of guarantee for access to the available capacity. After a maximum allowed waiting time T_{max} is reached, connection should be blocked based on the assumed outage probability B_i lower than threshold outage probability B_{max} determined based on the moment when the MNO will reach the guaranteed minimum capacity C_i, or

$$B_i \leq B_{max} \quad \text{for } O_i < C_i \tag{15.19}$$

There is an admission of the connection in case of existence of a single channel:

$$\sum_{i=1}^{N} A_i < C. \tag{15.20}$$

Connection is refused in that if no channel is available, T_{max} elapses. As elaborated earlier, here we yield that the total available channels are $C = 44$ for the data service. We assume $T_{max} = 15s$, average duration of connection of 12s, and data rate is 3.03 Mbps. Table 15.5 summarizes the simulation results for the achieved improvement compared to the case with a static assignment of 22 data channels, assuming four different fixed values for the load in Erlangs of MNO_2, O_2, for which we obtain value for the load of MNO_1, O_1 for particular blocking probability. The received value of O_1 is compared with the achieved capacity of the MNO_1 for a fixed share of the radio resources and by that the capacity gain is obtained.

It can be seen that when the traffic is high for the other MNO O_2 compared with the load of MNO O_1, there is a capacity decrease related to a basic case with 22 dedicated channels in most of the cases. However, with a slightly increased traffic of the second MNO, or reaching 87% of the load of the evaluated MNO O_1, with the use of the dynamic prioritization implemented with CRS, there is a 38% increase of the carried load of the MNO O_1 in comparison to its load in case of the fixed channel reservation, with 5% blocking probability.

Consequently, the average channel utilization η will be increased from 0.68 to 1.07, the value compared to the channel utilization in the case of a single MNO bringing an even capacity increase of 23%. Even more, if we compare this result with the result of the comparison

TABLE 15.5

Capacity Gains Achieved with Cognitive Radio Relative to a Fixed Channel Allocation in Case of Various Blocking Probabilities

Blocking Probability	Parameter	Value (%)			
2% [2]	O_2 [Erl] versus O_1 [Erl] [3]	3900	400	20	−78
	Capacity gain [4]	−91	−50	25	80
5% [5]	O_2 [Erl] versus O_1 [Erl] [6]	600	117	−13	−82
	Capacity gain [7]	−60	−8	38	120
10% [8]	O_2 [Erl] versus O_1 [Erl] [9]	180	54	−33	−85
	Capacity gain [10]	−23	0.5	38	170
20% [11]	O_2 [Erl] versus O_1 [Erl] [12]	70	5	−52	−89
	Capacity gain [13]	−8	−6	39	280

between the channels utilizations of only single and two MNOs in case of a fixed-channel reservation, the use of CRS with dynamical priority queuing in admission control shows a significant capacity improvement of 34%. This is also depicted in Figure 15.6.

15.9 Conclusion and Future Work

In this chapter, we propose a business valuation and cost-capacity modeling of the cognitive radio enabled beyond 4G- and 5G-based wireless heterogeneous networks. We evaluate the HetNets equipped with the advanced RATs such as LTE-A advanced, WiMax 2.0, IEEE 802.11ac, and forthcoming technologies supporting carriers within the mmW band considered as foundation for the capacity increase of the 5G layouts. 5G mmW MiBS sites ensure a sustainable operations of the mobile operators, except for the outdoor-to-indoor coverage provisioning when MiBSs with 4G LTE-A should still be the main choice with profitability more than 50%. The MiBS deployments using the CRSs bring satisfactory profit margins of up to 40% for the indoor coverage. WiMax 2.0 MaBS deployment shows a modest cost efficiency due to smaller capacity gains compared to other RATs.

Also, we propose the use of cognitive radio for guaranteeing QoS in case of capacity over-provisioning. Therefore, we present a method for the dynamic radio resources sharing with the cognitive radio between mobile networks that increase the capacity higher than 30%.

Our future work continues with techno-economic analysis in case of a nonuniform traffic distributions served by forthcoming 5G cellular networks.

Acknowledgments

We thank our families for their support and motivation.

References

1. International Telecommunication Union, Recommendation ITU-R M.1457-12 (01/2015). Detailed specifications of the terrestrial radio interfaces of International Mobile Telecommunications-2000 (IMT-2000).
2. International Telecommunication Union, Recommendation ITU-R M.2012-1 (2014). Detailed specifications of the terrestrial radio interfaces of International Mobile Telecommunications-Advanced (IMT-Advanced).
3. 3rd Generation Partnership Project (3GPP), Feasibility study for Further Advancements for E-UTRA (LTE-Advanced) (3GPP TR 36.912 version 11.0.0 Release 11) (2012–2010)
4. Institute of Electrical and Electronics Engineers, Std 802.16-2012 (2012). *IEEE Standard for Air Interface for Broadband Wireless Access Systems.* IEEE Std 802.16™-2012. (Revision of IEEE Std 802.16-2009). Aug. 2012.
5. Institute of Electrical and Electronics Engineers, IEEE Std 802.22-2011(TM) (2011). *Standard for Cognitive Wireless Regional Area Networks (RAN) for Operation in TV Bands.* July 1st, 2011.
6. Niu, Y. et al. (2015). *A Survey of Millimeter Wave (mmWave) Communications for 5G: Opportunities and Challenges.* Cornell University Library. arXiv:1502.07228v1, February 2015.
7. Akdeniz, M. R. et al. (2013). *Millimeter Wave Channel Modeling and Cellular Capacity Evaluation.* Cornell University Library. http://arxiv.org/abs/1312.4921, Dec. 2013.
8. Hang, Z. et al. (2013). Indoor 28 GHz millimeter wave cellular communication measurements for reflection and penetration loss in and around buildings in New York City. In *2013 IEEE ICC. Conference,* June 2013.
9. Rappaport, T.S. et al. (2013). Millimeter wave mobile communications for 5G cellular: It will work!. *IEEE Access Journal,* 1, 335–349. doi:10.1109/ACCESS.2013.2260813.
10. Rangan, S., Rappaport, T. Erkip, S. E. (2014). Millimeter wave cellular wireless networks: Potentials and challenges. *Proceedings of the IEEE,* 102(3), 366–385. doi:10.1109 /JPROC.2014.2299397.
11. Murdock, J. N. et al. (2012). A 38 GHz cellular outage study for an urban outdoor campus environment. In *Proceedings of the IEEE Wireless Communications and Networking Conference,* April 2012, Shanghai, pp. 3085–3090.
12. Khan, F., and Pi, Z. (2011). Millimeter-wave mobile broadband (MMB): Unleashing 3-300 GHz spectrum. In *Proceedings of the IEEE Sarnoff Symposium,* March 2011, Princeton, NJ.
13. Hossain, E. et al. (2015). *5G Cellular: Key Enabling Technologies and Research Challenges.* Cornell University Library. arXiv:1503.00674, Feb. 2015.
14. Roh, W. et al. (2014). Millimeter-wave beamforming as an enabling technology for 5G cellular communications: Theoretical feasibility and prototype results. *Communications Magazine, IEEE.* 52(2).
15. IEEE 802.15 WPAN Millimeter Wave Alternative PHY Task Group 3c (TG3c). Available at: http://www.ieee802.org/15/pub/TG3c.html.
16. Draft Standard for Information Technology–Telecommunications and Information Exchange Between Systems–Local and Metropolitan Area Networks–Specific Requirements–Part 11: Wireless LAN Medium Access Control (MAC) and Physical Layer (PHY) Specifications–Amendment 4: Enhancements for Very High Throughput in the 60 Ghz Band, IEEE P802.11ad/ D9.0, Oct. 2012.
17. Bock, C. et al. (2014,). Techno-economics and performance of convergent radio and fibre architectures. In *Transparent Optical Networks (ICTON), 2014 16th International Conference on IEEE,* Jul, 2014, Graz, pp. 1–4.
18. Shahab, H. (2014). An Innovative RAN Architecture for Emerging Heterogeneous Networks: The Road to the 5G Era. Dissertations and Theses, 2014–Present. Paper 320.
19. Johansson, K. (2007). Cost Effective Deployment Strategies for Heterogeneous Wireless Networks. PhD Dissertation. The Royal Institute of Technology, Stockholm, Sweeden.
20. Johansson, K. et al. (2004). Relation between base station characteristics and cost structure in cellular systems. In *Proceedings of the IEEE PMRC 2004,* Barcelona, Spain.

21. Johansson, K., and Furuskär, A. (2005). Cost efficient capacity expansion strategies using multi-access networks. In *Proceedings of the IEEE VTC*, May 2005, Beijing, China.

22. Johansson, K. et al. (2007). Modelling the cost of heterogeneous wireless access networks. *Int. J. Mobile Network Design and Innovation*, 2(2), 58–66. doi:10.1504/IJMNDI.2007.013805.

23. Markendahl, J., and Mäkitalo, Ö. (2010). A comparative study of deployment options, capacity and cost structure for macrocellular and femtocell networks. In *Proceedinga of the IOFC 2010*, Istanbul, September 2010.

24. Markendahl, J. (2011). Mobile Network Operators and Cooperation, PhD Dissertation. The Royal Institute of Technology, Stockholm, Sweden.

25. Frias, Z., and Pérez, J. (2012). Techno-economic analysis of femtocell deployment in long-term evolution networks. *EURASIP Journal on Wireless Communications and Networking 2012*, 288, pp. 1687–1499..

26. Mölleryd, B. et al. (2010). Mobile broadband expansion calls for more spectrum or base stations. In *European Regional ITS Conference*, Copenhagen, 13–15 September 2010.

27. Popescu, R. et al. (2013). Complementing macrocell deficits with either smallcells or Wi-Fi-willingness to choose based on the cost-capacity analysis. In *24th European Regional Conference of the International Telecommunication Society*, Florence, Italy, 20–23 October 2013.

28. Markendahl, J. et al. (2009). Business innovation strategies to reduce the revenue gap for wireless broadband services. *Journal Communications and Strategies*, 75(3rd quarter), 35.

29. Kang, D.H. et al. (2012) *Cost Efficient High Capacity Indoor Wireless Access: Denser Wi-Fi or Coordinated Pico-cellular?* Cornell University Library. November 2012. Retrieved from http://arxiv.org/abs/1211.4392.

30. Mölleryd, B. G. et al. (2010). Spectrum valuation derived from network deployment and strategic positioning with different levels of spectrum in 800 MHz. In *ITS Bi-annual Conference*, Tokyo, June 2010.

31. Tombaz S. et al. (2014). Is backhaul becoming a bottleneck for green wireless access networks? In *2014 IEEE International Conference on Communications (ICC) 2014*, Sydney, 10–14 June 2014.

32. Widaa et al. (2014). Toward capacity-efficient cost-efficient and powerefficient deployment strategy for indoor mobile broadband. In *24th European Regional Conference of the International Telecommunication Society*, Florence, Italy, 20–23, October 2013.

33. METIS Project (2013). Scenarios, requirements and KPIs for 5G mobile and wireless system, Document Number: ICT-317669-METIS/D1.1, 2013.

34. Khattab, A. et al. (eds.) (2013). *Cognitive Radio Networks From Theory to Practice*. Springer Science+Business Media, New York.

35. ITU. Report ITU-R SM.2152. (2009). *Definitions of Software Defined Radio (SDR) and Cognitive Radio System (CRS)*. International Telecommunication Union.

36. VTT. (2012). *Cognitive Radio Systems: Enabler for Intelligent Wireless Telecommunications*. VTT, Technical Research Centre of Finland..

37. Celebi, H. (2008). Location Awareness in Cognitive Radio Networks. PhD Dissertation. Graduate Theses and Dissertations. University of South Florida, Tampa, FL.

38. Haddad, M. et al. (2007) Spectral efficiency of cognitive radio systems. In *Global Telecommunications Conference, 2007, GLOBECOM '07*. IEEE, 26–30 November, Washington, DC, USA.

39. ETSI TR 136 913 V10.0.0 (2011-04) LTE: European Telecommunications Standards Institute 2011.

40. Cisco (2015). *Visual Networking Index: Global Mobile Data Traffic Forecast Update, 2014–2019*. February 2015 San Jose, CA: Cisco.

41. Analysis Mason (2010). Wireless network traffic 2010–2015. Cambridge, UK: Analysis Mason.

42. Holma, H. et al. (eds.) (2014). *HSPA+ Evolution to Release 12: Performance and Optimization*. Chichester, West Sussex, UK: John Wiley & Sons.

43. International Telecommunication Union, Report ITU-R M.2135-1. (2009). Guidelines for evaluation of radio interface technologies for IMT-Advanced, December 2009.

44. WIMAX Forum. (2010). *WiMAX and the IEEE 802.16m Air Interface Standard*. April 2010.

45. Institute of Electrical and Electronics Engineers, IEEE 802.16 Broadband Wireless Access Working Group. (2009). *IEEE 802.16m System Requirements.* September 24, 2009.
46. Xiao, Y. (2005). IEEE 802.11n: Enhancements for higher throughput in wireless LANs. *Wireless Communications, IEEE,* 12(6), 82–91 2005. doi:10.1109/MWC.2005.1561948.
47. Cisco. (2014). *802.11ac: The 5th Generation of Wi-Fi.* San Jose, CA: Cisco, 2014.
48. Nikolikj, V., and Janevski, T. (2015). State-of-the-art business performance evaluation of the advanced wireless heterogeneous networks to be deployed for the "TERA age." *Wireless Personal Communications, Special Issue on Recent Advances in Mobile and Wireless Networks,* 84(3), 2241–2270, D.J. Deng et al. (eds), Springer US, Science+Business Media New York, doi:10.1007/s11277-015-2491-2.
49. Perahia, E., and Gong, M.X. (2011). Gigabit wireless LANs: An overview of IEEE 802.11ac and 802.11ad. *Mobile Computing and Communications Review,* January 2011.
50. Blennerud, G. (2009). Don't worry—Mobile broadband is profitable. *Ericsson Business Review,* 2.
51. Motorola. (2011). Proven-Carier Grade Wi-Fi Solutions. Libertyville, IL, USA: Motorola, 2011.
52. Senza Fili Consulting. (2010). Compact base stations: A new step in the evolution of base station design squeezing out cost, volume, and complexity from WiMAX deployments. Retrieved from http://www.senzafiliconsulting.com/Home.aspx
53. Leijon, H. (2014). Extract from the Table of the Eralng B Formula. ITU, Retrieved October 30, 2014 from https://www.kth.se/social/upload/4fd8a33ff276547747000031/erlangt.pdf.
54. Johansson et al. (2004). Radio resource management in roaming based multi-operator WCDMA networks. In *2004 IEEE 59th Vehicular Technology Conference, 2004. VTC 2004-Spring.* (Vol. 4), May 2004, Los Angeles, USA. pp. 2062–2066, 17–19. doi:10.1109/VETECS.2004.1390637.

16

Integrating Cognitive Radio with OFDMA-Based Femtocell Networks: Interference Mitigation Strategies

Izwah Ismail, Mohd Dani Baba, Rhoma Erma Zaini, and Harwati Hashim

CONTENTS

16.1 Introduction

Wireless technology plays a dominant role in today's tremendous demand for mobile user communication. Therefore, improving its ability to provide higher data rates and better quality of services (QoSs) is an urgent requirement. Al-Rubaye and Cosmas [1] highlighted the potential of integrating the cellular communication system with the Internet Protocol (IP) technology in a long-term evolution (LTE) network. The main objective is to provide a seamless and high data-rate connection with an efficient cost for global roaming and user-customized personal services. The ongoing 4G cellular network deployment involves three accessible concepts: to apply the new techniques such as interchanging the interoperability microwave access (WiMAX) backbone station with the LTE network to increase the cell capacity; to utilize the reconfigurable technologies, such as the cognitive radio (CR) and advanced antenna systems, to enhance the spectral efficiencies; and to design a new network architecture for the mobile networks that boosts the capability to provide a seamless and robust connection. The integration of at least two of these concepts will contribute to the new generation of the cellular network that can be deployed to manage and handle the huge demand of high data traffic, while accomplishing the requirements of seamless mobility for various corresponding technologies.

The latest network provides its individual users full control over privacy and costs. This is a natural extension of the current technologies of broadband internet and 3G mobile networks such as the universal mobile telecommunications system (UMTS). This allows uninterrupted coverage for a user that changes terminals or switches unnoticeably between the underlying fixed and mobile networks [UMTS, wireless local area network (WLAN), etc.]. This is very important for the ad hoc networking and for a mobile user that travels among different terminals of a single network or the terminals of third parties. There are so many requirements for keeping the femtocell costs as low as possible for effectively competing against the ubiquitous Wi-Fi technology. Chandrasekhar and Andrews [2] show that the main challenge for the femtocell deployments is the interference with the macrocell base station (MBS).

Other femtocell requirements, including resource management, spectrum allocation management, providing QoS over an internet backhaul and allowing access to femtocells are also addressed. Cheng et al. [3] highlights that the term *quality of experience* provides a more adequate measure of how a service or application meets the user needs in practice, such as medical image or video quality, instant on-demand medical data availability, reliability during critical operations, and ease of the use. In addition, the handover and mobility are equally important when the future networks employ an IP-based environment for all the traffic requests as there are different types of femtocell handover schemes for voice, video, broadcasting media, and internet that can access the landline and wireless networks. Furthermore, power consumption is another important factor to be taken into consideration to be integrated in the future 5G solutions of the next-generation wireless networks.

Femtocells operate in the licensed spectrum of a cellular operator with a very low power. The radio in the femtocell is controlled by the service provider's core network, and it operates with the standard mobile phones with no special modifications. Nevertheless, Fratu et al. [4] proved that the reuse of the licensed cellular spectrum requires interference management between the femtocells and the umbrella macrocell. It is seconded by a study in [3] that points out that in a two-tier network which shares the same spectrum, two types of interferences appear—cross-tier and intra-tier. Hence interference mitigation gets more attention by both the academia and cellular industry. Generally, the two-tier network is illustrated as shown in Figure 16.1.

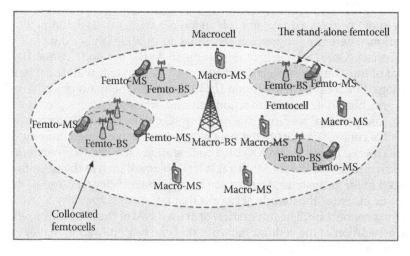

FIGURE 16.1
Macro–femto two-tier network.

This chapter describes a study on interference management by integrating the CR in the femtocell LTE-based network and thus enhancing the capacity and network coverage. Based on the literature review, the accessible frequency spectrum can be utilized efficiently by using the CR. Thus, the objective of this study is to improve the capacity of femtocell users (FUs) and also to utilize the available bandwidth efficiently and reduce the bandwidth scarcity. To be specific, there are two categories for the cell users: the primary users (PUs) and the secondary users (SUs). The results from the simulation show that the CR mechanism has the ability to improve the overall capacity of the active SUs.

This chapter is organized into following sections. Section 16.2 describes the interference coordination, followed by the interference management in Section 16.2.3. Section 16.3 serves to discuss the overview interference mitigation techniques and cognitive femtocell architecture, and Section 16.5 verifies the proposed cognitive femtocell network by using simulation and analyzes the result of this study. Section 16.6 summarizes the conclusion and suggests further work.

16.2 Interference Coordination

LTE as one of the orthogonal frequency division multiple access (OFDMA)–based networks aims to achieve a higher spectral efficiency. Hence, it may involve the use of the entire system's bandwidth in all the cells known as *Frequency Reuse 1* approach as stated in [5]. All subbands of the available bandwidth are assigned to each cell. Therefore, the requirement of an intercell interference coordination (ICIC) scheme becomes vital. Previous study conducted by Fratu et al. [4] indicates that the interference is one of the technical challenges that needs to be overcome before enhancing the spectrum efficiency. Consequently, both time and frequency domains have to use the ICIC-based schemes especially for a two-tier network as femtocell to reduce the interference.

As a promising solution, femtocells are introduced by the operator services and later provided to the subscribers when needed. The main goal of the femtocell deployment is to improve the capacity of the FUs as well as to efficiently utilize the available bandwidth and reduce its scarcity. With reference to the nature of femtocell [6], the self-organization or self-management is an important function for the operations of femtocell networks. In the two-tier network, femtocells and macrocells have to reuse the same set of frequencies from the licensed band. Due to limited resources, a signal interference occurs between the cells. The resulting technical challenge should be resolved for the successful deployment of the femtocells. Sections 16.2.1 through 16.2.3 describe a conventional femtocell network, spectrum sharing in the femtocell network, and the interference management.

16.2.1 Conventional Femtocell Network

Femtocell, also known as the home base station (BS), is a small, low-power access point and visually looks like an ordinary wireless router. These indoor access points are installed by the users, which creates a small wireless coverage area and connects the user equipment (UE) to the cellular core network through the subscribers' broadband internet access. Due to the attractive features of plug and play, femtocell attracts a lot of attention from indoor users as it provides good signal strength for a small service area and connects to the core network using a wired backhaul link. Conventional femtocell operates on a licensed spectrum. From the operator service provider's view, femtocells have advantages of low deployment cost and traffic offload over the macrocell.

Femtocell gateway controls and manages the femtocell base station (FBS), also known as femtocell access point (FAP), as shown in Figure 16.2 [7]. Its main function is to perform and decide the traffic routing for the core network. And the femto gateway also supports the femto-specific functionalities which are admission control, handover control, and interference management. Self-organizing network feature is very important for the operation of the femtocell network since femtocells are usually installed when demanded. However, due to the limited radio resources, macrocells and femtocells have to share the licensed frequency spectrum.

Key roles of femtocell in LTE services are as follows [8]:

• Speeds up the launch and deployment
• Enables services that encourage adoption
• Delivers superior performance where needed

Despite the benefits provided by deploying the femtocell network, the main concern is the interference management which is an important issue in a networking operation. Two types of interferences in this conventional two-tier network are as follows [9]:

1. Co-Tier Interference

    Co-tier or co-layer interference is the interference of signals caused at the femtocell due to immediate neighboring femtocells. This decreases the quality of communication. Co-tier interference occurs at the same network layer and is mainly among the immediate neighboring femtocells due to less distance between them.

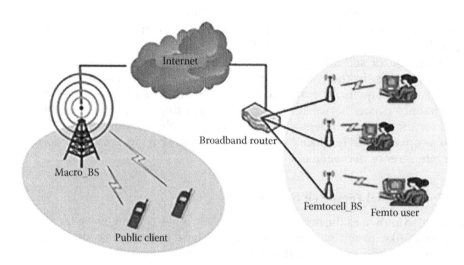

FIGURE 16.2
Basic femtocell-network architecture. (From Da Costa, G., and Cattoni, A., *IEEE Globecom 2010 Workshop*, 2010, pp. 721–725.)

2. Cross-Tier Interference

Interference in cross-tier occurs between different network elements. For example, the unwanted signals by the FAP cause interference to the downlink macrocell users (MUs) and likewise the unwanted signals by the MU at the uplink cause interference to the FAP user.

16.2.2 Spectrum Sharing in Femtocell Networks

As the current mobile technology, femtocell connects the macrocell service provider's network to the indoor subscribers using the standard broadband lines such as optical fiber. Femtocell is an access point which transmits at low power, extends the mobile coverage for indoor subscribers, and solves the problem of limited access to the macrocell network. Indoor subscribers are able to use the voice call and experience excellent data services. Unfortunately, the performance of femtocell architectures is limited by the available frequency spectrum [9]. One of the limitations of the femtocell network is that it operates on the same licensed spectrum as macrocell networks due to the limited radio resources. Spectrum sharing is not only a problem for the femtocell networks, but also for the WLAN and macrocell networks. Nonetheless, the traditional spectrum-sharing methods for WLAN and macrocell networks are not efficient in the femtocell networks.

In the OFDMA network architecture, most of the operators are allocated with two frequencies for use. All the available frequencies are separated into two parts for macrocell and femtocells. The frequency channel allocation helps reduce the cross-tier interference by allowing the femtocells to transmit on the unused second frequency. However, this still does not resolve the interference issue caused between two femtocells that operate on, say, two floors of a building. This scenario may also affect the QoS and capacity of each individual femtocell. Another alternative as suggested by Elleithy and Rao [10] is for mobile operators to implement a two-tier femtocell network by sharing the spectrum rather than splitting it between two individual femtocells.

As per studies conducted by the femto-forum, the main forms of interference that arises in the femtocells are mentioned as follows:

- Femtocells interfering with the BSs on the same frequency: A large number of femtocells operating on the same carrier frequency may increase the load on the overlaying macrocell, thereby reducing the capacity of the entire network.
- BSs interfering with the femtocells on the same frequency: This scenario is identical to the one mentioned above.
- Femtocells interfering with each other: If multiple femtocells operate close to each other, they produce a level of background noise that reduces the QoS of each femtocell.
- Cell phone signals received by both macrocells and femtocells: In some cases, when a mobile phone connects to a femtocell, the signal strength is strong enough to be received by the surrounding macrocell as well. This leads to a level of noise at the macrocell, which is beyond its tolerance level.

16.2.3 Interference Management

There are several studies in the literature reporting how femtocell deployment is able to greatly enhance the indoor coverage and accommodate an excellent user experience. The

FAP is user deployed and hence reduces the infrastructure, maintenance, and operational costs of the operator while at the same time providing good QoS to the end user and high network capacity gains. However, the mass deployment of femtocell faces a number of challenges among which the interference management is the most important, as the fundamental limits of capacity and achievable data rates mainly depend on the interference faced by the femtocell network. To cope with the technical challenges, including interference management, researchers have suggested a variety of solutions. These solutions vary depending on the physical layer of technology and the specific scenarios.

Interference management has becomes the main challenge for the femtocell deployment as a result of their ad hoc network nature [11]. Its function as a secondary layer network increases the intercell interference's value compared to the value before the deployment of the femtocell network especially in close access mode. The received signal power during transmission may become lower than the signal power from the potential interferer [7]. As a consequence, to ensure the femtocell operates efficiently, immediate attention for developing the inter-cell mitigation strategies is needed [12].

To overcome the penetration losses, the indoor users need high power from the serving BS. Zahir et al. [11] mention that when the overall system throughput is reduced, the other users will have less power. The needs of a high-capacity network would require a large number of outdoor BSs, which is too expensive. As a consequence, increasing the number of BSs also increases the burden on network planning and optimization. Excellent channel condition is compulsory to guarantee and maintain the higher data rates and QoS. Hence, femtocell has to ensure that it has the functionality of opportunistic spectrum access to make it intelligent. Therefore, to achieve this, an integrated femtocell and CR network is proposed as a solution [7]. Following are the three types of interference scenarios in a femtocell network:

1. Interference between the downlink femtocell transmission and UE served by MBS
2. Interference between the uplink transmission of UE served by the macrocell and femtocell receivers
3. Interference in both downlink and uplink transmissions among femtocells

Zahir et al. [11] pointed out that the femtocell will require some portions of spectrum from the operators for its operation. This can be a separate portion of the spectrum allocated by the operator or the same portion of spectrum used by the macrocell. In the case of same spectrum being used for femtocell (co-channel femtocell deployment), the issue of interference arises. This interference can be either between the neighboring femtocells or between femtocell and macrocell. In [7], a cognitive femtocell switching unit acts as a service coordinator between the femtocell and macrocell areas to guarantee the quality of radio service, spectrum utilization, and enables an excellent local handover management to reduce the unnecessary handovers between FBSs.

To address these problems, a cognition femtocell access point (CFAP) was introduced by Al-Rubaye et al. [12] to mitigate the interference. From the simulation result, variation of power level did not affect the signal-to-interference + noise (SINR) from the neighboring cells. The SINR level maintains a threshold level although the interference increases. In contrast, Viswanadh and Garimella [13] applied the graph coloring method for data scheduling to avoid the interference. The proposed scheme is to identify inter-femtocell interference by analyzing the received patterns observed by the mobile stations. Vasavada and Srivastava [14] extended this work by incorporating the CR technology into femtocells. From the experiments, the proposed interference identification method can successfully identify the real interferers while excluding the noninterfering femtocells from suspicious interferers.

Liu and Huang [15] proposed a spectrum allocation scheme based on the QoS graph coloring algorithm. The aim is to mitigate the interferences and maximize the spectrum efficiency. Different QoS targets were taken into consideration and achieved a trade-off between the fairness and spectrum efficiency. The simulation results provide better spectrum efficiency and average throughput. These findings contradict Xu et al.'s study [16], who argued that the traditional spectrum-sharing methods, for example the graph coloring method, are not efficient for a dense femtocells deployment. They proposed the joint allocation and fast power control scheme for downlink transmission in the overlay mode. The proposed scheme without any iteration achieved almost twice the average capacity and a much lower user blocking rate than the coloring method.

Similarly Xiang et al. [17] described the spectrum sharing in CR access networks using a framework based on a discrete time Markov chain model. This method enables an opportunistic secondary access to share the spectrum resources while the mutual interference is kept below acceptable levels. With the same objective, Gelabert et al. [18] conducted a spectrum-sensing experiment based on a Welch periodogram and applied it to a femtocell scenario where the cognitive femtocell base station (CFBS) is located in the same frequency band as the surrounding macrocell and neighboring femtocells.

Harjula and Hekkala [19] found that allocating the available PU power among the OFDMA subcarriers shows that a reduction of 5% spectral efficiency could be utilized to gain more than 15% in terms of the correct detection probability. And, a study by Herath et al. [20] is to maximize the throughput of the cognitive network while not affecting the performance of PUs by considering both downlink and uplink transmission scenarios in the cognitive network. By applying two-phase mixed distributed/centralized control algorithms that require minimal cooperation between the cognitive and primary devices, the coverage and throughput can be optimized. In addition to Herath et al. [20], Hoang et al. [21] provided a cognitive radio resource management (CRRM) scheme which is inspired by the spirit of the CR technology. The femtocell with the proposed CRRM can autonomously sense the radio resource usage of the macrocell and mitigate the interference. The optimum sensing period and radio resource allocation are proposed for the CRRM to achieve the full radio resource utilization while statistically guaranteeing the QoS requirement of the femtocell.

16.3 Interference Mitigation Technique

The finding of the present study highlights that the interference experienced by the femtocell network interrupts the capacity limits and achievement data rates. The mobile network architecture becomes a two-tier or two-layer network that consists of a macrocell network as the first layer and a femtocell network as the second layer or an ad hoc network [22]. Saquib et al. [23] proposed a scheme where if a Home eNode B (HeNB) is turned on, it identifies the adjacent neighbors and obtains the knowledge of the cognitive cells (CCs) used by the neighbors. The main idea of the scheme is that each HeNB estimates the co-tier interference based on the path-loss information, capitalizes the knowledge of the usage of CCs by the neighbors, and accesses the spectrum intelligently to minimize the interference. The selection of CC is done in such a way that each HeNB selects the CC which is not used by the neighbor, or the CC that is occupied by the furthest neighbor, or the CC that is occupied by the least number of neighbors.

A study by Xiang et al. [17] formulates the downlink spectrum sharing problem in the CR femtocell networks, and employs the decomposition theories to solve it. Simulation results indicate that the CR-enabled femtocells could achieve much higher capacity than the femtocell networks which do not employ an agile spectrum access. Another useful method in interference management justified by Sung et al. [24] is a joint power control and coverage scheme for a femtocell-based cognitive wireless metropolitan area network. In this scheme the power of each node to which BS a node connects is controlled to maximize the aggregate throughput. From [25], a flexible spectrum reuse scheme for interference mitigation is proposed. The frequency reuse pattern is cognitively determined according to the femtocell's environment. The proposed scheme regards the femtocell as a secondary system and macrocell as the primary system. Femtocell recognizes an interference signature from the network and intelligently reuses the proper channel modes to avoid the interference. The ability of the CR to detect and identify the interference based on different environments is managed autonomously.

Based on the review of the literature, the accessible frequency spectrum can be utilized efficiently by using the CR. The objective of this study is to improve the capacity of FUs and at the same time efficiently utilize the available bandwidth and reduce the bandwidth scarcity. To be specific, there are two categories of cell users, the PUs and SUs, by integrating the CR in the femtocell LTE-based network.

16.3.1 Spectrum Holes in CR

The CR offers a novel way of solving the spectrum underutilization problems. It does so by sensing the radio environment with a twofold objective: identifying the sub-bands of the radio spectrum that are underutilized by the primary (i.e., legacy) users. However, we must note that to achieve these goals in an autonomous manner, the multiuser CR networks will have to be self-organizing and able to respond to the surrounding wireless changes including the power adaptability requirements. The concept of spectrum mobility is illustrated in Figure 16.3.

Figure 16.3 shows the concept of spectrum mobility, for example, with assumption that several FUs also known as SUs are searching for the available spectrum holes, and fortunately there is available bandwidth in the global positioning system (GPS) spectrum at a 3-time unit. The FUs need to either strive for or share the bandwidth among them.

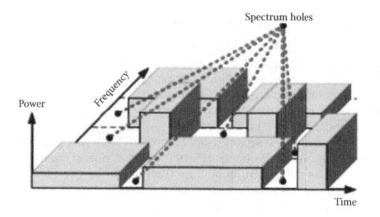

FIGURE 16.3
Spectrum mobility for a cognitive radio. (From Al-Rubaye, S., and Cosmas, J., *Self-Organization and Green Applications in Cognitive Radio Networks*, IGI Global, 2013.)

Furthermore, if several spectrum holes are available, the SUs may experience performance deterioration such as severe and massive interruptions.

16.3.2 CR Functions

CR interconnection of femtocell networks could be a part of the future internet wireless networks [1]. This new coexistence paradigm between the CR and femtocells is based on the predefined converged areas of services and the challenge is to combine the capacity of different resources to provide the broadband access to both stationary and mobile cognitive users. However, high throughput demands of the mobile end users may need more resources in future than what are currently available for the existing macrocell networks. Hence, femtocell networks will play a vital role in supporting the indoor environments, such as at the airports, hospitals, or houses. Enhancing the data delivery for the internet services could be creating a novel cross-layer framework in the gateway router. This improves the cognitive femtocells' flexibility and efficiency in accessing the spectrum. And, the new design concepts increase the system's reconfigurability to respond to real-time changes in the wireless environment.

After accessing the unlicensed spectrum, the cognitive operator can adopt different approaches to utilize the spectrum in a wireless overlay network. The principal approach is that the two-tier networks share the unlicensed spectrum such that the macrocell and femtocell operate in a co-channel frequency reuse. Other aspects are focusing on the resource management to avoid two-tier interference, where each radio-tier has more available aggregate spectrum but suffers from a higher cross-tier interference. Therefore, a potential increase in the energy efficiency while deploying a certain number of low-powered relay femtocell nodes can provide lower interference to both PUs and SUs at the same time. In order to achieve the target, Huang and Zhu [26] suggested that the self-configuration module for a cognitive femtocell architecture should include three components: spectrum mobility, spectrum sharing, and spectrum configuration.

16.3.3 Cognitive Femtocell Architecture

The MBS also known as the PU of the licensed spectrum is provided by the operators. Normally, MBS manages the mobile users and FBS manages the bulk traffic. The CR's spectrum sensing, spectrum management, spectrum sharing, and spectrum mobility functionalities, as defined in [27] are completed on the FBS. By integrating the CR with a femtocell, all types of user access schemes such as Communication Convergence are able to access the primary network. In the case where majority of the users of WLAN in the area covered by MBS and the modulation used for communication are based on WLAN, cognitive femtocell plays the role using its capability to sense and locate any available spectrum portions for the white spaces or spectrum holes that can allow the users to access the spectrum and provide connectivity to its users. They can collaborate and cooperate among the neighboring cognitive femtocells to sense the available spectrum accurately. If there is no available spectrum holes, femtocells have to use the licensed band to publish the connection.

Furthermore, there is a difference between the cognitive and traditional femtocell architectures [9]. For the purpose of coverage extension and interference mitigation, the cognitive femtocell may expand its range beyond the indoor communication as ordered by the MBS. The FBS cooperatively schedules its transmission parameters such that all clients can access the macrocell network whenever they need it. Client nodes are either equipped with the CRs or the traditional radios. With reference to Figure 16.4, private clients may be

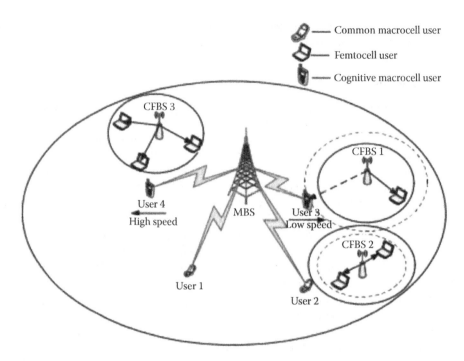

FIGURE 16.4
Cognitive femtocell architecture. (From Q. Li et al. *International Conference on Wireless Communications and Signal Processing (WCSP)*, pp. 2–6, November 2011.)

defined as users who own an FBS, thus freely associating with it, while public clients are nonfemtocell owners and are normally associated with the MBS.

CFBS is equipped with the cognitive functionalities. Therefore it can sense the radio environment within a certain range (defined as cognition range) to collect the information and receive the SINRs of cognitive users. The CFBS may also extend its coverage beyond the indoor communication by increasing the transmission power to access the cognitive users closer to it for the purpose of cross-tier interference mitigation. It is assumed that in the cognitive femtocell network, there are k CFBSs randomly deployed in the coverage area of a MBS, and three types of users which are defined as the following:

1. The common MUs that are only served by the macrocell BS.
2. The cognitive MUs that are normally associated with the MBS but can be accessed by the SUs using unlicensed bands by a nearby CFBS when its QoS is significantly deteriorated by the cross-tier interference.
3. The cognitive FUs that are served by the CFBS as a PU with licensed bands.

16.4 System Model and Assumption

Figure 16.5 shows the example of coexistence of a two-layer network. Assigning CR technology to the femtocell network makes the femtocell UEs to be able to recognize and utilize the spectrum opportunities from the licensed and unlicensed band, e.g., macrocell networks and TV broadcast systems.

The LTE-based femtocell network simulation scenarios consist of only 1 cell with 1 femtocell, 10 FUs, and 64 randomly distributed MUs. Throughout the simulation, the FUs are assumed to stay and move randomly around 10 m inside the femtocell. The distance between an FAP and an MBS is 1000 m. The simulation parameters are shown in Table 16.1.

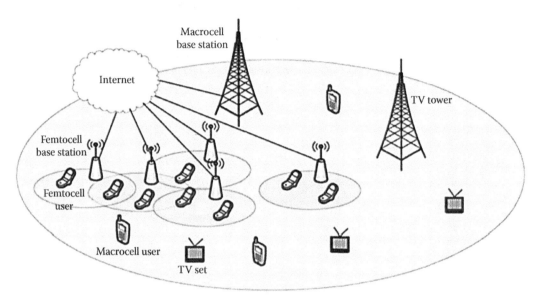

FIGURE 16.5
Coexistence between cognitive radio femtocells and primary systems such as macrocells and TV systems. (From Gelabert, X. et al., *Comput. Netw.*, 54, 2519–2536, 2010.)

TABLE 16.1

Simulation Parameters

Parameter	Unit	Value
System bandwidth	MHz	5
No. of subcarriers		512
Subcarriers bandwidth	kHz	375
Base station frequency	MHz	2000
Cell radius (M/F)	m	280/30
Path loss	dB	$\text{PL}_{mu} = 15.3 + 37.6 \log_{10}(d \text{ [m]}) + S^{out}$ (macrocell)
		$\text{PL}_{fu} = 38.5 + 20 \log(d \text{ [m]}) + 0.7 d_{2D,} \text{indoor} + 18.3n^{((n+2)/(n+1)-0.46)}$ (femtocell)
Indoor penetration loss	dB	12
Macrocell BS transmit power	dB	20
Femtocell BS transmit power	dBm	20
Power noise density	dBm/Hz	−144
Threshold at the CR	dBw	−111.6

16.5 Simulation Results and Analysis

When the CR technology is integrated with the femtocell network, it helps to optimize the femtocell coverage. From the observation in Figure 16.6, the value of the user's capacity increases when the distance of the CFAP increases from the MBS.

The major problem in the femtocell deployment is the interference due to the frequency sharing concept in a two-tier network. With reference to Figure 16.7, it shows that the capacity keeps increasing even though the FUs are increased. The numerical result indicates that the capacities of the FU for both the downlink and uplink CFAP are enhanced as the distance between the mobile base station and CFAP increases. Compared with the capacity for downlink and uplink scenario for a conventional FAP, the values are lower but still

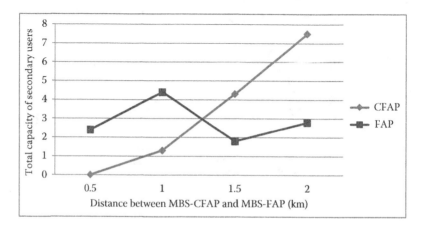

FIGURE 16.6
Total downlink capacity over distance of CFAP from MBS.

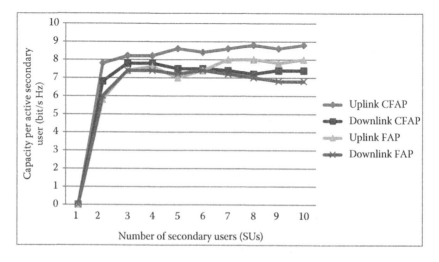

FIGURE 16.7
Secondary users network capacity.

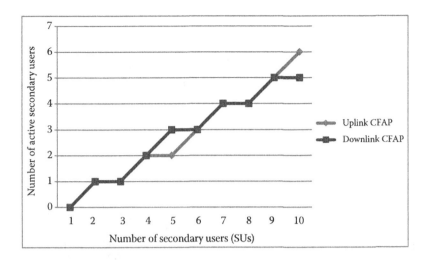

FIGURE 16.8
Number of active CogFem users.

around the same range. In a cognitive femtocell scenario, N number of channels are to be sensed. If the transmission time is divided into 40 slots and by using 5 channels, there will be 32 states (from 00000 to 11111). For example at the states of 00010, channels 1, 2, 3, and 5 are being idle while the SU which is the FU will be given the opportunity to transmit the data. The greedy algorithm approach will determine the best solution for the data transmission, although it merely takes into account the current spot and has no concern for the future issues. However, it still can be accepted since the characteristic of the CR is to adapt with the communication environment to reach the optimum network performance.

CR allows the femto-network to perform a periodical channel sensing to estimate the radio resource usage of the macro-network, shown in Figure 16.8. The number of femtocell active users eventually represents the estimation number of the radio resource usage. During the simulation, it is assumed that the opportunities for a channel involved two probabilities where α is the probability of the channel being busy and β is the probability of the channel being idle.

16.6 Conclusion and Future Work

This finding highlights the advantages of the CR-technology capability to increase the network capacity in an LTE-based femtocell network. This study has contributed to the knowledge related to the interference management on femtocell deployment by using the CR technology and the technical challenges that have to be overcome for the optimum deployment of femtocell and macrocell networks (two-tier networks). Thus, both femtocell and macrocell should be able to use the radio resources more effectively and efficiently as the femtocell will complement the macrocell indoor coverage. Further study will involve identifying the challenges on mitigating the interference issues and the user mobility management in the coexistence of femtocell with macrocell networks.

Acknowledgments

The authors would like to thank the Faculty of Electrical Engineering, Universiti Teknologi MARA for their support and assistance given to the authors in carrying out this research study.

References

1. S. Al-Rubaye and J. Cosmas, Technical challenges in 4G cognitive femtocell systems, In *Self-Organization and Green Applications in Cognitive Radio Networks*, Edited by A. Al-Dulaimi, J. Cosmas, and A. Mohammed. Pennsylvania, USA: IGI Global, 2013, pp. 1–25.
2. V. Chandrasekhar and J. Andrews, Uplink capacity and interference avoidance for two-tier femtocell networks, *IEEE Trans. Wirel. Commun.*, vol. 8, no. 7, 3498–3509, 2009.
3. S. Cheng, S. Lien, F. Chu, and K. Chen, On exploiting cognitive radio to mitigate interference in macro/femto heterogeneous networks, *IEEE Wirel. Commun.*, vol. 18, no. 3, 40–47, 2011.
4. O. Fratu, A. Vulpe, R. Craciunescu, and S. Halunga, Small cells in cellular networks: Challenges of future HetNets, *Wirel. Pers. Commun.*, vol. 78, no. 3, 1613–1627, 2014.
5. I. Ismail, M. D. Baba, and R. E. Zaini, Frequency reuse technique for femtocell LTE-Based network, in *Technology and Innovation Conference 2015 (TECHON)*, Kuching, Serawak, Malaysia, 2015, pp. 479–492.
6. L. Abdullah and M. D. Baba, Femtocell geo-location challenge: DSL approach as solution, in *2014 IEEE 5th Control and System Graduate Research Colloquium*, Shah Alam, Selangor, Malaysia, 2014, pp. 239–241.
7. G. Da Costa and A. Cattoni, Interference mitigation in cognitive femtocells, in *IEEE Globecom 2010 Workshop*, Miami, Florida, USA, 2010, pp. 721–725.
8. S. Lien, S. Member, C. Tseng, K. Chen, and C. Su, *Cognitive Radio Resource Management for QoS Guarantees in Autonomous Femtocell Networks*, In *2010 IEEE International Conference on Communications (ICC)*, Cape Town, 2010.
9. O. Akinlabi, B. Paul, M. Joseph, and H. Ferreira, A review of femtocell, in *International MultiConference of Engineers and Computer Scientists 2014*, Hong Kong vol. II. , 2014.
10. K. Elleithy and V. Rao, Femto cells: Current status and future directions, *Int. J. Next-Generation Networks*, vol. 3, no. 1, 1–9, 2011.
11. T. Zahir, K. Arshad, A. Nakata, and K. Moessner, Interference management in femtocells, *IEEE Commun. Surv. Tutor.*, vol. 5, no. 1, 293–311, 2013.
12. S. Al-Rubaye, A. Al-Dulaimi, and J. Cosmas, Spectrum handover strategies for cognitive femtocell networks, in *Femtocell Communications and Technologies: Business Opportunities and Deployment Challenges*, USA: IGI Global, 2012, pp. 85–102.
13. K. Viswanadh and R. M. Garimella, A cognitive femto cell access point in HetNets to mitigate interference, *Procedia Comput. Sci.*, vol. 46, pp. 1417–1424, 2015.
14. T. Vasavada and S. Srivastava, Review of fairness and graph coloring methods for data collection in wireless sensor networks, in *2013 Annual IEEE India Conference (INDICON)*, Mumbai, India, 2013, pp. 1–4.
15. C. Liu and P. Huang, Interference identification and resource management in OFDMA femtocell networks, in *Conference on 2014 IFIP*, Trondheim, Norway, 2014.
16. Z. Xu, Y. He, X. Xu, and F. Peng, QoS graph coloring spectrum allocation for femtocell in macro/femto heterogeneous network, in *8th International Conference on Communications and Networking in China (CHINACOM)*, Guilin, People's Republic of China, 2013, pp. 374–378.

17. J. Xiang, Y. Zhang, S. Member, T. Skeie, L. Xie, and S. Member, Downlink spectrum sharing for cognitive radio femtocell networks, *IEEE Syst. J.*, vol. 4, no. 4, 524–534, 2010.

18. X. Gelabert, O. Sallent, J. Pérez-Romero, and R. Agustí, Spectrum sharing in cognitive radio networks with imperfect sensing: A discrete-time Markov model, *Comput. Networks*, vol. 54, 2519–2536, 2010.

19. I. Harjula and A. Hekkala, Spectrum sensing in cognitive femto base stations using Welch periodogram, in *IEEE 22nd International Symposium on Personal, Indoor and Mobile Radio Communications*, Toronto, Canada, 2011, pp. 2305–2309.

20. S. Herath, N. Rajatheva, and P. Saengudomlert, Primary and cognitive user cooperative spectrum sensing in OFDMA air interface, in *2010 IEEE 71st Vehicular Technology Conference (VTC-2010 Spring)*, 2010, pp. 1–5.

21. A. Hoang, Y. Liang, and M. Islam, Power control and channel allocation in cognitive radio networks with primary users' cooperation, *IEEE Trans. Mob. Comput.*, vol. 9, no. 3, 348–360, 2010.

22. L. Yang, S. H. Song, and K. B. Letaief, Cognitive spectrum access in two-tier femtocell networks, in *IEEE ICC 2014-Wireless Communication Symposium*, Sydney, Australia, 2014, pp. 5354–5359.

23. N. Saquib, E. Hossain, B. L. Le, and D. I. Kim, Interference management in OFDMA femtocell networks: Issues and approaches, *IEEE Wirel. Commun.*, vol. 19, no. 3, 86–95, 2012.

24. N. Sung, J. P. M. Torregoza, W. Hwang, S. Lee, and H. Yoon, A joint power control and converge scheme in a cognitive-femtocell architecture for wireless networks for throughput maximization, *2010 8th IEEE International Conference on Industrial Informatics*, Osaka, Japan, July 2010, pp. 1025–1030.

25. H. Qing, Y. Liu, G. Xie, and J. Gao, Interference mitigation scheme for cognitive femtocell networks, in *IET Conference Publications*, Beijing, China, 2013, pp. 1–5.

26. L. Huang and G. Zhu, Cognitive femtocell networks: An opportunistic spectrum access for future indoor wireless coverage, *IEEE Wirel. Commun.*, vol. 20, no. 2, 44–51, 2013.

27. G. Andy, "The impact of femtocells on next generation mobile networks", in *3GPP Seminar*, Moscow, Russia, , 2010.

28. Q. Li, Z. Feng, W. Li, and P. Zhang, "Joint Access and Power Control in Cognitive Femtocell Networks," in *International Conference on Wireless Communications and Signal Processing (WCSP)*, November 2011, Nanjing, China, pp. 2–6.

Index